The Cambridge Companion to W. B. Yeats

This accessible and thought-provoking Companion is designed to help students experience the pleasures and challenges offered by one of the twentieth century's greatest poets. A team of international contributors examines Yeats's poetry, drama, and prose in their historical and national contexts. The essays explain and synthesize major aspects and themes of his life and work: his lifelong engagement with Ireland; his complicated relationship to the English literary tradition; his literary, social, and political criticism; and the evolution of his complex spiritual and religious sense. First-time readers of Yeats as well as more advanced scholars will welcome this comprehensive account of his career with its useful chronological outline and survey of the most important current trends in Yeats scholarship. Taken as a whole, this Companion is an essential introduction for students and teachers of Yeats.

THE CAMBRIDGE COMPANION TO
W. B. YEATS

EDITED BY

MARJORIE HOWES
Boston College

JOHN KELLY
St. John's College, Oxford

CAMBRIDGE UNIVERSITY PRESS
Cambridge, New York, Melbourne, Madrid, Cape Town,
Singapore, São Paulo, Delhi, Tokyo, Mexico City

Cambridge University Press
The Edinburgh Building, Cambridge CB2 8RU, UK

Published in the United States of America by Cambridge University Press, New York

www.cambridge.org
Information on this title: www.cambridge.org/9780521658867

First published 2006
Third printing 2008

A catalogue record for this publication is available from the British Library

ISBN 978-0-521-65089-2 Hardback
ISBN 978-0-521-65886-7 Paperback

CONTENTS

Notes on contributors *page* vii
Chronology of Yeats's life x
List of abbreviations xv

1 Introduction 1
MARJORIE HOWES

2 Yeats and Romanticism 19
GEORGE BORNSTEIN

3 Yeats, Victorianism, and the 1890s 36
GEORGE WATSON

4 Yeats and Modernism 59
DANIEL ALBRIGHT

5 The later poetry 77
HELEN VENDLER

6 Yeats and the drama 101
BERNARD O'DONOGHUE

7 Yeats and criticism 115
DECLAN KIBERD

8 Yeats, folklore, and Irish legend 129
JAMES PETHICA

9 Yeats and the occult 144
MARGARET MILLS HARPER

10 Yeats and gender 167
ELIZABETH BUTLER CULLINGFORD

11 Yeats and politics 185
JONATHAN ALLISON

12 Yeats and the postcolonial 206
MARJORIE HOWES

Select bibliography 226
Index 232

NOTES ON CONTRIBUTORS

Daniel Albright teaches English and comparative arts at Harvard University. He has edited Yeats's poems and written a number of books on nineteenth- and twentieth-century literature and music, including *Quantum Poetics: Yeats, Pound, Eliot, and the Science of Modernism* (1997) and *Untwisting the Serpent: Modernism in Music, Literature, and Other Arts* (2000).

Jonathan Allison is Associate Professor of English at the University of Kentucky and Director of the Yeats International Summer School. His publications include *Yeats's Political Identities* (1996), *Patrick Kavanagh: A Reference Guide* (1996), and *Poetry and Contemporary Culture* (ed. with A. M. Roberts, 2002). He is currently completing a history of modern Irish poetry and editing selected letters of Louis MacNeice.

George Bornstein, C. A. Patrides Professor of Literature at the University of Michigan, is the author of several books of literary criticism, including *Yeats and Shelley* (1970) and, most recently, *Material Modernism: The Politics of the Page* (2001). He has edited the two volumes of Yeats's early poetic manuscripts for the Cornell Yeats Series as well as the book *Letters to the New Island* for the *Collected Edition of the Works of W. B. Yeats*. He is currently finishing co-editing the *Early Essays* volume for the same series and working on a critical study entitled *The Colors of Zion: Blacks, Jews, and Irish a Century Ago*.

Elizabeth Butler Cullingford is Jane and Roland Blumberg Centennial Professor in English Literature and University Distinguished Teaching Professor at the University of Texas at Austin. Her publications include *Ireland's Others: Ethnicity and Gender in Irish Literature and Popular Culture* (2001; American Conference for Irish Studies Robert Rhodes Prize), *Gender and History in Yeats's Love Poetry* (1993; a Choice Outstanding Academic Book), and *Yeats, Ireland and Fascism* (1981). She is currently studying conflicting representations of nuns in Irish literature and popular culture, and working on a feminist cultural studies project that examines literary representations of the only child in the contexts provided by folklore, history, demography, and sociology.

Margaret Mills Harper is the author of *The Aristocracy of Art: Joyce and Woolf* (1990) and a forthcoming study of the occult and literary collaboration between Yeats and George Yeats. She is the co-editor of two volumes of *Yeats's "Vision" Papers* (1992 and 2001) and Professor of English at Georgia State University.

Marjorie Howes is Associate Professor of English and Co-director of the Irish Studies program at Boston College. She is the author of *Yeats's Nations: Gender, Class, and Irishness* (1996), the co-editor of *Semicolonial Joyce* (2000), and a contributor to *The Field Day Anthology of Irish Writing, Volume 4: Women's Writing and Traditions* (2002).

John Kelly is a Fellow of St. John's College, Oxford. He is the author of a number of scholarly publications, and is the general editor for *The Collected Letters of W. B. Yeats*, of which three volumes have been published to date.

Declan Kiberd is Professor of Anglo-Irish Literature and Drama at University College Dublin. He is the author of numerous scholarly books, including *Synge and the Irish Language* (1979), *Inventing Ireland: The Literature of the Modern Nation* (1995), and *Irish Classics* (2000). His work has won a number of awards, including the *Irish Times* Literature Prize for Non-Fiction, the Truman Capote Prize for Best Work of Literary Criticism in the English-Speaking World, and the Oscar Wilde Award for Literary Achievement.

Bernard O'Donoghue grew up in County Cork but since 1965 he has lived in Oxford, where he teaches medieval English and modern Irish literature at Wadham College. He has written on medieval love poetry, and is the author of *Seamus Heaney and the Language of Poetry* (1994). He was Director of the Yeats Summer School in Sligo in 2001 and 2002. He has published five volumes of poetry: *Poaching Rights* (1987), *The Weakness* (1991), *Gunpowder* (1995), *Here nor There* (1999), and *Outliving* (2003).

James Pethica teaches Irish and Modern British literature at Williams College, Massachusetts, and is currently at work on the authorized biography of Lady Augusta Gregory and a critical book on her creative partnership with Yeats. His publications include *Lady Gregory's Diaries 1892–1902* (1996), an edition of the drafts of Yeats's *Last Poems* (1997), and *Yeats's Poetry, Drama and Prose: A Norton Critical Edition* (2000).

Helen Vendler is the Porter University Professor at Harvard University. She is the author of books on Yeats, Stevens, Keats, Herbert, Shakespeare, and Heaney. Her new book, *Poets Thinking*, was published by Harvard University Press in 2004.

George Watson is Professor of Irish Literature in English at the University of Aberdeen. His publications include *Irish Identity and the Literary Revival: Yeats, Joyce, Synge and O'Casey* (1995, second edition; first edition 1979), *Drama* (1983), and *W. B. Yeats: Short Fiction* (1995). He has written many essays on Irish literature and cultural politics, and has lectured and taught extensively in Europe and the USA. He is on the editorial board of the *James Joyce Quarterly*, and was a founding member and later Vice Chairman of the British Association of Irish Studies (1990–5). He was Director of the W. B. Yeats International Summer School in Sligo, 1998–2000. He was Mellon Fellow of the National Humanities Center in North Carolina in 2000–1, and is currently working on a monograph on *The Ideology of Celticism in Scotland and Ireland 1760–1900*.

CHRONOLOGY OF YEATS'S LIFE

1865 *13 June* William Butler Yeats born in Sandymount, Dublin.
1867 John B. Yeats gives up law and moves to London to study art.
1871 Jack Butler Yeats born.
1872 *July* Family moves to Sligo.
1874 *October* Family moves back to London.
1877 Enters Godolphin School.
1881 Family moves to Dublin; Yeats enters Erasmus Smith High School.
1883 Hears Oscar Wilde lecture in Dublin.
1884 Attends Metropolitan School of Art; meets George W. Russell (AE).
1885 First meeting of the Dublin Hermetic Society.
First poems and *Mosada* published in *Dublin University Review*.
Meets Katharine Tynan and John O'Leary.
1886 Meets William Morris.
First Home Rule bill defeated.
1887 Family moves to London.
Meets Madame Blavatsky.
1888 Meets G. B. Shaw and Lady Wilde.
Fairy and Folk Tales of the Irish Peasantry
Joins Esoteric Section of Madame Blavatsky's Theosophical Society.
1889 *The Wanderings of Oisin and Other Poems*
30 January Meets Maud Gonne.
1890 Helps found Rhymers' Club.
7 March Joins the Order of the Golden Dawn.
Asked to resign from the Esoteric Section of the Theosophical Society.
1891 *John Sherman and Dhoya*
Representative Irish Tales
First marriage proposal to Maud Gonne.
1892 *The Countess Kathleen and Various Legends and Lyrics*
Irish Fairy Tales

1893 *The Celtic Twilight*
The Works of William Blake, co-edited with Edwin Ellis
Gaelic League founded by Douglas Hyde.
Second Home Rule bill defeated.
1894 *March–April The Land of Heart's Desire* produced in London.
Sees Villiers de l'Isle Adams's *Axël* in Paris.
1895 Edits *A Book of Irish Verse.*
Poems
1896 Meets Lady Gregory.
Affair with Olivia Shakespear.
Rosa Alchemica
Summer Visits Aran Islands.
December Meets J. M. Synge in Paris.
1897 *The Tables of the Law* and *The Adoration of the Magi*
The Secret Rose
End of affair with Olivia Shakespear.
July–November At Coole Park with Lady Gregory.
1899 *The Wind Among the Reeds*
The Countess Kathleen produced at Antient Concert Rooms in Dublin; opening of Irish Literary Theatre.
1900 *The Shadowy Waters*
1901 *October Diarmuid and Grania* produced in Dublin.
1902 Meets James Joyce.
2 April Cathleen ni Houlihan produced in Dublin.
Where There is Nothing
Dun Emer (later Cuala) Press established.
1903 *21 February* Maud Gonne marries Major John MacBride.
Ideas of Good and Evil
In the Seven Woods
The Hour-Glass
American lecture tour.
1904 *14 January The Shadowy Waters* produced in Dublin.
26–9 June Where There Is Nothing produced in London.
The King's Threshold
27 December On Baile's Strand produced at opening of the Abbey Theatre.
1905 Maud Gonne granted a separation from John MacBride.
November Abbey company on tour in England.
Stories of Red Hanrahan
1906 *Poems 1899–1905*
Edits *The Poems of Spenser.*

1907 *January* Riots over Synge's *The Playboy of the Western World.*
John B. Yeats moves to USA.
Deirdre
21 November The Unicorn from the Stars produced at the Abbey.
1908 *Collected Works in Verse and Prose*, eight volumes.
Affair with Mabel Dickinson.
1909 24 *March* Synge dies.
1910 Granted Civil List pension (150 pounds per year).
The Green Helmet and Other Poems
The Abbey Theatre continues production after death of King Edward VII.
1911 *September–October* With Abbey Players on American tour.
Meets Ezra Pound.
Synge and the Ireland of His Time
Plays for an Irish Theatre
1912 Meets Rabindranath Tagore.
The Cutting of an Agate
1913 *Poems Written in Discouragement*
November–January At Stone Cottage in Sussex with Ezra Pound.
1914 *January–April* American lecture tour.
4 *August* United Kingdom declares war on Germany.
Responsibilities: Poems and a Play
1915 *May* Hugh Lane killed on the *Lusitania.*
December Refuses a knighthood.
1916 *Reveries over Childhood and Youth*
4 *April At the Hawk's Well* performed.
24 *April* Easter Rising begins in Dublin.
3–12 May Leaders, including Major John MacBride, executed.
July–August Final marriage proposal to Maud Gonne, in Normandy.
1917 *March* Purchases Norman tower house outside Gort, Co. Galway; names it Thoor Ballylee.
August Marriage proposal to Iseult Gonne rejected.
20 *October* Marriage to Bertha Georgie Hyde Lees.
George Yeats begins automatic writing that becomes basis for *A Vision.*
The Wild Swans at Coole
1918 *Per Amica Silentia Lunae*
Moves to Oxford.
Robert Gregory killed in action in Italy.

Thoor Ballylee restored.
11 November End of First World War.
1919 *January* Irish War of Independence begins.
Two Plays for Dancers
26 February Birth of Anne Yeats.
The Player Queen produced in London.
1920 *January–May* American lecture tour.
1921 *Michael Robartes and the Dancer*
22 August Birth of Michael Yeats.
Four Plays for Dancers
Four Years
6 December Anglo-Irish treaty signed in London.
1922 *3 February* John B. Yeats dies in New York.
Becomes Senator in the Irish Free State.
June Civil War begins.
The Trembling of the Veil
Later Poems
Plays in Prose and Verse
Joyce's *Ulysses* published.
1923 *May* Civil War ends.
November Awarded Nobel Prize for Literature.
Plays and Controversies
1924 *Essays*
The Cat and the Moon and Certain Poems
1925 *January–February* Travels to Sicily and Rome.
The Bounty of Sweden
Early Poems and Stories
A Vision published privately.
1926 *15 January A Vision* delivered to subscribers.
Estrangement
Autobiographies
1927 *October Blast*
November Visits Algeciras, Seville, and Cannes.
1928 *The Tower*
Sophocles' King Oedipus
The Death of Synge
Resigns from the Senate.
Winters in Rapallo.
1929 *A Packet for Ezra Pound*
The Winding Stair
December–early 1930 Suffers Malta fever in Rapallo.

1930 Meets Virginia Woolf and Walter de la Mare.
17 November The Words upon the Window Pane produced at the Abbey.
1931 Receives honorary degree from Oxford.
Arranges an Edition de Luxe with Macmillan, London.
1932 *Stories of Michael Robartes and His Friends*
22 May Death of Lady Gregory.
Moves to Rathfarnam, Dublin.
Words for Music Perhaps
October–January American lecture tour.
1933 *The Winding Stair and Other Poems*
The Collected Poems of W. B. Yeats
1934 *Letters to the New Island*
April Undergoes Steinach operation in London.
Wheels and Butterflies
The Collected Plays of W. B. Yeats
The King of the Great Clock Tower
1935 *17 July* Death of George Russell (AE).
A Full Moon in March
Dramatis Personae
Arranges for the Dublin Edition with Charles Scribner's Sons, New York.
1936 *January* Illness in Majorca.
Edits *The Oxford Book of Modern Verse*.
1937 Revised edition of *A Vision*.
Essays, 1931–1936
Writes Introductions for Scribner Edition.
29 December New constitution for Éire comes into effect.
1938 *The Herne's Egg*
New Poems
10 August Purgatory produced at the Abbey Theatre.
Death of Olivia Shakespear.
1939 *28 January* Dies and is buried at Roquebrune, France.
Last Poems and Two Plays
On the Boiler
1940 *Last Poems and Plays*
1941 *17 September* Body reinterred in Drumcliffe churchyard, Co. Sligo.

ABBREVIATIONS

A — *Autobiographies*. Ed. William H. O'Donnell and Douglas N. Archibald. New York: Scribner, 1999.

CLI — *The Collected Letters of W. B. Yeats: Volume One, 1865–1895*. Ed. John Kelly. London and New York: Oxford University Press, 1985.

CLII — *The Collected Letters of W. B. Yeats: Volume Two, 1896–1900*. Ed. Warwick Gould, John Kelly, and Deirdre Toomey. London and New York: Oxford University Press, 1997.

CLIII — *The Collected Letters of W. B. Yeats: Volume Three, 1901–1904*. Ed. John Kelly and Ronald Schuchard. London and New York: Oxford University Press, 1994.

CT — *The Celtic Twilight*. London: Lawrence and Bullen, 1893.

E&I — *Essays and Introductions*. London and New York: Macmillan, 1961.

Ex — *Explorations*. Selected by Mrs. W. B. Yeats. London: Macmillan, 1962; New York: Macmillan, 1963.

GY — *The Gonne–Yeats Letters 1893–1938*. Ed. Anna MacBride White and A. Norman Jeffares. New York: Norton, 1993.

L — *The Letters of W. B. Yeats*. Ed. Allan Wade. London: Rupert Hart-David, 1954; New York: Macmillan, 1955.

LAR — *Later Articles and Reviews*. Ed. Colton Johnson. New York: Scribner, 2000.

LE — *Later Essays*. Ed. William H. O'Donnell. New York: Scribner, 1994.

LNI — *Letters to the New Island*. Ed. George Bornstein and Hugh Witemeyer. London and New York: Macmillan, 1989.

Mem — *Memoirs*. Transcribed and ed. Denis Donoghue. New York: Macmillan, 1972.

Myth — *Mythologies*. London and New York: Macmillan, 1959.

OTB — *On the Boiler*. Dublin: Cuala, 1939.

P&I *Prefaces and Introductions*. Ed. William H. O'Donnell. London and New York: Macmillan 1989.

SF *W. B. Yeats: Short Fiction*. Ed. G. J. Watson. Harmondsworth: Penguin Books, 1995.

SS *The Senate Speeches of W. B. Yeats*. Ed. Donald R. Pearce. Bloomington: Indiana University Press, 1960.

*UP*I *Uncollected Prose by W. B. Yeats*. Vol. I. Ed. John P. Frayne. London: Macmillan; New York: Columbia University Press, 1970.

*UP*II *Uncollected Prose by W. B. Yeats*. Vol. II. Ed. John P. Frayne and Colton Johnson. London: Macmillan, 1975; New York: Columbia University Press, 1976.

VA *A Critical Edition of Yeats's "A Vision"* (1925). Ed. George Mills Harper and Walter Kelly Hood. London: Macmillan, 1978.

VB *A Vision*. London: Macmillan, 1962 [1937].

VP *The Variorum Edition of the Poems of W. B. Yeats*. Ed. Peter Allt and Russell K. Alspach. New York: Macmillan, 1957.

VPl *The Variorum Edition of the Plays of W. B. Yeats*. Ed. Russell K. Alspach. London and New York: Macmillan, 1966.

CAMBRIDGE COMPANIONS TO LITERATURE

The Cambridge Companion to Greek Tragedy
edited by P. E. Easterling

The Cambridge Companion to Roman Satire
edited by Kirk Freudenburg

The Cambridge Companion to Old English Literature
edited by Malcolm Godden and Michael Lapidge

The Cambridge Companion to Medieval Women's Writing
edited by Carolyn Dinshaw and David Wallace

The Cambridge Companion to Medieval Romance
edited by Roberta L. Krueger

The Cambridge Companion to Medieval English Theatre
edited by Richard Beadle

The Cambridge Companion to English Renaissance Drama, second edition
edited by A. R. Braunmuller and Michael Hattaway

The Cambridge Companion to Renaissance Humanism
edited by Jill Kraye

The Cambridge Companion to English Poetry, Donne to Marvell
edited by Thomas N. Corns

The Cambridge Companion to English Literature, 1500–1600
edited by Arthur F. Kinney

The Cambridge Companion to English Literature, 1650–1740
edited by Steven N. Zwicker

The Cambridge Companion to English Literature, 1740–1830
edited by Thomas Keymer and Jon Mee

The Cambridge Companion to Writing of the English Revolution
edited by N. H. Keeble

The Cambridge Companion to English Restoration Theatre
edited by Deborah C. Payne Fisk

The Cambridge Companion to British Romanticism
edited by Stuart Curran

The Cambridge Companion to Eighteenth-Century Poetry
edited by John Sitter

The Cambridge Companion to the Eighteenth-Century Novel
edited by John Richetti

The Cambridge Companion to Gothic Fiction
edited by Jerrold E. Hogle

The Cambridge Companion to Victorian Poetry
edited by Joseph Bristow

The Cambridge Companion to the Victorian Novel
edited by Deirdre David

The Cambridge Companion to Crime Fiction
edited by Martin Priestman

The Cambridge Companion to Science Fiction
edited by Edward James and Farah Mendlesohn

The Cambridge Companion to Travel Writing
edited by Peter Hulme and Tim Youngs

The Cambridge Companion to American Realism and Naturalism
edited by Donald Pizer

The Cambridge Companion to Nineteenth-Century American Women's Writing
edlted by Dale M. Bauer and Philip Gould

The Cambridge Companion to Victorian and Edwardian Theatre
edited by Kerry Powell

The Cambridge Companion to the Literature of the First World War
edited by Vincent Sherry

The Cambridge Companion to the Classic Russian Novel
edited by Malcolm V. Jones and Robin Feuer Miller

The Cambridge Companion to the French Novel: from 1800 to the Present
edited by Timothy Unwin

The Cambridge Companion to the Spanish Novel: from 1600 to the Present
edited by Harriet Turner and Adelaida López de Martínez

The Cambridge Companion to the Italian Novel
edited by Peter Bondanella and Andrea Ciccarelli

The Cambridge Companion to the Modern German Novel
edited by Graham Bartram

The Cambridge Companion to the Latin American Novel
edited by Efraín Kristal

The Cambridge Companion to Jewish American Literature
edited by Hana Wirth-Nesher and Michael P. Kramer

The Cambridge Companion to Native American Literature
edited by Joy Porter and Kenneth M. Roemer

The Cambridge Companion to the African American Novel
edited by Maryemma Graham

The Cambridge Companion to Canadian Literature
edited by Eva-Marie Kröller

The Cambridge Companion to Contemporary Irish Poetry
edited by Matthew Campbell

The Cambridge Companion to Modernism
edited by Michael Levenson

The Cambridge Companion to American Modernism
edited by Walter Kalaidjian

The Cambridge Companion to Postmodernism
edited by Steven Connor

The Cambridge Companion to Postcolonial Literary Studies
edited by Neil Lazarus

The Cambridge Companion to Australian Literature
edited by Elizabeth Webby

The Cambridge Companion to American Women Playwrights
edited by Brenda Murphy

The Cambridge Companion to Modern British Women Playwrights
edited by Elaine Aston and Janelle Reinelt

The Cambridge Companion to Twentieth-Century Irish Drama
edited by Shaun Richards

The Cambridge Companion to Homer
edited by Robert Fowler

The Cambridge Companion to Virgil
edited by Charles Martindale

The Cambridge Companion to Ovid
edited by Philip Hardie

The Cambridge Companion to Dante
edited by Rachel Jacoff

The Cambridge Companion to Cervantes
edited by Anthony J. Cascardi

The Cambridge Companion to Goethe
edited by Lesley Sharpe

The Cambridge Companion to Dostoevskii
edited by W. J. Leatherbarrow

The Cambridge Companion to Tolstoy
edited by Donna Tussing Orwin

The Cambridge Companion to Chekhov
edited by Vera Gottlieb and Paul Allain

The Cambridge Companion to Ibsen
edited by James McFarlane

The Cambridge Companion to Flaubert
edited by Timothy Unwin

The Cambridge Companion to Proust
edited by Richard Bales

The Cambridge Companion to Thomas Mann
edited by Ritchie Robertson

The Cambridge Companion to Kafka
edited by Julian Preece

The Cambridge Companion to Brecht
edited by Peter Thomson and Glendyr Sacks

The Cambridge Companion to Walter Benjamin
edited by David S. Ferris

The Cambridge Companion to Lacan
edited by Jean-Michel Rabaté

The Cambridge Companion to Nabokov
edited by Julian W. Connolly

The Cambridge Companion to Chaucer, second edition
edited by Piero Boitani and Jill Mann

The Cambridge Companion to Shakespeare
edited by Margareta de Grazia and Stanley Wells

The Cambridge Companion to Shakespeare on Film
edited by Russell Jackson

The Cambridge Companion to Shakespearean Comedy
edited by Alexander Leggatt

The Cambridge Companion to Shakespeare on Stage
edited by Stanley Wells and Sarah Stanton

The Cambridge Companion to Shakespeare's History Plays
edited by Michael Hattaway

The Cambridge Companion to Shakespearean Tragedy
edited by Claire McEachern

The Cambridge Companion to Christopher Marlowe
edited by Patrick Cheney

The Cambridge Companion to Ben Jonson
edited by Richard Harp and Stanley Stewart

The Cambridge Companion to John Donne
edited by Achsah Guibbory

The Cambridge Companion to Spenser
edited by Andrew Hadfield

The Cambridge Companion to Milton, second edition
edited by Dennis Danielson

The Cambridge Companion to John Dryden
edited by Steven N. Zwicker

The Cambridge Companion to Aphra Behn
edited by Derek Hughes and Janet Todd

The Cambridge Companion to Samuel Johnson
edited by Greg Clingham

The Cambridge Companion to Jonathan Swift
edited by Christopher Fox

The Cambridge Companion to Mary Wollstonecraft
edited by Claudia L. Johnson

The Cambridge Companion to William Blake
edited by Morris Eaves

The Cambridge Companion to Wordsworth
edited by Stephen Gill

The Cambridge Companion to Coleridge
edited by Lucy Newlyn

The Cambridge Companion to Byron
edited by Drummond Bone

The Cambridge Companion to Keats
edited by Susan J. Wolfson

The Cambridge Companion to Mary Shelley
edited by Esther Schor

The Cambridge Companion to Jane Austen
edited by Edward Copeland and Juliet McMaster

The Cambridge Companion to the Brontës
edited by Heather Glen

The Cambridge Companion to Charles Dickens
edited by John O. Jordan

The Cambridge Companion to George Eliot
edited by George Levine

The Cambridge Companion to Thomas Hardy
edited by Dale Kramer

The Cambridge Companion to Oscar Wilde
edited by Peter Raby

The Cambridge Companion to George Bernard Shaw
edited by Christopher Innes

The Cambridge Companion to W. B. Yeats
edited by Marjorie Howes and John Kelly

The Cambridge Companion to Joseph Conrad
edited by J. H. Stape

The Cambridge Companion to D. H. Lawrence
edited by Anne Fernihough

The Cambridge Companion to Virginia Woolf
edited by Sue Roe and Susan Sellers

The Cambridge Companion to James Joyce, second edition
edited by Derek Attridge

The Cambridge Companion to T. S. Eliot
edited by A. David Moody

The Cambridge Companion to Ezra Pound
edited by Ira B. Nadel

The Cambridge Companion to W. H. Auden
edited by Stan Smith

The Cambridge Companion to Beckett
edited by John Pilling

The Cambridge Companion to Harold Pinter
edited by Peter Raby

The Cambridge Companion to Tom Stoppard
edited by Katherine E. Kelly

The Cambridge Companion to Herman Melville
edited by Robert S. Levine

The Cambridge Companion to Nathaniel Hawthorne
edited by Richard Millington

The Cambridge Companion to Harriet Beecher Stowe
edited by Cindy Weinstein

The Cambridge Companion to Theodore Dreiser
edited by Leonard Cassuto and Claire Virginia Eby

The Cambridge Companion to Willa Cather
edited by Marilee Lindemann

The Cambridge Companion to Edith Wharton
edited by Millicent Bell

The Cambridge Companion to Henry James
edited by Jonathan Freedman

The Cambridge Companion to Walt Whitman
edited by Ezra Greenspan

The Cambridge Companion to Ralph Waldo Emerson
edited by Joel Porte and Saundra Morris

The Cambridge Companion to Henry David Thoreau
edited by Joel Myerson

The Cambridge Companion to Mark Twain
edited by Forrest G. Robinson

The Cambridge Companion to Edgar Allan Poe
edited by Kevin J. Hayes

The Cambridge Companion to Emily Dickinson
edited by Wendy Martin

The Cambridge Companion to William Faulkner
edited by Philip M. Weinstein

The Cambridge Companion to Ernest Hemingway
edited by Scott Donaldson

The Cambridge Companion to F. Scott Fitzgerald
edited by Ruth Prigozy

The Cambridge Companion to Robert Frost
edited by Robert Faggen

The Cambridge Companion to Ralph Ellison
edited by Ross Posnock

The Cambridge Companion to Eugene O'Neill
edited by Michael Manheim

The Cambridge Companion to Tennessee Williams
edited by Matthew C. Roudané

The Cambridge Companion to Arthur Miller
edited by Christopher Bigsby

The Cambridge Companion to David Mamet
edited by Christopher Bigsby

The Cambridge Companion to Sam Shepard
edited by Matthew C. Roudané

The Cambridge Companion to Edward Albee
edited by Stephen J. Bottoms

CAMBRIDGE COMPANIONS TO CULTURE

The Cambridge Companion to Modern German Culture
edited by Eva Kolinsky and Wilfried van der Will

The Cambridge Companion to Modern Russian Culture
edited by Nicholas Rzhevsky

The Cambridge Companion to Modern Spanish Culture
edited by David T. Gies

The Cambridge Companion to Modern Italian Culture
edited by Zygmunt G. Barański and Rebecca J. West

The Cambridge Companion to Modern French Culture
edited by Nicholas Hewitt

The Cambridge Companion to Modern Latin American Literature
edited by John King

The Cambridge Companion to Modern Irish Culture
edited by Joe Cleary and Claire Connolly

I

MARJORIE HOWES

Introduction

Few modern writers have had careers as long, varied, and complex as W. B. Yeats. Born in 1865, he produced works that arguably belong to each of three major literary historical periods or traditions: the Romantic, the Victorian, and the Modernist. His thought was profoundly dialectical; for nearly every truth he made or found, he also embraced a counter-truth: a proposition that contradicted the first truth, was equally true, and did not negate it. He repeatedly remade himself as a writer, as a public figure, even as a person. And yet his life and work revolved around a few central preoccupations and themes: the Ireland of his day, the occult, sexual love, and the power of art to work in and change the world. In 1938, the year before he died, he wrote "The Spur," whose speaker accuses the reader of thinking it "horrible" that an old man should be filled with "lust and rage" and retorts "They were not such a plague when I was young. / What else have I to spur me into song?" (*VP* 591). The continuity Yeats asserts here is both genuine and false. If we turn from this poem to the early poetry expecting to see the young Yeats lusting and raging, we will be disappointed. The explicit embrace of lust and rage is a feature of Yeats's later years, when he cast himself as the wild, wicked old man to avoid settling into any of the more comfortable poses available to him: the venerable sage, the elder statesman, or the famous poet. All these roles appealed to him, and he adopted each of them at times, but he also drove himself beyond them, towards more risky personae. As he put it in "An Acre of Grass," "My temptation is quiet. / . . . Myself must I remake" (*VP* 575–6).

On the other hand, the continuity between the early and late work implied by "The Spur" is not simply spurious: there *is* a real continuity there. Yeats's early poems are not exactly lustful, but they do circle obsessively around desire and its objects. They depict a kind of desire that cannot be satisfied; it feeds off its own frustration, and it exceeds its objects. This desire is an eternal, disembodied force that sweeps across humanity; poems like "The Travail of Passion" describe what happens "When an immortal passion breathes in mortal clay" (*VP* 172). As for rage, Yeats's early works do not display the naked anger and the will to shock that one finds in many of the later poems, but they repeatedly portray speakers who are struggling, isolated, and embattled in some way; many are poet-figures. The speaker of "The Sad Shepherd," for example, tries to comfort himself by finding or creating sympathetic correspondences between his mood and his natural surroundings in the manner of the Romantic poets. But nature remains alien and indifferent to him; the shell to whom he tells his story "Changed all he sang to inarticulate moan / Among her wildering whirls, forgetting him" (*VP* 69). So we can and should discern, beneath the shifts and transformations that mark Yeats's career, the underlying threads that link all the phases of his work together.

Most of his major preoccupations were established quite early in his life. His lifelong interest in the theatre manifested itself in his earliest writings; his very first publications, in the spring of 1885, when he was just twenty, consisted of several lyrics and a verse play, *The Island of Statues*. Throughout his career, dialogue appealed to him because it allowed him to stage conflicts between opposing principles, voices, or moods. His earliest work was not Irish in its themes, but that same year Yeats met the ageing Fenian John O'Leary, and, at O'Leary's urging, joined the Young Ireland Society. This and his connection with another society, the Contemporary Club, brought Yeats into contact with a circle of nationalist intellectuals. He began to read Irish literature, and his subsequent publications bore the marks of that new interest. Over the next few years he began to establish himself as a freelance critic and editor. The year 1885 also attests to Yeats's early and enduring interest in spiritualism and the occult. That year he helped found the Dublin Hermetic Society, and in 1886 he met the charismatic Mohini Chatterjee, whose Eastern mystical philosophy was much in vogue in Theosophist circles. In the late 1880s he met Maud Gonne for the first time, and conceived one of the most famous unrequited passions in literary history. Within three months of their meeting (as Yeats later dated it), Gonne became pregnant by her lover Lucien Millevoye; Yeats would learn about Millevoye and their two children nearly ten years later. By 1890 he was living in London, and helped start the Rhymers' Club, a bohemian literary society with a significant homosexual subculture and a set of aesthetic ideas that participated in Decadence and Symbolism.

His early work often combines all these elements: nationalism, the occult, love, and contemporary avant-garde poetry. Perhaps the most famous examples are the Rose poems of *The Rose* (1893) and *The Wind Among the Reeds* (1899); the Rose is imagined variously as a symbol of eternal beauty, a bringer of apocalypse, an actual beloved, the priestess of an occult shrine, a figure for Ireland, a force for peace, and an incitement to war. For the poet–speaker, the complex and shifting symbolism of the Rose often helps him to structure relationships between conflicting imperatives. For example, "To the Rose upon the Rood of Time" uses the Rose to explore a tension between the search for the eternal, abstract, and transcendent, and the drive to remain rooted in the concrete, personal, and everyday: "Come near, come near, come near – Ah, leave me still / A little space for the rose-breath to fill! / Lest I no more hear common things that crave" (*VP* 101). "To Ireland in the Coming Times" invokes the Rose in order to take up another potential conflict: between Yeats's occult pursuits and his nationalist politics. The poem asserts their compatibility, but implicitly acknowledges that future readers may or may not agree. Yeats's poems of this period are more dreamlike and ornate than his later poems, but they are best approached without condescension; many of them are (in their own way) just as intellectually rigorous, complex, and concerned with conflict as his later works.

The Yeats of the early work also drew on the world of Irish myth and folklore to meditate in verse on the incompatibility of the natural and supernatural worlds. Critics sometimes label his early poems escapist, but this is somewhat misleading. The early work is full of speakers who yearn to escape from the everyday. But the escapism is nearly always qualified in some way. In some poems, such as "Fergus and the Druid," the speaker is granted access to a supernatural realm or knowledge, but pays too great a price: "now I have grown nothing, knowing all" (*VP* 104). In others the wish to escape is never fulfilled, and pursuing it ruins the speaker's life: examples in this vein include "The Man who Dreamed of Faeryland" and "The Song of Wandering Aengus." Still other poems represent the supernatural as alluring but also threatening; these include "The Hosting of the Sidhe" and "The Stolen Child." Finally, "The Lake Isle of Innisfree" (*VP* 117) offers a speaker whose nostalgia for an idealized Ireland is a product of city life among the "pavements grey," and whose wish to leave the city – "I will arise and go now" – will remain perpetually deferred. Yeats consistently combined an immense need for revelation, for belief, with an intense and critical skepticism; this makes it difficult to determine exactly what he believed and when. In any event, however, the world of the occult and the supernatural was real enough to him to pose genuine dangers.

Many of Yeats's early lyrics are love poems; the early Yeats explored love and desire in several different registers. Very early poems like "The Falling of the Leaves" and "Ephemera" adopt the world-weary pose favored by the Decadents. Yeats, who did not have his first sexual experience with a woman until he was over thirty, wrote at age twenty-four of "that hour of gentleness / When the poor tired child, Passion, falls asleep" (*VP* 80). Mostly, however, versions of romantic and sexual frustration dominate. And much of the imagery in these early poems also displays the influence of the poets of the 1890s. Female figures have dim, dewy, or half-closed eyes; they are "pearl-pale" (*VP* 158) or "cloud-pale" (*VP* 163), they have long, heavy hair and a generally sensuous atmosphere. As George Watson observes in his chapter (pp. 46–7), they look like pre-Raphaelite paintings. The speakers are lover–poet figures who are at the utter mercy of the beloved; their abasement ranges from the material – "But I, being poor, have only my dreams" (*VP* 176) – to the fatal and the apocalyptic.[1] However, these speakers often salvage significant personal and artistic power out of frustration and failure. The speaker of "He wishes for the Cloths of Heaven" may not have the cloths of heaven to offer his beloved, but instead he produces a poem whose intricate patterns of repetition create a beautiful, tapestry-like effect. Every rhyme in the poem, for example, involves the repetition of the same word; "cloths" is rhymed with "cloths," "light" with "light," and so on. To take another example, the jester in "The Cap and Bells" does capture the heart of the queen, though he has to die to do it.

In his early reviews and essays, Yeats was a forceful proponent and theorist of the Irish Literary Revival, even though, taken together, the early prose works suggest a changing struggle for definition as often as they demonstrate the articulation of a steady set of principles. The early poems proclaim Yeats's engagement with Ireland and Irish culture in various ways too. Some, like "The Ballad of Moll Magee" or "The Ballad of Father Gilligan," use a ballad measure to invoke the folk tradition and oral culture. Others link themselves to a specific landscape by using Irish place names. "The Ballad of Father O'Hart" refers to Coloony, Knocknarea, Knocknashee, Tiraragh, Ballinafad, and Inishmurray, all places in the Sligo area.[2] These references combine towns, natural features (a mountain, an island) and the folkloric associations of such places. The poem thus suggests a symbolic geography that maps relationships among the human, natural, and supernatural or mythic worlds, something the poems do in other ways as well. It also displays a geographical imagination that is profoundly local, rather than national, but that is harnessed in the service of a nationalist re-possession of territory. Other poems use figures out of Irish myth like Oisin, Fergus, and Cuchulain. The early Yeats's Ireland is alternately a homely, rural landscape populated by rustics, and an idealized, otherworldly place. In both cases Yeats associates it with childhood, and with extreme age. "Into the Twilight" claims that "Your mother Eire is always young" (*VP* 59), but this is the eternal youth of the ageless, ancient Ireland that Yeats consistently identified as the source of vital Irish culture and tradition.

While the twilit moods of the early Yeats might suggest impracticality and detachment from the material and public worlds, the early Yeats was also an active, assertive, even manipulative participant in the clubs and societies he founded and joined. He threw himself enthusiastically into the internal conflicts of organizations like the Theosophical Society and the Golden Dawn. He and his friends became noted for praising each other in their reviews; when he published his first novel, *John Sherman*, in 1891, he coached Katharine Tynan about her review: "you might perhaps, if you think it is so, say that Sherman is an Irish type. I have an ambition to be taken as an Irish novelist not as an English or cosmepolitan one chosing Ireland as a background [*sic*]."[3] The next year he fought a losing battle against Charles Gavan Duffy for control of a new series of books called the Library of Ireland. And he routinely orchestrated public controversies in the newspapers and magazines in order to promote his pet projects, such as the opening of the Irish Literary Theatre seven years later. While he often appeared to contemporaries as the impractical, otherworldly Celtic poet, in many respects Yeats was a shrewd judge of people, events, and opportunities.

By the early 1890s this combination had made him something of a public figure, and the years 1895–6 marked a new phase of his life and work. He published *Poems* (1895), a collected and revised edition of previously published poems, which would be a reliable seller for decades and create a steadier income than his previous work. He also moved out of his family house and got his own flat in London, began his first love affair (with Olivia Shakespear), and threw in his lot with a scandalous new literary magazine named *The Savoy* after the hotel where Oscar Wilde took his lovers.

But his life and work were about to incorporate still further new directions. He also met two people who were not part of his slightly racy milieu in 1896: Augusta Gregory and J. M. Synge. Yeats's interest in folklore and fairytales, and in their potential to help create an Irish national literature, predated his relationship with Gregory. He had already published *Fairy and Folk Tales of the Irish Peasantry* (1888), *Irish Fairy Tales* (1892), and *The Celtic Twilight* (1893), and, as James Pethica points out, his "early literary achievement rested significantly on his work as a folklorist" (p. 129). But his collaborations with Gregory enabled him to continue, and also to transform, this interest. Gregory would support him, and other members of his family, in various ways for decades. Her house in Galway became an important refuge for Yeats; he went there to recuperate from his exhausting involvement in various public controversies, and to find the peace conducive to writing poetry. In the summer of 1897 Yeats and Gregory formulated the idea of the Irish Literary Theatre, which opened in May of 1899 with the production of Yeats's *The Countess Cathleen* and Edward Martyn's *The Heather Field*. Synge came to symbolize for Yeats a kind of national art that drew energy and inspiration from the peasantry but that was also modern, innovative, even shocking. In the wake of the controversies that occurred when audiences protested against his plays *In the Shadow of the Glen* (1903) and *The Playboy of the Western World* (1907), Synge also came to symbolize the Irish public's unwillingness to accept such art.

In 1899 Yeats published *The Wind Among the Reeds*; it would be his last collection of poems for several years and marks the end of the early phase of his poetry. The elaborate notes Yeats originally appended to the volume dismayed some of his readers; his father wondered why he had written them.[4] The original title of "He wishes for the Cloths of Heaven" was "Aedh wishes for the Cloths of Heaven," and Yeats laboriously explained in a note that Aedh was a "principle of mind" and that he represented (in magical terms) "fire burning by itself" or (in other, but no less obscure terms) "the myrrh and frankincense that the imagination offers continually before all that it loves" (*VP* 803). Clearly, some new departure was called for. For the next few years after the turn of the century the Irish Literary Theatre, re-organized and re-named several times, would dominate his creative and business life. Yeats had a reputation in some quarters as a Fenian sympathizer, and he touted the new theatre in nationalist language, but many of the controversies about the theatre arose from his conflicts with various strands of nationalist opinion. His success as a playwright was uneven. *The Countess Cathleen* had been attacked for blasphemy and for its portrait of the Irish peasantry; on the other hand, the controversy over the play was good publicity for the opening of the theatre, which was generally regarded as a success. The 1901 production of *Diarmuid and Grania* (the product of a stormy collaboration between Yeats and George Moore) was received with hostility by nearly everyone, but the 1902 staging of *Cathleen ni Houlihan*, which Yeats and Gregory wrote together, was quite popular. Indeed, he would never achieve that kind of popularity with his plays again, and his commitment to an elite and symbolic – rather than popular and realistic – theatre would be strengthened in the coming years.

Meanwhile, although it took a back seat to his dramatic work for the moment, Yeats's poetry was also changing. In 1903 he published *In the Seven Woods*, a brief transitional volume, the first produced by Dun Emer (later Cuala) Press (run by his sisters). It indicated a new direction for his poetry, one that he described in these terms: "My work has got far more masculine. It has more salt in it."[5] The early themes and vocabularies are still apparent, but the difference between the volume's title poem and "The Lake Isle of Innisfree" (*VP* 117) is instructive. Both invoke the soothing sights and sounds of the natural world – birds, bees, vegetation – in order to escape from, or compensate for, the traumas of modern urban life. But while "The Lake Isle of Innisfree" simply mentions generic urban spaces – "the pavements gray" – "In the Seven Woods" (*VP* 198) refers to a more specific modern malaise: "Tara uprooted, and new commonness / Upon the throne." The poem's title, which refers to a part of the Gregory estate, and this reference to the coronation of Edward VII (following the death of Queen Victoria), indicate a more particular historical location for the speaker, as well as a new emphasis on class: the poem sets the vulgarity of modernity against the leisured refuge represented by Coole. Increasingly, over the course of the next several volumes, Yeats's critiques of the modern world targeted the middle classes. At the same time, the comfort the speaker of "In the Seven Woods" derives is all the more complete, because of (not despite) the fact that it is purely an exercise of will. "The Lake Isle of Innisfree" contains nothing as convincingly assertive as "I am contented, for I know that Quiet / Wanders laughing and eating her wild heart."

The year 1903 was also a watershed year in personal terms. Maud Gonne, who had repeatedly refused to marry Yeats, stunned him by embarking on an ill-considered, and immediately disastrous, marriage to Major John MacBride. Gonne turned to Yeats in a time of trouble, and he responded, giving her help and advice during a messy public scandal and separation. This was a pattern that would be repeated throughout their long friendship. On the other hand, his first American lecture tour, in the winter of 1903–4, was a great success. It brought him excellent publicity, a good sum of money, new skills as an orator, and new confidence in himself. He had lunch with President Roosevelt, and acquired an imposing fur coat. These personal developments contributed to a deliberate turn away from many of his earlier works and attitudes, as he reached for new modes that he formulated in terms of hardness, masculinity, and salt.

Accordingly, some poems of this period translate Yeats's new salty assertiveness into a productive ambiguity about some of his most cherished convictions or stances. "The Folly of Being Comforted," which first appeared in 1902, praises, but also gently satirizes, the ideal of an inexhaustible passion. In response to the well-meaning friend who suggests that the ageing of the beloved's body will decrease the speaker's tormented desire for her, the speaker's heart claims his position as the eternal lover for whom she will always be beautiful: "Heart cries, 'No, / I have not a crumb of comfort, not a grain.'" But the poem's closing lines have a double meaning: "O heart! O heart! if she'd but turn her head, / You'd know the folly of being comforted" (*VP* 200). On the one hand, this means that if she turned her head the speaker's passion would be ignited, as ever, and he would realize that the idea of drawing comfort from her declining physical beauty was folly. On the other hand, to "know the folly of being comforted" also means to "know" comfort in the sense of being comforted, even though it is folly – and, indeed, if she turned her head, he would see her ageing face. "Adam's Curse" (*VP* 204–6) strikes a similar pose about Yeats's romantic ideals, by holding to the value of "the old high way of love" while at the same time suggesting that this way has become exhausted, and now seems "an idle trade enough," the word "trade" implying disturbing links between that ideal and the fallen, materialistic world Yeats increasingly deplored.

Dimness and twilight, once attractive states connected with reverie and the supernatural, were now to be avoided. In the volumes that followed *In the Seven Woods*, Yeats embraces "reality," exposure, and directness, expressing his determination to "wither into the truth" ("The Coming of Wisdom with Time"; *VP* 261), praising "the lidless eye that loves the sun" ("Upon a House shaken by the Land Agitation"; *VP* 264), and declaring that he would give up his earlier preoccupation with ornament and mythology because "there's more enterprise / In walking naked" ("A Coat"; *VP* 320). He brought his poetic language closer to ordinary speech in diction and syntax, and embraced more irregular rhythms and rhymes. Failure and struggle, both personal and political, are confronted directly and defiantly, and Yeats's poems continued to locate him increasingly in a contemporary, rather than a mythic, Ireland. *Responsibilities* (1914) opens with the speaker's apology to his ancestors that he has "nothing but a book" to prove his, and his family's, "blood" ("Pardon, Old fathers"; *VP* 269–70), and closes with the bleak statement that "all my priceless things / Are but a post the passing dogs defile" ("While I, from that reed-throated whisperer"; *VP* 320–1). In between, Yeats meditates on public controversies, such as the Dublin Corporation's refusal to build an art gallery to house the pictures Hugh Lane proposed to donate, and private crises, such as his relationship with Gonne.

At the same time, after 1903 Yeats began to construct an increasingly elaborate mythology of class, in which he formulated his disenchantment with the modern world through ideas of middle-class corruption. The controversies over Synge's plays hardened his opinions about the capacity of popular audiences for appreciating good art, and his various struggles over the theatre made him particularly hostile to artists and actors he perceived as pandering to popular tastes or propaganda. In "The Fascination of What's Difficult" the frustrations of running the theatre (now re-named the Abbey), in which he was deeply involved, appear as "the day's war with every knave and dolt, / Theatre business, management of men" (*VP* 260). "These are the Clouds" laments that "all things at one common level lie" (*VP* 265), and "At Galway Races" mourns for a time "Before the merchant and the clerk / Breathed on the world with timid breath" (*VP* 266). Yeats reserved a special scorn and anger for middle-class Irish Catholics: "September 1913" paints a memorably unpleasant picture of them as grasping, timid materialists, who "fumble in a greasy till / And add the half pence to the pence / And prayer to shivering prayer" now that "Romantic Ireland's dead and gone" (*VP* 289).

Against the corruption of modern Ireland this mythology of class ranges a number of forces and examples. They are all firmly anti-utilitarian and anti-materialistic, a quality encapsulated by the dictum "'Only the wasteful virtues earn the sun'" (*VP* 270), and they share a commitment to the value of art, passion, honor, and lofty ideals. Some are actual aristocrats, like the "honour bred" (*VP* 291) Gregory and the noble patrons of the arts during the Italian Renaissance that Yeats invokes in "To a Wealthy Man . . ." Others belong to a kind of natural aristocracy, like the nationalist heroes of "September 1913" or Maud Gonne. If Yeats spent a good deal of time dividing the world into the corrupt and the noble during these years, he also wrote a number of poems in which a speaker confronts corruption within himself: the corruption of bitterness, anger, and scorn. "Paudeen" begins with an attack on middle-class Catholics, but the poem ends with the speaker's counter-assertion that "on the lonely height where all are in God's eye, / There cannot be, confusion of our sound forgot, / A single soul that lacks a sweet crystalline cry" (*VP* 291). And the closing poem of *Responsibilities* is able to "forgive" the circumstances that make the speaker and his ideals the "notorious" (*VP* 321) targets of public scorn.

These changes in Yeats's work were part of the development of literary Modernism. While Yeats often thought of himself as one of the "last romantics" (*VP* 491), the ways in which he remade his poetics during his middle and late periods gave him much in common with Modernism. In 1909 he met the younger poet Ezra Pound, who would become an important Modernist figure. They forged a lasting friendship and influenced one another's work, though Pound's influence on Yeats should not be overstated. As we have seen, Yeats had already begun to "modernize" his work. They spent three winters together sharing a cottage near Oxford from 1913 to 1915, Pound acting as Yeats's secretary. Yeats's growing emphasis on plain speech and harsh reality did not mean that he was simplifying the meaning of his poems. Rather, like many Modernists, he was using increasingly spare language to explore ever more complex and ambiguous states of mind. "The Cold Heaven," for example, begins with a simple, abrupt, declarative: "Suddenly I saw . . ." But, as is characteristic of the middle and late Yeats, the first eight and a half lines of the poem form a single, complex sentence. (Beginning readers of Yeats sometimes forget that most of his poems are written in sentences, and, helpfully, can be parsed like sentences.) The poem's opening exists in considerable tension with the ambiguities, even the "confusion" (a word the poem itself uses at one point), suggested by the poem's title and notoriously difficult lines such as: "And I took all the blame out of all sense and reason,

/ Until I cried and trembled and rocked to and fro, / Riddled with light" (*VP* 316). The symbols of this period were, like all his symbols, used in various ways to mean various things. While the sun often represented the harsh but salutary glare of truth, "Lines Written in Dejection" laments the loss of an imaginative world populated by mythical creatures: "wild witches," "holy centaurs," and the "heroic mother moon." In their place, the speaker has nothing but the sun, which he describes as "embittered" and "timid" (*VP* 343–4).

Embracing directness and reality also did not mean giving up his interest in the occult; on the contrary, Yeats pursued his interests in the supernatural energetically during these years. Hugh Lane died when the *Lusitania* was sunk in 1915 and a dispute erupted, one Yeats was to be involved in for years, about whether he had really meant to leave his modern art collection to Dublin or London. Besides his more practical efforts to resolve the issue in Dublin's favor, Yeats also got in touch with a medium he had been consulting for years, Elizabeth Radcliff, in the hope that the dead Lane might make contact through automatic writing (which he did not). Apart from the Lane controversy, Yeats was not particularly engaged in the events of the First World War. Before the War, the winter of 1913–14 brought another profitable American lecture tour. He spent his summers at Coole, and he and Pound were isolated from wartime London (at least to some extent) at Stone Cottage the next winter. He began writing his autobiography, looking back over his life as if his major achievements were behind him. They were not; a series of significant upheavals in his life, in the world around him, and in his work, were on the way.

Events in Ireland interested him more. Yeats was still involved in the Abbey Theatre, which had become an important Dublin institution. His earlier sympathy for the physical force republicanism of Fenianism had moderated into support for constitutional nationalism and, like many other observers, he had been anticipating Home Rule for several years. The Easter Rising of 1916, in which a small force of Irish nationalists declared an Irish republic and took over some Dublin buildings for nearly a week before being subdued by the British, came as a shock to Yeats, and he initially thought it was a foolish and destructive act by the rebels. Then, as the British government imposed harsh martial law and began to execute the rebels, public opinion began to shift. Yeats became increasingly sympathetic to the rebels and increasingly critical of the British government. He returned to Ireland in May and saw the devastation of the city center. The contempt of "September 1913" seemed to require some modification now. He began writing "Easter 1916," his deeply complex and ambivalent response to the Rising, though he would not publish the poem until 1920.

His personal life was also in turmoil. In the summer of 1916 he went to France, to propose marriage to Maud Gonne one last time (her husband John MacBride was one of the executed rebel leaders). Gonne refused him, and he turned his attention to her twenty-two-year-old daughter Iseult, to whom he proposed the next summer. She also refused him, after some vacillation. Almost immediately, in a decisive new departure, Yeats proposed to Georgie Hyde Lees (also known as George), whom he had known for several years, and she accepted him. When they were married in October of 1917, he was 52; she was 24. The marriage was hastily arranged, and Yeats's ambivalence and continuing preoccupation with Iseult were palpable. It was not an auspicious start, and the first week of the marriage was a difficult one. Then George initiated a decisive new departure of her own, one that was to change their lives. She told Yeats that she felt something was to be written through her, and produced the first of the "automatic writing" that would preoccupy the Yeatses for years to come, and out of which would grow the "System" of *A Vision*. George shared Yeats's occult interests; as Roy Foster has observed, "effectively, the 'automatic script' represents her own creative work,"[6] and the System itself is perhaps best thought of as a collaboration between the Yeatses.

Marriage brought new stability to Yeats's life, as well as new occult excitement. He paid tribute to this combination in "Solomon to Sheba" and "Solomon and the Witch," poems that explore fulfilled rather than frustrated desire, and link sexual satisfaction to knowledge or revelation. He also continued to write poems about both Gonne and Iseult; indeed, they are dominant figures in *The Wild Swans at Coole*, the expanded version of which appeared in 1919. Several occult poems in that volume arose from Yeats's enthusiasm over George's automatic writing and the emerging System, such as "The Phases of the Moon" and "The Double Vision of Michael Robartes." Yeats placed the latter poem at the end of the volume, perhaps suggesting that his destructive preoccupation with unattainable women had given way to an embrace of the natural and supernatural rewards of marriage. The speaker's vision makes him feel "As though I had been undone / By Homer's Paragon," suggesting Gonne, who Yeats associated with Helen of Troy, but the poem's close also implies an association between that visionary knowledge and the tranquillity his wife brought. His frenzy spent, the speaker recounts: "And after that [I] arranged it in a song / Seeing that I, ignorant for so long, / Had been rewarded thus / In Cormac's ruined house" (*VP* 384).

Personal and political events were also conspiring to root Yeats more firmly in Ireland. When he and George were married, Yeats had already bought an old Norman tower in County Galway. He Gaelicized its name to Thoor

Ballylee, and was fixing it up to make it habitable; the Yeatses would spend the summers there for about a decade, beginning in 1919. Meanwhile, political events in Ireland were increasingly turbulent. Popular reaction in Ireland to the government's harsh response to the Rising had paved the way to Sinn Fein electoral victories in 1918, and guerilla activity there was increasing. Yeats wrote "The Second Coming" (*VP* 401–2) and "A Prayer for my Daughter" (*VP* 403–6) during the unsettled months of 1919. Both express fears about a world apparently descending into chaos; like "Easter 1916," both are also meditations on various kinds of transition: historical, political, and personal. "A Prayer" celebrates the personal peace and stability that Yeats had found in marriage and fatherhood. The poem praises George's "glad kindness" and suggests that, in order to be happy, their baby Anne should become as much like George as possible, an assertion that tells us much more about Yeats's own happiness during this period than about his wife's. The speaker also identifies various threats to this tranquillity, including uncooperative women like Gonne and Yeats's own desires for them. "The Second Coming" is "A Prayer"'s companion poem in many respects. It places contemporary political turbulence in the context of the historical cycles of the System, but it also reaches over to resonate with the personal concerns of "A Prayer," which follows it in *Michael Robartes and the Dancer* (1921). The values represented by Anne – custom, ceremony, innocence – look even more fragile and endangered next to "The Second Coming"'s assurance that "The ceremony of innocence is drowned." And the horror of the rough beast's "rocking cradle" is magnified by its link to the baby's "cradle-hood and coverlid." That one poem can illuminate or comment on another poem, and that the poet arranged his volumes carefully with this in mind, are important principles for readers of Yeats.

"The Second Coming" ends with a question, a move that helps define the poetic style of the mature Yeats: "And what rough beast, its hour come round at last, / Slouches towards Bethlehem to be born?" (*VP* 402). That Yeatsian question is urgently literal but unanswerable. The question that ends "Leda and the Swan" is also literal and unanswerable, with the added difficulty of being ambiguous: "Did she put on his knowledge with his power / Before the indifferent beak could let her drop?" (*VP* 441). Is the speaker suggesting that Leda has already put on Zeus' power, or might she have neither knowledge nor power? And does "put on" mean "take on" or "simulate"? Other Yeatsian questions are rhetorical, such as "A Prayer"'s "How but in custom and in ceremony / Are innocence and beauty born?" (*VP* 406) or the series of questions that organizes "Sixteen Dead Men," which Yeats wrote after the executions of the rebel leaders. A few are literal and have obvious answers, like "The Tower"'s query "Does the imagination dwell the most /

Upon a woman won or woman lost?" (*VP* 413) – clearly, for Yeats, it was the latter. The second section of "The Tower" is organized around the principle of questioning. The speaker calls up "Images and memories / . . . For I would ask a question of them all" (*VP* 410).

Events in Ireland continued to generate more confusion and questions than answers. The Yeatses were dividing their time between England and Ireland, and the winter of 1919–20 brought another American lecture tour. But Yeats followed events in Ireland closely. As atrocities and reprisals on both sides increased, Yeats wrote "Reprisals," in which he addressed the ghost of Gregory's son Robert. Robert had been killed fighting for the British in World War I, and the poem calls for a reassessment of that cause in light of British violence in Ireland: "certain second thoughts have come / Upon the cause you served, that we / Imagined such a fine affair." It ends by numbering Robert among the "cheated dead" (*VP* 791). Yeats did not publish the poem because Gregory, not surprisingly upset by it, asked him not to. But the theme of being forced to question previously firm positions and convictions recurs in his poetry of this period. The new view the speaker reaches varies, however. For example, "The Fisherman" confronts the difference between "What I had hoped 'twould be / To write for my own race / And the reality" (*VP* 347), and rejects uncooperative real Dublin audiences in favor of the imaginary fisherman. In contrast, in "The People" the speaker lodges the same complaint about "The daily spite of this unmannerly town" (*VP* 352) but the poem invokes the voice of Maud Gonne to reprove him for it.

The great meditative poems of Yeats's middle period, such as "Meditations in Time of Civil War," and "Nineteen Hundred and Nineteen," often have narrative structures in which a speaker moves through a series of possible ideas or stances, enacting an often painful search for ways to make sense of, and come to terms with, contemporary events. He finished the latter poem in 1921, and originally titled it "Thoughts upon the Present State of the World," but later retitled it, probably for the numerological appeal of 1919. The poem utters laments for more humane, cultured, and promising times, some in the distant past, others in the more immediate past "seven years ago" when people "talked of honour and of truth" (*VP* 431), a reference to the optimism of 1912 (or 1914, depending on whether we subtract from 1919 or 1921), when Home Rule was widely expected and World War I had not yet begun. The speaker's anger against the forces of corruption and violence, for example the "drunken soldiery" (*VP* 429) of the British state, gives way to lacerating self-accusations, only to return later. His repeated efforts to cultivate the detachment of the artist or the mockery of the observer who, aware of the historical cycles of the System, understands the futility of human endeavor, are countered by calls for sincere engagement: "Mock mockers after that / That would not lift a hand maybe / To help good, wise or great" (*VP* 432). "Meditations in Time of Civil War" illustrates a similar determination to confront, without minimizing, the pain and uncertainty generated by turbulent and traumatic historical events.

With the establishment of the Irish Free State in January of 1922, and the beginning of the Civil War that spring, Yeats acquired a new public role in Ireland. He was appointed to the Irish Senate, and accepted with alacrity. He was eager to undertake public service and help shape the new Ireland, and took the Senate post at some personal risk; a number of senators' houses were burned during the Civil War. This phase of his life involved an imposing house on Merrion Square in Dublin, and the honor and financial stability (at least for a time) the Nobel Prize for Literature brought in 1923. The Abbey Theatre was doing well, and Yeats negotiated with the government to secure future funding. He began to advocate conservative government and the need to maintain public order; some of the political preoccupations of his late life began to emerge. Yeats took his Senate work seriously and thought that the senators were an elite group who could offer the new Ireland the leadership it needed. He continued to develop his myth of class; increasingly, he invoked the Protestant Ascendancy of the eighteenth century as a model for himself and the Senate. And he was still writing, though it would be 1928 before he would publish his next book of poems, *The Tower*.

But if he had a busy public life in the 1920s, he also became increasingly estranged from public opinion in Ireland. He protested government initiatives, undertaken in the years following the Civil War, to impose censorship and ban divorce. He became increasingly embattled and deliberately combative, and enjoyed outraging Dublin opinion; he did so with the publication of "Leda and the Swan." He also lent his support to another scandalous new journal, *To-morrow*, and was regularly attacked in the Catholic press for his lack of religious orthodoxy and his aristocratic (or "new Ascendancy") leanings. His famous speech to the Senate on divorce invoked the Protestant Ascendancy in a manner calculated to offend nearly everyone. Other forms of estrangement were less enjoyable. He published the first version of *A Vision* in 1925; it got a lukewarm reception from most readers. And his marriage had settled into a more domestic and predictable pattern; George's role as medium had faded, and with it much of the excitement of their marriage.

The end of Yeats's six-year Senate term marks the beginning of another phase in his life and works. He suffered his first serious illness in 1927, and began to spend winters abroad for his health. He determined to avoid public activities that took him away from his writing. He and George gave up spending the summers at Thoor Ballylee; 1928, the year he published *The Tower*, was also the year in which they stopped going to the actual tower. But he exploited the tower's symbolic potential with enormous skill and success. Both ruin and living fortification, in the poetry Yeats's tower is a symbol of elevation and isolation, genuine learning and false wisdom, strength and weakness. It is a vantage point from which the Yeats of this period contemplates his favorite themes, such as ageing, memory, mortality, and continuity. These themes operate on both public and private registers. In the beginning of "The Tower" the tower is a place of decay, as the speaker confronts old age, and considers giving up poetry for philosophy: "It seems that I must bid the Muse go pack" (*VP* 409). By the end of the poem, however, the tower has become a symbol for the speaker's self-assertion, his attempt to fix his legacy, his willful rejection of philosophy in favor of poetry, and his determination to come to terms with mortality. Thus the tower stands for both the "wreck of body" and the speaker's attempt to overcome that wreck through acts of will and imagination. It is, to borrow a phrase from "My House," one of his "Befitting emblems of adversity" (*VP* 420).

Yeats's next major volume, *The Winding Stair and Other Poems* (1933), also capitalizes on the symbolic potential of the tower, often, as its title suggests, examining the tower from the convoluted spaces within it. "A Dialogue of Self and Soul," for example, takes up a question similar to the one that began "The Tower": should the ageing poet give up anger, desire, and imagination – the things out of which he makes poetry – and embrace philosophical or religious states of mind as more fitting? The winding stair represents the difficult ascent towards those states of mind, the possibility of leaving the messy realities of human existence behind. The Soul asks the Self, "Why should the imagination of a man / Long past his prime remember things that are / Emblematical of love and war?" (*VP* 477). But the Self counters this argument: "A living man is blind and drinks his drop. / What matter if the ditches are impure?" (*VP* 478). By going down into the ditch, rather than up into the tower, the Self achieves a kind of blessedness and peace different from the one offered by the Soul. "Blood and the Moon" also offers a tower that is "Half dead at the top," this time to note the corruption of modern times. Yeats's towers are to be admired and aspired to, but there is always some qualifying factor that keeps them from being symbols of triumph or achievement. Repeatedly the Yeats of this period re-commits himself to lust, rage, and imagination, and begins the process of wanting to shed them all over again. At the same time, Yeats was also preoccupied with memory; he wrote several powerful elegies for dead friends during these years, such as "In Memory of Eva Gore-Booth and Con Markiewicz." Yeats also wrote a number of poems with elegiac sensibilities, poems that survey the ghosts of the past. These include "Among School Children," "All Souls' Night," "Coole Park and Ballylee, 1931," and "Coole Park, 1929."

Another kind of voice is apparent in Yeats's work of this period as well, particularly in the early 1930s, which were a time of great poetic productivity for him, particularly at Coole. This is the voice of short lyrics, often preoccupied with romantic and sexual themes. The Crazy Jane poems are the best known examples, but we should include sequences like "A Man Young and Old" and "A Woman Young and Old," poems about Tom the Lunatic, and other lyrics as well. There are a number of reasons why this mode is important to the middle and late Yeats. During the 1920s, he embraced erotic frankness, in part as a combative response to the social and sexual conservatism of the Irish government. It is no accident that Crazy Jane argues with a Bishop, or that, rather than rejecting religion, she offers an alternative metaphysics in which sexual and spiritual knowledge are linked. And this new departure has plenty of links to Yeats's earlier preoccupations. The sexually explicit Yeats of this period is interested in the delights of sheer physicality, but he is even more interested in finding ways to connect those delights with philosophical questions or revelations. Crazy Jane's claim that "Love has pitched his mansion in / The place of excrement; / For nothing can be sole or whole / That has not been rent" (*VP* 513) insists on the lowly physicalities of human desire. But it also re-works the central paradox of some of the Rose poems: the intersection of an abstract beauty or desire with the concrete particularities of the world.

This period of productivity did not survive the shock of Gregory's death in 1932, and for a time he feared that his creative life was coming to an end. At a time when, on a biographical level, increasing age and ill health meant that Yeats really might have written about "that hour of gentleness / When the poor tired child, Passion, falls asleep" (*VP* 80) or relinquished his angry and bitter commentaries on public events in favor of more restful topics, he refused to do anything of the kind. His interest in the Irish eighteenth century, in authoritarian forms of government, and the violent or degenerative historical changes he contemplated through contemporary events and the historical cycles of *A Vision* continued. In 1933–4 he had a brief period of enthusiasm for the Irish fascist Blueshirts. This was fading by the time he wrote some poems as "marching songs" for them, and he was still looking for a way to revive his creativity. As always, he turned to sexual desire, this time in a more clinical sense than usual; he underwent a vasectomy, which was then thought to increase sexual power. And he began a series of sexual adventures with various women.

Whatever combination of physical and psychological factors was responsible, the operation gave him an enormous creative boost. The late phase of Yeats's work, in the years leading up to his death in 1939, is marked by extraordinary productivity, extraordinary achievement, and some poems or moments that often make readers uncomfortable. Stylistic developments included increasingly sophisticated use of the refrain as a haunting commentary or counterpoint for a number of poems, ranging from the masterful "Long-legged Fly" to the self-interrogation of "Are You Content?" and "What Then?" to ballads and other modes as well. And his daring in matters of diction, rhyme, and rhythm continued to increase too. "News for the Delphic Oracle" pokes fun at an earlier Yeats poem, "The Delphic Oracle upon Plotinus," in part by replacing the "stately" diction of that poem, with its regular rhyme scheme and its reference to "the choir of Love" (*VP* 531), with a more unseemly vocabulary and more irregular formal features. The "choir of love" (*VP* 611) dissolves into this scene: "Foul goat-head, brutal arm appear, / Belly, shoulder, bum, / Flash fishlike; nymphs and satyrs / Copulate in the foam" (*VP* 612). Yeats returned to his central themes and modes while at the same time re-making himself, questioning himself, again.

He began editing *The Oxford Book of Modern Verse*; some of his choices would make it controversial, and it was not well reviewed. The inflammatory pamphlet "On the Boiler," which Yeats wrote partly in an effort to shore up the shaky finances of Cuala Press, expressed some disturbing opinions about violence, democracy, and eugenics. *Last Poems* contains "The Gyres," in which the speaker's determination to confront the traumas of historical change without despair takes him into the territory of the willfully inhumane. The poem's elegiac impulses – "A greater, a more gracious time has gone" – are overborne by a more violent and chaotic vision of loss – "Irrational streams of blood are staining earth" – and by the injunction to "Rejoice" rather than to mourn. Philosophically, there may be something to be said for a speaker who forces himself to accept the inevitable, even when it appears in its most horrific form, and to salvage something positive or powerful out of it. But this stance comes at a high price, and lines like "What matter though numb nightmare ride on top, / And blood and mire the sensitive body stain?" (*VP* 564) may continue to disturb us.

But in *Last Poems* as a whole Yeats is as self-aware as ever, and as careful to arrange his poems so that they comment upon one another. The last poem he wrote before his death, "The Black Tower," returns to his favorite symbol, giving it yet another twist. The black tower is guarded by "oath-bound men" (*VP* 635) who are both living and dead; their loyalty to the tower may be admirable or quite misguided. One of Yeats's last creative acts was to re-arrange the contents list for *Last Poems* so that "Under Ben Bulben," with its hectoring, assertive tone and it triumphalist ambitions to enable the poet to determine his own legacy, opens the volume (though this order is not reproduced in the *Variorum Poems*). The rest of the volume tears down the certainties proposed by "Under Ben Bulben," and brings the speaker to an acknowledgement that he cannot make final sense of his life, control his own death, or determine how he will be remembered. "The Man and the Echo" offers a counterpoint to "Under Ben Bulben," and returns to the Yeatsian mode of questioning, only to conclude that no firm conclusions about death or the afterlife are possible: "What do we know but that we face / One another in this place?" (*VP* 633). The brief lyric "Politics," which Yeats placed last in the volume, makes an appropriate final poem, with its closing insistence on the primacy of desire, the "wild, wicked old man," and his links to the younger Yeats: "But O that I were young again / And held her in my arms!" (*VP* 631).

NOTES

1. The most comprehensive treatment of Yeats's love poetry is Elizabeth Butler Cullingford's *Gender and History in Yeats's Love Poetry* (Cambridge: Cambridge University Press, 1993).
2. Yeats did not always spell these names as they are spelled on Irish maps today, so, while some identifications are easy, others remain somewhat more speculative. For example, A. Norman Jeffares surmises that "Tiraragh may be 'Teeraree (*Tír a ríg*), a townland in the parish of Kilmorgan, Co. Sligo'" (*A Commentary on the Collected Poems of W. B. Yeats* [Stanford: Stanford University Press, 1968], p. 17).
3. Quoted in R. F. Foster, *W. B. Yeats: A Life I: The Apprentice Mage 1865–1914* (Oxford and New York: Oxford University Press, 1997), p. 111.
4. *Ibid.*, p. 217.
5. *Ibid.*, p. 287.
6. R. F. Foster, *W. B. Yeats: A Life II: The Arch-Poet 1915–1939* (Oxford and New York: Oxford University Press, 2003), p. 107.

2

GEORGE BORNSTEIN

Yeats and Romanticism

W. B. Yeats summoned the term "romantic" in his poetry for two of his most famous proclamations. Both were characteristically memorial, one invoking his political mentor John O'Leary against the background of the Dublin strike and lockout of 1913, and the other honoring his literary patron and collaborator Lady Gregory shortly after her estate at Coole Park had been sold to the government in 1927. The first came in the refrain of the poem that we now know as "September 1913": "Romantic Ireland's dead and gone, / It's with O'Leary in the grave" (*VP* 289).

The second inaugurated the last stanza of "Coole Park and Ballylee, 1931":

> We were the last romantics – chose for theme
> Traditional sanctity and loveliness;
> Whatever's written in what poets name
> The book of the people; whatever most can bless
> The mind of man or elevate a rhyme.
>
> (*VP* 491–2)

The question arises, what do these two uses of the term – one political and one literary – have to do with each other? A lifelong if sometimes ambivalent Romantic, Yeats saw literature and politics as intertwined, even when he opposed the reduction of literature to mere opinion. For him "Romantic Ireland" meant that large-minded attitude beyond the mere calculation of economic or political advantage that he saw in the present, an attitude for him incarnated in his sometime Fenian mentor John O'Leary. It was O'Leary who taught Yeats that "there is no fine nationality without literature, and ... the converse also, that there is no fine literature without nationality" (*LNI* 12). If O'Leary turned Yeats to Ireland, Lady Gregory turned him to the Irish folk in particular. "Whatever's written in what poets name / The book of the people" turned out to mean on the one hand both the large body of Irish mythic tales (such as those of Cuchulain) still widely recited in Irish in the countryside of Yeats's day and on the other hand the body of folklore including stories of fairies, social resistance, and striking personalities. Uniting Yeats's conception of both the political and the literary was the notion of imagination, described in "Coole Park and Ballylee, 1931" as "whatever most can bless / The mind of man or elevate a rhyme." Whatever Yeats's shifting cultural and political allegiances, his appropriation of the Romantic idea of imagination lay behind his disparate activities, enabling him to aim at what in *A Vision* he called simplification through intensity rather than dispersal.

Yeats's Romantic avowals abound in his prose even more than in his poetry. "I was a romantic in all," he wrote retrospectively on the first page of the first draft of his autobiography (*Mem* 19). Later in the draft, he elaborated his meaning in a context characteristically mingling literature and politics. After confessing "a blind anger against Unionist Ireland" partly for its deprecation of Irish literature, whether written in Irish or in English, Yeats turned to his own early strategic difficulties in committees and speeches. "I had, a romantic in all, a cult of passion," he declared (*Mem* 84). That cult of passion would survive many vicissitudes of Yeats's adult life: the loss of Maud Gonne, the dissolution of his idealistic nationalist hopes under the stress of the downfall of Parnell, the riots over *The Playboy of the Western World*, the Dublin strike and lockout of 1913, the controversy over a municipal gallery for the Lane pictures, and the brutality of the Civil War. It marked one of the many ways in which John O'Leary and Lady Gregory both earned their status as last Romantics.

As must already be obvious, Yeats's ideas on Romanticism call into question current notions of periodicity. On the one hand, Yeats tended to think of literary Romanticism in terms of "the Big Six" figures we identify today – Blake, Wordsworth, Coleridge, Byron, Shelley, and Keats (like most readers of the late nineteenth and early twentieth centuries, he knew little of recently rediscovered female Romantics like Joanna Baillie, Anna Barbauld, or Felicia Hemans). On the other hand, he saw Romanticism as spiraling out from there to include a poetic tradition from Dante and Spenser through Milton and the Big Six and on up to the present. In that sense Romanticism denoted not a specific historical epoch but rather a set of qualities that began much earlier, reached one peak of development in the Romantic period proper, and remained available to later artists like himself. Yeats regularly maintained the importance of Romanticism to his own epoch. For instance, he ringingly opened his 1890 review of an arts and crafts exhibition at William Morris's by declaring that "The movement most characteristic of the literature and art and to some small extent of the thoughts, too, of our century has been romanticism" (*LNI* 108).

That view continued into the twentieth century, where Yeats liked to pose as last Romantic even while promoting a Romantic Modernism in poems, in prose, and in his controversial edition of *The Oxford Book of Modern Verse*. In that way he resembled other Modernists like Wallace Stevens or Dylan Thomas, both of whom defined themselves against the anti-Romantic views of, say, T. S. Eliot or Ezra Pound. But being one of a seemingly endless succession of last Romantics did not mean simple repetition or imitation. On the contrary, the Romantic impulse led to an almost Poundian urge to "make it new." Wallace Stevens expounded his own definition of a "new romantic" in a letter glossing his poem "Sailing After Lunch." "When people speak of the romantic, they do so in what the French commonly call a *pejorative* sense," wrote Stevens. "But poetry is essentially romantic, only the romantic of poetry must be something constantly new and, therefore, just the opposite of what is spoken of as the romantic. Without this new romantic, one gets nowhere."[1]

Yeats would have joined Stevens in that endorsement, with the added proviso that not only Romanticism but even one's own Romanticism would change over time. In probing Yeats's relation to Romanticism, we must always ask *when* we mean; the multiple and shifting nature of those relationships demands a diachronic rather than synchronic mapping. At first Yeats sought to be a *fin de siècle* reincarnation of the original Romantics: he wore a shirt like Shelley's, and tied his tie in the manner of Byron. His poems, too, reflected their strategies and values. Isolated, impassioned Byronic heroes flicker through the plays and poems of the 1880s and 1890s, and so does a vocabulary derived neither from the contemporary age nor from Irish literature but rather from the English poets at the beginning of the century. As this early phase wore on, Yeats's re-working of Romanticism deepened. He came to value the Intellectual Beauty extolled by Shelley and to try to suggest it in his own Rose poems. Shelley's articulation of his imaginative creed in the great essay "A Defence of Poetry" gave Yeats sanction for his own views in the controversies from Parnell to the *Playboy* riots. He himself badly needed a rationale for a literature that could rise above partisan politics and the rancors of "opinion," almost always a negative word for Yeats. Shelley had written not only "A Defence of Poetry" but virtually a defense of Yeats's poetry, finding that address to the imagination always served both country and humanity better than mere advancement of correct opinion. And from Blake in this early period Yeats took more ideas about imagination, including its capacity to oppose nature. He found too in Blake a unified conception of the poetic book as embracing not only the words of the text but also the pattern of arrangement of the poems, the illustrations that accompanied them, and the entire physical layout of a volume.

Exploring Yeats's early relation to his two favorite Romantics, Shelley and Blake, lights up both Yeats's early Romanticism of the 1880s and 1890s and the magnitude of his swerve away from it during the first two decades of the twentieth century.[2] He thought that Shelley had influenced his life as well as his art the more profoundly of the two. Shelley "had shared our curiosities, our political problems, our conviction that, despite all experience to the contrary, love is enough; and unlike Blake, isolated by an arbitrary symbolism, he seemed to sum up all that was metaphysical in English poetry," he decided. "When in middle life I looked back I found that he and not Blake, whom I had studied more and with more approval, had shaped my life" (*E&I* 424). Shelley's influence helped shape Yeats's attraction to a large-minded politics, to an idealized love for Maud Gonne, and to the pursuit of esoteric wisdom.

All three areas – politics, love, and esoterica – informed Yeats's first and most substantial essay on his precursor, "The Philosophy of Shelley's Poetry" (1900). There Yeats explored Shelley's attraction to the Platonic notion of Intellectual Beauty as a master key to his philosophy, finding that it underlay his attitudes toward both literature and life. Shelley's lovers thus emerge as lovers of ideal beauty, his revolutionaries as lovers of an ideal social order, and his students in their towers as devotees of an ideal esoteric wisdom. He admired particularly Shelley's triad of "Alastor" (as Yeats mistakenly called the anonymous hero of the quest romance *Alastor*), Athanase, and Ahasuerus, all of whom sought esoteric lore as Yeats would himself. Indeed, their towers partly lay behind his own eventual choice of a tower as a summer home. The essay also paid attention to problems of presenting such ideas in vivid verse. Yeats tracked particularly Shelley's use of recurrent patterns of symbolism, such as rivers, towers, sun, moon, and above all the evening star. Not surprisingly, he evolved an analogous web of images in his own poetry, including tree, mask, sun, moon, and especially tower.

A good place to see Shelley's influence on Yeats's early poetry is the work now grouped under the rubric "The Rose" in the collected volumes. In his own notes to that section, Yeats repeatedly identified the Rose as his version of Intellectual Beauty and compared and contrasted it to that of Shelley, noting carefully that "the quality symbolized as The Rose differs from the Intellectual Beauty of Shelley and of Spenser in that I have imagined it as suffering with man and not as something pursued and seen from afar" (*VP* 842). Otherwise, the Rose mirrored Shelley's various incarnations of Intellectual Beauty just as its deployment from poem to poem mirrored Shelley's own recurrent imagery. Yeats worried particularly over how he could be a devotee of the Rose and of Irish nationalism at the same time. That concern surfaces notably in the opening and closing poems of *The Rose*. In the first one, "To the Rose upon the Rood of Time," the list in which the speaker seeks eternal beauty includes not only the nature around him but also explicitly

Irish legends such as those of Fergus and Cuchulain. In the last, "To Ireland in the Coming Times," the poet seeks to "accounted be / True brother of a company / That sang, to sweeten Ireland's wrong" and explicitly asks to "be counted one / With Davis, Mangan, Ferguson" (*VP* 137–8). He argues about Intellectual Beauty that "When Time began to rant and rage / The measure of her flying feet / Made Ireland's heart begin to beat" (*VP* 138) and therefore that in singing Intellectual Beauty he is being profoundly Irish as a poet. The high-minded sentiment might have surprised his hard-up neighbors in Dublin, let alone those who surrounded him when he was in England. And Yeats's conjunction of art and nationalist politics could come across with unintended humor. His early friend the writer Katharine Tynan recalled in her autobiography:

> I remember one very wet night, after we had been to a meeting of the Protestant Home Rule Association, when we waited in Westmoreland Street for a tram; I in my smart clothes, my high-heeled French shoes, standing in a pool of water; the wind driving the rain as it does only in a seabound city; Willie holding the umbrella at an acute and absent-minded angle which could shelter nobody, pouring the while into my ears [Shelley's poem] *The Sensitive Plant*. It was a moment to try a woman's temper, and mine did not stand the trial well.[3]

Katharine Tynan's water-soaked French shoes may serve as apt emblem of the exasperation that not only Yeats's friends but also Yeats himself felt as they looked back on his stance toward both English Romanticism and Irish politics during the last dozen years of the nineteenth century. Yeats himself famously portrayed the period as one when cultural nationalism superseded parliamentary politics and thus prepared the way for the Easter Rising and War of Independence. "The modern literature of Ireland and indeed all that stir of thought which prepared for the Anglo-Irish war, began when Parnell fell from power in 1891," Yeats recalled in the lecture he gave to the Royal Academy of Sweden when he won the Nobel Prize. "A disillusioned and embittered Ireland turned from parliamentary politics; an event was conceived . . ." (*A* 410). As Roy Foster has pointed out, this claim hardly accounts for the considerable vigor of Irish parliamentary politics between the fall of Parnell and the Easter Rising.[4] It accounts rather better for Yeats's view of a change in his own positions as part of the remarkable series of self-remakings that constitute his literary career. Whatever pressure the death of Parnell put on Yeats's development, key political events after 1900 intensified it and demanded a different strategy. The controversies over *The Playboy of the Western World* and the Dublin Municipal Gallery, and the strike and lockout of 1913, demanded a literature taking more account of events in the actual world, a stance that would later allow Yeats to bear witness to the

Troubles from the Easter Rising through the Civil War. Accordingly, Yeats abandoned his early aestheticism, which now made his early poetry seem escapist even to himself. "I have myself . . . begun . . . a movement downwards upon life, not upwards out of life," he wrote to his friend Florence Farr Emery in 1906 (*L* 469).

Yeats had so identified his early poetic self with Shelley that the remaking was bound to dethrone his former idol. At times Yeats thought to do that in unusual ways, as when he recalled that "when I found my verses too full of the reds and yellows Shelley gathered in Italy, I thought for two days of setting things right . . . by eating little and sleeping upon a board" (*E&I* 5). But sleeping on a board proved ineffective, and Yeats entered upon a deeper critique, one that tended to project the flaws of his own early verse onto his predecessor. That drive culminated in the second of his two essays on Shelley, "*Prometheus Unbound*" (1932), an indictment as hostile as his earlier essay had been celebratory. The Shelley of the earlier essay had envisioned a far-off future reign of Intellectual Beauty rather than a mere political revolution, had a wide and comprehensive vision of life, and had urged writers to exclude mere opinion from their works. In contrast, Yeats wrote in the later essay that "Shelley the political revolutionary expected miracle, the Kingdom of God in the twinkling of an eye . . .was terrified of the Last Day like a Victorian child," and could not attend to "the whole drama of life" (*E&I* 419–23). Yeats still retained enough admiration as late as "Under Ben Bulben" to summon Shelley's Witch of Atlas to join the Shee and the monastics around the Mareotic Lake, but clearly the period of his Shelleyan devotion had ended.

Blake fared more evenly in Yeats's lifelong admiration, though as with Shelley the period of greatest admiration was the 1890s. It was then that Yeats wrote the two major essays on Blake – "William Blake and the Imagination" and "William Blake and His Illustrations to *The Divine Comedy*" – which he would later collect in *Ideas of Good and Evil*. It was then, too, that he collaborated with Edwin Ellis on the elaborate three-volume *Works of William Blake: Poetic, Symbolic, and Critical*, much of it based on consultation of original manuscripts and which contained in print for the first time several works, including *An Island in the Moon*. Some of those manuscripts belonged to the heirs of the painter John Linnell, himself part of Blake's original circle. Yeats recalled in his autobiography that "one old man sat always beside us, ostensibly to sharpen our pencils but perhaps really to see that we did not steal the manuscripts, and they gave us very old port at lunch, and I have upon my dining-room walls their present of Blake's Dante engravings" (*A* 145). Yeats himself took responsibility for most of the commentary in the edition. That resulted in some insights remarkable for their time but also in others that perhaps did not need a great poet to ferret them out, like the injunction that "Any student of occultism . . . should especially notice Blake's association of black with darkness."[5]

Perhaps the most important way that Blake influenced Yeats was through his doctrine of contraries. In his difficult late book of esoteric philosophy *A Vision* Yeats recalled, "my mind had been full of Blake from boyhood up and I saw the world as a conflict – Spectre and Emanation – and could distinguish between a contrary and a negation. 'Contraries are positive', wrote Blake, 'a negation is not a contrary'" (*VB* 72). Those contraries served Yeats well in his movement downward upon life. Pairs of antinomies infiltrated his poetry: ideal and actual, art and nature, good and evil, the country of the young and Byzantium among them. Behind Crazy Jane's insight that "'Fair and foul are near of kin, / And fair needs foul,' I cried" (*VP* 513) lurk the dialectics of Blake's contraries. The same notion showed up in his politics, too, in the give and take between the ideal and the actual Ireland, between England and Ireland, and between reality and justice. Unlike his Shelleyan youth, he now had no expectation that the good would triumph. Recalling O'Leary's "romantic conception of Irish Nationality," he pledged allegiance to "that ideal Ireland, perhaps from this out an imaginary Ireland, in whose service I labour" (*E&I* 246).

One particular pair of contraries especially fascinated Yeats: that of art and nature. In contrast to the stereotype of nature-loving Romantic poets, Blake saw physical nature as antagonist to imagination, always ready to lead it astray. "Great things . . . depend on the Spiritual & not on the Natural World," he told one of his correspondents in 1802, and a quarter century later spoke longingly of "Leaving the Delusive Goddess Nature."[6] Yeats took over Blake's projection of nature and art or intellect as contraries or antinomies. In "Coole Park, 1929," for example, he celebrates "Great works constructed there in nature's spite," where the rhyme word "spite" carries overtones suggesting both "in spite of" and "in order to spite" nature. Similarly, in a draft of "Sailing to Byzantium," the speaker exclaims "I fly from nature to Byzantium."[7] Like Blake's, Yeats's imaginative speakers seek to move beyond nature into a more permanent world of spirit or intellect or art. In the late "An Acre of Grass" he invokes Blake along with two of Shakespeare's most passionate characters in an effort to get beyond the merely physical world:

> Grant me an old man's frenzy,
> Myself must I remake
> Till I am Timon and Lear
> Or that William Blake
> Who beat upon the wall
> Till Truth obeyed his call; . . .
>
> (*VP* 576)

Yeats's "four years' work upon the 'Prophetic Books' of William Blake" enhanced his awareness of the importance of material features (or what we now call "bibliographic codes"[8]) of the text. Indeed, his and Ellis's edition of *The Works of William Blake* was the first to print facsimiles of all the known engraved prophecies. There Yeats noticed how the overall design included more than the mere text of the words, and that illustration and layout could profoundly affect reception. Blake exploited such components constantly. Those versions of "The Tyger" that depict the fearsome beast of the words as the gentle pussycat of the illustration, for example, open up multiple levels of ironic readings. A painter's son and would-be painter himself in his youth, Yeats came from an environment that sharpened his sensitivity to physical features of the book, as did not only his study of Blake, but also his early devotion to William Morris during the Kelmscott phase, and to French Symbolist poetry. From his teens onward Yeats himself responded fervently to the physical form of the literature that he read, especially that in the Romantic tradition. "My own memory proves to me that at 17 there is an identity between an author's imagination and paper and bookcover one does not find in later life. I still do not quite separate Shelley from the green covers, or Blake from the blue covers and brown reproductions of pictures, of the books in which I first read them," he wrote to a designer working on a collected edition of his own work. "I do not separate Rossetti at all from his covers" (*L* 691). Blake had gone farther than any other Romantic poet in controlling the bibliographic codes of his own poetry, just as Rossetti and then Morris had than any Victorian one (except Emily Dickinson, who won her control by sacrificing print publication). Young Yeats clearly longed for input into the bibliographic codes of his own poetry and sought to influence the choice of designer and format for the *Poems* collection of 1895.[9]

He got his chance after the turn of the century. With the founding of Dun Emer (later Cuala) Press by his sisters in 1903, Yeats acquired a small press outlet that he would use for all the main volumes (or parts of volumes) of his poetry in the twentieth century. The format of the press provided a stable bibliographic code. His sister Elizabeth had trained with William Morris's partner Emery Walker in preparation for running the enterprise. That association provided a pedigree running back through Morris's socialist medievalism to the medieval revival engineered by the Romantics themselves, particularly in works that Yeats loved such as Keats's "The Eve of St. Agnes." The Cuala custom of setting its type high on the page with larger external than internal margins echoed both Morris and medieval book design and implied an alternative to methods of capitalist mass production. At the same time, the manufacture of the books in Ireland using Irish materials gave a nationalist inflection to their contents. The opening title pages trumpeted their Irish place of publication and the prominent closing colophons printed in red boasted of their Irish provenance. Even when the books appeared in somewhat larger editions from Macmillan, Yeats still insisted on having a say in their presentation, often collaborating with designers like T. Sturge Moore or Charles Ricketts.

In that way the physical appearance of the volumes matched Yeats's largest claim as a reviser of Romanticism: to have fastened it to an Irish national landscape. That became his way of being both a devotee of Intellectual Beauty and of the patriotic poets Davis, Mangan, and Ferguson. The internationalism of Shelley had bothered him from the start:

> I could not endure, however, an international art, picking stories and symbols where it pleased. Might I not, with health and good luck to guide me, create some new *Prometheus Unbound*; Patrick or Columcille, Oisin or Finn in Prometheus' stead; and, instead of Caucasus, Cro-Patrick or Ben Bulben? Have not all races had their first unity from a mythology that marries them to rock and hill? (*A* 166–7)

Such a hybrid art became his aim. He of course did go on to write of Oisin instead of Prometheus and most famously of Ben Bulben rather than Caucasus, all the while proclaiming himself a "last romantic." The hybridity of a Romantic stance and Irish content enabled him to correct flaws not only of Shelley but also of Blake, who he thought should have been more rooted and less obscure. "He was a man crying out for a mythology, and trying to make one because he could not find one to his hand," mourned Yeats, who wished that Blake had "gone to Ireland and chosen for his symbols the sacred mountains" (*E&I* 114). Yeats even tried to claim a partial Irish background for his own Rose symbol, citing James Clarence Mangan's "My Dark Rosaleen" and Aubrey de Vere's "The Little Black Rose" as precedents.

The key figure in Yeats's turn from adolescent cosmopolitanism to his more familiar nationalism was, of course, John O'Leary. "From these debates, from O'Leary's conversation, and from the Irish books he lent or gave me has come all I have set my hand to since," recalled Yeats in *Autobiographies* (*A* 104). O'Leary had directed Yeats not just to large-mindedness, but to a way of combining Romanticism with Irishness into an original synthesis. That was another meaning of "Romantic Ireland." So, too, was the diction of that poem, one of the first in which we hear Yeats's truly modern voice. Before the turn of the century, Yeats had indeed sought to marry Irishness and Romanticism, but he had still written about Irish materials in the manner of the English poets. We can hear a different note in the famous first stanza of "September 1913":

What need you, being come to sense,
But fumble in a greasy till
And add the halfpence to the pence
And prayer to shivering prayer, until
You have dried the marrow from the bone?
For men were born to pray and save:
Romantic Ireland's dead and gone,
It's with O'Leary in the grave. (*VP* 289)

The very phrases that are sometimes attacked by critics eager to arraign Yeats for insufficient sympathy with the Irish Catholic middle classes, like "fumble in a greasy till" and "For men were born to pray and save," have another virtue here: they no longer echo the diction and meters of the English Romantics but instead belong to the cadences of literary Modernism, particularly in its Irish inflections. Just as the speaking voice in Wallace Stevens is recognizably American, the voice here is resolutely Irish in allusions (Ireland, O'Leary) and cadence. As the poem goes on, both its overt sense and the implicit gesture of its language and meter suggest the irony of its own refrain. For the tone of indignation joins with the materials of language and overt sense of the words to suggest that Romantic Ireland is not dead after all: rather, it lives on in the remarkable voice uttering the poem, the voice of O'Leary's greatest disciple, full of hybridity and passion at once. It is the characteristic note of Yeats's great mature poetry.

We can glimpse the complex impact of Romanticism on the mature Yeats by looking at one of his finest poems, "The Tower." That work, of course, displayed not just any tower, but in particular the late medieval one at Ballylee, which Yeats bought in 1917 and after extensive restoration summered in with his family for a decade beginning in 1919. The tower is thus not merely a trope but rather a physical structure in Ireland itself. Indeed, its very name embodies part of Yeats's nationalist project. When he bought the tower, people called it "Ballylee Castle"; Yeats himself re-named it Thoor Ballylee as a gesture toward the Gaelic language, with "Thoor" being his version of the Irish word Tor (tower). Yeats featured the building in major poetry from "In Memory of Major Robert Gregory" to "Coole Park and Ballylee, 1931," including "Meditations in Time of Civil War," "The Phases of the Moon," and "Blood and the Moon." It also inspired the title of two of the major volumes of that period, *The Tower* and *The Winding Stair.*

The meanings spiraled outwards but always retained their association with the actual tower, and so with Yeats's project to de-anglicize English Romanticism.[10] Yeats exploited the appearance of towers in disparate traditions but always particularly stressed the Romantic and the Irish, sometimes in the same utterance. In a note to *The Winding Stair and Other Poems* of 1933, for instance, he proclaimed:

> In this book and elsewhere I have used towers, and one tower in particular, as symbols and have compared their winding stairs to the philosophical gyres, but it is hardly necessary to interpret what comes from the main track of thought and expression. Shelley uses towers constantly as symbols . . . Part of the symbolism of *Blood and the Moon* was suggested by the fact that Thoor Ballylee has a waste room at the top . . . (*VP* 831)

Not given to hiding these meanings under a bushel, he paraded them even more explicitly in the poetry itself. "Blood and the Moon" invokes towers from ancient Alexandria and Babylon before going on to cite one from Shelley's *Prometheus Unbound*: "And Shelley had his towers, thought's crowned powers he called them once" (*VP* 480). Similarly, in "The Phases of the Moon" he ascribes his choice of the tower to recollection of "the far tower where Milton's Platonist / Sat late, or Shelley's visionary prince" (*VP* 373). Shelley's Athanase studying hermetic philosophy in his tower lies behind Yeats studying esoteric doctrine in *his*.

Remaking Romanticism by fastening it to Irish earth operates in both form and content throughout the great lyric that forms Part II of "The Tower." The first stanza reads:

> I pace upon the battlements and stare
> On the foundations of a house, or where
> Tree, like a sooty finger, starts from the earth;
> And send imagination forth
> Under the day's declining beam, and call
> Images and memories
> From ruin or from ancient trees,
> For I would ask a question of them all.
> (*VP* 409–10)

The Romantics invented the format of the Greater Romantic Lyric, in which an individual speaker in a definite setting confronts the landscape, and the interplay between mind and setting constitutes the poem. Such poems often exhibit a three-part structure in which the speaker begins in a state of detachment from the landscape; interacts with it through imagination and memory in the second section, which often involves changes in place and time; and then comes back out with new insight or understanding in the third. Wordsworth did that in "Tintern Abbey," Coleridge in "The Eolian Harp" or "Frost at Midnight," and Keats in "Ode to a Nightingale."[11] Yeats does that here, too, when he "send[s] imagination forth" to encounter images of passionate intensity, all of which are Irish ones associated with the particular landscape around Thoor Ballylee. Mrs. French and her serving-man, the poet Raftery and beauty Mary Hynes, Yeats's own character Red Hanrahan, and the "ancient bankrupt master of this house" all inhabited the Galway landscape surrounding the tower. And, of course, the speaker of the poem was in his non-poetic life a member of the Irish Senate. Such national materials enable Yeats to take a form associated with the English Romantics and turn it to his own Irish ends.

The Irish components of the tower and landscape match those of the very books in which the poem first appeared, the Cuala Press edition of *October Blast* (1927) and the Macmillan edition of *The Tower* (1928), which combined *October Blast* with two other predecessors. In both instances "The Tower" came second in the sequence, immediately after "Sailing to Byzantium." The bibliographic coding of *October Blast* highlighted its Irishness. The title page, for instance, gave the place of publication ("Dublin Ireland") equal billing with the author "William Butler Yeats" by setting it in type of the same size. The font for both title page and the poem itself was Caslon Old Style, a typeface much favored by Dublin printers during Yeats's admired eighteenth century. Yeats's own note to the poem explained that "The persons mentioned are associated by legend, story, and tradition with the neighbourhood of Thoor Ballylee or Ballylee Castle where the poem was written." And the closing colophon, printed in red, insisted on the Irish components of the physical volume. "Here ends 'October Blast': by William Butler Yeats," it read. "Three hundred and fifty copies of this book have been printed on paper made in Ireland, and published by Elizabeth Corbet Yeats at the Cuala Press, 133 Lower Baggot Street, Dublin, Ireland."[12] Title page, typeface, note, paper, and colophon all proclaimed the book to be "Made in Ireland" of Irish materials. In this way the material volume matches both the Irish components of the poem "The Tower" and those of the physical tower itself. Yeats punned on those analogies through his use of the word "characters" in his short verse "To be Carved on a Stone at Thoor Ballylee," with which he had ended his previous volume, *Michael Robartes and the Dancer*:

I, the poet William Yeats,
With old mill boards and sea-green slates,
And smithy work from the Gort forge
Restored this tower for my wife George;
And may these characters remain
When all is ruin once again. (*VP* 406)

Just as the mill boards, green slates, and smithy work from the Gort forge restored the physical tower, so did the Irish paper, Caslon typeface, and printing work from Cuala Press enable construction of the poetic one. The word "characters" reminds us of both enterprises, suggesting as it does both intense personalities on the one hand and the physical letters of which the words are composed on the other.

When Yeats collected the three Cuala volumes for the first time into the *Tower* volume of his verse, the poems lost their original bibliographic coding. Yeats tried to make up for that by involving himself actively with the format of the volume, making sure that his favorite designer Sturge Moore got the commission for the cover. Moore had collaborated with Yeats on other covers and produced one of his best designs for this one. Their correspondence indicates Yeats's particular concern that the tower on the cover refer to Thoor Ballylee in particular. Yeats wrote: "I am also sending you some photographs of the Tower. I need not make any suggestions, except that the Tower should not be too unlike the real object, or rather that it should suggest the real object. I like to think of that building as a permanent symbol of my work plainly visible to the passer-by. As you know, all my art theories depend upon just this – rooting of mythology in the earth."[13] In the end, Moore created a striking design of the tower stamped in gold on a green background. He included the cottages at the side (symbolic of folk tradition next to the aristocratic castle) and delighted Yeats by having the tower reflected in the stream (symbolic of existence) below. "I think that the Tower is recognisably your Tower and not anyone else's," wrote Moore.[14]

In thinking of Romanticism from his tower, Yeats did not limit himself to the English Romantics, but pondered instead that large-mindedness associated in his mind with John O'Leary in politics and Lady Gregory in literature, as we saw in "September 1913" and "Coole Park and Ballylee, 1931." He found magnanimity earlier, too, particularly in Dante and Spenser as precursors of Romanticism. He associated both of them with that term, in his youth attaching them to it and in his maturity often contrasting them to the Romantics themselves. He recalled his early devotion to Dante this way: "When I was fifteen or sixteen my father had told me about Rossetti and Blake and given me their poetry to read; and once at Liverpool on my way to Sligo I had seen [the picture] *Dante's Dream* in the gallery there . . . and its colour, its people, its romantic architecture had blotted all other pictures away" (*A* 114). That early aesthetic devotion did not last. Later, especially in the decade between the poem "Ego Dominus Tuus" and the book *A Vision*, he exalted Dante as a sort of perfected Romantic, free of the flaws of Keats and Shelley. In *A Vision*, for instance, he assigned Dante to the same phase seventeen that housed both himself and Shelley, and contrasted Dante to

Shelley in this way: "Dante, having attained, as poet, to Unity of Being, as poet saw all things set in order . . . and was content to see both good and evil. . . . Dante suffering injustice and the loss of Beatrice, found divine justice and the heavenly Beatrice, but the justice of *Prometheus Unbound* is a vague propagandistic emotion and the women that await its coming are but clouds" (*VB* 144).

Yeats read Spenser through Romantic eyes as well. Indeed, in his teens he associated Spenser particularly with Shelley, writing a narrative poem in Spenserian stanzas and a series of plays "in imitation of Shelley and of Edmund Spenser" (*A* 81). His notes and marginalia for his own edition of Spenser in 1906 refer continually to Blake, Shelley, and Keats, as when he compares a magic boat in *The Faerie Queene* to Shelley's boats, or remembers of the "cords of wire" binding Satyrane that "Blake has chords or nets of wire."[15] The harshness of Spenser's opinions as a colonial administrator in *A View of the Present State of Ireland* troubled Yeats, but he sought to maneuver around them by thinking of Spenser as divided between a positive, poetically symbolic, aristocratic, and Anglo-French delight in the senses, and a negative, prosaically allegorical, middle-class, and Anglo-Saxon allegiance to the emerging state. In that way he tried to avoid the vituperation of Karl Marx, who dismissed Spenser as "[Queen] Elizabeth's arse-kissing poet."[16] Instead, Yeats cited Spenser's political image for the Earl of Leicester and his successors admiringly in the late poem "The Municipal Gallery Revisited," where he called it "An image out of Spenser and the common tongue" (*VP* 603). Similarly, he would enlist Dante for the *terza rima* of one of his last poems, "Cuchulain Comforted."

Dante and Spenser were major poets of both vision and politics, of course, as Yeats himself hoped to become. Rather than linger on Yeats's invocation of them, I turn instead to the summoning of Yeats himself by a contemporary poet who aspires to the same balance, Seamus Heaney. *Crediting Poetry*, Heaney's Nobel Prize lecture of 1995, in important ways rewrites Shelley's "A Defence of Poetry" for a modern artist and modern times. Heaney even uses one of Shelley's most famous images for poetry when he seeks to credit poetry "for being itself and for being a help, for making possible a fluid and restorative relationship between the mind's centre and its circumference," a formulation that echoes Shelley's famous definition of poetry as "at once the centre and circumference of knowledge."[17] In the lecture Heaney prominently and movingly invokes Yeats, the last Irish poet before himself to win the Nobel Prize. "Nobody understood better than he the connection between the construction or destruction of a political order and the founding or foundering of cultural life"[18] writes Heaney, while noticing that in conjuring his friends John Synge and Lady Gregory into his own speech

Yeats had chosen to emphasize the "local" aspects that his own work also embodied. Heaney finds the breadth of Yeats's vision embodied best perhaps in one of the poems from "Meditations in Time of Civil War," namely "The Stare's Nest by my Window," where the window is that of Thoor Ballylee. The famous last stanza reads:

> We had fed the heart on fantasies,
> The heart's grown brutal from the fare;
> More substance in our enmities
> Than in our love; O honey-bees,
> Come build in the empty house of the stare.
> (*VP* 425)

Calling attention to the extraordinary triangulation triggered by the triple rhyme *fantasies*, *enmities*, and *honey-bees* in that passage, Heaney argues that it

> satisfies the contradictory needs which consciousness experiences at times of extreme crisis, the need on the one hand for a truth-telling that will be hard and retributive, and on the other hand the need not to harden the mind to a point where it denies its own yearnings for sweetness and trust . . . Yeats's work does what the necessary poetry always does, which is to touch the base of our sympathetic nature while taking in at the same time the unsympathetic reality of the world to which that nature is constantly exposed.[19]

I think that Heaney gets Yeats exactly right here, and would dissent only from the notion that such insights apply solely "at times of extreme crisis." For when are we not in times of extreme crisis one way or another? What Heaney singles out here is the large-mindedness that undergirds Yeats's poetry at its best, and that Yeats saw underlying a Romantic tradition in poetry that stretched from Dante, Spenser, and Milton through the Romantics themselves and on to the writers of his own time. Were he to return from the grave (surely something he would have liked), Yeats might even have found it in one of his most courageous modern champions. It is that large-mindedness, and not the accidents of mere chronology, that generates imagination's true passion rather than opinion's sectarian hatred. Yeats identified it as a Romantic characteristic in the one usage of the word "romantic" in his poetry that we have not mentioned yet but with which I would like to close this chapter. The prose draft reads: "Passion in Shakespeare was a great fish in the sea, but from Goethe to the end of the Romantic movement the fish was in the net. It will soon be dead upon the shore."[20] That notion follows Yeats's mature sense that the large-mindedness and passion that he originally had assigned to poets of the Romantic period itself had flowed even more fully in Renaissance writers like Spenser or Shakespeare and was in danger of withering altogether in the present day. As he put it more memorably in *The Winding Stair and Other Poems*:

> Shakespearean fish swam the sea, far away from land;
> Romantic fish swam in nets coming to the hand;
> What are all those fish that lie gasping on the strand?
> (*VP* 485)

NOTES

1. *Letters of Wallace Stevens*, ed. Holly Stevens (Oxford and New York: Alfred A. Knopf, 1970), p. 277.
2. For a fuller mapping of Yeats's changing relation to Shelley, see my *Yeats and Shelley* (Chicago: University of Chicago Press, 1970) and Harold Bloom's *Yeats* (Oxford and New York: Oxford University Press, 1970). For more information on Yeats and Blake see Bloom's book and also Hazard Adams, *Blake and Yeats: The Contrary Vision* (New York: Russell & Russell, 1968 [1955]); Deborah Dorfman, *Blake in the Nineteenth Century: His Reputation from Gilchrist to Yeats* (New Haven: Yale University Press, 1969); and Margaret Rudd, *Divided Image: A Study of William Blake and W. B. Yeats* (London: Routledge & Kegan Paul, 1953).
3. Katharine Tynan Hinkson, *Twenty-Five Years: Reminiscences* (London: J. Murray, 1913), p. 219.
4. For a good discussion of this see the essay "Protestant magic" in R. F. Foster's *Paddy and Mr. Punch: Connections in Irish and English History* (London and New York: Penguin Books, 1993), especially p. 229.
5. *The Works of William Blake: Poetic, Symbolic, and Critical*, ed. Edwin John Ellis and William Butler Yeats, 3 vols. (London: Bernard Quaritch, 1893), Vol. I, p. 313.
6. *The Poetry and Prose of William Blake*, ed. David Erdman with commentary by Harold Bloom (Garden City: Doubleday, 1965), pp. 688, 708.
7. For a transcription of the drafts and commentary on them, see Jon Stallworthy, *Between the Lines: Yeats's Poetry in the Making* (Oxford: Clarendon Press, 1963), Chapter 5, especially p. 94.
8. This term was coined by Jerome McGann in *The Textual Condition* (Princeton: Princeton University Press, 1991), Chapter 2, *passim*, and elaborated as a concept in his *Black Riders: The Visible Language of Modernism* (Princeton: Princeton University Press, 1993). For extended applications to Yeats see my essay "Yeats and textual reincarnation: 'When You Are Old' and 'September 1913,'" in *The Iconic Page in Manuscript, Print, and Digital Culture*, ed. George Bornstein and Theresa Tinkle (Ann Arbor: University of Michigan Press, 1998), pp. 223–48, and David Holdeman, *Much Labouring: The Texts and Authors of Yeats's First Modernist Books* (Ann Arbor: University of Michigan Press, 1997).
9. For an account of those issues see my essay "What is the text of a poem by Yeats?" in *Palimpsest: Editorial Theory in the Humanities*, ed. George Bornstein and

Ralph G. Williams (Ann Arbor: University of Michigan Press, 1993), pp. 167–93.

10. I have discussed this at greater length from a somewhat different viewpoint in "Romancing the (native) stone: Yeats, Stevens, and the Anglocentric canon," in *The Romantics and Us*, ed. Gene W. Ruoff (New Brunswick: Rutgers University Press, 1990), pp. 108–29.
11. For more on the Greater Romantic Lyric see M. H. Abrams, "Structure and style in the Greater Romantic Lyric," in *From Sensibility to Romanticism*, ed. Frederick W. Hilles and Harold Bloom (London and New York: Oxford University Press, 1965), pp. 527–60. I discuss the form's application to Yeats more fully in "Yeats and the Greater Romantic Lyric," in *Poetic Remaking: The Art of Browning, Yeats, and Pound* (University Park, PA: Penn State University Press, 1988), pp. 51–69. For more on Yeats and Romantic authors other than Blake and Shelley, see my *Transformations of Romanticism in Yeats, Eliot, and Stevens* (Chicago: University of Chicago Press, 1976), and James Land Jones, *Adam's Dream: Mythic Consciousness in Keats and Yeats* (Athens: University of Georgia Press, 1975).
12. W. B. Yeats, *October Blast: Poems* (Dublin: Cuala Press, 1927), p. 26.
13. *W. B. Yeats and T. Sturge Moore: Their Correspondence 1901–1937*, ed. Ursula Bridge (London: Routledge & Kegan Paul, 1953), p. 114.
14. *Ibid.*, p. 114.
15. These annotations are discussed in "The making of Yeats's Spenser," in my *Poetic Remaking*, which also contains a chapter on "Yeats's Romantic Dante."
16. Translation mine. See Karl Marx, *The Ethnological Notebooks of Karl Marx*, ed. Lawrence Krader (Assen: Van Gorcum, 1972), p. 305: "Elizabeths Arschküssende Poet Spenser." I owe awareness of this remark to the edition of Edmund Spenser, *A View of the Present State of Ireland*, ed. Andrew Hadfield and Willy Maley (Oxford: Blackwell, 1997), p. xii, which has a helpful section entitled "Spenser in Ireland."
17. Seamus Heaney, *Crediting Poetry: The Nobel Lecture* (New York: Farrar Straus Giroux, 1996), p. 10. For Shelley, see Percy Bysshe Shelley, *Shelley's Poetry and Prose*, ed. Donald. H. Reiman and Sharon B. Powers (New York: Norton, 1977), p. 503.
18. Heaney, *Crediting Poetry*, p. 40.
19. *Ibid.*, pp. 47, 53.
20. A. Norman Jeffares, *A New Commentary on the Poems of W. B. Yeats* (London: Macmillan, 1984), pp. 279–80.

3

GEORGE WATSON

Yeats, Victorianism, and the 1890s

Yeats was in a literal sense a Victorian. Born in 1865 in what may be called the high noon of the Victorian period, he lived thirty-six of his seventy-four years "in the great peace of Queen Victoria and amid all the social and spiritual conditions prevailing through her realms."[1] One would not, however, find too many critics ready to characterize Yeats as a Victorian – indeed, that Yeats was irredeemably hostile to everything Victorian has been an article of critical faith. His own comments are pungent. His best known assault on qualities that he associated with Victorian poetry comes in the sprightly, controversial introduction to *The Oxford Book of Modern Verse* (1936), where he condemns its irrelevant descriptions of nature, its scientific and moral discursiveness, along with "the political eloquence of Swinburne, the psychological curiosity of Browning, and the poetical diction of everybody" (*LE* 183). Then, after describing the late Victorian poets of the nineties, many of whom he knew well and who tried to define themselves in revolt against what may be called mainstream Victorian aesthetic and moral positions, Yeats goes on: "Then in 1900 everybody got down off his stilts; henceforth nobody drank absinthe with his black coffee; nobody went mad; nobody committed suicide; nobody joined the Catholic church; or if they did I have forgotten . . . Victorianism had been defeated" (*LE* 185). If "Victorianism" had been defeated, the battle with it had been a vigorous one, and had shaped Yeats's sensibility in profound ways. The impact has been seen mainly as negative, as taking the form of rejection, but it is more complicated than that. Yeats owed more than he cared to admit to Matthew Arnold, and it is during the years up to 1901 that he forged his aesthetic philosophy. Yeats in part created or constructed his version of Victorianism, and in creating it and living it, in grappling with the substance as well as the shadow of the Victorian age, he forged lifelong aesthetic and philosophical positions.

In the first place, Yeats hated the sterilities (as he saw them) of Victorian scientific rationalism. He linked science, which "I had grown to hate with a monkish hate" (*A* 91–2) with naturalism, and condemned both, using as a kind of shorthand abusive refrain the names of the scientific philosophers T. H. Huxley and John Tyndall alongside the realist French painters Carolus Duran and Bastien-Lepage. His praise of his acquaintances and friends in the Rhymers' Club was that "not one had hearkened to the feeblest caw, or been spattered by the smallest dropping from any Huxley, Tyndall, Carolus Duran, Bastien-Lepage bundle of old twigs" (*A* 149). Naturalism as an offshoot of "science" was an aesthetic mode entirely antipathetic, Yeats believed, to the operation of true imaginative powers, because it enforced a mechanical passivity in the mere recording of sense impressions. The imagination became a mirror, not a lamp. Further, an art based on the "philosophy" of Victorian science was incapable of creating beauty. All through his autobiographical writing, Yeats excoriates those nineteenth-century artists whose naturalist canons, derived as he believed from the scientific Zeitgeist (the spirit of the age), offended everything in him that he owed to his visionary exemplars, Blake and Shelley. His own early poem, "The Song of the Happy Shepherd" (written in 1885), which stands at the entrance to his collected poems, contrasts the "grey truth" of the physicists and astronomers with the visionary truth only to be found in those who reject the scientific universe:

Seek, then,
No learning from the starry men,
Who follow with the optic glass
The whirling ways of stars that pass –
Seek, then, for this is also sooth,
No word of theirs – the cold star-bane
Has cloven and rent their hearts in twain,
And dead is all their human truth.

(*VP* 66)

Behind the aesthetic objection to Victorian scientific rationalism lay an essentially religious hostility. Though born into the Protestant Church of Ireland, Yeats quite early discovered that he was not or could not be at all orthodox. Yet he had an essentially religious temperament:

> I was unlike others of my generation in one thing only. I am very religious, and deprived by Huxley and Tyndall, whom I detested, of the simple-minded religion of my childhood, I had made a new religion, almost an infallible Church of poetic tradition, of a fardel of stories, and of personages, and of emotions, inseparable from their first expression, passed on from generation to generation by poets and painters with some help from philosophers and theologians. I wished for a world where I could discover this tradition perpetually.
>
> (*A* 115)

Victorian scientific secularism thus reinforced powerfully positions he had derived from Blake and Shelley, helping to produce in reaction Yeats's most deeply held and enduring poetic beliefs in the centrality of art as a conduit of essential and transcendental truth. Here too one sees the origins of his eclecticism – that "fardel" of which he speaks – in which poets rubbed shoulders with philosophers, theologians, and artisans; his belief in the value of tradition; and his commitment to an essentially heroic art.

In a powerfully mythologized reading of English history, Yeats opposes "Merry England" to Victorian England, and in doing so constructs the set of antithetical values out of which he would create the dynamics of his own poetry. Briefly, Merry England (Yeats means, roughly speaking, the late medieval to early Renaissance period) has imagination and eccentricity, and does not count the cost; Victorian England is utilitarian and Puritan. Yeats most frequently attacked Victorian literature on the grounds of its narrow moralism. He is repeatedly severe on what he sees as an ethical bias in the literary attitudes and critical principles of two quintessential Victorians, Matthew Arnold and George Eliot. He frequently alludes, and always with hostility, to Matthew Arnold's dictum that poetry should be "a criticism of life." He is even more antagonistic to George Eliot, who fails to provide Yeats with what he sees as an inescapable quality of great art, namely joy: "She seemed to have a distrust or a distaste for all in life that gives one a springing foot . . . she knew so well how to enforce her distaste by the authority of her mid-Victorian science" (*A* 95).

In the 1901 essay, "At Stratford-on-Avon" (*E&I* 96–110), Yeats can be seen actively constructing his Victorian period. He is no respecter of conventional literary periodization: as with his Romanticism, his Victorianism denotes not a specific historical epoch but rather a set of qualities that began much earlier, and reached a peak of development in the Victorian period proper. It is instructive to watch a great poet work through critical analysis to creative vision, as in the 1901 essay. In it, he compares George Eliot unfavorably with the less judgemental Balzac: "Great literature has always been . . . the Forgiveness of Sin, and when we find it becoming the Accusation of Sin, as in George Eliot, who plucks her Tito in pieces with as much assurance as if he had been clockwork, literature has begun to change into something else" (*E&I* 102). Yeats goes on to find this same moralism in the Shakespearean critics of the Victorian age, and to unite it to utilitarianism, another quality he particularly despised: "They and she grew up in a century of utilitarianism, when nothing about a man seemed important except his utility to the State, and nothing so useful to the State as the actions whose effect can be weighed by reason" (*E&I* 102). The argument develops into a partisan account of Shakespeare's characters, in particular Richard II and Henry V, and of those critics – such as the unfortunate Edward Dowden of Trinity College Dublin, who becomes a particular whipping boy – who hold up the "'sentimental,' 'weak,' 'selfish' and 'insincere'" Richard, and contrast him to "'Shakespeare's only hero,'" Henry V. This error is due, Yeats implies, to the deformations caused by the vulgar worship of efficiency and success common in the Victorian period; and in the case of the hapless Dowden by the added factor of his Irish envy and misunderstanding of where lay the true secret of what had made England great. She was not made by her Dombeys and her counting houses, by the power of Victorian moralism and utilitarianism, but by "people of wildness and imagination and eccentricity": "The Accusation of Sin produced its necessary fruit, hatred of all that was abundant, extravagant, exuberant, of all that sets a sail for shipwreck, and flattery of the commonplace emotions and conventional ideals of the mob, the chief Paymaster of accusation" (*E&I* 105).

In this essay, and in the introduction that he wrote in 1902 to a selection of the poems of Edmund Spenser, Yeats vigorously manipulates for his own larger imaginative purposes two Englands of the mind, "Merry England" and an England of the Puritan and the merchant. The latter has clear affinities with his portrait of Victorian England. Yeats elides the sixteenth and the nineteenth centuries as he imagines one of Spenser's admiring contemporaries come back to life in a drabber present: "If one of those poets who threw his copy of verses into the earth that was about to close over his master were to come alive again . . . he would find nothing [in England now] but the triumph of the Puritan and the merchant – those enemies he had feared and hated. . ." (*E&I* 364). The sweeping generalizations and intensely personal emphases of this reading of English history anticipate the Yeats who would schematize the whole of human history in *A Vision*. "The courtly and saintly ideals of the Middle Ages were fading, and the practical ideals of the modern age had begun to threaten the unuseful dome of the sky" (*E&I* 106). For all the tone of defeat and regret, Yeats found imaginative energy in the contemplation of this decline. The contrast played a vital part in Yeats's elaboration of a set of antithetical values that would inform all his work. "Sin," "argumentative," "utilitarianism," "reason," "efficiency," "vulgar," "success," "commonplace," "the mob," "Puritan," "merchant" – all of these negative terms coalesce in the unceasing Yeatsian critique of the modern commercial and secular world, and its sterile art predicated on the ethical and the utilitarian. This is the context out of which comes a characteristic emphasis in the poems – "the noisy set / Of bankers, schoolmasters, and clergymen / The martyrs call the world" ("Adam's Curse"; *VP* 205); "the merchant and the clerk" breathing on the world with "timid breath" in "At Galway Races" (*VP* 266); those who "fumble in a greasy till" in "September 1913" (*VP* 289). In the other corner, as it were, are those who have "wildness and imagination and eccentricity," all who "[set] a sail for shipwreck." In these and like phrases Yeats anticipates an equally characteristic poetic emphasis – on those who have "the wasteful virtues" that "earn the sun" ("Pardon, Old Fathers"; *VP* 270); on those who "weighed so lightly what they gave" ("September 1913"; *VP* 290); on all those, heroic and gay, who come "proud, open-eyed and laughing to the tomb" ("Vacillation"; *VP* 501); and on those who are driven to their shipwreck by "a lonely impulse of delight" ("An Irish Airman Foresees his Death"; *VP* 328).

What Yeats disliked in the art of the Victorians, then, was its strong emphasis on the pulpit rather than the altar, its view of art as morally improving, directed to conduct and behavior rather than to mystery and vision. As he writes in "Art and Ideas" (1913), still looking to the pre-Puritan past as a stick with which to belabor the present:

> I think that before the religious change that followed on the Renaissance men were greatly preoccupied with their sins, and that to-day they are troubled by other men's sins, and that this trouble has created a moral enthusiasm so full of illusion that art, knowing itself for sanctity's scapegrace brother, cannot be of the party. We have but held to our ancient Church, where there is an altar and no pulpit . . . and turned away from the too great vigour of those who, living for mutual improvement, have a pulpit and no altar. (*E&I* 350–1)

To sum up, he felt that the ethical and improving bent of Victorian literature, especially when vented in poetry, adulterated the essential business of art, which was to reveal timeless truths, and that its palpable design on its readers produced a banality of rhetoric rather than the beauty of rhythm and word that alone was conducive to vision.

However, there were ways in which Yeats engaged more positively with the Victorian age into which he was born. In particular, the relation between Yeats and Matthew Arnold needs re-scrutiny. Arnold died in 1888, when Yeats was twenty-three. Despite his constant attacks on Arnold's notion of art as a criticism of life, which he refers to in his first published review (of the poetry of Sir Samuel Ferguson; *UP*1 81–104), he was to conduct a covert dialogue with the most famous Victorian critic for a good part of his life. He had clearly read Arnold carefully, and quite extensively. Where Arnold speaks of "the dialogue of the mind with itself"[2] as a disfiguring introspectiveness in modern poetry, Yeats confirms the diagnosis, and writes of "the sad soliloquies of nineteenth century egoism" (*UP*1 103). Where Arnold writes in his poem "The Scholar Gypsy" (1853) of the "strange disease" of modern life, "with its sick hurry, its divided aims," Yeats hopes that the study of Irish legends will save Irish readers from "that leprosy of the modern – tepid emotions and many aims" (*UP*1 104). He had made a kind of pilgrimage to Oxford in 1889, the year after Arnold's death, and quotes approvingly, even lovingly, from "The Scholar Gypsy" in his essay on "Magic" in 1901 (*E&I* 38).

Arnold confirmed in Yeats the belief that art, even tragic art, must be instinct with joy. Yeats read with excitement and approval Arnold's "Preface to First Edition of *Poems* (1853)," in which Arnold explains his exclusion of "Empedocles on Etna" from the collection. Certain situations are unsuitable for poetic representation, writes Arnold: "They are those in which the suffering finds no vent in action; in which a continuous state of mental distress is prolonged, unrelieved by incident, hope, or resistance; in which there is everything to be endured, nothing to be done."[3] Yeats was famously and controversially to take up Arnold's point in excluding the poets of the Great War from *The Oxford Book of Modern Verse*: "I have rejected these poems for the same reason that made Arnold withdraw his *Empedocles on Etna* from circulation; passive suffering is not a theme for poetry" (*LE* 199). This was not a passing judgement. The views that Arnold expressed on the need for art to assert joy, and Arnold's concern about the introspective, even solipsistic character of modern poetry, were congenial to Yeats right through his career.[4]

Arnold's interest in the Celt, and his belief in the power of art and criticism to raise the cultural level of a nation, and to stem the tide of vulgarity and of Philistinism, were as important to Yeats as his rejection of passive suffering as a poetic subject. In 1866, Arnold published *On the Study of Celtic Literature*, based on the lectures he had given at Oxford as Professor of Poetry in the previous academic year. In them, Arnold, from a position that he himself admitted to be one of the deepest ignorance of the original languages and literatures involved, created a potent stereotype of the Celt. This had an enormous influence on the Irish Literary Revival, and especially, for a time, on the young Yeats, the chief spirit in that revival. Arnold's purpose was to argue for the establishment of a Chair of Celtic at Oxford, but he was also trying to inaugurate a change in political and cultural hostilities between Britain and Ireland. There is no need to rehearse here the details of Arnold's portrait of the Celt, spiritual, melancholy, in love with beauty, nor to argue the case that his portrait did indeed powerfully shape Yeats's art and criticism in his early years.[5] However, Yeats denied that Arnold's lectures had had any impact on him. In his essay of 1897, "The Celtic Element in Literature," he said that "I do not think any of us who write about Ireland have built any argument upon [Arnold's ideas]" (*E&I* 174). Even more vehemently, he wrote in 1900 to D. P. Moran, the acerbic and skeptical editor of *The Leader*, that he had not quoted Arnold's essay "on a hundred platforms," and that Arnold had not understood that "Celtic" characteristics more correctly describe "the qualities of the early races of the world" (*UP*II 241).

Why was Yeats so eager to deny any influence on his work, even though Arnold's picture of the Celt is on the whole complimentary? At a simple level, one can agree that "it would be too painful for an evangelizing Celt to admit, even to himself, that he had got any substantial share of his gospel from an Englishman – even a good Englishman, now dead."[6] The denial of Arnold would have been even more urgent in an argument with Moran, the pugnacious proponent of "Irish Ireland," who had savaged Yeats's literary movement.[7] Moran's opposition, moreover, reflects a key shift in the balance of patriotic power between the terms "Celtic" and "Gaelic," in which, during the 1890s, use of the Irish language began to be *the* authentic marker of nationalist integrity. Further, there was the incontrovertibly awkward fact that for all Arnold's admiration for the Celt, he saw him as essentially inferior to the Saxon in one vital area. He is "sentimental," by which Arnold means that he is "always ready to revolt against the despotism of fact" (a phrase he borrows from Henri Martin's chapter on the Celts in his *Histoire de France*). He cannot match the Saxon in the practical arts of making "doors that open, windows that shut, razors that shave, coats that wear."[8] Most of all, this readiness to revolt against the despotism of fact renders him unfit to govern himself. So, Arnold implies, the Saxons would continue in their dull and muddy-mettled but practical way to run the show, but the Celts would be most welcome at the banqueting board of the British Isles, because they would supply the music, the charm, and the imagination. The "Celtic nations" were of purely antiquarian interest, and of significance in the present only because of what their literature and art had contributed to an enchanting strand of "English" literature. For an Irishman with aspirations to being a national poet to buy into this package, as it were, was to endorse the colonial relationship.

If Yeats did understand the imperialist implications of Arnold's portrait of the Celt, why did he nevertheless flirt with something so risky? There has been a consensus after the impact of Edward Said's *Orientalism* (1978) that Yeats's early Celticizing poetry and prose show him trapped in colonialist contradiction.[9] However, it is of more relevance here to ask why and where did Yeats find Arnold's Celticism so useful, and how does it fit into his poetic development? First, Arnold – whatever his imperial goals – asserted the reality of racial difference. Ethnological and racial theories saw their great flourishing in the Victorian period, and no word appears more often in

Arnold's writings than "race."[10] As Lionel Trilling says, "Science, the anthropology of his day, told him that the spirit of a nation – what we might call its national style – is determined by blood or race and that these are constants, asserting themselves against all other determinants such as class, existing social forms, and geographical and economic environment."[11] Arnold embraces the whole of the racial assumption, and therefore earnestly distinguishes between the "genius" of the Teuton and the Saxon and the Norman and the Celt. What Yeats found so useful about this was that the best known and perhaps most prestigious literary critic of his day acknowledged a racial type called Celtic, and the distinctiveness of its literature. Further, unlike most other imperial Englishmen, he spoke of it with admiration, however politically qualified. If there was a racial type called Celtic, "Celtic writing" could be guaranteed. This was no small consolation to the young Yeats. Driven by the desire to establish and mold a literary movement, he faced difficulties. As John Frayne points out, Yeats knew that his claims for the worth of nineteenth-century Irish literature, including that of his own generation, rested on shaky foundations; however, "Yeats's main hopes depended . . . not upon individual talents but upon racial types" (*UP*1 54). The confidence of the young Yeats's propaganda for the Irish Literary Revival was based not only on his own great talents, but on the Celtic gene-pool. He did not have to rely on a substantial record of achievement; all he had to do was to raise to consciousness the creative characteristics of the Celtic race. In this, Arnold was an invaluable if suppressed ally.

Further, Arnold's emphasis in *On the Study of Celtic Literature* on the Celt as above all passionately melancholy – "their manifold striving, their adverse destiny, their immense calamities"[12] – the Celt as defeated but heroic in defeat, greatly impressed Yeats. Stereotype it might be, but it was preferable to the stereotype of Pat the comic Irishman with his bulls and his blunders. In that early review of Ferguson's Celticizing poetry, Yeats praises him for giving the lie to the calumny of England that "we are men of infirm will and lavish lips," and claims instead, in a very Arnoldian way, that the Celt has above all others a "faithfulness to things tragic and bitter." He goes on: "Those who have it, alone are worthy of great causes. Those who have it not, have in them some vein of hopeless levity, the harlequins of the earth" (*UP*1 87). This contrast between Arnold's tragic but dignified Celt and the hopeless levity of the harlequin becomes the basis for Yeats's version of the history of his own time, projected in characteristically aesthetic terms and through the personae of the two greatest Irish leaders of the nineteenth century: "I had seen Ireland in my own time turn from the bragging rhetoric and gregarious humour of O'Connell's generation and school, and offer herself to the solitary and proud Parnell as to her anti-self, buskin followed hard on sock" (*A* 167). This aestheticised version of history was deeply embedded in Yeats's sensibility: hence, in "Easter 1916," motley is laid aside, and the terrible beauty of tragedy replaces the casual comedy.

There is another concern Yeats shared with Arnold. Yeats was acutely aware of the role he had imposed on himself as one who wanted to mold the nation, as one of those who "sang, to sweeten Ireland's wrong" ("To Ireland in the Coming Times"; *VP* 137). At bottom he believed in the role of the poet-critic as one vitally concerned with the shaping of the social polity. For all their temperamental differences and differing rhetoric, Arnold and Yeats are both serious and even earnest men, both poets and cultural critics, and both believed deeply that art had a social function. Yeats may have used Arnold's phrase about literature being a "criticism of life" as a shorthand stick with which to beat the narrowly moralistic strain of Victorian writing, and he may have preferred that the religion of art should be enacted on an altar rather than preached from a pulpit. He was, however, too honest a reader not to see that Arnold transcends that narrow moralism, and that in his own way he too, like Yeats, links the morality of art to the enhancement of life rather than to its repression. As Terry Eagleton says of Arnold:

> His writing plays a vital role in shifting the whole meaning of morality in English discourse away from duties and prohibitions, and back to a more traditional sense of morality as an inquiry into the quality of a whole way of life . . . it concerns itself less with some abstract code of conduct than with the texture of felt experience.[13]

Finally, Yeats knew that in Arnold the cultural critic he had an ally in the fight that both waged in their respective societies against what Arnold called Philistinism. Arnold has made the term "Philistine," the thick-witted, materialistic, opinionated, utilitarian, vulgar, and complacent member of the middle class so current a term of abuse that it needs no glossing, for his own time or indeed for ours. The key text is *Culture and Anarchy* (1869), but the attack had been mounted pretty comprehensively two years earlier in the pages of *On the Study of Celtic Literature*. Indeed, Lionel Trilling sees the latter work as primarily a treatise on the failure of the Victorian middle class, with the Celt providing the salutary (and highly idealized) contrast: "Speaking for the Celt, Arnold speaks for . . . the style of the dream and the ideal, of all that is the opposite of getting and spending, the Philistine activities which have laid waste the powers of England."[14] Getting and spending, the valuation of getting on, the utilitarianism that he saw as the true enemy of vision and dream, and the enemy of what Arnold called "disinterestedness" – these were Yeats's foes too. In an interesting passage in an article in July, 1892, published in *United Ireland*, Yeats shows how carefully he had read Arnold, and how smoothly he was able to transfer Arnold's terminology to the discussion of Irish Philistinism, which he identified with Trinity College Dublin. Yeats begins with a description of his sense of depression at the contemplation of his fellow readers in the National Library:

> Nobody in this great library is doing any disinterested reading, nobody is poring over any book for the sake of the beauty of its words, for the glory of its thought, but all are reading that they may pass an examination . . . [Trinity College] has gone over body and soul to scholasticism, and scholasticism is but an aspect of the great god, Dagon of the Philistines. "She has given herself to many causes that have not been my causes, but never to the Philistines," Matthew Arnold wrote of Oxford. Alas, that we can but invert the sentences when we speak of our own University – "Never to any cause, but always to the Philistines." (*UP*1 232–3)

The passage is contemporaneous with Yeats's rows with Sir Charles Gavan Duffy and his supporters over the kinds of books – strong on patriotic sentiment, weak on anything resembling artistic merit – that they wanted to publish in a New Irish Library series intended to nurture the Irish imagination. It presages later rows over *The Playboy of the Western World*, and over the Hugh Lane bequest of pictures to Dublin on the condition that a suitable gallery be built. Yeats's instinctive hatred of Philistinism was confirmed by Arnold's association of it with lumpen Saxonism, the antithesis of which is the passionate idealism of the Arnoldian (and Yeatsian) Celt.

Yeats often gives the impression that in Victorian literature there was only that moral and ethical bias that he saw as a distortion of the true aim of art. Yet there were other and different poetic traditions or groupings in a period as long as the Victorian. Especially significant to Yeats were the Pre-Raphaelite movement, and then the poetry of the 1890s, the work of those whom he was to call in *Autobiographies* "The Tragic Generation."

Yeats said of himself that he began "in all things Pre-Raphaelite" (*A* 114) and his *Autobiographies* pays full homage to the paintings of Rossetti, Morris, and Burne-Jones, as well as to the poetry of Morris and Rossetti.[15] Introduced as a very young man to Pre-Raphaelitism by his father and his circle, Yeats initially enjoyed its art, pictorial and literary, for the remoteness of its subject matter and its mood from the material, social, and psychological realities of Victorian life. Its delight in color and pattern – Pre-Raphaelite art might be said to aspire to the condition of tapestry – its sensuousness, its remote and exotic subject matter provided one of the bases for the stress on the primacy of the purely aesthetic, which was to be taken up with such enthusiasm in the nineties. Morris and Rossetti concern themselves with the picturesque and decorative details of a medieval never-never land, vaguely Arthurian, and self-consciously exotic. Yeats does not much use the romantic quasi-medieval that was a particularly favored Pre-Raphaelite mode. However, in his earliest poetry his settings are indeed remote, Arcadian or Indian, as for example in "The Song of the Happy Shepherd," "The Cloak, the Boat, and the Shoes" (from *The Island of Statues*, "an Arcadian play in imitation of Edmund Spenser" [*A* 98]), and the Indian poems in the volume *Crossways* (1889). Of course, very early on his settings do become Irish; yet for an English readership they would still have had the glamor of exotic remoteness.

One particular aspect of Pre-Raphaelite art is notably represented in Yeats's own poems of the nineties, collected in *The Wind Among the Reeds* (1899). The women or Woman of the poems is obviously derived from the paintings of Rossetti, especially his *Sibylla Palmifera*, his *Lilith*, and his *Venus Syriaca*. The thick and flowing hair, the long throats, the heavy eyelids and the rapt eyes at once sensual and spiritual, the air of nobility and mysterious sadness – all the features of the Rossetti paintings are to be found in Yeats's poems, where hair is long and heavy and dim, and the lover will be hidden by it or drown in it; where eyes are "passion-dimmed" or "dream-dimmed"; and where the incantatory rhythms suggest the sense of mysterious ritual. "He gives his Beloved certain Rhymes" is characteristic, with its compound adjectives, hieratic gestures, and hypnotic use of parataxis (the linking of clauses by the word "and"), a marked feature in much of the early poetry:

> You need but lift a pearl-pale hand,
> And bind up your long hair and sigh;
> And all men's hearts must burn and beat . . .
> (*VP* 158)

This woman is eternally alluring, but eternally unattainable; but the worship and pursuit of her is the visionary quest that alone makes life meaningful, as for wandering Aengus:

> Though I am old with wandering
> Through hollow lands and hilly lands,
> I will find out where she has gone,
> And kiss her lips and take her hands;
> And walk among long dappled grass,
> And pluck till time and times are done
> The silver apples of the moon,
> The golden apples of the sun.
> (*VP* 150)

It is clear that this type of woman in both portrait and poem is a more fitting subject for the kind of art that favors the altar over the pulpit. Yeats points to the connections between the notion of "pure" poetry, the Pre-Raphaelites, and his contemporaries in the Rhymers' Club in his memoir of "The Tragic Generation":

> Woman herself was still in our eyes, for all that, romantic and mysterious, still the priestess of her shrine, our emotions remembering the *Lilith* and the *Sibylla Palmifera* of Rossetti; for as yet that sense of comedy which was soon to mould the very fashion-plates, and, in the eyes of men of my generation, to destroy at last the sense of beauty itself, had scarce begun to show here and there, in slight subordinate touches, among the designs of great painters and craftsmen. It could not be otherwise, for Johnson's favourite phrase, that life is ritual, expressed something that was in some degree in all our thoughts, and how could life be ritual if woman had not her symbolical place? (*A* 234)[16]

Delight in ritual, in the formal, in the vaguely sacramental, is a feature of the art of the period, manifested in diverse ways in the elaborate prose of Walter Pater, in the exploitation of the aesthetic side of Catholic ritual in the poetry of Lionel Johnson and Ernest Dowson, and in the jeweled artificiality of Oscar Wilde's conversation. Yeats's own ornate prose in the stories of *The Secret Rose*, his absorption in the mysteries of the Order of the Golden Dawn, the labor he expended on trying to construct with Maud Gonne and others a Celtic Mystical Order on an island in Roscommon, are all testimony to the centrality of ritual to his creative imagination. In the poetry, delight in ritual is manifested in the rhetorical devices of inversion, parataxis, repetition, and above all in the "wavering, meditative, organic rhythms" (*E&I* 163) that produce an effect of incantation, of the priest at his shrine, as in the exquisite artifice of the 1899 poem "He wishes for the Cloths of Heaven." However, as we shall see later, for Yeats ritual was not an end in itself, not – as it often is in the poems of Johnson and Dowson – merely decorative and atmospheric, but a means towards revelation; ritual was thus based on genuine if heterodox religious impulse.

Yeats played a significant part in shaping the cultural atmosphere of the 1890s. He saw much to commend in the Aesthetic or Decadent movement, in part because it reflected his own hostility to aspects of the Victorian literary ethos. However, his great and enduring strength as a writer was his willingness to move beyond fixed positions, to embrace the contraries without which, as his master Blake had said, there is no progression. His road was the road of *Hodos Chameliontos* – the Path of the Chameleon (*A* 215) – the winding, swerving, shifting path of the artist. His reservations about and conflicts with the tenets of the Aesthetic movement are as significant for an understanding of his art as his assent to its broad position. In fact, it is in the nineties that one can best see Yeats forging the artistic beliefs that would make him one of the truly great poets of the century to come.

In his 1898 essay with the classic *fin de siècle* title "The Autumn of the Body," Yeats sees his own progress from "externality" to "spirituality" as emblematic of a larger change in the poetic weather. "When I first began to write I desired to describe outward things as vividly as possible," he tells us, but now finds that he has lost the desire of describing outward things, and prefers the "spiritual and unemphatic." He now understands that this change is part of a struggle "all over Europe" against "that picturesque and declamatory way of writing, against that 'externality' which a time of scientific and political thought has brought into literature" (*E&I* 189). He turns to the Victorians, attacks their discursive inclusiveness, and proclaims that the new poetry will be a poetry of contraction, of condensed focus: "The poetry which found its expression in the poems of writers like Browning and Tennyson . . . pushed its limits as far as possible, and tried to absorb into itself the science and politics, the philosophy and morality of its time; but a new poetry, which is always contracting its limits, has grown up under the shadow of the old" (*E&I* 190–1). The critical mentors behind this kind of statement are A. H. Hallam and Pater. Yeats consistently praised Hallam's 1831 essay on the poetry of Tennyson[17] as one of the key documents of nineteenth-century criticism, and in 1893 claimed that the essay had first explained "the principles of the aesthetic movement" (*UP*I 276). In "John Eglinton and Spiritual Art" (1898), he praises Hallam's attempt to distinguish between a "pure" poetry, "art free and unalloyed" in Hallam's words, and poetry with an alien admixture of reflection. Hallam, Yeats believes, stands for "a poetry of sensation rather than of reflection" and against the poetry of Wordsworth which (in Yeats's words) "'mixes up' anecdotes and opinions and moral maxims for their own sake – the things dull temperaments can understand" (*UP*II 130). Yeats is very clear that Hallam's essay is intensely relevant to the aesthetic debate of his own time. In an 1898 review he calls it "a profound essay [which] defines more perfectly than any other criticism in English the issues in that war of schools which is troubling all the arts" (*UP*II 89). In particular, he praises Hallam's valorizing of "sensation" over "reflection."

Hallam's emphases are reinforced in Yeats's mind by the writings of Pater, to whom the poets of the 1890s "looked consciously . . . for our philosophy." *Marius the Epicurean* contained "the only great prose in modern English" (*A* 235), while *Studies in the History of the Renaissance* was doctrinal to the whole generation. Yeats not only placed its famous description of the *Mona*

Lisa, arranged by him in blank verse, at the opening of *The Oxford Book of Modern Verse*, but was profoundly influenced by several aspects of Pater's aesthetic philosophy. Especially important to him were Pater's stress on the primacy and intensity of the given particular moment, and his emphasis on the importance of artistic impression and how all that is not essential to it must be purged away. Yeats was the more ready to incorporate into his own poetry Pater's emphasis on the "privileged moment," since he would have linked the idea to Blake's view of the transforming power of the creative moment. As he writes in 1900 in "The Theatre": "If one studies one's own mind, one comes to think with Blake that 'every time less than a pulsation of the artery is equal to six thousand years, for in this period the poet's work is done, and all the great events of time start forth, and are conceived in such a period, within a moment, a pulsation of the artery'" (*E&I* 172). Yeats's art, as well as his early theories, owes much to the notions he derived from Hallam and Pater. He eschews reflection and recollection in favor of a concentrated lyricism designed to evoke a mood without commentary, as in the characteristically short poem "He reproves the Curlew," where the bird's cry "brings to my mind / Passion-dimmed eyes and long heavy hair / That was shaken out over my breast" (*VP* 155). The "disjunction of sensation from judgment," and the criterion of intensity are central to the creation of modern literature.[18] In the shift from Victorian discursiveness to the modernist poetry of the image, Pater and the impact of his philosophy on the poets of the nineties, including Yeats, plays a significant part.

Yet despite his general approval of Hallam and Pater as allies against externality and discursiveness in poetry, Yeats had critical reservations, and to understand these is to understand how the poet remade his style and his conception of art in the new century. In his diary for 1909, he recants his support for Hallam. Having set out his familiar version of Hallam's distinction between the "pure" Keats and Shelley and the "impure" Wordsworth who "mixed up popular morality" with his work, Yeats goes on to say:

> I now see that the literary element in painting, the moral element in poetry, are the means whereby the two arts are accepted into the social order and become a part of life and not things of the study and the exhibition. Supreme art is a traditional statement of certain heroic and religious truths, passed on from age to age, modified by individual genius, but never abandoned. (*A* 361–2)

The position informally adopted in the diary is developed in the key essay of 1914, "Art and Ideas" (*E&I* 346–55), which looks back not just on Hallam but on the "pure poetry" movement of the nineties. Yeats gently mocks his adherence to the canon of writing poetry where everything except sensation is winnowed away – "I was always discovering some art or science that I might be rid of." He admits the usefulness of the "new formula" derived from Hallam and Pater in freeing his generation from the moralizing "zeal and eloquence" of the earlier Victorians, as a switch to drive geese from the roads. In the end, however, the poetry of sense impressions is not enough for Yeats: "Yet those delighted senses, when I had got from them all that I could, left me discontented" (*E&I* 348). He was aware of the dangers of a disabling subjectivity inherent in the methods of the kind of poetry that he and his companion Rhymers committed themselves to write. Perhaps the self could know nothing but its own experiences? What if, as Yeats wrote in the late poem "The Statues," "Mirror on mirror mirrored is all the show" (*VP* 610)? Asserting the primacy of impressions, Pater had written rather chillingly in the conclusion to his *Studies in the History of the Renaissance*: "Every one of those impressions is the impression of the individual in his isolation, each mind keeping as a solitary prisoner in its own dream of a world."[19]

Yeats finds the antidote to the solipsism of Paterian impressionism in what in one of his late poems he was to call "the book of the people" (*VP* 492). Echoing Arnold's rejection of an art based on "the dialogue of the mind with itself" and his own critique of "the sad soliloquies of nineteenth century egotism," he explains in "Art and Ideas" how he had come early to turn away from the beautiful but chilly Palace of the Aesthetes to a more robust and more nurturing first world: "I filled my imagination with the popular beliefs of Ireland, gathering them up among forgotten novelists in the British Museum or in Sligo cottages. I sought some symbolic language reaching far into the past and associated with familiar names and conspicuous hills that I might not be alone amid the obscure impressions of the senses" (*E&I* 349). The resource of the legends and "popular beliefs of Ireland" was not available to Johnson, Dowson, and the other Rhymers, alone amid the obscure impressions of the senses. Thus, in "The Tragic Generation" Yeats suggests that Pater's philosophy, urging the pursuit of impressions, and a strenuous aesthetic contemplation freed from all public interests, produced the intolerable strains that led to the premature deaths or breakdowns of his contemporaries of the nineties. That philosophy, Yeats writes in a startling metaphor, "taught us to walk upon a rope tightly stretched through serene air, and we were left to keep our feet upon a swaying rope in a storm" (*A* 235).

The art of the inner world of impressions and finely tuned sensibilities, of truth to the private quest for self-realization, is a lesser art, says Yeats in "Art and Ideas," than that of "the centuries before the Renaissance," when art was not separated off from the common pursuits of life, the art of the "old abounding, nonchalant reverie": "Impressions that needed so elaborate a record did not seem like the handiwork of those careless old writers one imagines squabbling over a mistress, or riding on a journey, or drinking round a tavern fire, brisk and active men" (*E&I* 348). In the poem "Ego Dominus Tuus," written soon after the essay, Yeats rejects the solipsism and inner-directedness of Pater's aesthetic ideal, to embrace instead the heroic and active agenda of that older, abounding world where art is not the sole preserve of "the sedentary man out of reach of common sympathy":

> *Hic.* And I would find myself and not an image.
>
> *Ille.* That is our modern hope, and by its light
> We have lit upon the gentle, sensitive mind
> And lost the old nonchalance of the hand;
> Whether we have chosen chisel, pen or brush,
> We are but critics, or but half create,
> Timid, entangled, empty and abashed,
> Lacking the countenance of our friends.
>
> (*VP* 367–8)

The valuation of that old nonchalance of the hand condemns not only the subjectivity of the aesthetic philosophies derived from Pater, but also their passivity. Yeats was clearly uneasy in the nineties with what he saw as the subjection of Symons and Johnson to the impressionism that Pater had recommended.[20] In his diary for 1909 he writes: "Surely the ideal of culture expressed by Pater can only create feminine souls. The soul becomes a mirror not a brazier" (*A* 352). Yeats's roots in the great Romantics, with their conception of the imagination as a lamp rather than as a mirror, is very evident here, as are his masculinist assumptions. His most comprehensive verdict on the progress of poetry in his time, in his introduction to *The Oxford Book of Modern Verse*, brings together his criticism of all the Victorians, the school of Tennyson, and the school of Pater:

> When my generation denounced scientific humanitarian preoccupation, psychological curiosity, rhetoric, we had not found what ailed Victorian literature. The Elizabethans had all these things, especially rhetoric . . . The mischief began at the end of the seventeenth century when man became passive before a mechanized nature; that lasted to our own day with the exception of a brief period between Smart's *Song to David* and the death of Byron, wherein imprisoned man beat upon the door. (*LE* 194)

Passivity, mimesis and impressionism are all enemies of the active, heroic, and tragic imagination. Passivity and impressionism go together, and the "ailment" has continued right to the present. The mischievous older Yeats mocks the "creativity" of his contemporaries by suggesting that they merely record in loose free verse whatever is fortuitously present, and produces his own parodic "poem": "I am sitting in a chair, there are three dead flies on a corner of the ceiling" (*LE* 195). The poetry of three dead flies, of impressionism, will not do. Yeats's own poetry written in the twentieth century moves away from the purity of Pater's aesthetic idealism towards a more robust inclusiveness. He had been confirmed by that idealism in crucial ways, but in the end had to go beyond it. He wrote in 1906: "we should ascend out of common interests, the thoughts of the newspapers, of the market-place, of men of science, but only so far as we can carry the normal, passionate, reasoning self, the personality as a whole" (*E&I* 272). The admiration for the hyper-refined sensibilities in Pater, Maeterlinck, Verhaeren, Stéphane Mallarmé and Villiers de l'Isle Adam is supplanted by a "delight in the whole man – blood, imagination, intellect, running together" (*E&I* 266).

One aspect of the *fin de siècle* nurtured in Yeats one of the most fruitful strains in his sensibility. The sense of imminent revelation appealed greatly to him. Looking back from 1922, he titled his autobiographical account of the decade of the 1890s *The Trembling of the Veil*. He recalled that Mallarmé had said that "his epoch was troubled by the trembling of the veil of the Temple," and that "as those words were still true, during the years of my life described in this book," he had named it accordingly (*A* 111). At the time, during the nineties, he saw it all around him, in the work of Mallarmé, of Villiers de l'Isle Adam, of Maeterlinck, and closer to home in Symons, Johnson, and Dowson: "I see, indeed, in the arts of every country those faint lights and faint colours and faint outlines and faint energies which many call 'the decadence,' and which I, because I believe that the arts lie dreaming of things to come, prefer to call the autumn of the body" (*E&I* 191).

Yeats's epithet "faint" does indeed accurately describe the mannered and attitudinizing art of much of the work of the Decadents, in which the impending end slides rather too easily from *fin de siècle* to the more portentous *fin du globe*, and in which an extreme attenuation is very marked – Maeterlinck, says Yeats, sets before us "faint souls, naked and pathetic shadows already half vapour and sighing to one another upon the border of the last abyss" (*E&I* 190). Yeats is more robust. For him, the apocalypse is always connected with genuine spiritual revelation, with vision, and is independent of a date in the calendar. The persistence of his apocalyptic vision beyond 1900 is proof, and it issues in some of his very greatest poems – "The Magi," "The Second Coming," "Nineteen Hundred and Nineteen," "Leda and the Swan," "Two Songs from a Play," and "Meru" among them. But even in his earliest work, from "The Wanderings of Oisin" to the poems of the late nineties, there is a sense of elemental energy – what Harold Bloom calls "apocalyptic vitalism" in the manner of Blake, Shelley, and Nietzsche – that is not to be found in the work of his contemporaries in the nineties.[21] From the early "The Wanderings of Oisin" onwards, Yeats's work is instinct with a sense of the genuineness of the otherworld and the power of its superhuman inhabitants. In "The Hosting of the Sidhe," for example, the fairy host are as far as it is possible to be from the domesticated denizens at the bottom of English gardens. They converse with the elements of fire and air, they are in furious motion (accentuated by the hammering rhythm), and their passage stuns the human watcher:

> The winds awaken, the leaves whirl round,
> Our cheeks are pale, our hair is unbound,
> Our breasts are heaving, our eyes are agleam,
> Our arms are waving, our lips are apart;
> And if any gaze on our rushing band,
> We come between him and the deed of his hand,
> We come between him and the hope of his heart.
>
> (*VP* 140–1)

The energy and personal force Yeats brought to his art of apocalyptic vision in his great later poems is universally admired; yet their origins clearly lie in the 1890s. This is especially obvious in the ornate stories collected in *The Secret Rose* (1897). The last three stories, which form a kind of triptych, "Rosa Alchemica," "The Tables of the Law," and "The Adoration of the Magi" are particularly heavy with the *fin de siècle* sensibility, and the style is highly reminiscent of Pater. In them, the characters seek out or encounter the visionary moment that will bring a new dispensation. In all three stories, artistic and religious vision are closely linked. In "The Tables of the Law," for instance, the protagonist Aherne has discovered a new heterodox gospel based allegedly on a rare book written by a twelfth-century Cistercian. This will sweep away the Commandments of the Father and the Son and replace them with a new religion. Interestingly, this seems to be a religion of art, which will "reveal the hidden substance of God which is colour and music and softness and a sweet odour" (*SF* 206). This artistic–religious creed is inevitably subversive of the status quo in its very extremism – Aherne has always believed, he tells us, that "the beautiful arts were sent into the world to overthrow nations, and finally life herself, by sowing everywhere unlimited desires, like torches thrown into a burning city" (*SF* 202). "The Adoration of the Magi" provides the first example of Yeats's powerfully heterodox versions of the Christian story of the Epiphany. Here the three Magi are three old Irishmen who travel to Paris to receive their mysterious revelation, that "the immortals" are about to overthrow the present era and inaugurate a new one, from the lips of a dying prostitute. In "Rosa Alchemica," as in all the stories, the narrator is passionately aware of another world that transcends the material one, and whose fringes once again can only be glimpsed or apprehended through the art that he collects:

> All those forms, that Madonna with her brooding purity, those rapturous faces singing in the morning light, those bronze divinities with their passionless dignity, those wild shapes rushing from despair to despair, belonged to a divine world wherein I had no part; and every experience, however profound, every perception, however exquisite, would bring me the bitter dream of a limitless energy I could never know, and even in my most perfect moment I would be two selves, the one watching with heavy eyes the other's moment of content. (*SF* 181–2)

In this story, as in "The Tables of the Law," we can recognize the Yeatsian visionary, whose imagination is always at the end of an era, wearing his *fin de siècle* clothes.

Yeats was an expert cultural politician, and used the Aesthetic or Decadent movement to shape his Irish movement and present it in a flattering yet not wholly uncritical light before both English and Irish readers. Thus, he could pick up on that sense of sophisticated ennui and hyper-refined artificiality in the ethos of the Decadent movement and contrast it with the vigor and energy of the Irish Renaissance, as he does in 1892 in an article "Hopes and Fears for Irish Literature," published in the *United Irishman*:

> It is not possible to call a literature produced in this way the literature of energy and youth. The age which has produced it is getting old and feeble, and sits in the chimney-corner carving all manner of curious and even beautiful things upon the staff that can no longer guide its steps. Here in Ireland we are living in a young age, full of hope and promise – a young age which has only just begun to make its literature. It was only yesterday that it cut from the green hillside the staff which is to help its steps upon the long road. (*UP*1 249)[22]

However, what Ireland may have in creative energy is offset by its lack of craftsmanship and art, its inability to come in any way near the labor and dedication needed "to articulate sweet sounds together" (*VP* 205), which Yeats says in "Adam's Curse" is harder than breaking stones: "But side by side with this robustness and rough energy of ours there goes most utter indifference to art, the most dire carelessness, the most dreadful intermixture of the commonplace" (*UP*1 249). What Irish art needs desperately is what the literary men of France and England have in abundance, and what it needs to learn is "a little of their skill and a little of their devotion to form, a little of their hatred of the commonplace and the banal" (*UP*1 250). In this way,

Yeats uses the Aesthetic movement to rebuke the Philistine Irish assumption that patriotic sentiments alone are sufficient to make good art, and to battle against the legacy of Thomas Davis and the Young Ireland poets. "Today we are paying the reckoning with much bombast," wrote Yeats in 1894 (*P&I* 104); the example of the poets of the Aesthetic movement would be useful in Yeats's project of the "deDavisisation of Irish literature."

Who did Yeats think he was writing for? What was the nature of his audience? His early work dances an elaborate gavotte between patriotism and Aestheticism. Thus, the Irish poets whose naïveté and crudity Yeats lamented had nevertheless one great lesson to teach him, or rather to reinforce in him. They bore witness to the absolute necessity of a national audience. In his late (1937) essay "A General Introduction for my Work," Yeats acknowledges the lifelong importance to him of Thomas Davis and the other poets of the *Nation* school, to whose work he was introduced by John O'Leary: "I saw even more clearly than O'Leary that they were not good poetry. I read nothing but romantic literature; hated that dry eighteenth-century rhetoric; but they had one quality I admired and admire: they were not separated individual men; they spoke or tried to speak out of a people to a people; behind them stretched the generations" (*E&I* 510). At the same time, Yeats was strongly attracted to the notion of an aristocratic and coterie art, and approved of the ways in which Aesthetic and Decadent writers were willing to confront, shock, or ignore the bourgeoisie. He wrote to O'Leary in 1897, at the height of his involvement with the Aesthetic and Symbolist movements of the nineties, that his volume of stories *The Secret Rose* was "an honest attempt towards that aristocratic esoteric Irish literature, which has been my chief ambition. We have a literature for the people but nothing yet for the few" (*L* 286).

In the end, however, "the people" win the battle for his allegiance, notwithstanding his attraction to the elaborate artifice in Decadent literature. The tension between esoteric interests and patriotic commitment is registered in "To Ireland in the Coming Times":

Know, that I would accounted be
True brother of a company
That sang, to sweeten Ireland's wrong,
Ballad and story, rann and song;
Nor be I any less of them,
Because the red-rose-bordered hem
Of her, whose history began
Before God made the angelic clan,
Trails all about the written page.
(*VP* 137–8)

If the patriotic impulse is the stronger, the question of the nature of his audience greatly exercised Yeats during the nineties. The impulse to the "aristocratic esoteric" literature and its "fit audience though few" was strengthened by his involvement with the Decadents and Symbolists. He loved to quote "Villiers de l'Isle-Adam's proud words, 'As for living, our servants will do that for us'." (*A* 236), and was clearly attracted to this fine haughtiness. Like his friends in the Rhymers' Club, who "never made a poorer song / That [they] might have a heavier purse" ("The Grey Rock"; *VP* 273), Yeats spurned the hated commercial and Philistine middle class, as visible in Ireland as in England. Yet how to reach "the people"? One ingenious solution is to be found in his 1901 essay "What is 'Popular Poetry'?". Here, Yeats asserts that the art of the coterie *is* the art of the people, or at least of the people who matter: "There is only one kind of good poetry, for the poetry of the coteries, which presupposes the written tradition, does not differ in kind from the true poetry of the people, which presupposes the unwritten tradition. Both are alike strange and obscure, and unreal to all who have not understanding" (*E&I* 8). In the same year, however, he seems less convinced of the value of "coteries," and asserts with great eloquence in the essay "Ireland and the Arts" the primacy of a kind of art that goes beyond the specialized and rarefied, and in its "symbolic language reaching far into the past" (*E&I* 349) goes beyond also the rootless impressionism of his contemporaries: "I would have Ireland re-create the ancient arts, the arts as they were understood in Judaea, in India, in Scandinavia, in Greece and Rome, in every ancient land; as they were understood when they moved a whole people and not a few people who have grown up in a leisured class and made this understanding their business" (*E&I* 206).

Yeats's relation to the literature and critical theories of the nineties is, therefore, shifting and variable, a mix of attraction to the call of "high art" and rejection of its esoteric remoteness from life, delight in its elaborate artificiality and a yearning for something more like "the book of the people." Similarly, his relation to the earlier Victorian period is not as monolithically hostile as it has been painted. In short, Yeats cannot be understood without being placed firmly in the Victorian context. As Nietzsche, whom Yeats was to call "that strong enchanter," wrote in *The Use and Abuse of History*: "For as we are merely the resultant of previous generations, we are also the resultant of their errors, passions and crimes: it is impossible to shake off this chain. Though we condemn the errors and think we have escaped them, we cannot escape the fact that we spring from them."[23]

NOTES

1. John Eglinton, *Irish Literary Portraits* (London: Macmillan, 1935), p. 17.
2. Sir Arthur Quiller-Couch, Introduction, in *The Poetical Works of Matthew Arnold* (London: Oxford University Press, 1942 [1909]), p. 1.
3. *Ibid.*, pp. 2–3.
4. See Ronald Schuchard, "Yeats, Arnold, and the morbidity of Modernism," *Yeats: An Annual of Critical and Textual Studies* 3 (1985), 88–106, for a full account of Yeats's assent, with Arnold, to Schiller's assertion that "all art is dedicated to joy."
5. See J. V. Kelleher, "Matthew Arnold and the Celtic revival," in *Perspectives in Criticism*, ed. H. Levin (Cambridge, MA: Harvard University Press, 1950), pp. 197–221.
6. *Ibid.*, p. 205.
7. Moran wrote a number of essays in the late 1890s, which were published in book form in 1905 as *The Philosophy of Irish Ireland*. This is a representative passage: ". . . an intelligent people is asked to believe that the manufacture of the beforementioned 'Celtic note' is a grand symbol of an Irish intellectual awakening. This, it appears to me, is one of the most glaring frauds that the credulous Irish people ever swallowed" (*The Philosophy of Irish Ireland* [Dublin: James Duffy and Co., n.d. (1905)], p. 34).
8. Matthew Arnold, *On the Study of Celtic Literature*, in *The Works of Matthew Arnold*, vol. v (New York: AMS Press, 1970), p. 92.
9. See among others Seamus Deane, *Celtic Revivals: Essays in Modern Irish Literature 1880–1980* (London and Boston: Faber and Faber, 1985); David Cairns and Shaun Richards, *Writing Ireland: Colonialism, Nationalism, and Culture* (Manchester: Manchester University Press, 1988); Declan Kiberd, *Inventing Ireland: The Literature of the Modern Nation* (Cambridge, MA: Harvard University Press, 1996); Marjorie Howes, *Yeats's Nations: Gender, Class, and Irishness* (Cambridge: Cambridge University Press, 1996).
10. Frederic E. Faverty, *Matthew Arnold the Ethnologist* (Evanston: Northwestern University Press, 1951), p. 10.
11. Lionel Trilling, *Matthew Arnold* (New York and London: Harcourt Brace Jovanovich, 1949), pp. 232–3.
12. Arnold, *Celtic Literature*, p. 126.
13. Terry Eagleton, "Sweetness and light for all," *TLS*, 21 January, 2000, 14–15.
14. Trilling, *Matthew Arnold*, p. 238.
15. See Elizabeth Bergmann Loizeaux, *Yeats and the Visual Arts* (New Brunswick: Rutgers University Press, 1986).
16. Lionel Johnson, with Ernest Dowson and Arthur Symons, were the members of the Rhymers' Club who mattered most to Yeats's imagination and memory. Of Johnson, Yeats wrote: "He was the first disciple of Walter Pater whom I had met, and he had taken from Walter Pater certain favourite words which came to mean much for me: 'Life should be a ritual', and we should value it for 'magnificence', for all that is 'hieratic'" (*Mem* 26).
17. A. H. Hallam, "On some of the characteristics of modern poetry, and on the lyrical poems of Alfred Tennyson," in *The Writings of Arthur Hallam*, ed. T. H. Vail Motter (London: Oxford University Press, 1943).

18. Denis Donoghue, *Walter Pater, Lover of Strange Souls* (New York: Knopf, 1995), p. 319.
19. Walter Pater, *Studies in the History of the Renaissance* (London: Macmillan, 1873), p. 209.
20. See Carol T. Christ, *Victorian and Modern Poetics* (Chicago: University of Chicago Press, 1984), *passim*; Linda Dowling, *Language and Decadence in the Victorian Fin de Siècle* (Princeton: Princeton University Press, 1986), pp. 244–83; Dwight Eddins, *Yeats: The Nineteenth Century Matrix* (Alabama: University of Alabama Press, 1971), pp. 79–127.
21. Harold Bloom, *Yeats* (Oxford and New York: Oxford University Press, 1970), p. 33. For Yeats, the otherworld, or what he sometimes calls the "Unseen Life," is real. The Immortal Moods are the creative powers behind the universe. As he writes in "The Moods" (1895), they "are the labourers and messengers of the Ruler of All . . . Everything that can be seen, touched, measured, explained, understood, argued over, is to the imaginative artist nothing more than a means, for he belongs to the invisible life, and delivers its ever new and ever ancient revelation" (*E&I* 195).
22. The theme recurs frequently in his writings of this time, especially in his *Letters to the New Island*. See "The Rhymers' Club" (1892): ". . . the literature of Ireland is still young, and on all sides of this road is Celtic tradition and Celtic passion crying for singers to give them voice. England is old and her poets must scrape up the crumbs of an almost finished banquet, but Ireland has still full tables" (*LNI* 60), and "The New National Library" (1892): "In England I sometimes hear men complain that the old themes of verse and prose are used up. Here in Ireland the marble block is waiting for us almost untouched, and the statues will come as soon as we have learned to use the chisel" (*LNI* 66–7).
23. Friedrich Nietzsche, *The Use and Abuse of History*, trans. Adrian Collins (New York: Bobbs-Merrill, 1949), p. 21.

4

DANIEL ALBRIGHT

Yeats and Modernism

When Yeats died in January 1939, he quickly became the ghost that haunted Modernism. First to register the shade's presence was W. H. Auden, who wrote his famous elegy "In Memory of W. B. Yeats" in February 1939:

> Now he is scattered among a hundred cities
> And wholly given over to unfamiliar affections . . .
> The words of a dead man
> Are modified in the guts of the living. . . .

For Auden, Yeats is a distasteful Orpheus, whose corpse dismembers into the scattered leaves of his volumes of poetry, undergoing a queasy process of digestion in the guts of his readers. Auden gives the distinct impression that Yeats might have been a much more satisfactory meal:

> You were silly like us . . .
> [Time] Worships language and forgives
> Everyone by whom it lives;
> Pardons cowardice, conceit,
> Lays its honours at their feet.
>
> Time that with this strange excuse
> Pardoned Kipling and his views,
> And will pardon Paul Claudel,
> Pardons them for writing well.[1]

He does not directly call Yeats a timid, vain, blustering fascist, but by treating Kipling, Claudel, and unspecified cowardly and conceited poets as parallel cases, he leaves such characterizations open as a possibility.

In an essay in the *Partisan Review* (Spring, 1939), "The Public v. the Late Mr. William Butler Yeats," Auden, wearing the mask of the "Public Prosecutor," goes further: he says that Yeats did nothing to "create a juster social order, he felt nothing but the hatred which is born of fear":

> Of all the modes of self-evasion open to the well-to-do, Nationalism is the easiest and the most dishonest. . . . Still, it has often inspired men and women to acts of heroism and self-sacrifice. For the sake of a free Ireland the poet Pearse and the countess Markiewicz gave their all. But if the deceased did give himself to this movement, he did so with a singular moderation . . . What are we to say of a man whose earliest writings attempted to revive a belief in fairies and whose favourite themes were legends of barbaric heroes with unpronounceable names, work which has been aptly and wittily descried as Chaff about Bran?[2]

The defense attorney in Auden's imaginary debate tries a few mild rebuttals of these points, but with less verve and conviction. In 1939 Auden saw Yeats's ghost as a fussy and inept specter, and yet (as the elegy suggests in a slightly noncommittal fashion) a figure of astonishing force, a river, a fountain in the heart's desert, a manifestation of something great. Even the bland glance at the thermometer at the opening ("O all the instruments agree / The day of his death was a dark cold day") can be interpreted either as the sign of a preference for objective fact over mythy nonsense, or as the symptom of desolation of the landscape from the master's death, as if Yeats were the Grail King from Eliot's *The Waste Land*. It is impossible to get a clear fix on Auden's attitude toward Yeats; one may feel that Auden scribbles mustaches on Yeats's face to defend himself from his overwhelming cultural authority. The whole elegy works at once to manifest Yeats's ghost and to exorcise it: even Auden's adoption, in the last part of the poem, of Yeats's almost-patented form of catalectic trochaic tetrameter suggests the power of the ghost to usurp the soul of his elegist. Auden ridicules Yeats's spooks, but seems determined to become a spirit-medium in spite of himself. Because "Under Ben Bulben," Yeats's tetrameter elegy to himself, was not published until February 1939, and then only in three Irish newspapers, the literary historian may feel a certain shiver that the ghost was trying to show itself forth simultaneously through the *Irish Times* and through Auden's empathic intelligence.

The ghost's next important apparition occurred around August 1942, when T. S. Eliot was writing drafts for the so-far unsatisfactory second part of "Little Gidding":

> Then, changing face and accent, he
> declared with another voice:
>
> These events draw me back to the
> streets of the speech I learned early
> in life. I also was engaged in the
> battle of language. My alien people

with an unknown tongue claimed
me. I saved them by my efforts –
you by my example: yet while I
fought the darkness I also fought the
light, striving against those who
with the false condemned the true.
Those who have known purgatory
here know it hereafter – so shall you
learn when enveloped by the coils
of the fiery wind, in which you
must learn to swim.[3]

The ghost goes on to say that his "spirit parted from the southern shore" – Yeats died in the south of France – and to add other details that tend to identify him with Yeats, though Yeats's name never appears. As air-raid warden Eliot moves through the dismantled streets of London, he seems to inhabit a purgatory that contains one and only one shade, as if Tradition had fined itself down to a sole Individual Talent, that of Yeats. Like Auden, Eliot seems eager to deface the mighty ghost: Eliot makes him confess that he fought the light as well as the darkness, as if his anarchic strength were so great that nothing whatever, good or bad, could stand before him. In *The Waste Land* Eliot imagined a Thunder Word, *DA*, an utterance of such force that it might restore vitality to a slack, exhausted culture; in "Little Gidding" he imagines a Thunder Speaker, a furious wraith who seems to energize and to destroy; to prophesy and to lacerate; to sustain, even if that sustenance has the bitter taste of shadow fruit. The ghost seems an abstract of the whole culture of the English language, in all its triumph and failure.

In both Auden's poem and Eliot's, the ghost is so intimate with the elegist that every excoriation of the ghost seems a form of self-excoriation. As Auden wrote many years later, Yeats "has become for me a symbol of my own devil of inauthenticity [. . . his poems] make me whore after lies."[4] This almost repeats Eliot's complaint that Yeats's "'supernatural world' was the wrong supernatural world. It was not a world of spiritual significance, not a world of real Good and Evil, of holiness or sin, but a highly sophisticated lower mythology summoned, like a physician, to supply the fading pulse of poetry with some transient stimulant so that the dying patient may utter his last words."[5] For Auden and Eliot, Yeats was *false*: he wrote potent, unforgettable poetry without caring whether the content was good or evil, truth or error. In the elegy, Auden calls him "A way of happening, a mouth," a line that may insinuate that Yeats was all mouth and no brain, a blank megaphone, the Decadents' *poésie pure* incarnate. Still, he looms.

What Harold Bloom calls the anxiety of influence usually leads to a more elegant and subtle subversion of the great father-poet than this hectoring of Yeats. Auden and Eliot seem to see themselves as walking in Yeats's footsteps, just as Chaucer, at the end of *Troilus and Criseyde* (written 1382–6), asks his "litel book" to "kis the steppes where as thow seest pace / Virgile, Ovide, Omer, Lucan, and Stace." But Auden and Eliot seem to find themselves confronted with a path that leads straight to purgatory, if not to hell. Has poetry itself, in a dying culture, simply become a form of lying? The extraordinary prosiness of Auden's and Eliot's later works might suggest that with Yeats the art of poetry has reached its end.

But perhaps Yeats could stimulate his successors precisely because his rhetorical vehemence seemed disconnected from any discipline except the discipline of poetic form. If he struck Auden and Eliot as amoral, evasive, indifferent to truth, he nevertheless reminded them that poetry is incantation, spell, charm – an art dedicated not to correctness but to power. Auden and Eliot were suspicious of the poet's archaic and magical aspect – Auden once wrote that the purpose of poetry is "by telling the truth, to disenchant and disintoxicate."[6] But it is impossible to disenchant without some prior enchantment, and it may be that Yeats and his drabber successors form a single whole. The long tradition of British poets, from the savage bards who could make trees walk by casting spells, to the refined sorcery of Yeats, may find its complement and antidote in the later Modernism of Eliot and Auden. But perhaps disillusionment is itself a flattering illusion, and the poet who whores after lies may not always go in the wrong direction.

According to my records, the third visitation of Yeats's ghost occurred in 1945, in a detention camp in Pisa:

> . . . I recalled the noise in the chimney
>   as it were the wind in the chimney
>   but was in reality Uncle William
>   downstairs composing
>   that had made a great Peeeeacock
>   in the proide ov his oiye
>   had made a great peeeeeeecock in the . . .
> made a great peacock
>   in the proide of his oyyee
>
>   proide ov his oy-ee
>   as indeed he had, and perdurable
>
>   a great peacock aere perennius . . .[7]

In this passage from Ezra Pound's Canto LXXXIII, memories of Yeats seem to intensify into a sort of "clairaudience." Pound recalls a moment from the winter of 1913–14, when he and Yeats lived in a cottage in Sussex learning the craft from one another: Yeats was bawling his poem "The Peacock" out loud, to test its cadences as he invented it. Now, in 1945, the finished poem disarticulates itself into wind, pneuma, sheer inspiration. Yeats's organ seems to fill vast spaces with sound, as if he, so intimate with transcendence, has become after death the voice of imagination itself.

For Yeats's successors, then, Yeats was both god and idol, the ark of the covenant and the golden calf.

If Yeats became a ghost that haunted Modernism, Modernism was also a ghost that haunted Yeats. Yeats often casts himself as the enemy of Modernism. If Eliot condemns Romanticism as "fragmentary . . . immature . . . chaotic,"[8] Yeats asserts "We were the last romantics" (*VP* 491). Again and again, Yeats flogs the Modernist poets for their sloppiness of construction ("All out of shape from toe to top" [*VP* 639]) and flatness of diction. He never pretends to understand the concept of free verse; the best that he can say of an ametrical poem that he finds reasonably attractive, Pound's "The Return," is that it seems like a brilliant improvisation that "has not got all the wine into the bowl" (*LE* 193). When, in the introduction to *The Oxford Book of Modern Verse* (1936), the elderly Yeats sums up his response to contemporary poetry, he finds a writhe, a seethe, a degenerate mess: "Nature, steel-bound or stone-built in the nineteenth century, became a flux where man drowned or swam; the moment had come for some poet to cry 'the flux is in my own mind'" (*LE* 195). Most of all Yeats despises the absence of metaphor, the dead plod, in advanced recent poetry: he even offers a little caricature of a Modernist poem: "It has sometimes seemed of late years . . . as if the poet could at any moment write a poem by recording the fortuitous scene or thought, perhaps it might be enough to put into some fashionable rhythm – 'I am sitting in a chair, there are three dead flies on a corner of the ceiling'" (*LE* 194–5). As Yeats says elsewhere, this rejection of imagination reminds him of the sedate bewigged poetry of the Augustan age: "Technically we are in a state corresponding to the time of Dryden . . . We are developing a poetry of statement as against the old metaphor. The poetry of to-morrow will be finely articulated fact. T. S. Eliot fascinates us all because he is further on towards this consummation than any other writer."[9] It seems that Modernist poetry paradoxically combines all the worst aspects of banality and incomprehensibility.

And yet, one might venture to argue that there is not a single feature that Yeats ascribes to Modernist poetry that cannot be found in Yeats's own poetry. Vulgar diction starts to intrude in the late 1930s: "His rod and its butting head / Limp as a worm"; "Belly, shoulder, bum, / Flash fishlike"

(*VP* 575, 612). Much earlier, at the time of his winters in Sussex with Pound, there come experiments with something like free verse. Compare Pound's "The Return" with a passage from Yeats's play *At the Hawk's Well*:

See, they return, one, and by one,
With fear, as half-awakened;
As if the snow should hesitate
And murmur in the wind,
    and half turn back;[10]

Her heavy eyes
Know nothing, or but look upon stone.
The wind that blows out to sea
Turns over the heaped-up leaves at her side;
They rustle and diminish. (*VPl* 401)

It is difficult to find any technical reason for declaring one passage freer than the other: each has irregular line lengths, and an iambic pulse unsteadied by extra syllables in odd positions. If anything, more wine spills out of Yeats's bowl than Pound's.

As for Modernist fortuitousness, dependency on casual observation, we can even find a Yeats poem not far removed from "I am sitting in a chair, there are three dead flies on a corner of the ceiling":

The bees build in the crevices
Of loosening masonry, and there
The mother birds bring grubs and flies.
My wall is loosening . . . (*VP* 424)

This is a somewhat unfair example, since Yeats instantly proceeds to take the scenery as a metaphor for his spiritual state, and the stanza concludes with a prayer: "honey-bees, / Come build in the empty house of the stare." On the other hand, might not the imaginary Modernist poet have meant the three dead flies as an emblem of despondency, torpor? Does not Yeats himself mean to say something about the inner life of Modernism by referring to the three dead flies?

One aspect of bold artistic ambition is the desire to be complete; and Yeats may have felt, consciously or unconsciously, that he had to incorporate the methods and themes of Modernism in order to comprehend in himself the whole round of art. Similarly Igor Stravinsky, in old age, fitfully abandoned his tonal style and adopted an idiosyncratic version of Arnold Schoenberg twelve-tone methods. Stravinsky waited until Schoenberg's death in 1951 before attempting something that might be read as capitulation; Yeats, however, did not have the luxury of trying to outlive Pound, Eliot, and Auden, and so had to fight them and to accommodate them at the same time.

Many of those whom we call the High Modernists were born in the 1880s: Ludwig Kirchner, Pablo Picasso, Igor Stravinsky, Béla Bartók, Virginia Woolf, Anton Webern, James Joyce, D. H. Lawrence, Pound, Alban Berg, and T. S. Eliot, for example. Yeats was born in 1865, during a decade far less richly productive of English writers; but if we look beyond the confines of English literature, we find in the 1860s the birth years of a number of important Modernists, or precursors to Modernism, such as Claude Debussy, Gustav Klimt, Richard Strauss, Vassily Kandinsky, and Henri Matisse. All of them were profoundly influenced by the aesthetic of Symbolism, the artistic movement that leads most directly into Modernism.

Accounts of the origin of Modernism often begin with Charles Baudelaire, partly because Baudelaire's *The Painter of Modern Life* (1864) gave such prestige to the term *modern*:

> *this solitary mortal endowed with an active imagination, always roaming the great desert of men . . . is looking for that indefinable something we may be allowed to call "modernity,"* for want of a better term to express the idea in question. *The aim for him is to extract from fashion the poetry that resides in its historical envelope, to distil the eternal from the transitory . . . Modernity is the transient, the fleeting, the contingent; it is one half of art, the other being the eternal and the immovable . . . You have no right to despise this transitory fleeting element, the metamorphoses of which are so frequent, nor to dispense with it. If you do, you inevitably fall into the emptiness of an abstract and indefinable beauty.*[11]

Of course, if Modernism is defined as the art of fugitive urban junk – posters for last week's cabaret singers ungluing in the rain, orange peels flushing into the sewers – Yeats is the least Modernist of poets. Many Modernists were at home in cities; one rarely encounters a major character in a novel by Joyce or Woolf who would feel comfortable milking a cow. But Yeats's attitude towards the pavements grey, despite the fact that he lived in Dublin or London for most of his life, was contempt: "When I stand upon O'Connell bridge in the half-light and notice that discordant architecture, all those electric signs, where modern heterogeneity has taken physical form, a vague hatred comes up out of my own dark" (*E&I* 526).

On the other hand, Baudelaire was also the poet of "Correspondences," which defines nature as a temple where living pillars utter confusing words – man passes through a forest of symbols that stare at him with an intimate gaze. This is the sonnet that gave an important push to the Symbolist movement. In fact, the tension in Baudelaire's aesthetic between the "transitory fleeting element" and "abstract and indefinable beauty" – between the city's detritus and transsensuous sanctity – helped to generate Modernism itself. In his occult book *A Vision* (1925) Yeats expresses this tension as an eternal competition between objective (factual, ugly) and subjective (symbolic, beautiful), continually boring into one another in the peculiar arrangement he called a double gyre – a set of intersecting cones. Yeats feels that the Modernist artists were to some extent failures, in that their work shows a grotesque floundering between realistic and mythic/hallucinatory elements:

> Mr Ezra Pound, Mr Eliot, Mr Joyce, Signor Pirandello . . . either eliminate from metaphor the poet's phantasy . . . or . . . break up the logical processes of thought by flooding them with associated ideas or words that seem to drift into the mind by chance; or . . . set side by side as in "Henry IV," "The Waste Land," "Ulysses," the *physical primary* – a lunatic among his keepers, a man fishing behind a gas works, the vulgarity of a single Dublin day prolonged through 700 pages – and the *spiritual primary*, delirium, the Fisher King, Ulysses' wandering. It is as though myth and fact . . . have now fallen so far apart.
>
> (*VA* 211–12)

This is not a bad reading of Modernism: a heap of urban garbage weirdly juxtaposed with antique glamor. Professors like to teach *Ulysses* by stressing the points of connection between Homer's *Odyssey* and Joyce's novel; but much of the pleasure lies in the bitonal clash, the discord between the two texts.

From a Symbolist point of view – from Yeats's point of view – the objective or realistic elements exist only as a sort of colorful wrapping paper that half disguises, half reveals the bright ineffabilities within. As Thomas Carlyle put it in 1836, man's "Life is properly the bodying forth" of the Invisible, and "In a Symbol there is concealment and yet revelation."[12] As Jean Moréas put it in the Symbolist manifesto of 1886,

> Symbolic poetry, the enemy of "instruction, declamation, false sensibility, and objective description," seeks to clothe the Idea in a tangible form which will not be that poetry's object but which, while serving to express the Idea, will remain subordinate. Nor must the Idea itself be seen stripped of the sumptuous robes of external analogy; for the essential characteristic of symbolic art is never to go so far as the conception of the Idea in itself. Thus, in this art, neither scenes from nature nor human actions nor any other physical phenomena can be present in themselves: what we have instead are perceptible appearances designed to represent their esoteric affinities with primordial Ideas.[13]

Symbolist art, then, is an aesthetic of strip-tease, an unveiling of something (intense, devastating) that can never be shown quite naked, lest the spectator, like Semele, perish from over-apprehension. This explains why the Symbolists keep reviving again and again the story of Salome (who never had a dance of the seven veils until Oscar Wilde gave her one in his 1893 play): Richard Strauss in his 1905 opera; Yeats in the story "The Binding of the Hair" (1896) and the plays *The King of the Great Clock Tower* (1934) and *A Full Moon in March* (1935); and Klimt in his 1901 *Judith* (presumably the severed head belongs to Holofernes, not John the Baptist, but the woman's eyes-half-shut, head-thrown-back, lips-faintly-parted look of sexual languor tends to make the spectator think first of Salome). The art work becomes the garment of shimmering gold, the erogenous zone beneath which some bulge of meaning makes itself felt.

Yeats is always happier with symbols drawn from the traditional stock of conventions than with symbols drawn from modern life. For Yeats, such fact-scenes as a man fishing behind the gas works could never align themselves properly with a myth, a meaning – so *The Waste Land* looks to him like a bunch of industrial photographs arbitrarily pasted onto the story of Parsifal or Adonis, like a tin can tied to a dog's tail. It took a later generation of Modernists to savor the dissonance between fact and myth with full appreciation of the aesthetic possibilities. Nevertheless Yeats's works, like those of all the Symbolists, are full of the most up-to-date references, though the contemporaneity is sometimes occluded. The Viennese public that first saw Klimt's *Judith* regarded it as a disturbing portrait of a contemporary upper-class Jewish woman, and Klimt's volumeless, intricate style reflects the most recent artistic trends. Strauss's music characterizes Salome as a creature of pure chromatic glitz, sometimes slithering out of tonality altogether. And Yeats furnishes his play *The King of the Great Clock Tower* with the movable abstract sets that the visionary director Gordon Craig had devised for a famous early-twentieth-century production of *Dido and Aeneas*: "*an inner curtain . . . may have a stencilled pattern of dancers . . . one sees to left the King and Queen upon two thrones, which may be two cubes. There should be two cubes upon the opposite side to balance them . . . The background may be a curtain hung in . . . a semi-circle of one foot Craig screens, so painted that the blue is darker below than above*" (*VPl* 990, 992). Yeats aspires to a sort of timelessness, but the conventions of his eternity are those determined by the Cubism of Picasso and the dramaturgy of the Noh play as revealed by a Japanese dancer who had studied with the Denishawn modern dance company in New York. Another sign of Yeats's engrossment with Modernist abstraction can be found in his last play, *The Death of Cuchulain*, in which Cuchulain's severed head is represented by "*a black parallelogram, the size of a man's head. There are six other parallelograms near the backcloth*" (*VPl* 1061). The more fervently Yeats tries to disencumber himself of the modern world, the more deeply the modern world imprints itself upon his work.

The first aesthetic movement fully to rejoice in the technological present – and in that sense the first Modernist movement – thrust itself on Europe in 1909, when Filippo Tommaso Marinetti published his Futurist manifesto in *Le Figaro*. For Baudelaire, the city was a zone of detachment, where a distinguished, nearly extinguished observer could gaze into shop windows, or contemplate a spectral throng of passing strangers; for Marinetti, the city was a zone of power, the buzzsaw of motors on the street, the silent buzz of electric wires above, an outspew of signifiers. For Marinetti, an art work should aspire to the brute certainty of the laws of physics: "To substitute for human psychology, now exhausted, the lyric obsession with matter . . . The warmth of a piece of iron or wood is in our opinion more impassioned than the smile or tears of a woman."[14] Furthermore, art should attune itself to the radiation that permeates the universe – as he wrote, collaborating with some futurist painters, in the "Technical Manifesto of Futurist Painting": "All things move, all things run, all things are rapidly changing . . . moving objects constantly multiply themselves: their form changes, like rapid vibrations, in their mad career. Thus a running horse has not four legs but twenty . . . Who can still believe in the opacity of bodies, since our sharpened and multiplied sensitivity has already penetrated the obscure manifestations of the medium? Why should we forget in our creations the doubled power of our sight, capable of giving results analogous to those of X-rays?"[15]

Yeats, of course, detests most of the things that Marinetti loved. He purges his poetic vocabulary of technological words. As he explains to Virginia Woolf, such words as *steam roller* were altogether dead to his ear: "He said that the spade had been embalmed by 30 centuries of association; not so the steam roller. The great age of poetry, Shakespeare's age, was subjective; ours is objective; civilisations end when they become objectified. Poets can only write when they have symbols. And steam rollers are not covered in symbolism – perhaps they may be after 30 generations."[16] For Marinetti, the shock, the crush, imparts to the steam roller the most potent symbolic value, while the spade has long since sunk into the realm of the boring; for Yeats, symbolic value can be imparted only by age and long use – no word is fit for poetry unless your great-grandfather uttered it.

And yet, Yeats is fascinated by what he loathes, and technology, obliquely or directly, makes a strong appearance in his writing. Aerial warfare especially haunts him, from the symbolical "brazen hawks" whose "innumerable clanging wings . . . have put out the moon" to the quite explicit evocation,

"Aeroplane and Zeppelin will come out, / Pitch like King Billy bomb-balls in" (*VP* 427, 565). A canceled passage from "Under Ben Bulben," also on the theme of aerial bombardment, shows Yeats's closest approach to Futurism:

So what's the odds if war must come
From Moscow, from Berlin, or Rome.
Let children should an aeroplane
Some neighbouring city pavement stain,
Or Should the deafening cannon sound
Clasp their hands & dance in a round.
The passing moment makes it sweet
When male & female organ meet[17]

The poem cuts from exploding bombs to dancing children to orgasm. Marinetti wrote odes to his femme fatale, the machine gun; Yeats here toys with a similar confusion of the erotic and technological. Yeats's great-grandfather surely never used the word *aeroplane*; and yet a device that can provoke such powerful glee may indeed be fit for use in a poem.

Even the robot, that science-fiction gadget familiar from Karel Čapek's *R.U.R.* (1921) and Fritz Lang's film *Metropolis* (1927), has a role to play in Yeats's imagination. Ezra Pound, in his more demonic aspect, could appear to Yeats as a big doll or robot: "Mr. Pound, not transfigured but transfixed contemplat[ing] the race . . . until hatred turns the flesh to wood and the nerves to wire."[18] And when Yeats considers the future society of AD 2000 – the end of our modern, thing-driven, fact-ridden civilization, according to his historical system – he has a vision of gigantic puppets chomping or manipulating small human figures:

> with the last gyre must come a desire to be ruled or rather, seeing that desire is all but dead, an adoration of force spiritual or physical, and society as mechanical force be complete at last.
>
> Constrained, arraigned, baffled, bent and unbent
> By those wire-jointed jaws and limbs of wood
> Themselves obedient,
> Knowing not evil and good.
>
> A decadence will descend . . . what awaits us, being democratic and *primary*, may suggest bubbles in a frozen pond – mathematical Babylonian starlight.
> (*VA* 213)

Technology may be Moloch, a general smashing or petrifying of things, but it does not lack poetic interest.

The machine is exceedingly sinister in Yeats's work, as his version of a mock mechanical Creation suggests:

> Locke sank into a swoon;
> The Garden died;
> God took the spinning-jenny
> Out of his side. (*VP* 439)

Yeats discovers the robot not only in the spinning-jenny but also in *The Waste Land*'s typist, whose verse-movement seems to him as mechanical as the gramophone she plays "with automatic hand": "in *The Waste Land* there is much monotony of accent" (*LE* 191). But if Yeats hates machines, he likes electromagnetic radiation just as much as the Futurists did. Giacomo Balla painted objects that decompose into fields of force (*Street Lamp*, 1909); Luigi Russolo painted objects generated from the vibration-patterns of sound (*Music*, 1912). If Yeats, following Blake, rejects the Newtonian model of the clockwork cosmos in which dead objects swing inexorably around other dead objects, Yeats hopes that post-Newtonian physics may be far more congenial – may even find experimental proof for the existence of the phenomena he witnesses during spiritualist séances:

> I once heard Sir William Crookes tell half a dozen people that he had seen a flower carried in broad daylight slowly across the room by what seemed an invisible hand. His chemical research led to the discovery of radiant matter, but the science that shapes opinion has ignored his other research that seems to those who study it the slow preparation for the greatest, perhaps the most dangerous, revolution in thought Europe has seen since the Renaissance, a revolution that may, perhaps, establish the scientific complement of certain philosophies that in all ancient countries sustained heroic art. (*VPl* 569)

Crookes was the physicist who developed the cathode ray tube by sending an electric current through rarefied air. The "radiant matter" mentioned by Yeats has nothing to do with radioactivity, but instead refers to a fourth state of matter, beyond solid, liquid, or gas, that Crookes (incorrectly) described. Crookes noticed that cathode rays caused certain substances to phosphoresce; and it seemed to Yeats that Crookes's scientific and psychic researches were converging – that ectoplasm was receiving a sort of public confirmation. Marinetti looked forward to an art of pure radiation: "The reception amplification and transfiguration of vibrations emitted by matter[.] Just as today we listen to the song of the forest and the sea so tomorrow shall we be seduced by the vibrations of a diamond or a flower."[19] It is of course a long way from Madame Blavatsky to Marconi, and yet both Yeats and Marinetti hoped for a poetry in which potent vibrations far beyond the visible spectrum would enter into the field of knowing.

During and just after the Great War, starting in the cabarets of Zurich and Berlin, the Modernist movement stared directly at its limits. How far could art go towards a radical attack on the assumptions that governed its own operation and reception? How far could art go towards a disengagement of itself from history, from canons of beauty, from the human mind itself? Here, in the world of Dada, artists performed experiments in dismembering art: Tristan Tzara, for example, generated poems by cutting up newsprint into individual words, mixing them in a hat, and pulling them out one by one. Here is the art that Yeats sets himself against, "All out of shape from toe to top" – indeed it had no purpose except to investigate the aesthetics of out-of-shape. And yet, from a certain point of view, the Dadaists were behaving like magicians, who have always looked for inspiration to random designs, the pattern of dregs in the bottom of teacups, the flight of birds, the twist of intestines, a word chosen by chance from Virgil or the Bible. Yeats's magic was purposive and consequential, unlike the magic of the Dadaists, but they were alike hoping for revelation from disordered fields or from the null set.

According to the mythology of Yeats's *A Vision*, personality types close to the full moon, Phase 15, are lost in imaginative reverie, while personality types close to the new moon, Phase 1, are lost in contemplation of objective truth. Therefore, those personality types that fit into the last few days of the lunar month, Phases 26, 27, and 28, lead useful lives only insofar as they try to cure themselves of desire, try to accept the physical world exactly as it is. For most of the phases, Yeats lists human exemplars, such as Keats in Phase 14, and Blake (and Maud Gonne) in Phase 16, since Romantic poets and beautiful women manifest the maximum degree of imagination. But for the extremely objective phases, Yeats mentions no specific people, except for Socrates and Pascal in Phase 27, the phase of the Saint – most of those born in these phases have too little personality to leave any trace in the historical record. Abandoned to the sheer factuality of things, they cannot register any traces of themselves against the unyielding background of hard objects and hard ideas. And yet, Yeats likes to correlate his phases of human personality with artistic movements; and if I read his descriptions of Phases 26 and 28 correctly, Yeats is thinking of people who might be called Dadaists:

Phase 26 is called the Hunchback, or the *Multiple Man*:

> All the old abstraction, whether of morality or of belief, has now been exhausted . . . there is an attempt to substitute a new abstraction, a simulation of self-expression . . . He is all emphasis, and the greater that emphasis

> the more does he show himself incapable of emotion, the more does he display his sterility. If he live amid a theologically minded people, his greatest temptation may be to defy God, to become a Judas who betrays, not for thirty pieces of silver, but that he may call himself creator . . . "The Hunchback is his own *Body of Fate*." (*VB* 177–8)

Body of Fate is Yeats's technical term for the objective world as it manifests itself to a particular person. Therefore, the Hunchback has in effect turned into a *thing*: incapable of having a finite personality, he is simply a deformation, a lump of clay not yet shaped into a man.

If Yeats's Hunchback, utterly incoherent and unimaginative, were to become an artist, he could do little more than to exhibit his own falseness by means of spasms of nihilistic defiance. This is one interpretation of what the Dadaists in fact did. In Yeats's play about Judas, *Calvary* (1920), the Roman soldiers perform a "dance of the dice-throwers" for Christ's cloak, and, in a note to the play, Yeats tells a story about an old Arab who has spent his life worshiping God's Chance: "If I should throw from the dice-box there would be but six possible sides on each of the dice, but when God throws He uses dice that have all numbers and sides" (*VPl* 790). I know no better description of the God of Dada, the random number generator from whom the universe streams. As Tzara said, "Everything is incoherent . . . There is no logic . . . The acts of life have no beginning and no end. Everything happens in a completely idiotic way."[20] If the Hunchback points the way towards identification of the human subject with exterior chaos, Yeats's Fool, at Phase 28, has fully achieved it: "He is but straw blown by the wind, with no mind but the wind and no act but a nameless drifting and turning" (*VB* 182). It is as if he were cut up and put inside Tzara's hat.

Of all the radical aspects of Modernism, Surrealism came closest to touching Yeats. By the early 1920s the disintegrating force of Dada had reached such a pitch that it managed to disintegrate itself; and from its orts and scraps André Breton cobbled together a movement that he called, borrowing a term that Apollinaire had coined in 1917, Surrealism. Surrealism can be conceived as a psychologizing of Dada, in that it displaced the *locus* of random from the exterior universe to the human mind: as Breton defined it in the *Surrealist Manifesto*, "SURREALISM, n. Pure psychic automatism . . . Dictation of thought in the absence of all control exercised by reason."[21] Breton experimented with methods for hearing the inspired voice, the dictation of the unconscious, by cultivating states of trance, waiting, and then at last transcribing the mysterious words and images that appeared. Breton gave a famous example of words that "*knocked at the window*" of his mind: "'There is a man cut in two by the window' . . . it was accompanied by a feeble visual representation of a walking man sliced halfway up by a window perpendicular to this axis of his body."[22]

Breton's automatism had the cachet of Freud and the literary avant-garde. But Yeats was pursuing a surprisingly similar automatism, under the far less reputable aegis of occult research. Yeats records in his autobiography some of his sessions with MacGregor Mathers, a quixotic, war-obsessed visionary: when Yeats closed his eyes and Mathers held a cardboard symbol to Yeats's head, "there rose before me mental images that I could not control: a desert and black Titan raising himself up by his two hands from the middle of a heap of ancient ruins. Mathers explained that I had seen a being of the order of Salamanders because he had shown me their symbol" (*A* 161). In this light, Yeats's poem "The Second Coming" (1920) looks like a transcript of an automatic process of image-evocation. The poet empties his mind until it becomes a *tabula rasa*; then in the blank desert there appear complicated intra-ocular effects ("Reel shadows of the indignant desert birds") and in the center a vision, more virtual than actual, of a sphinx-Antichrist, "slouch[ing] towards Bethlehem to be born" (*VP* 402). Breton sought what he called convulsive beauty; and Yeats's poems often record both images of terrible beauty and the processes of imaginative convulsion that bring them into being.

Yeats differs from Breton in that his rigid stanza forms, his extraordinary syntactical control, impose a sort of discipline on the imaginative act. Yet sometimes that very discipline could impose a sense of the automatic. "Sailing to Byzantium" (1927) begins with a leisurely, somewhat loose stanza about Ireland's salmon falls and mackerel-crowded seas, but ends with a stanza in which the poet imagines himself transfigured after death into a golden bird – written in tick-tock iambs, this stanza gives the feel of a key winding the mechanical bird's mainspring. It is a powerful conclusion, this twitter of hammered gold and gold enameling; and yet it verges on a whole world of Modernist toys, as in Stravinsky's Hans Christian Andersen fable *The Nightingale* (1914) – the artificial nightingale is Stravinsky's true heroine, not the real one – George Antheil's *Golden Bird* (1921), and Paul Klee's *Twittering Machine* (1921). One of the sources of Surrealism's force is a certain shivery sense that the voice of the unconscious or transconscious has little of human pertinence to say – that its dictate is something inanimate, vain, a measured seizure, a rote chirp. It makes us uncomfortable to think that its deepest oracle may scarcely serve to keep a drowsy emperor awake.

In the last year of his life, when Yeats was decrying the out-of-shape-from-toe-to-top as loudly as he could, he was also experimenting more intently than ever before with seriously shapeless ways of writing, as in "High Talk" (1938), a poem about a stilt-walker:

All metaphor, Malachi, stilts and all. A barnacle goose
Far up in the stretches of night; night splits and the dawn breaks loose;
I, through the terrible novelty of light, stalk on, stalk on;
Those great sea-horses bare their teeth and laugh at the dawn.

(*VP* 623)

Yeats does not quite indulge in the slosh of images that André Breton could produce, but he comes close: "Ah, to take a bath, a bath of the Romans, a sand bath, an ass's milk sand bath . . . To travel on the back of a jellyfish, on the surface of the water, then to sink into the depths to get the appetite of blind fish, of blind fish that have the appetite of birds that howl at life."[23] This passage is from *The Immaculate Conception* (1930), a text in which Breton tries to find prose equivalents for various mental diseases. As Yeats's speaker admits that he and his world consist entirely of metaphor, he seems to lose any sense of what these tropes are metaphors for: they seem to become free radicals, figures of speech incapable of terminating in meaning, metaphors for nothing in particular, simply constituents of a landscape deliquescing into ecstasy. This is an essentially Surrealist state of referencelessness: barnacles, geese, sea-horses, it is all an uncontrolled teeming of words, just as Breton's text continually deviates into inconsequence. The recklessness of Yeats's last year can scarcely be exaggerated. Sometimes he casts a cold eye on life and death; other times he undergoes strange seizures of giddiness and frivolity, as when, in his play *The Herne's Egg*, a man enters "*leading a Donkey, a donkey on wheels like a child's toy, but life-size*" (*VPl* 1014). One explanation of the origin of the word *dada* is that it is a child's word for hobby-horse; Yeats promotes the hobby-horse to a character in an apocalyptic farce.

It could be argued that Yeats's *A Vision* is the greatest of all Surrealist experiments. Based on years and years of George Yeats's trances, in the form of both automatic writing and transcriptions of voices she uttered while she slept, *A Vision* never falters in its attempts to rationalize the unrationalizable: the messages from the unconscious, or from beyond death, seem all the eerier because they exercise such strong resistance to interpretation. Breton's texts, by contrast, have a certain stressless feel, because Breton, a trusting man, rarely calls them into question. I have previously quoted some of the passages from *A Vision* that describe the failure of the human subject to constitute itself before the disorderliness, the defunction of things; perhaps no *Modernist* text is more intimate with chaos.

The strenuous geometry of *A Vision*, with its diagrams of gyres and cones and midnight things, does not lessen the feel of chaos's hand at work. Nothing is more formless than arbitrary form: when the form imposed is the wrong form for the content, or when the content is such that any form would be the wrong form, then form does not serve to articulate or illuminate. Yeats deplores the arbitrary form he found in Cubist painting: "I feel in Wyndham Lewis's Cubist pictures an element corresponding to rhetoric arising from his confusion of the abstract with the rhythmical. Rhythm implies a living body, a breast to rise and fall, or limbs that dance, while the abstract is incompatible with life" (*VA* 11). And yet, he repeatedly describes *A Vision* as an essentially Cubist book: "the whole philosophy was so expounded in a series of fragments which only displayed their meaning, like one of those child's pictures which are made up out of separate cubes, when all were put together" (*VA* 11). This childishness is not something clumsy and immature, but the high childishness of High Modernism itself: "now that the system stands out clearly in my imagination I regard [the gyres] as stylistic arrangements of experience comparable to the cubes in the drawing of Wyndham Lewis and to the ovoids in the sculpture of Brancusi" (*VB* 25). Yeats fights Modernism as hard as he can, only to find himself acknowledging that he is Modernist to the marrow of his bones. But this paradox is itself typical, for the Modernist often travels a road as far as it will go, only to wind up in some exactly opposite place.

NOTES

1. W. H. Auden, *The English Auden*, ed. Edward Mendelson (New York: Random House, 1977), pp. 242–3.
2. *Ibid.*, pp. 390–1.
3. Helen Gardner, *The Composition of Four Quartets* (New York: Oxford University Press, 1978), p. 186.
4. Humphrey Carpenter, *W. H. Auden: A Biography* (Boston: Houghton Mifflin, 1981), p. 416.
5. T. S. Eliot, *After Strange Gods: A Primer of Modern Heresy* (New York: Harcourt Brace, 1933), p. 51.
6. W. H. Auden, *The Dyer's Hand* (New York: Random House, 1962), p. 27.
7. Ezra Pound, *The Cantos of Ezra Pound* (New York: New Directions, 1995), pp. 533–4. Horace (*Odes* III.30) intended his poems to be *aere perennius*, more lasting than bronze.
8. T. S. Eliot, *Selected Essays* (New York: Harcourt Brace, 1960), p. 15.
9. E. H. Mikhail, ed. *W. B. Yeats: Interviews and Recollections*, Vol. II (New York: Barnes & Noble, 1977), p. 200.
10. Ezra Pound, *Personae* (New York: New Directions, 1926), p. 74.
11. Vassiliki Kolocotroni *et al.*, eds. *Modernism: An Anthology of Sources and Documents* (Chicago: University of Chicago Press, 1998), pp. 106–7. The translator here is P. E. Charvet.
12. Thomas Carlyle, *Sartor resartus* (London: J. M. Dent, 1975), pp. 164–5.

13. Cited in Robert L. Delevoy, *Symbolists and Symbolism* (New York: Rizzoli, 1982), p. 71.
14. Filippo Tommaso Marinetti, *Marinetti: Selected Writings*, trans. R. W. Flint and Arthur A. Coppotelli (New York: Farrar, Straus, and Giroux, 1972), p. 87.
15. Cited in Caroline Tisdall and Angelo Bozzolla, *Futurism* (New York: Thames and Hudson, 1989), pp. 33, 35.
16. Virginia Woolf, *The Diary of Virginia Woolf, Vol. III, 1925–1930*, ed. Anne Olivier Bell, assisted by Andrew McNeillie (New York: Harcourt Brace Jovanovich, 1980), p. 330.
17. Jon Stallworthy, *Vision and Revision in Yeats's Last Poems* (Oxford: Clarendon Press, 1969), pp. 163–4.
18. George Mills Harper, *The Making of Yeats's "A Vision": A Study of the Automatic Script*, Vol. II (Carbondale: Southern Illinois University Press, 1987), p. 28.
19. Filippo Tommaso Marinetti and Pino Masnata, "La radia," trans. Stephen Sartarelli, in *Wireless Imagination*, ed. Douglas Kahn and Gregory Whitehead (Cambridge, MA: MIT Press, 1992), p. 267.
20. Robert Motherwell, ed. *The Dada Painters and Poets: An Anthology* (Cambridge, MA: Belknap Press, 1981), pp. 250–1.
21. André Breton, *Œuvres complètes*, Vol. I, ed. Marguerite Bonnet (Paris: Editions Gallimard, 1988), p. 328.
22. *Ibid.*, pp. 324–5.
23. André Breton, *What is Surrealism? Selected Writings*, ed. Franklin Rosemont (New York: Pathfinder, 1978), p. 50. This passage was translated by John Ashbery.

5

HELEN VENDLER

The later poetry

If we arbitrarily divide Yeats's fifty-four years of publishing into thirds, "late Yeats" would cover the years 1920–39. By 1920, when he was fifty-five, Yeats felt that his heart had grown old (as he said in "The Wild Swans at Coole"). He had given up his hope to marry Maud Gonne (to whom he had proposed, for the last time, in 1916), had married George Hyde Lees, had become a father at the birth of his daughter Anne, and, when lecturing in America, had seen his failing father for the last time (J. B. Yeats died in 1922). Yeats had already moved into a retrospective mode by writing, in 1914, the first of his autobiographical essays, called *Reveries over Childhood and Youth*, to be followed, in 1922, by *The Trembling of the Veil*. He was spending summer weeks in his tower at Ballylee, making it his symbol of age, endurance, fortitude, and wide observational power. He and his wife were ardently pursuing the practice of automatic writing, which had led, in 1918, to the first sketch – called *Per Amica Silentia Lunae* – of the occult materials that would receive their fullest form in the 1926 publication of *A Vision*.

In another person's life, this period of late middle age might have been a quiet and intimate one, but Yeats could not be indifferent to the larger world of politics. After 1914, events in Europe, England, and Ireland took on destructive forms. During World War I (1914–18), many Irish enlisted and died in the British forces, among them Lady Gregory's son Robert. In 1916, a symbolic rebellion against British rule in Ireland, deliberately raised at Easter to suggest an aura of religious resurrection, had been put down by British troops, and its leaders – several of them personal friends of Yeats, two of them poets – were executed as traitors. In 1920, the British parliament passed the Government of Ireland Act, partitioning the country into the six counties of Northern Ireland (still governed by England) and the Republic of Ireland, which was granted independence. Political strife intensified, martial law was declared, and, upon the ratifying of the Anglo-Irish Treaty by the Irish parliament in 1922, civil war broke out in Ireland between the nationalists who did not want to settle for partition, and those who accepted the treaty. These ungovernable events and others further afield (such as the Russian Revolution in 1917) brought home to Yeats, as nothing lyric or occult could have done, the uncontrollable forces of violence by which lives of individuals are threatened. Things unthinkable began to happen, summed up by Yeats in his great political poem, "Nineteen Hundred and Nineteen":

> Now days are dragon-ridden, the nightmare
> Rides upon sleep: a drunken soldiery
> Can leave the mother, murdered at her door,
> To crawl in her own blood, and go scot-free.
> (*VP* 429)

The incident of the murdered mother (killed by the British irregular squads known – because of the color of their uniforms – as the "Black and Tans") happened in the neighborhood of Yeats's tower. Human violence had come into close view, and this time innocent civilians, not armed forces as in the 1916 Easter Rising, were among the victims.

Yeats's most recent volume of poetry, *The Wild Swans at Coole*, had mentioned the World War but only briefly, in the largely private elegies for Robert Gregory: "Shepherd and Goatherd," "In Memory of Major Robert Gregory," and "An Irish Airman Foresees his Death." (There was a fourth, more political elegy, called "Reprisals," which, at the request of Lady Gregory, was not published: it placed her son "among the other cheated dead.") Yeats deliberately refused to write directly about the War. His concise and classical epigram "On being asked for a War Poem" claims the right, even in time of war, to direct himself to lyric and private verse:

> I think it better that in times like these
> A poet's mouth be silent, for in truth
> We have no gift to set a statesman right;
> He has had enough of meddling who can please
> A young girl in the indolence of her youth,
> Or an old man upon a winter's night. (*VP* 359)

But that was when the war was England's. As soon as war moved onto Irish soil, Yeats could not keep silent. When he wrote, it was not "to set a statesman right," but to meditate, like his mythical hero Cuchulain in "Cuchulain Comforted," on "wounds and blood" (*VP* 634).

The first volume of poetry published in the last third of Yeats's writing life was *Michael Robartes and the Dancer* (1921). Although Yeats had privately published his stirring "Easter 1916" before the 1917 publication of *The Wild Swans at Coole*, he held it back until the furor of the event had died down. It appeared – together with other poems about the Rising and its dramatis personae – in the 1921 volume, companioned by the second famous poem of the volume, apocalyptically entitled "The Second Coming," an altogether more archetypal poem about the turn of history toward violence. In the third famous poem of the volume, "A Prayer for my Daughter," the random storms of the world threaten even Yeats's newborn child. In these three poems, we can see three characteristic modes of late Yeats: the historic, the archetypal, and the personal. Together with his other late poems, they raise the question whether Yeats is the "last romantic" (as he said himself) or the first Modernist. Some critics have been unwilling to grant him the Modernist label, because he wrote within traditional genres and verse-forms. Others see that the originality, insouciance, and even blasphemy in his employment of those genres and those forms removes him from Romantic and Victorian modes of writing, and makes him rather the first of the iconoclastic Modernists writing in English.

As I have said, in "Easter 1916" we can see Yeats's first mode, a properly historical one, as he refers to "this man" and "this other man" among the participants in the Easter Rising, and finally names them as they would be known to history: "MacDonagh and MacBride / And Connolly and Pearse." For this "historical mode," Yeats chose the rapid *abab* trimeters that became one of his most powerful poetic symbols of a natural Irish aristocracy of being. These half-hexameters – the epic measure split in two – go to the drumbeat of an implied tetrameter, in which the fourth foot is silent: x′ x′ x′ [x′].

This man had kept a school
And rode our wingèd horse;
This other his helper and friend
Was coming into his force.
(*VP* 392)

The pause at each line-break would be represented, if the piece were reassembled into hexameters, by the medial cesura:

This man had kept a school // and rode our wingèd horse;
This other his helper and friend // was coming into his force.

The greater briskness of the trimeter form breaks the narrativity of the epic hexameter into short, nervous lines; and Yeats's *abab* quatrains emphasize, by coming to a rhyme-word at the end of each three-beat line, that these are complete lines in themselves, rather than half-hexameters. On the other hand, by running his quatrains together, so that the sense-unit need not coincide with the rhyme-unit, Yeats de-emphasizes the quatrain-form in relation to the larger stanzas into which the quatrains fit.

Yeats chose to inscribe into the poem the historic date of the Easter Rising – the twenty-fourth day of the fourth month of 1916 (24/4/16) – by making stanzas of sixteen lines (nos. 1 and 3) alternate with stanzas of twenty-four lines (nos. 2 and 4); all stanzas are assembled from four-line units. This unusual form of extreme numerological control has an element of Yeatsian magic behind it: if technique were to make something happen on the page, it had to be intimately linked, by some means, to the originating cause. (Yeats was more likely to practice this sort of magic in his earlier verse, but he never forsook it utterly; we see it reappear in "Nineteen Hundred and Nineteen," in which, as my student Nathan Rose pointed out to me, part II has two stanzas, part III has three stanzas, part IV has four lines, part V has five five-line stanzas; and part VI is composed in continuous rhyming sixains.)

If Yeats's first mode is historical, the second, as I have said, aspires to the archetypal, and even the apocalyptic. All particular historical reference is suppressed as Yeats opens "The Second Coming" (*VP* 401–2) with the impersonal stance of an epic viewer-from-above of the entire earth: "Things fall apart; the centre cannot hold." This opening becomes the octave of a "failed" impersonal blank-verse sonnet. The poem cannot continue in the impersonal mode; it cannot write its own sestet. Therefore Yeats re-begins the poem, in line 9, as a sonnet in the first person, which then, as one man's lyric perspective, can find its sestet. When a lyric poet utters in a sonnet huge vatic lines such as "everywhere / The ceremony of innocence is drowned," his genre – which depends on an interior point of emotional reference – is endangered. Yeats consequently stops short after his last of these impersonal statements – "The best lack all conviction, while the worst / Are full of passionate intensity" – and re-opens the poem in the first-person mode: "a vast image out of *Spiritus Mundi* / Troubles my sight." The personal conclusion follows in the now "successful" sestet: "I know / That twenty centuries of stony sleep / Were vexed to nightmare by a rocking cradle." Yeats could not have completed the poem without the mutation from the voice of the cosmic sage to the voice of the located "I." The apocalyptic declaration of the poem – that the 2,000 years of Christian hegemony are ending, and that a new sphinx-like force that will govern the next 2,000 years is "slouch[ing] towards Bethlehem to be born" – is nonetheless not made entirely in declarative form. "I know *that* . . ." is followed by "And *what* rough beast. .?" (italics mine). The non-parallel syntax shows that the poet's knowledge is limited. He is convinced that a new force is imminent, for which the cosmic cradle has been set rocking; yet what sort of beast it will be is as yet undetermined. Unlike the canonical Apocalypse, the Modernist apocalyptic utterance is not certain of its visions.

The third of Yeats's modes in the famous poems of this volume is the intimate lyric one. It appears in conjunction with several themes: marriage, the old-age waning of hatred and desire ("Demon and Beast"), and the birth of his daughter ("A Prayer for my Daughter"; *VP* 403–6). The last of these poems might more properly have been entitled "A Prayer that the Ill-Fortune that Fell on my Mother and my Beloved May Not Fall on my Daughter." Yeats's wishes for his infant daughter (wishes sometimes mistakenly represented as patriarchal and limiting) are an apotropaic gesture, warding off the curse of beauty that led Maud Gonne (as it had led Helen of Troy and Venus herself) to mate with a fool; warding off, too, the curse of hatred that chokes the mind and that had destroyed Maud Gonne's inner peace; and warding off as well the curse that had fallen on Yeats's mother when she married a feckless man who never settled her in a stable house, but shifted her round from lodging to lodging until she sank into permanent depression and illness. Haunted by the evils that had befallen the two women dearest to him in his youth, Yeats prays for his daughter,

> May she be granted beauty and yet not
> Beauty to make a stranger's eye distraught . . .
> It's certain that fine women eat
> A crazy salad with their meat
> Whereby the Horn of Plenty is undone . . .
> O may she live like some green laurel
> Rooted in one dear perpetual place . . .
>
> . . . to be choked with hate
> May well be of all evil chances chief . . .
>
> And may her bridegroom bring her to a house
> Where all's accustomed, ceremonious . . .
> How but in custom and in ceremony
> Are innocence and beauty born?
> Ceremony's a name for the rich horn,
> And custom for the spreading laurel tree.

Yeats, who nowhere in his poetry wrote autobiographically about his sad mother, here imagines for her the life she should have had, rooted in a familial "accustomed" place, a place where she could be happy. Since his daughter is as yet an unknown quantity, he can only hope to launch her on a life less full of distress than his mother's, less full of folly and hatred than Maud Gonne's ("I thought my dear must her own soul destroy, / So did fanaticism and hate enslave it" ["The Circus Animals' Desertion"; *VP* 630]. Yeats's guilt towards two beloved women – feeling that he ought to have been able to save them and yet not having succeeded – shadows and underlies the poem for his daughter, which finds exoneration for that guilt in the conviction that one can save only oneself by banishing past and present hatred from the mind:

> . . . all hatred driven hence,
> The soul recovers radical innocence
> And learns at last that it is self-delighting,
> Self-appeasing, self-affrighting,
> And that its own sweet will is Heaven's will.

The three modes that I have identified as historical, apocalyptic, and intimate continue to be of use to Yeats in his next volume, *The Tower* (1928). But they are joined there by a fourth mode, which I will call the comprehensive one – a mode that attempts to survey an entire life from beginning to end, and say something that is true of the whole rather than of a single episode or a single mood. In a youthful poem of 1899, Yeats had regarded the "fire-born moods" (*VP* 142), despite their existential transience, as substantively eternal, and the true subject of lyric. Old age, however, must go beyond "moods" to a philosophical enquiry into the entire life. This late audit in *The Tower* – though conducted with great force, depth, and intelligence in the title poem and "Sailing to Byzantium" – finds its most complete and beautiful form in the *ottava rima* Romantic ode called "Among School Children." A poem in *ottava rima* consists of pentameter stanzas rhymed in two asymmetric parts, a sestet and a couplet: *abababcc*. As its name suggests, it originated in Italy, but it had been used in English by such predecessors of Yeats as Shelley and Byron; it appears in Yeats's poetry as a consequence of his 1907 trip to Italy in the company of Augusta Gregory. As a Renaissance form, *ottava rima* implied to Yeats aristocratic poise, custom, and ceremoniousness (aesthetic qualities of life never present in his father's and mother's rented lodgings, but amply evident in Lady Gregory's comfortable, welcoming, and peaceful house at Coole Park). Yeats was to use *ottava rima* memorably in almost a score of reflective poems. These range from "Sailing to Byzantium" to "The Circus Animals' Desertion" and they include the first poems in the sequences "Meditations in Time of Civil War" and "Nineteen Hundred and Nineteen," and the two Coole Park poems.

Both "Sailing to Byzantium" and "Among School Children" scrutinize and debate Yeats's life-choices; but the first is conceived mythically, the second autobiographically: the first is classical in organization, the second apparently wayward. The symmetry of "Sailing to Byzantium" (*VP* 407–8) can be seen not only in the fact that the rhyme ending its first half ("come . . . Byzantium") is perfectly mirrored in the rhyme ending the second half ("Byzantium . . . come"), but also in the fact that the "country" scene of the first stanza – which portrays a heterosexual company, lovemaking, birds in the trees, and a "sensual music" – is analogously replicated in the "city" scene of the last stanza – a company of "lords and ladies of Byzantium," a "drowsy" Emperor ("drowsy" was for Yeats a word allied with the sleep of sensuality), a bird on a golden bough, and a historical and prophetic music "Of what is past, or passing, or to come." In between the alternatives of "that country" and "the holy city" is placed a (rejected) third place, called "God's holy fire," in which an ascetic and asexual company of male sages lives in eternity and sings the praises of God.

For Yeats, medieval Byzantium represented a culture in which the sacred and the profane were in aesthetic balance: the artificers of Byzantium not only produced religious artifacts of eternity (such as the mosaics of the cathedral of Hagia Sophia, Holy Wisdom, with their gold background representing the holy fire) but also worldly artifacts of time (secular enameled golden birds for the Emperor's court). Where, thinks Yeats, do I belong now that I must leave the country of lovemaking and "sensual music?" It is understandable that for a moment he thinks of abandoning his body ("a dying animal"), as he prays to the sages to consume away his heart (the source of sensual love) because it is still, in spite of his dying body's impotence, "sick with desire." If the sages were to gather what is left of him – minus his body and his heart – "into the artifice of eternity," he would join the company of Isaiah, Jeremiah, and the other sages in heaven, a heaven "visible" to the devotee who looks "through" the gold of the sacred mosaic to the eternity it represents iconographically. Yeats chooses instead to take on the form of an artifice of time, the golden bird that sings in all tenses, past, present, and future. He will remain – though unmated himself – in a heterosexual and secular company. The rhapsodic move to odal address to a transcendent order – "O sages standing in God's holy fire" – is dropped at the end of the poem in favor of an ironic and tempered view of the company Yeats would like to keep. The golden bird sings the kind of music – not a "vertical" religious hymn but a "horizontal" hymn of life's changes – that is found in Yeats's *Collected Poems*.

The most comprehensive of all Yeats's late poems, "Among School Children" (*VP* 443–6) also rises to an odal address, but does not forsake it for a worldly irony in the manner of "Sailing to Byzantium." After a deliberately mundane and autobiographical beginning in which Yeats the senator (who bitterly sees himself at sixty as a "scarecrow" and a "smiling public man") visits children in kindergarten and is shown round by the nun in charge, his mind wanders to what Maud Gonne might have looked like as a child of their age. But then, cruelly, his imagination shows her to him as she now is at sixty, "hollow of cheek." This despairing diptych of Maud young and old is succeeded by a second diptych of the poet himself young and old: we see a male child as a "shape" upon his mother's lap, and then encounter him at the poet's age, "with sixty or more winters on its head," as his own mother judges that, given what her son has become at sixty, she should not have borne and raised him.

The learning on which the children in the schoolroom are embarking is thought by humanists to lead to the highest spiritual efforts – and yet, when Yeats thinks of those who have carried it farthest – Plato the philosopher of the invisible ideal, Aristotle the philosopher of the solid real, and Pythagoras the philosopher of the aesthetic – he reduces them to physical scarecrows like himself. The success of the mind does not compensate for the failure of the body. As a backdrop to the individual scarecrows that he and Maud Gonne have become, we see stretch the scarecrow-frieze of all past thinkers and creators. It is at this low point that the poem resorts to odal address, calling out to all the idols created and worshiped by human beings. The lover idolizes the object of his passion; the nun idolizes in her piety the divinity symbolized by the statues before which she prays; the mother, in affection, idolizes her child. And yet these objects of devotion, one and all, end up breaking the hearts of their worshipers. Yeats calls out bitterly to our idealized objects – and breaks off, unable to continue his address to them:

> . . . O Presences
> That passion, piety or affection knows,
> And that all heavenly glory symbolise –
> O self-born mockers of man's enterprise . . .

The marring of the erotic body by Christian asceticism (even if the soul is thereby enhanced), the marring of the emotions by the despair of the unrequited lover-poet (even if the beauty of art is born from the wreck of erotic hope), the marring of the eyes of the philosophers by their midnight study (even if wisdom is the product) seem to be the bitter results, in old age, of piety, passion, and learning.

At this lowest point, the poem is rescued – at the last possible moment – by a massive re-conceiving of life. Hitherto, life has been indexed by its two determining points – its promising inception and its betrayed close. Now, with a mighty effort, Yeats begins to think of life in two new ways. He perceives it, first, as an ongoing organic process that continues, always, even in age, to bear the blossoms of perpetually efflorescing inner energy: "O chestnut-tree, great-rooted blossomer, / Are you the leaf, the blossom or the bole?" Though the image of the sturdy "blossomer" inseparable into its parts is a consoling one, the blossoming of the tree is involuntary, its effort seasonal: in these respects, Yeats knows, it differs from human creativity. In a final burst of inspiration, Yeats replaces the image of the chestnut tree with another – that of the self-choreographing dancer (such as Loie Fuller) who – with the continual "brightening glance" of creative invention – spontaneously conceives of and executes, to the music imposed by Fate, a self-born, self-identifying pattern: "O body swayed to music, O brightening glance, / How can we know the dancer from the dance?" This is not an external image "that passion, piety or affection knows"; it is an internal image that the self makes of the self. The dancing dancer represents living as a continually invented creative act extended over time. One is not, then, in terms of identity, either the child one was or the scarecrow one is: one's identity is the linear shape self-choreographed throughout life, a shape never ceasing to evolve, and continuous from childhood to death. By "rewriting" Wordsworth's "Ode: Intimations of Immortality" – a comparably comprehensive and philosophical poem on the compensation of loss by creativity – in Modernist (individual, wayward, secular) fashion, Yeats found a way to be more than his less-than-human enameled singing bird or blossoming chestnut tree. The fully human portrait of the dancer inventing a dance to the music of time reconceives life as a fluid motion, a voluntary cooperation with, and interpretation of, one's fated location in historical time and space.

Many of Yeats's most ambitious late poems take up these themes of identity, culture, and wisdom, refracting them in different emphases. As his meditations grew more elaborate, Yeats often turned to sequences as a form of combining, while distinguishing, different foci of attention. His sequences are not isometric (that is, the poems are not all of the same shape, as Shakespeare's sonnets – with a few exceptions – are); they may contain poems of different stanza form, different length, and different symbolic systems. I want to chart, in order to show the ambition of the Yeatsian sequence, the seven individual poems that make up "Meditations in Time of Civil War," a poem written in the midst of a national crisis that came to Yeats's own threshold, a crisis in which he saw the definitive end of the Protestant Ascendancy in Ireland. The sequence begins with "Ancestral Houses" (*VP* 417–18) (forty lines), an ornate *ottava rima* debate about the relation between the violence (such as Cromwellian dictatorship) that imposes hegemony, and its results in subsequent aesthetic productions such as the culture of the "Big House"; its verse-form suggests Yeats's sympathy with the aristocratic Protestant elite, without whom art, he fears, cannot exist. In direct contrast to "Ancestral Houses" is the second poem, "My House" (*VP* 419–20) (thirty lines), comprising three ten-line stanzas of a shape invented by Yeats to symbolize the complexity of the aged mind. Though all the stanzas observe the same rhyme (a sestet – *abcabc* – followed by an embraced quatrain – *deed*) and the same line-lengths (553553; 3335), the unfamiliarity of such untraditional patterns of rhyme, and the oddity of lines – such as those in the quatrains – in which lines that rhyme do not exhibit the same line-length – make this a formalist house, yes, but a distinctly Modernist one.

In the third poem of "Meditations in Time of Civil War," Yeats takes us inside his house to see his table, on which he has placed a symbolic object, an ancient Japanese sword wrapped in embroidery. Its admonitory masculine presence, softened by its feminine cloth, brings the influence of the past into the present in which Yeats must forge works of art at his table. "My Table" (*VP* 421–2) (thirty-two lines) is composed of eight continuous quatrains with no white space between them: these rhyme in couplets *aabb*, in which two tetrameters are followed by two trimeters (4433). This unstable "rocking" measure, like the poem, oscillates between the "noble" past and the ignoble present. And what of the future? Meditating on the inclination of all things to decay, and wondering about his own progeny, the poet returns in the fourth poem, "My Descendants" (*VP* 422–3) (twenty-four lines) to the ceremonial *ottava rima* measure of "Ancestral Houses." Since no systems or constructs can last, and his family may well decline, the tower, which itself will sink into ruin, will at best commemorate him, his wife, and Lady Gregory.

These four poems just described may be thought of as the "run-up" to the center of "Meditations in Time of Civil War," the poem – much shorter than its predecessors – called "The Road at my Door" (*VP* 423–4) (fifteen lines) in which successively two soldiers, "An affable Irregular" and "A brown Lieutenant," each representing one side of the Irish conflict, pass the time of day with Yeats at his tower. Yeats, envying these men of action, turns away, "caught / In the cold snows of a dream." The five-line tetrameter stanzas rhyme *abaab*, prolonging the "normal" quatrain into the rare cinquain and "delaying" the expected *b*-rhyme. Such delay in stanza length and in return of the *b*-rhyme suggests, I think, Yeats's reluctance to abandon the active world for his aesthetic "chamber." (Compare Keats's comparable prolongation of his ten-line odal stanza by an eleventh line in "To Autumn" in order to express his reluctance to encounter winter.) The *b*-rhymes all end in "n" or "m," connecting these three cinquains to each other by recurrent sound, though this effect may not be noticed except in hindsight, after we read the next poem.

Deprived of the fantasy of political action, certain that all human constructions will decay, that there will be no more ancestral houses, that his descendants may lose heart, and that his tower and his table will come to ruin, Yeats finds nowhere to turn, in the sixth poem of his sequence, except to nature, to the honeybees building a nest in the abandoned nesting-place of the starlings, in a fissure in the rock-wall of the tower. "The Stare's Nest by my Window" (*VP* 424–5) (twenty lines) repeats the *abaab* cinquains of "The

Road at my Door," making sure we perceive these poems as "fraternal" if not "identical" twins. As in "The Road at my Door," each cinquain of "The Stare's Nest by my Window" possesses the same *b*-rhyme, but it is a far more "hearable" rhyme (in the broad vowel-sound "air") than the sometimes slant *b*-rhymes of the earlier poem ("man," "sun," "uniform," etc.). The sound "air" is reinforced since each stanza ends with the same refrain-prayer to the honeybees: "Come build in the empty house of the stare." This yearning poem – facing the worst of the random civil strife ("Last night they trundled down the road / That dead young soldier in his blood") – acts as a "counter-spell" to its predecessor, "exorcising," by using the identical stanza-form, the poet's envy of men of action. Yeats prays instead for the traditional "sweetness" (honey) and "light" (candle-wax), which are the products of the labor of bees (often used to symbolize poets). Cultural violence cannot be changed by hatred, by military action, but only by culture's evolution into more peaceful counter-forms, created by meditation and love.

Yeats's extraordinarily titled last poem, "I See Phantoms of Hatred and of the Heart's Fullness and of the Coming Emptiness" (*VP* 425–7) (forty closing lines, "magically" matching the opening forty lines of the first poem, "Ancestral Houses"), consists of eight-line stanzas rhyming in quatrains, *ababcdcd*. It is written in rough epic hexameters suitable to the sweeping mist, the wind, and the images of a troop of violent men that at first bewilder and perturb the Hamletian "mind's eye" of the poet. The poem becomes calmer as the image of a raging crowd is replaced by images of unicorn-borne ladies full of erotic loveliness and "self-delighting reverie"; but they in turn give way to images of a menacing and indifferent fate, "The innumerable clanging wings that have put out the moon." (These images may be seen as representative of the four themes that have preoccupied the poet – violence, love, art, and annihilation.) As the poem comes to an end, Yeats turns once again away from the active life to reiterate his devotion to these images rising from his "daemonic" or unconscious mind: "The abstract joy, / The half-read wisdom of daemonic images, / Suffice the ageing man as once the growing boy." Yet the poet cannot – though he "matches" the end-poem of his sequence to the opening-poem in forty-line extension – duplicate in "I See Phantoms of Hatred" the initial "civilized" *ottava rima* with which his sequence began ("Ancestral Houses") and which was continued in "My Descendants." He will conclude with an eight-line stanza, yes – but he will abandon the *ottava rima* rhyme scheme, and the stately pentameter, in favor of restless enjambed quatrains and an unsettled turbulent hexameter.

Such a long sequence (201 lines written over two years) – with its tonal and stanzaic variety, its internal self-reference, its weighing of the claims of action and art – suits the enormous confusion of civil war. Yeats's other long non-isometric sequences – "The Tower," "Nineteen Hundred and Nineteen," "Blood and the Moon," "Vacillation," and "Supernatural Songs" – could be "mapped" in comparable ways, as a set of responses to a historical and personal reality too complex to be examined in anything other than a multifaceted way. The stanza-forms chosen for such non-isometric sequences often bear either ideological or "magical" meaning, as I have said above concerning those in "Nineteen Hundred and Nineteen." In "Blood and the Moon" (*VP* 480–2), for instance, poems I, III, and IV all consist of three quatrains in "embraced rhyme," *abba*: but since the first of these poems – an epigram serving as epigraph – is written in trimeter, whereas poems III and IV are written in pentameter, the effects at beginning and end are vastly different. Such a conjunction of similarity accompanied by difference is intended to show that "something" is the same at the end of the sequence (poem IV) as at the beginning (poem I): we are still within the triadic subject of earthly blood, celestial moon, and the winding stair between the two; we are still in the "conclusive" mood of embraced (rather than alternate) rhymes. However, the initial epigrammatic mockery has by the end been replaced by meditative debate between violence and the ideal, blood and the moon, power and wisdom. What has intervened to make this happen? In between the epigrammatic epigraph of I and the dual (and brilliant) blood-and-moon meditations of III and IV comes the astonishing poem II, six lurching, irregular tercets rhyming *aaa*, with lines ranging in length from five to nine beats:

> And God-appointed Berkeley that proved all things a dream,
> That this pragmatical, preposterous pig of a world, its farrow that so solid seem,
> Must vanish on the instant if the mind but change its theme.

What can such a "preposterous" form imply? By its rhyme, it traps its language: every line in a stanza must end with the same sound. And yet in line-length it looses its language immoderately; one never knows how long any line will stretch. These tercets concern themselves with history, a history enumerating the long line of surveying beacon-towers antecedent to Yeats's own (Alexandria's and Babylon's real towers, Shelley's spiritual ones) and enumerating also the line of Anglo-Irish writers in which Yeats inscribes himself – Goldsmith, Swift, Burke, and Berkeley. These are writers who represent vastly different life-forms, from indolent Oliver Goldsmith, to Dean Swift with his "blood-sodden breast," to Burke the political philosopher, to Bishop Berkeley who "proved all things a dream." Yet because they are writers, they all responded to reality with "intellectual fire." Poem II of "Blood and the Moon," then, represents Yeats as a writer on the "stair" – that tower-passage between the blood of the earth and the moon of the ideal – where such is the contention among systems of thought and systems of violence, the individual and the state, that (although the architectural spiral of the stair remains, like the rhymes, constant from step to step), the warring forces felt on the stair twist the stanzas into different (and often ugly) shapes. The categorizing act of the mind, when it is not poised at the top of the tower in the radiance of the heavenly moon or at the foot of the tower contemplating earthly blood, shakes and blurts on the stair connecting the two.

Yeats's "lighter" late sequences – "A Man Young and Old" in *The Tower*, "A Woman Young and Old" and "Words for Music Perhaps" in *The Winding Stair*, and "The Three Bushes" in *Last Poems* – are the "lyric" counterparts to the powerful sequences of "epic" or esoteric intent. Because they are dominated by the "ballad Yeats" (by contrast to the philosophic and historical Yeats), these sequences – for the most part immediately accessible, non-topical, non-political, non-historical, short, and vividly concise – have been among Yeats's most popular poems. "Man" and "Woman" retell immemorial stories of the course of sexual life – infatuation, lovemaking, happiness or despair, death of one or the other of the lovers, and philosophical resignation. Of the eleven parts of "Man," ten are written in the ballad stanza (a four-line *abab* stanza of alternating tetrameter and trimeter) or in a prolonged (six-line) version of it; poems I, II, IX, and X of the eleven poems of "Woman," too, are composed in variants of the ballad stanza, and its other parts, though all unique, choose simple, stanzaic forms.

In the ballad-poems of "Words for Music Perhaps," Yeats created the characters "Crazy Jane" and "Tom the Lunatic," personae who can express the poet's occult beliefs with a plainness of language far from occult jargon, as we see in Crazy Jane's famous reply to the Bishop (who, when he was a curate, driven by his own covert sexual desire for Jane, expelled her lover Jack the Journeyman from the parish). Adjured by the Bishop to leave her "foul sty" for a "heavenly mansion," Jane replies:

"Fair and foul are near of kin,
And fair needs foul," I cried . . .

"A woman can be proud and stiff
When on love intent;
But Love has pitched his mansion in
The place of excrement;
For nothing can be sole or whole
That has not been rent."

(*VP* 513)

Tom the Lunatic, too, speaks Blakean truths in bluntly physical trimeters: "'The stallion Eternity / Mounted the mare of Time, / 'Gat the foal of the world'" (*VP* 529).

But not all of "Words for Music Perhaps" is pre-empted by the "low-born" personae who descend from Yeats's early Wordsworthian characters such as Moll Magee and the Fiddler of Dooney. For example, Yeats included among his pieces "for music perhaps" one of his most touching and austere love poems, "After Long Silence" (*VP* 523). It is set as a tryst: a man and a woman who were once lovers (in biographical fact, Yeats and his first mistress and life-long friend, Olivia Shakespear) are once again able to meet after years apart. In their rendezvous, they are protected from death-resembling night and eye-disillusioning light by curtains and shades, as they return to their perennial discussion of love, that "supreme theme of Art and Song." Yeats's poem is not initially presented as a narrative. Its first, verbless speech-act offers a title – "Speech after long silence" – set off by a semicolon. This is followed by a judgement ("It is right . . . / That we descant") to which is appended (after a colon) a philosophical epigram: "Bodily decrepitude is wisdom." Only in the very last eight words does the speaker's voice arrive at narration:

Speech after long silence; it is right,
All other lovers being estranged or dead,
Unfriendly lamplight hid under its shade,
The curtains drawn upon unfriendly night,
That we descant and yet again descant
Upon the supreme theme of Art and Song:
Bodily decrepitude is wisdom; young
We loved each other and were ignorant.

The sting in the poem comes not only from the fact that in their tryst in old age these former lovers can now only talk of love, not enact it; pain is also audible in Yeats's profound opening gratitude that he and Olivia Shakespear can still talk – since "all other lovers" (without exception) are either estranged (as was Maud Gonne) or dead. This dreadful alienating silence of old age is inserted as a participial absolute, as were the warding off of night and light, all three preventing, for a while, the syntactic completion of the initial judgement, "It is right." Only after naming all the drawbacks can the poet proceed to that validation, "That we descant." The past, unmusical "long silence" is assuaged by this harmonic unison in antiphonal descant; and the "composed," old-age acquiescence in what is still possible is manifest in the "through-composed," embraced rhymes of the two pentameter-quatrains that make up the poem. Yet within this harmony there lurks the asymmetry of the division of the poem into four unequal parts: the four-word summary-title; the long judgement; the curt four-word epigram "Bodily decrepitude is wisdom"; and the brief words of imperfect-tense narrative. And another asymmetry is also present: in lines 2–6, the sentiment and the line concur without interruption, while in lines 1 and 7 the pentameter is unsettled by cesurae that disrupt the balance. The most evident prosodic effect is the lingering, yearning suspension of the single word "young" over the last line-break. "Young, / We loved each other" is in fact the single piece of "pure" narrative; the conclusion of the poem, by contrast, returns to a present judgement on the lovers' imperfect capacities at that vanished time: "[We] were ignorant."

Yeats's genius in poetic composition can be judged by looking at the first draft of this poem, which focuses on the initial shock Yeats feels when he enters the room and finds that Olivia Shakespear's hair has turned white since he has last seen her. With the reactive self-irony that marks his late phase, he realizes that she must be experiencing the same shock, because his hair has turned white as well. This crudely realistic beginning is dropped, but the visual shock remains, deflected by the hiding of "unfriendly lamplight" under a shade. Here is the whole first draft:

Your hair is white
My hair is white
Come let us talk of love
What other theme do we know
When we were young
We loved each other and were ignorant.[1]

The many processes of thought, language, and rhythmic choice required to transform such a bare sketch into the ceremonious and beautiful epigram "After Long Silence" lie behind Yeats's remark in "Adam's Curse" that "A line will take us hours maybe" (*VP* 204).

But the beautiful simplicities of "Words for Music Perhaps" represent only one pole of Yeats's work in *The Winding Stair* (1933). Returning in that volume to the theme of Byzantium, he produced his densest metaphysical poem, "Byzantium" (*VP* 497–8), in which he imagines an afterlife considerably more agonized than that of the bird in the Emperor's court at the close of "Sailing to Byzantium." Now we see the dying as they are borne to Byzantium on the backs of dolphins, across buffeting seas. As they land, they are expected to enter the purgatorial flames of the smithies, flames that are seen writhing on "the Emperor's pavement" (where they are reproduced in mosaic). Those purgative flames will consume rage and lust, the "fury" and the "mire" of human veins, and reduce the dying person to a simple (i.e. non-complex) pure spiritual substance, which will then be able to sing. The shell of the body will remain as a ghostly mummy, wound in its shroud (Yeats had seen the memorial sculpture of Donne upright, bound in his shroud, in St. Paul's).

At midnight, as the poem dramatically begins, the great gong of the cathedral of the Holy Wisdom, Hagia Sophia, forces the "unpurged" daylight images to recede, so that the "purged" images of night can replace them, awakened by the cocks of Hades who announce midnight, as the cocks of earth announce dawn. The white-lit dome of the cathedral, high in the sky, disdains, from its religious sublimity, the squalid emotions of mortal men. Yeats then has two visions: in the first, he sees the mummy he will become if he enters the purifying flames; in the second, he sees the singing bird – a golden bird on a golden bough – that he will become once he is purged of complexity. Like the cathedral gong, this bird scorns "Common bird or petal / And all complexities of mire or blood."

These visions are difficult for Yeats to enunciate: in the familiar "*O quam te memorem*?" – "By what name shall I call thee?" – of Virgil, he names each thing three times, each time refining his conception. Is what I see "an image, man or shade?" he wonders, and then decides that the mummy is more like a ghost than like a man, but (because it occurs in his poem) more like an image than like a shade. He calls it by a name drawn from Coleridge's self-epitaph: "I call it death-in-life and life-in-death." The mummy-image cannot sing: its mouth has no moisture and no breath. Similarly, in contemplating the golden bird – a symbol of the formed and changeless posthumous voice of his *Collected Poems* – Yeats does not know whether to call it by its "natural" name, "bird," or by its name as an artifact, "golden handiwork." There is one other name that occurs to him: the preservation of natural forms (e.g. birds) by human art (of the goldsmith, of the wordsmith) is nothing less than a "miracle" – something to be amazed by and wonder at.

These two visions – of the mummy, of the bird, of body and soul, image and miracle – have postponed the moment when the (putatively dying) Yeats must decide whether or not he will step into the magical fire and be purged of the "complexities of fury." It is characteristic of late Yeats that every time the speaker glances at the churning emotions of the living they are seen at a slightly different angle – fury of veins, complexities of blood, complexities of fury, furies of complexity. The shifts in naming represent the bewilderment of all human beings before their own sufferings:

> All that man is,
> All mere complexities,
> The fury and the mire of human veins . . .
> And all complexities of mire or blood . . .
>
> Where blood-begotten spirits come

And all complexities of fury leave,
Dying . . .

Marbles of the dancing floor
Break bitter furies of complexity,
Those images that yet
Fresh images beget . . .

Of course, Yeats the poet cannot bring himself to abandon human complexities, and so, instead of stepping into the divine flames ("flames begotten of flame," a theological phrase), and undergoing the "agony" of the separation of body and soul in the "dance" of transformation, he turns his back on the flames and instead excitedly re-contemplates (with a glance at Coleridge's "Kubla Khan") the "dolphin-torn" and "gong-tormented" sea that brought him to Byzantium. The poem ends in an eternal standoff, as the breakwater of the smithies breaks the waves of arriving complexities, while the complexities defiantly continue to beget "fresh images." Thanatos and Eros exist in a continual clash of value. It is neither a mummy nor a golden bird that speaks the last stanza: it is (to use J. B. Yeats's words about Blake) "the man himself, revolting and desiring."

Between 1935 and 1939 (a period during which everyone realized that a new war was about to erupt), Yeats's poetry becomes more and more an elegy for culture – sometimes a raging protest, sometimes a mournful aspiring to a Buddhist quietism. In his most scornful sequence, "Supernatural Songs," Yeats invents a surrogate named Ribh (a hermit disturbed by the arrival in Ireland of St. Patrick's version of Christianity), who cholerically remarks – as Patrick preaches the Hellenized doctrine of the male Trinity, Father, Son, and Holy Spirit – "An abstract Greek absurdity has crazed the man." Ribh argues that sex and procreation underlie all valid religious trinities: "Man, woman, child (a daughter or a son), / That's how all natural or supernatural stories run" (*VP* 556). Ecstatic, reading in the dark by the light of the intercourse of "angels" (in fact the dead tragic lovers Baile and Aillinn), Ribh promulgates – in swinging pentameter stanzas – anti-Christian doctrines:

Why should I seek for love or study it?
It is of God and passes human wit.
I study hatred with great diligence,
For that's a passion in my own control . . .

Thought is a garment and the soul's a bride
That cannot in that trash and tinsel hide:
Hatred of God may bring the soul to God.
(*VP* 558)

Yet by the end of this sequence – after a ragged gothic poem ("What Magic Drum") in which we see the Trinitarian "selving" of a primitive godhead as the father-God assumes "Primordial Motherhood," thereby engendering a cub to the chthonic music of a "magic drum" – Yeats subsides into a classically balanced Shakespearean sonnet, "Meru," in which he bids a coded farewell to the Ascendancy and the British Empire: "Egypt and Greece, good-bye, and good-bye Rome!" (*VP* 563). Having accepted the falling into decay of his own culture, he can assume the quietism of those Buddhist monks who have so overcome their bodies that they can lie naked to the snow and winds of Mt. Everest. They know that every culture is transient, that even man's sturdiest monuments last but a day. Even the golden bird of "Byzantium" is no longer thought of by Yeats as immortal.

A poet elegizing a dying culture is tempted to believe that some cause has brought about its imminent death. Yeats was not immune (especially in prose) from ascribing the death of "Romantic Ireland" to the rising Catholic middle class. But "The Gyres" (*VP* 564–5) represents Yeats's more profound view: it is not an alien and hostile culture (say, that of the Catholic nationalists) that has "driven out" the beauty and worth of Protestant high culture. No, each culture dies of having exhausted its own intellectual, imaginative, and ethical powers:

> Things thought too long can be no longer thought,
> For beauty dies of beauty, worth of worth,
> And ancient lineaments are blotted out.

The poet places his hope in the motion of the gyres that will – after the destruction of contemporary Western culture – resurrect an older form of life, inhabited by men of action, "Lovers of horses and of women." Yeats's agitation at the flux of the world is contained here by his ceremonious *ottava rima* stanzas, just as in "Lapis Lazuli" (*VP* 565–7) the same agitation (displaced onto "hysterical women") is contained by the equanimity of Chinese art. Yeats's carved piece of lapis lazuli is a descendant of Keats's Grecian urn: just as Keats goes beyond what is represented on the urn to imagine the "green altar" to which the sacrificial procession directs itself, and the deserted "little town" from which it issued, so Yeats moves beyond the actual representation of two Chinese sages and their servant as they climb a mountain towards a "little half-way house" and imagines them there after they have completed their journey:

> . . . I
> Delight to imagine them seated there;
> There, on the mountain and the sky,

On all the tragic scene they stare.
One asks for mournful melodies;
Accomplished fingers begin to play.
Their eyes mid many wrinkles, their eyes,
Their ancient, glittering eyes, are gay.

The tragic joy of "The Gyres," the gaiety of Shakespearean tragic heroes who "do not break up their lines to weep" in "Lapis Lazuli," and the Buddhist gaiety of the Chinese sages can arise (out of Nietzsche) because Yeats has decided to focus on the second half of the gyre – the half of rebuilding. "All things fall and are built again, / And those that build them again are gay." But what of those who fall as their cultures fall around them? Doubts creep into Yeats's eschatological scenario when, in "A Bronze Head" (*VP* 618–19) – a poem about Maud Gonne written in the seven-line "rime royal" stanza (*ababbcc*) that he reserved for her and for the company of his lovers in "Hound Voice" – he focuses on his beloved's "vision of terror" that had "shattered her soul." Her marvelous complexity of being ("Which of her forms has shown her substance right?") has been reduced to a single staring eye contemplating the fall of culture:

Or else I thought her supernatural;
As though a sterner eye looked through her eye
On this foul world in its decline and fall;
On gangling stocks grown great, great stocks run dry,
Ancestral pearls all pitched into a sty,
Heroic reverie mocked by clown and knave,
And wondered what was left for massacre to save.

This agonized speculation is far from the equanimity of the Indian hermits on Everest or the Chinese sages in their half-way house. It suggests that though Yeats reached out for images of tranquillity and even gaiety, gleaned from his own culture (Shakespeare) or from cultures remote in time or space (China, India), he remained open to his own disturbed angers of loss. Sometimes, in prose, these sorrows gave rise to rant (as in the late pamphlet *On the Boiler*); sometimes, in life, they led Yeats to folly (as in his brief interest in the fascist Blueshirts); but contained in poetry, they found their own perilous means of balance. After all, though the sages are "gay," they ask for "mournful melodies"; after all, in spite of decline and fall, the last word in "A Bronze Head" is "save."

Such balance can be seen in the best of Yeats's late poetry. Although he laments, in part I of "The Circus Animals' Desertion" (*VP* 629–30), that he is bereft of themes, he has been looking for them in the wrong place – at the top of the ladder of imagistic and intellectual idealization. "Those masterful images" of his past work (described in the wonderfully compact narrative of part II) "grew in pure mind," he declares – but out of what did they begin? "A mound of refuse." In reaching down to the sources of his art he reiterates the great theme of his old age, broached in "Byzantium" – a recognition of rage and lust, the fury and the mire of human veins. "I must lie down where all the ladders start / In the foul rag-and-bone shop of the heart." The discovery is not agitated, as it was in the fluctuating line-lengths of the "Byzantium" stanza: instead, in "The Circus Animals' Desertion," the acceptance of necessity ("I must lie down") is contained within the formal equanimity of the *ottava rima*, as it was in "The Gyres."

The "filthy tide" of the modern, which is nonetheless generative, a "formless spawning fury," is similarly contained by the *ottava rima* of "The Statues" (*VP* 610–11). This poem tracks the spread of aesthetic representations inherited from Greece as they pass from culture to culture: Phidian statues, with their underlying armature of Pythagorean mathematical proportions, gave Greece dominance over Persia; and when, through the conquests of Alexander, Greek statues came to India, they influenced statues of the Buddha. Within Buddhism, the forms of the Greek statues came to one cultural terminus; and that cultural dark of the moon is marked as such by the presence of a witch's familiar: "Grimalkin crawls to Buddha's emptiness." Where will the Greek forms find their next incarnation? Now that the poet Padraic Pearse has summoned, during the Easter Rising, an archetypal cultural image – that of Cuchulain – to his side, it falls to the Irish to bring their archetypal images to a Greek perfection:

> When Pearse summoned Cuchulain to his side,
> What stalked through the Post Office? What intellect,
> What calculation, number, measurement replied?
> We Irish, born into that ancient sect,
> But thrown upon this filthy modern tide
> And by its formless spawning fury wrecked,
> Climb to our proper dark, that we may trace
> The lineaments of a plummet-measured face.

Yeats had become expert in finding, for his *ottava rima*, interesting rhymes and slant-rhymes, and rhyme-words with different numbers of syllables. Here, "intellect," "sect," and "wrecked" offer a case in point. There is an exhilaration for the reader in seeing a difficult rhyme so high-handedly brought off, whether through relatively common words, as in this instance, or (earlier in the poem) through exoticism (the rhyme, e.g., of the monosyllabic "these" with the quadrisyllabic "immensities," and the trisyllabic "Salamis").

At the end of his life, Yeats departed from the comprehensive and the apocalyptic modes in favor of "posthumous" poems, in which he represented himself as already dead – whether buried in Sligo, being judged by posterity, living in an afterlife, or singing a ghostly refrain of dead warriors:

Under bare Ben Bulben's head
In Drumcliff churchyard Yeats is laid.
("Under Ben Bulben"; *VP* 640)

You that would judge me, do not judge alone
This book or that, come to this hallowed place
Where my friends' portraits hang and look thereon;
Ireland's history in their lineaments trace.
("The Municipal Gallery Revisited"; *VP* 603–4)

A man that had six mortal wounds, a man
Violent and famous, strode among the dead.
("Cuchulain Comforted,"
13 January, 1939; *VP* 634)

There in the tomb stand the dead upright,
But winds come up from the shore:
They shake when the winds roar,
Old bones upon the mountain shake.
("The Black Tower,"
21 January, 1939; *VP* 635)

The latter two of the poems quoted were written during the last fortnight of Yeats's life: he died in France on 28 January, 1939. Of the deathbed poems, "The Black Tower" (with its italicized refrain of the unquiet dead) is another ballad version of the besieged nationalists in the General Post Office during the Easter Rising. "The men of the old black tower," their food and wine gone because of the long siege, nonetheless "lack nothing that a soldier needs" because they have kept their oath to their dead king: "Those banners" of the enemy will not be allowed entrance to their tower. "Stand we on guard oath-bound!" But against the heroic claims of martial action, commemorated in this folk-form, Yeats sets the claims of the contemplative life, commemorated in the earlier deathbed poem, "Cuchulain Comforted," which is couched in the most intricate poetic form of European high culture, Dante's linked *terza rima*.

To understand "Cuchulain Comforted," we must recall that Yeats's imagined afterlife in *A Vision* contained a phase called "The Shiftings," during which one has to live a life opposite to one's earthly existence: only thus can the soul become complete. Cuchulain, who has spent his life as a solitary leader of warriors, is told by a group of bird-like shades, once he enters the afterlife, that he must submerge his individuality in collective action, and that the collective he must join is composed not of warriors but of "'Convicted cowards all, by kindred slain / 'Or driven from home and left to die in fear'." He must sew his own shroud (an act normally reserved for women): "'We thread the needles' eyes, and all we do / All must together do.'" Through his obedience, Cuchulain is allowed to sing with his new companions, but it is an unearthly "song" without familiar melody or language, a pure avian vocalization:

They sang, but had nor human tunes nor words,
Though all was done in common as before;

They had changed their throats and had the throats of birds.

These last two "posthumous" poems, "The Black Tower" and "Cuchulain Comforted," aim at an unearthly music beyond the human. Other death-poems in which the speaker hovers on the edge of the posthumous – for example "The Man and the Echo" (*VP* 632–3) – remain largely within the bounds of human striving, speaking of "the spiritual intellect's great work" of ensuring that "all's arranged in one clear view." Yet the work of the intellect is ever interrupted by the sound of suffering:

Up there some hawk or owl has struck,
Dropping out of sky or rock,
A stricken rabbit is crying out,
And its cry distracts my thought.

These two human poles – the passions and sufferings of life on the one hand and, on the other, the work of the mind and hand to understand and represent them – contend in Yeats's thought. Without the "cold eye" of contemplation no art is made; without the "refuse" of the rag-and-bone shop of the heart, no life is lived. In the third part of the 1928 sequence "The Tower," in the brisk trimeter *abab* quatrains of "Easter 1916," Yeats had (prematurely) written a will, in which he vowed to "make" his soul fit for death. He will do this by thought and study, coming to spiritual peace in spite of a rising hierarchy of terrible happenings in old age:

Now shall I make my soul,
Compelling it to study
In a learned school
Till the wreck of body,
Slow decay of blood,
Testy delirium

Or dull decrepitude,
Or what worse evil come –
(*VP* 416)

What, we ask, could be a worse evil than the wreck of body, impotence, choleric wandering of mind, or lack of mentality itself? Yeats tells us: worse than all these is "the death of friends." And worst of all is the death of those one has loved – the "death / Of every brilliant eye / That made a catch in the breath." In Yeats's hierarchy, the spiritual (companionate, aesthetic, and sensual) losses of friends and lovers pierce far more anguishingly than physical deficits. And yet, even those excruciating spiritual losses must finally be folded into the tranquil swan-song willed by the poet.

Yeats intensifies the moment of death by "deleting" the last line of his will, so that absence replaces presence. His trimeters have been rhyming in quatrains; but the last "quatrain" is merely a tercet, as my lines marking the quatrain-divisions show:

Till the wreck of body . . .
. . . .
The death of friends, or death
Of every brilliant eye
That made a catch in the breath –
Seem but the clouds of the sky
. . . .
When the horizon fades,
Or a bird's sleepy cry
Among the deepening shades.
* * * * [-y]

Of course, the final incomplete quatrain is made to seem complete by the fact that its *b*-rhyme – "cry" – matches the *b*-rhymes of the preceding full quatrain ("eye, sky"). Together with this powerful deletion at the end of "The Tower" we can place an equally strategic deletion in Yeats's own epitaph in "Under Ben Bulben." In draft, his epitaph was a complete quatrain, repeating (to a passing horseman) the usual generic "Stay, traveler, and recall the one who here lies dead," before bidding him to be on his way:

Draw rein; draw breath
Cast a cold eye
On life, on death;
Horseman, pass by.
(*L* 913)

In a master-stroke, Yeats deleted the first line, creating a "defective quatrain" which suggests that the "missing" rhyme must be "breath" – that which the buried body lacks:

Cast a cold eye
On life, on death.
Horseman, pass by!
* * * [breath]

In deleting the first line, Yeats refused the conventional beginning to an epitaph, such as we find in Coleridge's "Stop, Christian passerby! Stop, child of God!" By such small touches, modernity is attained within tradition.

Although Yeats's late poems often arise from gripping political and personal occasions – World War I, the Easter Rising, the Civil War, Irish independence, the death of friends, the recapitulation of life, the advent of a second war, the preparation for death – it is not their themes alone that give these poems their monumental solidity, precision, and musicality. It is their underlying (and frequently intricate) structure that gives them architectural strength; it is Yeats's lexical eloquence that provides them with their striking formulations; and it is his ear for rhythmic and dramatic speech that makes them quotable. Though they use conventional genres – elegy, prophecy, love poetry, the legacy, the ballad, the posthumous poem – each genre is refreshed in Yeats's hands, so that while recognizing the convention, we also recognize the Yeatsian originality of handling. And though the late poems avail themselves of conventional stanza-forms – quatrains, couplets, the sonnet form, *ottava rima*, *terza rima* – they bend these to new syntactic shapes or new kinds of usage, as in the use of Dantesque *terza rima* in the purgatorial elegy for Cuchulain, or the use of the stately *ottava rima* to speak ironically of Yeats's thematic "circus animals" – "lion and woman and the Lord knows what." It was by bending to his own formidable will the resources of poetry in English – thematic, generic, and formal – that Yeats, above all in the later poems, made himself a Modernist, and made Irish poetry modern.

NOTE

1. A. Norman Jeffares, *A Commentary on the Collected Poems of W. B. Yeats* (Stanford: Stanford University Press, 1968), p. 383.

6

BERNARD O'DONOGHUE

Yeats and the drama

In a note to his play *At the Hawk's Well* in 1916, Yeats said "I need a theatre; I believe myself to be a dramatist" (*VPl* 415). T. S. Eliot declared in his 1940 anniversary lecture on Yeats: "I do not know where our debt to him as a dramatist ends – and in time, it will not end until that drama itself ends."[1] Yet, putting it at its most positive, there can be few major dramatists about whose standing there is so little critical consensus as Yeats. He was a prolific writer of plays throughout his life; only Shaw, of the major playwrights in English of his time, wrote more. His earliest writings are dramatic, from the "Arcadian play" *The Island of Statues* in 1885 onwards,[2] and in the late 1880s he is already discussing with George Russell and John O'Leary the possibility of writing poetic drama. Throughout his life he described his literary achievements in terms of the dramatic.

Yet from the first his plays had at best an uncertain critical reception. Moreover, it was an uncertainty with which Yeats himself seemed to be in sympathy, to judge from what he says about the stage in his great, career-summarizing late poem "The Circus Animals' Desertion." After mentioning his early (and favorite) play *The Countess Cathleen*, the poem concludes by expressing reservations about his involvement with drama as a whole: "Players and painted stage took all my love, / And not those things that they were emblems of" (*VP* 630). This final judgement recorded in the poetry seems to be that Yeats's creative career lost its way through concern with the stage: an impression seemingly confirmed in the poem's familiar last stanza, which advocates a return to "the foul rag-and-bone shop of the heart," implicitly leaving aside all theatrical effects. It is a return to an old theme: at earlier moments of disillusion Yeats had expressed the same regrets, as in "The Fascination of What's Difficult" in the *Green Helmet* volume (1910), written at the height of his most concentrated involvement in "theatre business" (*VP* 260) and partly motivated by such events as the negative audience response to Synge's *The Playboy of the Western World* at the Abbey Theatre in 1907. The finality of this negative view of his theatre work seems to be confirmed in the late, bitter diatribe *On the Boiler* (1938), when he writes "I have wondered if I did right in giving so much of my life to the expression of other men's genius" (*Ex* 415).

Yet the definitive nature of this anti-theatre judgement has to be balanced against the fact that Yeats intended his final volume, *Last Poems and Two Plays*, left uncompleted at his death, to end with the brilliant, harsh play *Purgatory*. Furthermore, the view that it was the "painted stage" itself rather than what it emblematized that usurped Yeats's love is a reminder that his significance for the drama was not confined to his role of playwright. As one of the founders of the Irish National Theatre, which developed into the Abbey, and as one of its directors who remained involved in its programs for over a quarter of a century, Yeats was vitally concerned with "theatre business" as what he called the "management of men" ("The Fascination of What's Difficult"; *VP* 260). This poem, while it puts a "curse on plays" and their distracting of the holy-blooded, Olympian Pegasus of poetry from his proper calling, still finds the theatrical difficulties – management of men and the rest – a "fascination." Besides, even if it is secondary and a distraction from his primary work as poet, Yeats still sees his activity in the theatre as a matter of great cultural moment in Ireland. Even more strikingly, in the 1906 *Samhain* essay reprinted in "The Irish Dramatic Movement" (the extensive section of *Explorations* [pp. 71–259], which collected Yeats's essays on the theatre first published in *Samhain* and *Beltaine*), he had called the gift of a theatre by Annie Horniman the occasion to begin his "real business" (*Ex* 210).

Still, whatever his ambitions for his theatre business, Yeats's judgement of its relative marginality seems on balance to mirror the general critical standing of his plays. Quite apart from the wider difficulties with Abbey productions, he had good reason to be discouraged by the reception of his own plays in their time – in the face of his self-nurtured artistic arrogance – because of the way contemporary fashion was against his symbolically inclined drama, setting the scene for the following half-century. It was the age of what Shaw perceptively characterized as "Ibsenism." Although Yeats had earlier admired the modernizing virtues of some aspects of Ibsen, linking him with Maeterlinck, he expressed his detestation for "Ibsenism" in the work of both Shaw and Ibsen. Yeats's dislike of this naturalist drama is well traced by Katharine Worth's "Yeats, Maeterlinck and Synge," in her crucial 1978 study of Yeatsian drama and its aftermath.[3]

It could be seen as Yeats's bad luck that Ibsenist realism took such an absolute hold on drama in England and Ireland at exactly the moment when in other parts of Europe the theatre was in impatient revolt against it. An unbroken tradition, traced by Worth, of less naturalistic drama remained largely unacknowledged in English. This alternative dramatic history offered a decidedly more promising context in which Yeats might gain a central place in the twentieth-century canon. Symbolic drama (the term is warranted by Yeats's own employment of it) such as Yeats's has been a strong alternative presence in the theatre since the late nineteenth century. Such drama, by contrast with the very full naturalistic stage-directions in Shaw, conveys its stage atmosphere impressionistically by such devices as the Cubist staging through the use of colored screens which Yeats adopted enthusiastically from Gordon Craig, for example in the production of his 1914 play *The Hour-Glass*.[4] And if it is felt that the formal concerns that Yeats developed from Craig might seem relatively trivial compared to the capacity of realistic drama to represent the great public events of the time, we should remember that Craig collaborated with Stanislawski in the Moscow Arts Theatre in the greatest new departure in theatrical presentation of the century. Terence Brown's fine 1999 critical biography of Yeats ends by raising the striking possibility that "Yeats's greatest contribution to world drama is to be found in the more general impact of his collaborator Gordon Craig's concept of total theatre," as well as with the more orthodox view that the plays "have enjoyed a very remarkable afterlife indeed" in their influence on Beckett, who preferred *At the Hawk's Well* to the "whole unupsettable applecart" of Shaw.[5]

This tradition is authoritatively traced in Worth's book which, as its title indicates, sees Yeats as the source of a lineage that culminated in Beckett, the end-of-century's most venerated dramatist in English. In her campaigning study, Worth aims at once to restore the plays to their proper European context and to argue that that tradition was the primary one for post-Romantic European drama. Yeats's dramatic world belongs formally to the Symbolist tradition of Maeterlinck as mediated through Symons, a heritage that had been noted periodically since Edmund Wilson's *Axel's Castle* in 1931. Within that tradition Worth makes great claims for Yeats as the fountainhead of Modernist drama, even if by the time of his death – in the year before Eliot's lecture – Yeats was not so much lamenting the quality of his plays as their chances of being performed at all. Now, half a century on from the first performance of Beckett's *Waiting for Godot*, we might expect less naturalistic drama to be better received. Already in his discussion of the Cuchulain plays in 1974, four years before Worth's study, Reg Skene had taken it that the battle *had* been won, saying that the public had been made "aware that there are exciting alternatives to naturalism in the theatre."[6] Predictably, Worth's occasional writings on Yeats in the 1990s emphasize their new popularity on the stage.[7] And Yeats's drama *is* now to some degree better received in the theatre; there is more chance of seeing his plays at the turn of the new century than there was thirty years ago. In 1989 James Flannery began the grand project of staging the whole corpus with the full quintet of Cuchulain plays, which played to packed houses in Dublin. In a less systematic but also effective popularizing venture, the Abbey toured in 1998–9 with a brilliant linked tableau made up of Synge's *Riders to the Sea* and *In the Shadow of the Glen*, and ending with Yeats's powerful and disturbing late play *Purgatory*.[8] Both these ventures showed beyond doubt that at least some of Yeats's plays can have enormous power in the theatre: a matter I will return to in evaluating them at the end of this chapter.

But to understand how significantly positive a development those two stagings were in the history of the plays' reception we might recall how slighted the plays had been. They were found wanting from the first general critics of Yeats onwards. Louis MacNeice, in his canon-forming *The Poetry of W. B. Yeats* (1941), said the plays were "little more than charades."[9] Eric Bentley in *In Search of Theater* in 1953 remarked "it cannot be said that Yeats has much of a reputation as a playwright."[10] Even the approvers rarely approved without reservation. Peter Ure's pioneering study, saluted as the first major criticism of the plays, starts by conceding their negative reputation: "Yeats's plays have not, generally speaking, been much regarded by his modern critics."[11] The qualified nature of Ure's admiration is also indicated by the fact that his book was thematically organized and unduly selective, leaving out of consideration altogether eight of the *Collected Plays*, among them some of the most central such as *Cathleen ni Houlihan* and *The Cat and the Moon*. Even Helen Vendler, at the end of her instructive reading of *The Player Queen* and its textual developments, concludes that "this is material intrinsically better suited to reflective poetry than to comedy," and that "*The Herne's Egg* suffers from somewhat the same uncertainty of direction":[12] not as censorious as Harold Bloom, who concludes his discussion of the latter play by calling it "as bitter as it is confused, and every kind of a failure."[13] Flannery believes that Yeats's theatrical ideas are of greater significance than the plays themselves.[14] Una Ellis-Fermor was primarily concerned with the impact of Yeats on the Irish dramatic movement as a whole, and is accordingly often most concerned with matters of production, even if she does claim that her account of the Irish theatre turned into a book primarily on Yeats in the course of its writing.[15] Few readers or viewers of the plays would accuse these judgements of ungenerosity; even amongst the enthusiasts there was little agreement, either in judgement or approach. Thus Terence Brown's authoritative recent evaluation of Yeats still concludes that, by contrast with the poetry, "Yeats's plays have found few advocates beyond enthusiasts in the academy . . . Even in Ireland and at the Abbey Theatre his drama is scarcely part of the living repertoire. Revivals are dutiful or marked by opportunistic eccentricities of production."[16]

As far as readers of Yeats are concerned, even the most committed tend to reserve the right to ignore the plays altogether, or just to bring them in where they cast light on the poems, under the assumption that they are the products of a writer whose Muse was really the lyric. It is easy to multiply examples of cases where the plays are brought in for passing clarification in this way, starting with Yeats himself and his famous allusion to *Cathleen ni Houlihan* in his late poem "The Man and the Echo": "Did that play of mine send out / Certain men the English shot?" (*VP* 632). Similarly, everyone learns that the lines in "The Circus Animals' Desertion" – "And when the Fool and Blind Man stole the bread / Cuchulain fought the ungovernable sea" (*VP* 630) – refer to the play *On Baile's Strand* (1904), in which Cuchulain, made mad by having killed his son, fights the sea in frenzy. Most readers assimilate this knowledge, but are less likely to be inspired to seek out the play and read it than to marvel at the wonderfully Yeatsian adjective "ungovernable."

Some modest increase in stage-popularity, perhaps a belated recognition of Yeats's own constant attention to drama, was cautiously anticipated by the critics. A. S. Knowland wrote in 1983 "the time has come when the characteristic features of Yeats's plays – masks, dance, stylization of language and movement – may not seem quite so strange."[17] Such discussions of the plays as those by Ure, Flannery, Vendler, and Liam Miller, and particularly those in Worth's tradition, did give them greater critical presence. In tracing the consistency of Yeats's obsession with the theatre, Miller sees the contact with the Japanese Noh in 1913 as revelatory of the "ideas he had been trying to express in dramatic form since he had begun to write for the stage thirty years before,"[18] arguing further that Yeatsian drama was not just an important alternative tradition in modern theatre but represented more fully (as Fenollosa claimed for the Noh) the fundamental framework of world drama as it flourished in Greece in the fifth century before Christ. That is, Yeats's kind of drama was in the mainstream of theatrical history, and modern "naturalism" is the aberration. Such advocates of a less purely realist theatre were able to point forward, as Beckett himself does,[19] to a tradition leading on to late O'Casey, Beckett, and other Modernist drama.

Predictably of course, many of the critics who most revere Yeats as fountainhead of modern drama in English (Brown's "enthusiasts in the academy") had always taken exception to the view that his drama was secondary,[20] long before the acceptance of *Purgatory* or the more frequent stagings since the 1980s. These critics stress the centrality of drama throughout his long career: he composed several plays while still in his teens, of which *Mosada* has come nearest to canonical acceptance nowadays (though still short of inclusion in the *Collected Plays*). These very early uncollected plays might equally be called eclogues or dramatic dialogues or Platonic colloquies; versions of all these forms occur in Yeats's poems. The metamorphosis of *The Golden Helmet* into *The Green Helmet* was partly a question of genre – whether it was a dramatic poem or play; it was finally established in the *Collected Plays* as "An Heroic Farce," dated 1910. Such constant attention by Yeats to the plays and their forms shows that the dramatic remained an intrinsic part of his poetic *œuvre* as he conceived it, and had been there from the outset. The double life in *Collected Plays* and Yeats's poetic volumes of *The Shadowy Waters* is a further indication that the absolute separation of the two literary forms is finally not possible for Yeats. A comparison of the prose "Acting Version" with the verse text in *Collected Plays* is an indication, I argue at the end of this chapter, of the greater sureness of the language of the poems generally. Still, the most conclusive evidence of Yeats's enduring concern with the plays is the revisions that he made constantly throughout his life. For example, the 1892 text of *The Countess Cathleen* had four major revisions, in 1895, 1901, 1912, and 1919; *The Player Queen* and *The King's Threshold*, like *The Green Helmet*, both underwent changes that radically affected their generic, theatrical, and ethical meanings. To see how obsessive Yeats's rewritings of plays were, often in response to particular stagings, one only has to look at the frequent articles on the matter in the issues of Richard Finneran's journal *Yeats: An Annual of Critical and Textual Studies* and Warwick Gould's *The Yeats Annual*, as well as the discussion throughout Vendler's 1963 study. S. B. Bushrui says that the verse-plays between 1900 and 1910 were "much revised in the light of their effect on the stage."[21]

The mainstream criticism of the poetry too had sometimes acknowledged this self-evaluation of Yeats as essentially a poet concerned with the drama. Harold Bloom, in his 1970 study of Yeats, which reclaimed him as a visionary Romantic poet, said that "Yeats's most typical poem is a dramatic lyric that behaves as though it were a fragment in a mythological romance."[22] This had also been the main drift of two important books by Thomas Parkinson, who saw Yeats's work for the Irish National Theatre as the crucial element in his poetry's development.[23] It is a view well founded in the poet's own claims, most famously in his Nobel Prize address on "The Irish Dramatic Movement," which begins by attributing his eligibility for the prize to qualities nurtured in the drama as much as in poetry: "Perhaps the English committees," he said, "would never have sent you my name if I had written no plays, no dramatic criticism, if my lyric poetry had not a quality of speech practised upon the stage" (*A* 410).

The magnificent language of Yeats's later lyric poetry was incubated in the plays; the plays must finally be seen not as competing with the poems but as in collaboration with them, especially in the case of a writer who was so concerned with the unity of his achievement as Yeats. It is true that from

1889 (when he met Maud Gonne) onwards, Yeats wanted to be a major poet before all else, and all was grist to that mill; but the kind of poet Yeats aimed to be was radically determined by his view of the theatre. He said more than once, in various formulations, that the highest form of poetry was dramatic. Yeats's plays, like those of T. S. Eliot, were part of his poetic output; but they were an enormously important part of it. By the end of the twentieth century, Yeats's insistence that the best poetry is dramatic and his stress on the dramatic nature of his own imagination were paid more attention, and the unconditional superiority of the late "lust and rage" (*VP* 591) poems over the plays was less unquestioned, especially in the case of *Purgatory*.

Moreover, claims for his centrality in the history of drama are securely founded in Yeats's own many pronouncements about the theatre throughout his career, most prominently in the essays in *Explorations*. In his essay on "The Theatre" in *Ideas of Good and Evil* (1900), Yeats declares the resolve of himself and his colleagues in the Irish Literary Theatre to "escape the stupefying memory of the theatre of commerce" by writing plays that "will be for the most part remote, spiritual, and ideal" (*E&I* 166). The "theatre of commerce" thereafter recurs with triumphant obsession as a term of disapproval for naturalistic drama. Escape from this commercial stupefaction was achieved to a significant degree by the changes in the conception of theatre and staging mentioned already, such as the Symbolist notions of staging derived from Craig, first seen by Yeats in Craig's stage-set for *Dido and Aeneas* in 1901. Another major factor here was the Japanese theatrical tradition to which Yeats was introduced by Ezra Pound, as he describes in "Certain Noble Plays of Japan," first published in April, 1916 (*E&I* 221–37). There Yeats explains how some principles taken from the classical Japanese Noh plays – the use of masks and statuesque gestures rather than displays of emotion – collaborated with European Symbolist drama derived from Maeterlinck to provide him with a new and distinctive kind of theatre.

Yeats was consistently opposed to "the theatre of commerce"; otherwise, as with his poetry, his career as dramatist is a strange mixture of consistency and what he called the "remaking" of himself. Richard Ellmann, in *Yeats: The Man and the Masks*, suggests a useful period-division of the plays: "early playwriting" (suggesting that the products of this were not always conclusive individual works), "plays of the middle period," and "later plays."[24] But any historical categorizing is of limited usefulness because Yeats changed the texts so much; it has to be borne in mind too that the dates in *Collected Plays* are not always dates of composition and, up to 1910, often not the dates of the final, much revised versions. There are of course other ways of categorizing: by theme or subject, for example. Flannery's Cuchulain quintet, for instance (the subject of Skene's 1974 study), incorporates plays of very different dates. The four plays brought together as a logical and temporal grouping in *Collected Plays* are already out of the sequence of their composition: *At the Hawk's Well* (1917), *The Green Helmet* (1910), *On Baile's Strand* (1904), and *The Only Jealousy of Emer* (1919). No doubt the last play, *The Death of Cuchulain* (1939), which remains last in *Collected Plays*, would have been brought back to complete the sequence if Yeats had lived to re-organize the volume. Ure, as I have said, takes a strictly thematic approach, of rather an odd kind, making a primary division into "Applied Arts" (*The Countess Cathleen*, *The King's Threshold*, and *Deirdre*) and "The Mystery To Come" (fifteen of the other plays, excluding eight from the *Collected Plays* but incorporating *Where There Is Nothing* amongst "The Beasts"). The Cuchulain group is brought together, but in order of composition rather than the narrative order reconstructed in *Collected Plays* and most discussions. A coherent classification and a lucid introduction to all the plays included in the Macmillan *Collected Plays* is provided by Anthony Bradley in *William Butler Yeats*.[25]

Categorization, however, remains a problem; here I will return to Ellmann's categories for a short historical outline. The "early playwriting" concluded with the preliminary, uncertain allegory of Irish politics (or Maud Gonne's politics) in the first version of *The Countess Cathleen* in 1892 (when Yeats was twenty-seven), and the folksy twilight of *The Land of Heart's Desire* (1894). The next is Yeats's most sustained dramatic period both as playwright and as man of the theatre, the first decade of the twentieth century. This period was dominated by collaboration and ended in frustration. The most effective moment was the appearance of *Cathleen ni Houlihan* in 1902 with Maud Gonne in the title role, Yeats's most assertive nationalist political statement, but even this was a collaboration with Lady Gregory, who became increasingly disposed to claim authorship of it.[26] *Diarmuid and Grania* was written in collaboration with George Moore in 1900, and left uncollected by agreement of both authors. One of Yeats's longest and most re-worked plays, the didactic *Where There Is Nothing*, first appeared in 1902 but was still being worked on nearly twenty years later. That too has not survived into the canonical *Collected Plays*. So the enduring product of this very active theatrical period is disproportionately meagre.

Ellmann's observations are a persuasive and aphoristic account of the waxing and waning of the plays' powers in this period; the reworkings are treated authoritatively by S. B. Bushrui.[27] Ellmann picks up Yeats's own phrase from "The Fascination of What's Difficult," about his ailing Pegasus, which labors "As though it dragged road-metal" (*VP* 260), and links the "irritating air of bravado and snobbery" in these lyrics to the way that "his dramas show the effect of much theorizing." Unlike Flannery, Ellmann sees the theorizing in this period as having a negative influence on the plays, especially on their language, of which he comments brilliantly "something seems to be wrong with their breathing."[28] After *The Green Helmet* (dated 1910) there is a short gap before a new and highly significant development, Yeats's encounter with the Japanese Noh plays to which he was introduced by Ezra Pound, as noted already. Ellmann argues that the impact of the Noh effected a dramatic improvement in the plays' language, offering Yeats "a form of drama where all could be symbolic instead of merely half symbolic as in his Irish heroic dramas and his early miracle plays."[29] It is certainly true that there is a sustained power in the language of the plays designed according to the principles of the Noh (as Yeats understood them) which had not been achieved in any of his previous stage-writing.

It is striking too that in this period (from 1913 onwards), the drama became more experimental as the poetry became more rooted in real events. Form is foregrounded in the plays through dance and masks and Edmund Dulac's lanterns, as well as through Craig's Cubist staging. There is a theatrical thrill in the stark opening words of *At the Hawk's Well* quite unlike anything that preceded them in the plays:

I call to the eye of the mind
A well long choked up and dry
And boughs long stripped by the wind.
(*VPl* 399)

The poet's most authoritative biographer, R. F. Foster, has suggested that in general the plays offer direct material to the researcher of Yeats's life in a way that the poetry does not; at this stage of Yeats's career the reverse appeared to be the case. For example, "Easter 1916" was written in the same year as this beautiful but ageless Noh-derived Cuchulain play. It was staged twice, in two London society drawing-rooms, in April, 1916, the month of both the explanatory essay on "Certain Noble Plays of Japan" and the momentous events commemorated in Yeats's greatest history poem, "Easter 1916." Indeed, given the private – almost *samizdat* – circulation of the poem in September, 1916, which waited nearly three years for its public appearance, the staging of the play before a small audience of London friends is oddly like the circumstances of the delayed unveiling of "Easter 1916." In any case, there is a sustained sureness about these sparely expressed "plays for dancers" beyond any other group of dramatic writings in Yeats's career. And it is striking too that this sureness carried over into the more overtly political 1916 play *The Dreaming of the Bones*, which, almost uniquely within Yeats's dramatic *œuvre*, does mix the symbolic and the historical successfully within the stylistic framework of the Noh.

This is the stage of Yeats's writing life, 1913–20, when the high claims made by the play-enthusiasts have their most convincing justification. Although it is not evident from the unreliable dating of the individual works on the contents page of the *Collected Plays*, theatrical activity became secondary in the 1920s when Yeats's (always prolific) prose-writing career was at its height in the construction of *A Vision*, and of course the magnificent poetic achievements of *The Tower* and the beginning of *The Winding Stair* were being built. In fact the plays of the period 1920–34 – the "later plays" section of Ellmann's tripartite division – are relatively over-represented, compared, for instance, with the first decade of the century when some notable plays were uncollected. The impressive versions of Sophocles and the plays on the severed head theme are all included, whereas there is no evidence in the *Collected Plays* of earlier plays that Yeats had worked on at great length, such as *Where There Is Nothing*. Finally there is an eerie double swan-song with the opinionated but effective *Purgatory* (1938) where the theatrical force of the events has to survive the play's repugnant underlying politics, and the beautiful revenant play in which Yeats at last completes the Cuchulain cycle with *The Death of Cuchulain*, written, astonishingly, in the weeks leading up to his own death.

I want to end by returning to examine what seems to be a continuing failure of Yeats's plays to attract major attention in the theatre, despite the advocacy of the enthusiasts in the academy (sometimes the theatrical academy, by scholar-directors such as Sam McCready), and offering some tentative explanations. The first is that the plays are still rarely criticized in terms of their substance and subjects: in crude terms, what their meaning is. It is a remarkable fact that Ure's 1963 pioneer study remains the only attempt, convincing or not, to suggest an overall thematic enterprise or subject: that all the plays are about art or the transcendent. Ure rightly praises the "supremely thrilling" theatrical moment in *The Resurrection* when the empirical Greek recognizes that "the heart of the phantom [Christ] is beating";[30] but he is unusual in having an overall *reading* of the plays that can embrace that event's significance. A second problem is that too often formal radicalism is claimed for the plays while the reactionary tendency of what that radicalism expresses is ignored: the familiar Modernist dilemma. Worth demonstrates the theatrical Stanislawskian brilliance of *The Hour-Glass*, and shows (what is unquestionably the case) how the odd couples in *On Baile's Strand* or *The Cat and the Moon* influence and anticipate *Waiting for Godot*. She also explains the origins of the comically irascible Old Man who speaks the long prologue to *The Death of Cuchulain* (1939) and infamously seems to argue for Yeats's "fit audience though few," usually read as claiming elitism and exclusiveness for Yeats's dramatic practice. Worth claims that "the self-aware Old Man is perhaps the most important archetype Yeats developed from the Maeterlinckian mode and in turn handed on to Beckett,"[31] going on to warn against taking him too unironically as Yeats's mouthpiece. In a much-quoted sentence the Old Man explains "I wanted an audience of fifty or a hundred, and if there are more, I beg them not to shuffle their feet or talk while the actors are speaking" (*VPl* 1051). The problem is that Worth, in warning against identifying that voice as Yeats's, has to recognize that the anti-democratic views it declares, however comically, are not that averse to Yeats's own in that period. Writers are as answerable for what they borrow as for what they invent. Symbolist staging, after all, could serve drama that was more obviously democratic than Yeats's was; it was used by Brecht in his agit-prop Marxist plays.

This is not to make a crude demand for a naturalistic form or moral, nor is it an accusation of disingenuousness in the critics who ignore Yeats's ideology in dramatic contexts; the problem is that Yeats himself sends out inconsistent signals. If it is argued that it was not clear what *Waiting for Godot* or *Endgame* is about, we might reply that those plays unmistakably represent a tragic-ironic view of the human condition. Besides, there is nothing in Beckett that leads us to expect the naturalistic; we are in a consistently surreal world. By contrast, Yeats, in plays such as *Where There Is Nothing* or *The Words upon the Window-Pane*, blurs the generic bearing of his kind of theatre by moving uncertainly between the realistic and the mythological: what Ellmann called "the half symbolic." It is surely remarkable that two of Yeats's most important plays exist in radically different generic versions: *The Player Queen*, tragic or comic; and *The King's Threshold*, tragic or reconciled in its conclusion. Yeats can use the same material to argue radically opposed views of the world.

Such uncertainty is perhaps related to Yeats's vague intimation that, when plays express the writer's opinion, they are working against their own dialectical nature, which is *not* to express opinion directly. The Yeats who advised his baby daughter that "An intellectual hatred is the worst" and that "opinions are accursed" (*VP* 405) implies that opinion must be kept out of art, whether poetry or drama. But the strong opinions voiced in Yeats's late controversial prose, especially in the "Tomorrow's Revolution" section of *On the Boiler* (*Ex* 417–28), are reflected much more damagingly in *Purgatory* than in the classic calm of "Why should not Old Men be Mad?". An appreciation of the theatrical power of that play has to believe that its political implication is secondary.

This may also suggest an explanation for another factor in the plays' failure to achieve major popularity in the repertoire: the narrowness and, for the most part, esotericism of their themes. There is a major difference between the poetry and plays in this way. Although the later poems do have a considerable mythopoeic element – Crazy Jane and Greek legend, for instance – there is a good proportion of the everyday of general experience as well (in "Politics," the "A Woman Young and Old" sequence, and the "Coole Park" biographical reveries for example). As "The Circus Animals' Desertion" says, the plays do indeed seem incapable of doing anything "but enumerate old themes" (*VP* 629). The repetition of mythic subjects – the *Salomé*-derived severed head, the displaced poet, ancient and increasingly anachronistic Irish heroes – prevents the staging of the matters that were crucial in the confessional poetry. It is remarkable, for example, how little of the material of the plays is concerned specifically with ageing, in the case of the greatest poet of ageing in the language. An exception is *At the Hawk's Well*, arguably Yeats's finest play.

The final – and I think most conclusive – problem with Yeats's dramatic writing has to do with language: ironically, given that his poetic language is arguably his greatest glory. The high gravity of language in the Noh-influenced plays for dancers was only a temporary cure for the defective breathing diagnosed by Ellmann in the earlier plays. Even the language of *Purgatory*, for all its compulsiveness and affinity with the diction of great late poems such as "High Talk," is distractingly unstable in the theatre. For example, within the same minute the Boy has to say the Shakespearean "your wits are out again" and the colloquial "my grand-dad got the girl and the money" (*VPl* 1042–3). An instructive contrast between Yeats's ease with his language in poetry and his lack of it in drama is provided by the opening exchange in *The Shadowy Waters* in the poetic volumes:

> I am so tired of being bachelor
> I could give all my heart to that Red Moll
> That had but the one eye. (*VP* 222)

The vividness of this odd language works well in the poetic dialogue. But in the play the Second Sailor's semi-Kiltartanese is distracting: "It is a hard thing, age to be coming on me, and I not to get the chance of doing a robbery that would enable me to live quiet and honest to the end of my lifetime" (*VPl* 318). "Enable" is a different register from "and I not" (we might contrast Synge whose intricate language is always perfectly sustained). The irony is that Yeats's dramatic language, which was such a powerful instrument in his poetry, is often disablingly deficient in the plays which, as he claimed in his Nobel essay, were its workshop.

So where can a case in favor of Yeats's drama be confidently made, at the end of what I am aware reads as something of a counsel of despair? A start might be made by taking the four plays in James Pethica's excellent

Norton Critical Edition of *Yeats's Poetry, Drama, and Prose*.[32] Pethica chooses the early Gregory collaboration *Cathleen ni Houlihan*; the early Symbolist Cuchulain play *On Baile's Strand*; the Noh-influenced Cuchulain play *At the Hawk's Well*; and the harsh, late-Modernist one-act *Purgatory*. What I have called uncertainty of direction in the plays could, on the evidence of this group, be called imaginative variety. Above all, there is the fact that the heritage of *Godot* and other aspects of Beckett's extraordinary theatre are to be found here. In an astonishingly prophetic review of Yeats's volume *Plays and Controversies*, the anonymous *Times Literary Supplement* reviewer foresaw this Banquo-like fate for Yeats's plays, concluding that "some day the influence from them will enter the modern, the popular theatre and be powerful there; but they themselves never will."[33] Maybe that is not an ignoble epitaph.

NOTES

1. T. S. Eliot, "Yeats," in *On Poetry and Poets* (New York: Noonday Press, 1970 [1943]), p. 307.
2. The discussion here will mostly be confined to the twenty-six plays included in the standard Macmillan *Collected Plays* (2nd edn. 1952, or later reprints). *The Island of Statues* and other dramatic writings before *The Countess Cathleen* (1892) are not in the *Collected Plays*, but are in VPl. They are also being published as part of the great Cornell series of facsimile editions of the complete works of Yeats.
3. Katharine Worth, *The Irish Drama of Europe from Yeats to Beckett* (London: Athlone Press, 1978).
4. There are several good accounts of Yeats's collaboration with Craig. See, for example, Chapter 10 of James W. Flannery, *W. B. Yeats and the Idea of a Theatre: The Early Abbey Theatre in Theory and Practice* (New Haven: Yale University Press, 1976) and also R. A. Cave, "Stage-Design as a Form of Dramatic Criticism," in *Irish Literature and Culture*, ed. M. Kenneally (Gerrards Cross: Colin Smythe, 1992), pp. 72–89.
5. Terence Brown, *The Life of W. B. Yeats: A Critical Biography* (Oxford: Blackwell, 1999), p. 382.
6. Reg Skene, *The Cuchulain Plays of W. B.Yeats* (London: Macmillan, 1974), p. xi.
7. See, for instance, her review of a stage performance: "*The Words upon the Window-Pane*: a female tragedy" (*Yeats Annual* 10 [1993]), 135–58.
8. *Shadows. A Trinity of Plays by J. M. Synge and W. B. Yeats* [no editor credited] (London: Oberon Books for the Royal Shakespeare Company, 1998).
9. Louis MacNeice, *The Poetry of W. B. Yeats* (London and New York: Oxford University Press, 1941), p. 196.
10. Eric Bentley, *In Search of Theater* (New York: Alfred A. Knopf, 1953), p. 315.
11. Peter Ure, *Yeats the Playwright: A Commentary on Character and Design in the Major Plays* (London: Routledge & Kegan Paul, 1963), p. 1.
12. Helen Hennessy Vendler, *Yeats's "Vision" and the Later Plays* (Cambridge, MA: Harvard University Press, 1963), p. 138.

13. Harold Bloom, *Yeats* (Oxford and New York: Oxford University Press, 1970), p. 426.
14. See Flannery, *W. B. Yeats and the Idea of a Theatre.*
15. Una Ellis-Fermor, *The Irish Dramatic Movement* (London: Methuen, 1939).
16. Brown, *The Life of W. B. Yeats,* p. 382.
17. A. S. Knowland, *W. B. Yeats: Dramatist of Vision* (Gerrards Cross: Colin Smythe, 1983), p. xv.
18. Liam Miller, *The Noble Drama of W. B. Yeats* (Dublin: Dolmen Press; Atlantic Heights, NJ: Humanities Press, 1977), p. 192.
19. Quoted in Anthony Roche, *Contemporary Irish Drama: From Beckett to McGuinness* (Dublin: Gill and Macmillan, 1994), p. 24.
20. Often quite violently: Ulick O'Connor says "Anyone who can read Yeats's plays and not say he's a dramatist is a fool" (reviewing Flannery's Dublin stagings in *Yeats: An Annual of Critical and Textual Studies*, ed. R. J. Finneran [Ann Arbor: University of Michigan Press, 1992], p. 186).
21. S. B. Bushrui, *Yeats's Verse-Plays: The Revisions, 1900–1910* (Oxford: Oxford University Press, 1965), p. vii.
22. Bloom, *Yeats,* p. 70.
23. See Thomas Parkinson, *W. B. Yeats, Self-Critic: A Study of His Early Verse* (Berkeley: University of California Press, 1951) and *W. B. Yeats: The Later Poetry* (Berkeley: University of California Press, 1964).
24. Richard Ellmann, *Yeats: The Man and the Masks* (New York: Norton, 1978).
25. Anthony Bradley, *William Butler Yeats* (New York: Ungar, 1979).
26. See James Pethica, "'Our Kathleen': Yeats's Collaboration with Lady Gregory in the Writing of *Cathleen ni Houlihan*," *Yeats Annual*, ed. Warwick Gould 6 (1988), pp. 3–31.
27. Bushrui, *Yeats's Verse-Plays.*
28. Ellmann, *The Man and the Masks*, p. 183.
29. *ibid.*, p. 214.
30. Ure, *Yeats the Playwright*, p. 126.
31. Worth, *The Irish Drama of Europe*, p. 145.
32. James Pethica, ed. *Yeats's Poetry, Drama, and Prose* (New York: Norton, 2000).
33. *Times Literary Supplement*, 10 January, 1924, repr. in *W. B.Yeats: The Critical Heritage*, ed. A. Norman Jeffares (London: Routledge & Kegan Paul, 1977), p. 24.

7

DECLAN KIBERD

Yeats and criticism

The critical writings of poets often have surprisingly little to do with their own work. This sometimes has an obvious enough cause: poets are usually poor and must take in whatever reviewing work comes their way. But there are other, more interesting reasons for this state of affairs. An artist such as T. S. Eliot seems to have seen his critical essays as a sort of elaborate smokescreen thrown up around his poetry and plays, the better to keep their magic and mystery inviolate.[1] The famous meditations on Milton, on the metaphysical poets, and on tradition itself have little enough in the end to do with *The Waste Land* or *Four Quartets*, despite the heroic and desperate efforts of scholars to posit some connections. When Eliot wrote of the need in all healthy art to make a separation between the man who suffers and the mind which creates, he may have come as near to critical autobiography as he dared.[2]

Not so with W. B. Yeats. Though he was, in his youth, far more dependent than Eliot on whatever reviewing came his way, he had a happy knack of using every kind of artist as a means of exploring himself. Criticism, as he practiced it, was really an overflow of his autobiography, a way of sharing the readerly experience with a wider audience. Subsequent Irish poets have written good criticism – notably Patrick Kavanagh and Seamus Heaney – but they have often been fearful of writing too much. Heaney has spoken of an artist's need to remain capable of accident and surprise, and of the consequent danger of becoming overly self-conscious in the creative process. You might, he warns, come to believe more in the critical coroner in yourself than in the person open to the unexpected.[3] As if to illustrate that warning, some very good poets like Matthew Arnold can be shown to have grown into powerful critics, but at a real cost to their own art. Yeats, however, never felt in any danger of being immobilized by the practice of criticism. On the contrary, he seems again and again to equate the critical with the creative act. In his aesthetic, a mind can never create until it is split in two: and poetry, being a quarrel with the self, is really just a form of autocritique.

Perhaps what saved Yeats from feeling violated by criticism was the fact that even his prose worked more by instinct than reason, being a mode of sublimated poetry. "He had been almost poor," he writes of Wilde, "and now, his head full of Flaubert, found himself with ten thousand a year" (*A* 224). The juxtaposition of elements involves the suppression of certain links in the expository chain, but the hypnotic rhythms establish the electric connections. Or consider this sentence: "A friend of Strindberg's, in delirium tremens, was haunted by mice, and a friend in the next room heard the squealing of the mice" (*A* 214). This comes just a couple of pages after Yeats has asked whether modern civilization might be "a conspiracy of the subconscious" and whether what seemed logical to the mind might be no more than automatic impulse (*A* 211).

Yeats achieved a real profundity of thought because he was willing to say things that he did not fully understand until long afterwards. What Eliot said of poetry – that it should always be able to communicate before it was fully understood – Yeats believed also of criticism: "It is so many years before one can believe enough in what one feels even to know what that feeling is" (*A* 105). He considered himself a medium for ideas as well as for emotions, and both ideas and emotions often seemed far stronger than his individual self. Hence his father's affectionate put-down: "You want to be a philosopher, Willie, but are only a poet."[4] Yeats's technical gift with language stood well in excess of his analytic power: but this was as it should be, because to any artist the half-said thing is what fascinates. He did not consider this a state peculiar to himself, but employed the case of J. M. Synge as an example of the need for an artist to achieve objectivity by a form of self-criticism.

The poems written by Synge in the 1890s had been mawkish and sentimental, because they were excessively subjective in their brooding over time and fate: they were in fact a bleak confirmation of the quip that all bad poetry springs from genuine feeling. But once Synge discovered an equivalent something outside himself for every mood within – as he did among the stones and fields of Aran – then he began to possess his theme and his true language, because he was able for the first time to submit those things to cool analysis:

> Whenever he tried to write drama without dialect he wrote badly, and he made several attempts, because only through dialect could he escape self-expression, see all that he did from without, allow his intellect to judge the images of his mind as if they had been created by some other mind. His objectivity was, however, technical only, for in those images paraded all the desires of his heart. (*A* 263)

This is, of course, a passage in Yeats's *Autobiographies*, and fittingly so, since it is also an account of how he too escaped the brooding melancholy of his own early work by seeking an image without rather than within. In that early work, Yeats had tried to be true to emotion but had often lapsed into sheer sentimentality (as he later admitted himself) for want of thought.

Part of Yeats's power as a critic is his honest account of the limits of analytic insight. If man can only ever embody a truth that he may never know, it behooves the critic not to make excessive claims. Perhaps the most sustained idea through all of Yeats's writing is the limited importance of any one idea: "Those men that in their writings are most wise / Own nothing but their blind, stupefied hearts" (*VP* 370) or "Opinion is not worth a rush" (*VP* 385). The classic example is, of course, "The Circus Animals' Desertion": "I sought a theme and sought for it in vain, / I sought it daily for six weeks or so" (*VP* 629). Here the poet discovers that his lack of a given theme is his greatest gift to others and his ultimate freedom to become and be himself. That poem may have its roots in an old Sligo tale about a tramp who came at nightfall to a farmhouse, in hopes of a bed and breakfast. "Fine," said the farmer and his family, "but first you must tell us a story," since this was the time-honored pay-off for such hospitality. However, the poor tramp had no story and so he could not stay. He trudged through the rainy twilight to another house, only to encounter the same problem. Again, he was expelled. In outrage by now, he went on to a third house, where he complained with eloquent bitterness of the meanness of the people in the previous two farmsteads. And *that* was his story, told with such fire as to delight his hosts, who gave him his straw bed and cake.

Yeats's story was also that he had no story. His search, as R. P. Blackmur said, was more for a mode of expression than for a dogma to express[5] – hence his far greater interest as a critic in matters of form than of content. All the most interesting ideas were old ideas: it was only by its style that a work of art could make a telling claim upon posterity. It could do this by infusing a sort of awareness into any form of its own workings as a medium.

This means, of course, that much of Yeats's poetry is also an act of profound literary criticism, self-aware in an enabling way rather than self-conscious in a manner that might only cloud its effect. Again and again, the major poems of Yeats supply not only their own lines but also (in other lines) the critical apparatus by which they might be interpreted, in keeping with that Symbolist aesthetic which demands a poetry that delivers not just an image but the light by which it can be illuminated. That fusion of the creative and the critical is well explored in "A Prayer for Old Age":

God guard me from those thoughts men think
In the mind alone;
He that sings a lasting song
Thinks in a marrow-bone. (*VP* 553)

How this works in practice may be seen in "The Municipal Gallery Revisited," when an eight-line stanza breaks off with a throb of anguish in its penultimate line for the destruction of Coole Park: "And now that end has come I have not wept; / No fox can foul the lair the badger swept –" before making way in the new stanza for an act of criticism: "(An image out of Spenser and the common tongue)" (*VP* 603). Yeats glosses the previous line by recalling a strange blend of sources, from popular lore and from Spenser's elegiac account of the death of the Earl of Leicester. The same technique is used in the lead-up to the closing section of "Lapis Lazuli":

Two Chinamen, behind them a third,
Are carved in lapis lazuli,
Over them flies a long-legged bird,
A symbol of longevity . . . (*VP* 566)

There are two ways of treating such a technique. The first is to see it as a Symbolist tactic of the sort already indicated, by which the poet can assert the proud self-sufficiency of the poem, which includes not just its text but its interpretation. The second is to recognize it as a somewhat more defensive ploy by which a poet, nervous of losing his audience's understanding, gently guides the reader's response along the desired lines.

When Yeats set about founding a national literature, he made it very clear that the gathering of an interpretative community was an intrinsic part of the process. "Does not the greatest poetry always require a people to listen to it?" he asked (*E&I* 213); and he remarked in "The Fisherman":

All day I'd looked in the face
What I had hoped 'twould be
To write for my own race
And the reality. (*VP* 347)

The problem with any newly gathered audience may be that it lacks interpretative confidence, being more used to seeing itself interpreted by others. Much of Yeats's criticism, outside his poems as well as within them, is his attempt to coach that gathered audience in the protocols of a true reading. The implication is clear: the Irish, so long "read" by others, must now learn how to read themselves. The mob would only be bonded into a people when their lyric effusions were accompanied by acts of self-explanation and self-analysis. In Yeats's aesthetic, criticism is but another kind of literature, and literature but another means of criticism. Moreover, his works, filled with the half-said thing, yearn for completion in the act of being read. In a strict sense, they are only completed when they are criticized.

This is a view of art found most often in postcolonial writing. When Toni Morrison, the black American novelist, was asked why she writes the kind of books she does, her reply was simple: "because they're the kind of books I want to read." Her colleague Alice Walker interprets this to mean that as an exponent of an emergent literature she must do the work of two: "She must (first of all) be her own model, as well as (secondly) being the artist attending, creating, learning from, realizing the model, which is to say herself."[6] Yeats expressed the same idea even more beautifully when he spoke of "the tradition of myself" (*A* 342), a special identity possible only to him in the act of writing and solely for its duration. All writers of a minority group in a majority language face that challenge: since freedom cannot be won *in* the available forms, it must somehow be won *from* them. A writer in conditions of perfect freedom begins with the easy assurance that literature is but one of the social institutions to project desirable values, and that the judiciary, the civil services, and the colleges can do so as well. A writer in an oppressed community knows that the desirable values can be fully embodied only in the written word: hence the daunting seriousness with which literature is taken by subject peoples. *Style* is the means by which W. B. Yeats or Alice Walker dramatizes a freed consciousness, to which others can aspire. This self exists only within the writing, and also up ahead in some future social formation. Walker herself has insisted that she writes more for "the adults one's children will become than for the children one's 'mature' critics often are."[7]

In effect, such critics must write themselves into existence as models, before going on to read and decode that new self. According to the account given of him in Yeats's *Autobiographies*, this is precisely what his own gifted father failed to do: and so the son could see the older man only in fragments, before going on to "complete" that broken, gapped narrative by an act of criticism. Such a critique is the highest compliment, for all truly great moments in culture are achieved by an act of analytic opposition. Those who read an age in its own spirit are soon forgotten; those who oppose that spirit somehow penetrate through to its deeper meanings. Whenever a country produces a man or woman of genius, it produces a critic, because he or she is never quite like its official idea of itself. George Bernard Shaw was too much in harmony with the modern age to be its truest critic (despite his addiction to the play of ideas): but Yeats, forever opposing the spirit of the times, could become their radical analyst (despite his belief in the superior value of emotion).

An early and neglected poem of Yeats, "His Dream" (*VP* 253–4), contains many clues to the ideal relationship between artist and interpretative community:

I swayed upon the gaudy stern
The butt-end of a steering-oar,
And saw wherever I could turn
A crowd upon a shore.

And though I would have hushed the crowd,
There was no mother's son but said,
"What is the figure in a shroud
Upon a gaudy bed?"

The speaker isn't in full control of his oar, for it sways him: and this may be an image of Yeats's addiction to the "gaudy" phraseology of the 1890s (the "butt-end" of Romantic tradition). He looks at the crowd upon the shore, whose fashionable tastes he has fed. The choice is the familiar Yeatsian one between expressing and exploiting your material: the performer here keeps his eye on the audience and so risks a betrayal of his subject and risks losing his audience. In effect, the poet has been asking others, cowardly in themselves, to do his living for him – in the manner of the Tragic Generation of the 1890s.

The scene may be based on that biblical setting in which Jesus preached to the multitude from a boat: and, if so, it has implications for Yeats's attempt to assume the role of a national bard or poet. For he goes out onto the waters in the boat, moving away a little from the crowd precisely so that he may be free to envisage its members as a community. He tries to "sway" that crowd by his leadership, but his effect is limited, even ludicrous. They talk rudely during his performance, not about him but about "a thing" – the very word used of a dead body wrapped in a wet sail (a "shroud") in J. M. Synge's *Riders to the Sea*.[8] If sailing out from land betokens death, that shroud may be made for the end of the tradition:

And after running at the brim
Cried out upon that thing beneath
– It had such dignity of limb –
By the sweet name of Death.

This shifts Synge's deathly "thing" back to Coleridge's life-in-death (from "The Rime of the Ancient Mariner"), developing the notion of a Romantic tradition nearing its demise:

Though I'd my finger on my lip,
What could I but take up the song?
And running crowd and gaudy ship
Cried out the whole night long,

Crying amid the glittering sea,
Naming it with ecstatic breath,
Because it had such dignity,
By the sweet name of Death.

The poet would prefer not to speak, but finds himself forced to adopt the prevailing Romantic fashion, while he cannot fail to jeer at its redundancy by the close. He may be admitting his failure to evoke a respectful silence in which his own true voice would be heard: but he is certainly casting himself in the role of an early Modernist officiating over the last rites of Romanticism in this opening lyric of *The Green Helmet and Other Poems* (1910). It was, we remember, in or about December, 1910 that human nature changed, according to Virginia Woolf. The only answer to corruption by the sentimentalist audience is a vigilant criticism, by which the entertainer will ensure his credentials as an artist.

Much of Yeats's writing in the first decade of the new century concerned his attempt not just to gather an audience for a national literature, but also to educate it in the necessary freedoms that should be enjoyed by artists. Essays like "The Irish National Theatre and Three Sorts of Ignorance" sought to combat the prescriptive, propagandist art favored by town councilors, pious clerics, and narrow-gauge nationalists. But such work was only a beginning. Even with the audience actually gathered, Yeats felt it necessary to provide in his plays the sort of critical commentary by which they could be more fully understood – as when Naoise says near the moment of his death in *Deirdre* (1907):

What need have I, that gave up all for love,
To die like an old king out of a fable,
Fighting and passionate? What need is there
For all that ostentation at my setting?
I have loved truly and betrayed no man.
I need no lightning at the end, no beating
In a vain fury at the cage's door.

(*VPl* 373)

It was a lesson he was to enforce many years later in a poem called "The Old Stone Cross":

> But actors lacking music
> Do most excite my spleen,
> They say it is more human
> To shuffle, grunt and groan,
> Not knowing what unearthly stuff
> Rounds a mighty scene . . .
> (*VP* 599)

He enforced it again in "Lapis Lazuli," which repeats the now-familiar suggestion that tragedy should be a joy to the one who dies, since he or she is set free of life rather than deprived of it:

> All perform their tragic play,
> There struts Hamlet, there is Lear,
> That's Ophelia, that Cordelia;
> Yet they, should the last scene be there,
> The great stage curtain about to drop,
> If worthy their prominent part in the play,
> Do not break up their lines to weep.
> They know that Hamlet and Lear are gay;
> Gaiety transfiguring all that dread.
> (*VP* 565)

Such lines were, in the first instance, critiques of bad acting, but also of the vulgar expectations that appeared to license such self-indulgence on the part of ham-actors. As always, the artist who deferred excessively to the audience is exposed as a cheap performer.

Deference might, of course, take subtler forms, but it was no less regrettable for that. Through his father, John Butler Yeats, the young poet came to know Edward Dowden, professor of English at Trinity College Dublin, and arguably the most prestigious and fashionable critic of the later Victorian period.[9] In his youthful days, Yeats loved to call with his father at Dowden's for an early morning discussion of poetry, and he was deeply grateful for the inspiration and encouragement provided during those visits. But, over the years, he came to see Dowden as an example of a man who "will not trust his nature" and wasted it therefore in a professional career spent assessing the opinions of others. He had succumbed to the "chief temptation of the artist, creation without toil" (*A* 171). As a result, he failed to be either a poet or a sage, becoming a mere provincial. In contrast to Dowden, Yeats proposed the artist-hero Synge, as a man who never bothered to read the newspapers or the opinions of his contemporaries, but who was alone with the great classic authors (*E&I* 329–30).

Synge was great because his nature was strong and trusted enough to be able to embrace its own opposite: and so he became a sick man picturing energy. This could only be done by those brave enough to incorporate the harshest possible criticism into their own art-works. So, *The Playboy of the Western World* contains not only the gorgeous excess of Hiberno-English but also a shrewd analysis of the costs and limits of such blarney, as Synge has the sophistication to raise some doubts about the very medium through which these doubts are expressed. When Pegeen Mike says near the end that "there's a great gap between a gallous story and a dirty deed,"[10] she is voicing the essential criticism of the codes to which the play, nevertheless, adheres.

This is an example of Scott Fitzgerald's test of a first-rate intelligence: "the capacity to hold opposed ideas in the head without losing the ability to function."[11] Hence, Yeats's belief that "a writer must die every day he lives, be reborn, as it is said in the Burial Service, an incorruptible self, that self opposite of all that he has named 'himself'" (*A* 336). The problem with those nationalist zealots who had attacked the art of Synge was that they had confused criticism with complaint: yet even they, in time, would learn to embrace their opposites, just as Ireland had gone from the bragging rhetoric of Daniel O'Connell to the passionate reticence of Charles Stuart Parnell. "When loathing remains but loathing, world or self consumes itself away, and we turn to its mechanical opposite" (*A* 192). For just this reason, nationalism and unionism were in real danger of becoming sad reflections of one another's less admirable features. There is a link in Yeats's mind between criticism and the death of all utterance: and so it is no surprise that he should have referred to the burial service of the Anglican Church as a model. To criticize a text is to complete it, and to complete it is effectively to kill it (to consume it "away"). This is also why Yeats sees all poetry as a near-death experience.

Such a criticism, which ends with the Protestant burial service, begins at the very outset of *Autobiographies* with the voice of conscience. Self-examination, though soon discarded in this melodramatic form, becomes the prevailing method of the ensuing volumes. Daniel T. O'Hara has compared initial and revised passages of set-piece scenes and finds "the incorporation into the text of a critical history of its own antithetical method of interpretation."[12] He sees Yeats embarked on a mission to become his own ideal and exemplary reader, a mission that is somehow triumphantly concluded in "Ego Dominus Tuus" (a poem that is a kind of history of criticism and a criticism of history over the previous fifteen-hundred years). At much the same time as Yeats was implementing this exacting program, James Joyce was installing the reader as the true wanderer in the labyrinth of *Ulysses*, the ultimate decoder "*lisant au livre de lui-même*" ("reading in the book of himself").[13] And, of course, a whole range of postmodern Irish writers, from Flann O'Brien to Brendan Behan, included passages of autocriticism in their novels or plays.

Yeats was the first major Irish writer to do this. One consequence has been – for him as well as for those who followed – a severe underestimation of his importance as a critic. His personal quarrel with Dowden concerning the Ireland of their time fed not only his dramatic treatments of the Cuchulain legend but also his meditative essays on Shakespeare. Complaining that the scientistic, efficiency-worshiping Victorian theorists had misread *Richard II* as a play that exalted Bolingbroke and devalued the despised King, Yeats chose to recast the contrast in terms that suggested a clash between the doomed poetic complexity of Richard and the merely administrative guile of his assailant and dethroner. In other words, he reinterpreted it in Arnoldian terms as a version of what England had done in Ireland. This he went on to re-imagine in the constrast between King Conchubar and the hero Cuchulain in plays like *On Baile's Strand* (1904), the former being astute, cunning, and worldly, the latter impulsive, poetic, and reckless of his own interest.

In one sense, by creating a cycle of Cuchulain plays, Yeats was merely making available to Irish audiences a myth of national self-explanation to set alongside Shakespeare's Henriad cycle: but his rewriting of the Bolingbroke–Richard saga in terms that showed the doomed poet as the moral and emotional center of the play helped to underwrite his own drama criticism, which had as a result a palpable influence on later developments in Shakespeare scholarship. That thinking was most fully expressed in the essay "At Stratford-on-Avon," which is a thorough repudiation of a Victorian scholarship that saw Richard as "weak" and "sentimental" and Henry V as "Shakespeare's only hero": "These books took the same delight in abasing Richard II that schoolboys do in persecuting some boy of fine temperament, who has weak muscles and a distaste for school games" (*E&I* 104). Obviously, Yeats felt (as always) an autobiographical stake in this criticism. Memories of being bullied at the Godolphin School in London were still painfully clear. But Dowden, who first made the fashionable reading "eloquent and plausible," is identified as leader of the critical bullies: "He lived in Ireland, where everything has failed, and he meditated frequently upon the perfection of character that had, he thought, made England successful, for, as we say, 'cows beyond the water have long horns'" (*E&I* 104). Disputing Dowden's version, Yeats averred that England was made by imaginative adventurers rather than by tame administrators: "to suppose that Shakespeare preferred the men who deposed his king is to suppose that Shakespeare judged men with the eyes of a Municipal Councillor weighing the merits of a Town Clerk" (*E&I* 105). Yeats suggests that Dowden's followers further coarsened these readings "at a moment of imperialistic enthusiasm" (*E&I* 104). So congealed did some of the more "robust" readings of *Richard II* become that – despite the warnings against them first issued by Walter Pater, or maybe it was because of them – A. P. Rossiter could comment that "there is something in Richard which calls out the latent homosexuality of critics."[14] It was only with the emergence of a postcolonial criticism, which tended to see Shakespeare's peripheral characters as central to a play's meaning, and with the willingness of such readers to go with the flow of his poetry, that Yeats's reversal in the interpretation of the Henriad took hold.

Today, it is possible to read many of the major critical essays written by Yeats in the first decade of the twentieth century as founding documents in the movement for cultural decolonization. Philip Edwards has shown how Yeats used the plays of Shakespeare like captured weapons turned on an old enemy:[15] and the same feat has been performed by writers from India to the West Indies.[16] This was the decade in which Yeats's productions as a poet slowed at times to a standstill, partly because of his activity in building up and writing for the Abbey Theatre, but also because he was so busy providing the critical underpinning of modern Irish thought.

He supported Douglas Hyde's campaign for the recognition of Irish as a secondary school subject by the Board of Education and as a fit subject for matriculation into the universities. But he went even further, arguing that Hiberno-English – the dialect spoken by country people who still thought in Irish while using English words – should be given official recognition: "Let every child in Ireland be set to turn a leading article or a piece of what is called excellent English, written perhaps by some distinguished member of the Board, into the idiom of his own countryside" (*Ex* 95). Had this been done, it would have anticipated by some decades the debate about the validity of using dialect in African-American texts: but the people's minds were so colonized that they felt ashamed of the emerging "lingo" rather than proud of its expressive subtlety. Yeats's hope was that, if the dialect were employed in such prestigious activities as university lectures, newspaper editorials, and church sermons, the people would soon take a proper pride in the idiom forged out of the trauma of language-loss in nineteenth-century Ireland: but it was not to be.

Yeats's achievements as a critic are in most ways linked to his role as the leading theorist of the Irish Renaissance. The major elements of *Essays and Introductions* refer either to the exemplary value of works from the English Renaissance (Shakespeare and Spenser), or to those radical authors (Blake,

Shelley, and Morris) who sought to hold England true to its own foundational principles. Or else they refer to contemporary exponents of national renaissance, whether Synge in Ireland or Tagore in India. The writings collected in *Explorations* draw heavily (for the first half of the volume, in fact) on the work of building and consolidating the Abbey as the one national institution in occupied Ireland. What they also testify to is the struggle of one great figure to remain an artist and to defend the autonomy of art in a time of political crisis. Later, Yeats would make of this the great theme of "Meditations in Time of Civil War," but he rehearsed it in plays like *The King's Threshold* (1904) and in the majestic essays published in *Beltaine* and *Samhain*.

The notion that an indigenous Irish criticism is a flower of recent growth – say, after 1970 – has been much canvassed by the current generation of scholars: but the critical essays of Yeats, Wilde, Synge, and Joyce, as well as their autocritical passages in creative texts, give the lie to it. The problem is the old Arnoldian one: achievements in analytic thought by Irish writers tend to be obscured by their lyric performances as artists, and by the fact that many have chosen to conceal their shrewdest acts of criticism within the works of art. Joyce's rereading of Shakespeare, for example, is embedded in *Ulysses*, with the result that few Yeatsians have noticed just how much support it offers to the man who the more youthful Joyce said was too old to be helped.[17]

Even less remarked on are the implications of all this for criticism of Yeats's work by others. Because he himself supplied, so to speak, the light by which his writings might be read, that criticism which is descriptive rather than interpretative has been generally the most helpful. In other words, a simple description of what it is like to read a poem, including in that experience its own self-readings, will often be far superior to more audacious or intrepid attempts to say "it really means X or Y." The heroic phase of Yeats criticism was dominated by attentively descriptive close readers: Richard Ellmann, A. Norman Jeffares, T. R. Henn, Helen Vendler, and Thomas Whitaker. All of these used Yeats's articles and essays in ways that scholars of Eliot could never employ his – as somehow continuous with the creative texts. Though it may seem tautological to put it like this, the best, fullest readings are Yeatsian.

This has given rise to suspicions and to problems. Some of Yeats's detractors feel that such maneuvers allow the poet too much latitude in dictating the conditions of his own reception. There is, for instance, in the commentary of Seamus Deane a smoldering resentment against the fact that, in order to be a major critic of Yeats's work, you have to buy absolutely into that work on its own set terms.[18] "Pythagoras planned it" – but what? "I have met them at close of day" – but whom? The Yeats poem never phases itself in with the protocols of polite literature: rather it assumes absolute, unconditional intimacy. This is a major source of his power as a poet, but also of his tendency to disturb those who fear lines that are often striking without being lucid, charged without being clear.

Such nervousness is understandable, but hardly conclusive. The worst that can be said against a Yeats poem usually turns out to have been said already, and far better, within the poem itself. And if it has not been said there, it will surely be said by Yeats in another lyric, perhaps even the next one in a collection. As John Unterecker pointed out many years ago, the best way of reading one poem by Yeats is often to go on to another, which may provide the essential criticism of the earlier one.[19] For, though Yeats has properly called forth some of the finest critics to study poetry in the last century, not one of them has produced a reading of his work that is better than his own: and, though he has had many poetic emulators, none has produced a body of critical thinking and appreciation to stand beside his own. He is the greatest poet-critic in the English language since Coleridge.

NOTES

1. See Mario Praz, "T. S. Eliot as a critic," in *T. S. Eliot: The Man and His Work*, ed. Allen Tate (Harmondsworth: Penguin, 1971), pp. 262–77; and Austen Warren, "Eliot's literary criticism," in *ibid.*, pp. 277–97.
2. Cited by Hugh Kenner, *The Invisible Poet: T. S. Eliot* (London: Harcourt, 1969), p. 103.
3. Seamus Heaney, *Preoccupations: Selected Prose 1968–1978* (London: Faber and Faber, 1980), p. 103.
4. Joseph Hone, ed., *J. B. Yeats: Letters to His Son 1869–1922* (London: Faber and Faber, 1969), p. 103.
5. R. P. Blackmur, "W. B. Yeats: Between Myth and Philosophy," in *Yeats: A Collection of Critical Essays*, ed. John Unterecker (Englewood Cliffs: Prentice Hall, 1963), pp. 64–79.
6. Alice Walker, *Living by the Word: Selected Writings 1973–1987* (London: Women's Press, 1988), p. 71.
7. *Ibid.*, p. 76.
8. J. M. Synge, *Collected Works: Plays 1*, ed. Ann Saddlemeyer (London: Oxford University Press, 1968), p. 23.
9. Terence Brown, *Ireland's Literature: Selected Essays* (Totowa, NJ: Lilliput Press; Barnes & Noble, 1988), pp. 29–48.
10. J. M. Synge, *Collected Works: Plays 2* (London: Oxford University Press, 1968), p. 169.
11. F. Scott Fitzgerald, *The Crack-Up, with Other Pieces and Stories* (Harmondsworth: Penguin, 1968), p. 39.
12. Daniel T. O'Hara, *Tragic Knowledge: Yeats's Autobiography and Hermeneutic* (New York: Columbia University Press, 1981), pp. 23ff.

13. James Joyce, *Ulysses: Student's Annotated Edition*, ed. Declan Kiberd (London: Penguin, 1992), p. 239.
14. Quoted by Kenneth Muir, introduction to William Shakespeare, *Richard II* (New York, New American Library, 1963), p. xxviii.
15. Philip Edwards, *Threshold of a Nation* (New York: Cambridge University Press, 1979), pp. 98–101.
16. See Declan Kiberd, *Inventing Ireland: The Literature of the Modern Nation* (London: Jonathan Cape, 1995), pp. 276–7.
17. *Ibid.*, pp. 269–81.
18. Seamus Deane, *Celtic Revivals: Essays in Modern Irish Literature 1880–1980* (London and Boston: Faber and Faber, 1985).
19. See John Unterecker, *A Reader's Guide to William Butler Yeats* (London and New York: Noonday Press, 1959).

8

JAMES PETHICA

Yeats, folklore, and Irish legend

By the time Yeats was twenty-one, two concerns had already emerged as central in his writing. One, which endured little changed throughout his life, was his rejection of late-Victorian scientific rationalism in favor of Romantic forms of knowledge. His placement of "The Happy Shepherd" at the start of *Collected Poems* self-consciously signals the centrality of this choice to the formation of his canon. Claiming that the materialist approach of science has yielded only "Grey" and inhuman forms of truth, the poem declares that the realm of imagination, for all its uncertainty, offers the best chance of self-knowledge and solace in a "sick" and hurried world (*VP* 64–5). The second concern, also enduring, but to which Yeats's relationship was often vexed and always evolving, was his desire to identify himself specifically as an Irish writer, and to assert the distinctiveness of "Irishness" as a cultural identity.

His interest in Irish folklore and heroic legend would bring these two seemingly separate preoccupations into intense and productive conjunction, particularly in the first two decades of his career. Folklore and legend offered him subject matter that contrasted sharply with the orthodoxies and concerns of the contemporary urban world, but that he was able to claim as distinctively Irish and draw on in creating master-myths of Irish nationality. As a storehouse of uncanny phenomena, ancient wisdom expressed in metaphorical or allegorical forms, and traditional models of story-telling, folklore appealed to him on occult, philosophical, and literary grounds. Heroic legend likewise attracted him both emotionally and intellectually, since he believed that only heroic action allowed the full expression of selfhood, and thus made possible the kind of passionate, heroic poetry he aspired to write (*UP*1 84).

Until the publication of *Poems* (1895), Yeats's early literary achievement rested significantly on his work as a folklorist. Of the ten volumes he had written or edited by 1894, three were works of folklore: *Fairy and Folk Tales of the Irish Peasantry* (1888), *Irish Fairy Tales* (1892), and *The Celtic Twilight* (1893); and two others – *Stories from Carleton* (1889) and

Representative Irish Tales (1891) – contain material of significant anthropological and folkloric interest. While the youthful Yeats "tried many pathways" (*VP* 845) in the 1880s in search of anti-materialist forms of truth, infuriating his rationalist father with his early enthusiasm for Theosophy and Esoteric Buddhism and his burgeoning interest in the occult, he quickly recognized the value of folklore and legend as an imaginative resource and as a potential foundation of national identity. In his earliest published prose works, two articles on the poetry of Samuel Ferguson written in 1886, he declares confidently that "great legends . . . are the mothers of nations" (*UP*1 104), and that Irish legendary materials offer "living waters for the healing of our nation" (*UP*1 82). These sentiments reflect his enthusiasm for the newly formed Dublin Young Ireland Society, which sought to promote Irish nationalist feeling by popularizing and encouraging Irish writing, and whose name recalled the patriotic Young Ireland movement of the 1840s. Inspired by John O'Leary, a Fenian who returned to Dublin in 1885 after spending twenty years in exile for advocating armed resistance to British rule, Yeats began to read widely in Irish literature and history, and he later recalled somewhat hyperbolically that from "[Young Ireland Society] debates, O'Leary's conversation, and from the Irish books he lent or gave me has come all I have set my hand to since" (*A* 104). By 1889 his belief in the necessity of a vital literary tradition for the construction of national identity had become a settled dictum – "there is no fine nationality without literature, and . . . no fine literature without nationality" (*LNI* 12).

Yeats's reading, however, quickly made it clear to him that Ireland lacked a coherent literary tradition. With the contours of the country's social and intellectual life deeply marked both by its colonial status, and by what Lady Gregory would term the "two great landslips" of its nineteenth-century history – the famine, and the shift from Irish-speaking to English-speaking amongst all but a small minority[1] – continuities of national culture, let alone of literary culture, seemed few. The body of writings from which a tradition might be constructed included texts in English, but also in the Irish language; writings that derived from English literary models, but also from Irish ones; work by writers who repudiated political connection with Britain, and by those who upheld it; and writings by those who sought a British audience, as well as by those who sought an Irish one. The effort to construct a tradition from these divergent literary products of a colonized culture would be Yeats's constant concern, and difficulty, over the next decade. He would repeatedly urge from around 1889 that Irish writers "ought to take Irish subjects" (*LNI* 31), but the question of what defined authentic "Irishness" would become progressively more vexed as the country's literary revival gathered momentum in the 1890s.

Oral culture, which he regarded as embodying unbroken, ancient traditions, initially attracted Yeats precisely since it offered a milieu seemingly immune to the linguistic and political dislocations visible in the published literary record, and one in which essential national characteristics might be revealed. In his introduction to *Fairy and Folk Tales of the Irish Peasantry*, he enthusiastically claimed that the Celts of the Irish western seaboard had remained untouched by "the Spirit of the Age," and that the folk tales still to be discovered amongst them offered an uncorrupted link with the distant Irish past and to a "visionary" knowledge now lost to "people of the cities" (*P&I* 3–5). In making such claims, Yeats was working within an established intellectual tradition. The notion that folk stories are repositories of experience and emotion more powerful and authentic than the artificial culture and art of the educated had become popular in the late eighteenth century as part of the Romantic movement's advocacy of emotion over intellect. German critic Johann von Herder, for instance, argued that the *Kultur des Volkes* ("culture of the people") embodied a primal engagement with fundamental questions about humanity's place in the cosmos, and thus revealed essential transhistorical truths about human experience. Such views contributed to the sensational popularity of the poetry published by James Macpherson in the 1760s, which purported to be the work of Ossian, a Gaelic warrior-poet from an unspecified remote period of pre-history. Macpherson's "Ossianic" poems – in fact merely adaptations and imitations of Gaelic material he had gathered in Scotland – were in vogue for more than a decade, and influenced many foundational Romantic texts, even after their recent origin had been exposed.

In the wake of Macpherson's success, Romantic popularization of folk culture flourished, gradually ushering in more systematic collections such as *Kinder- und Hausmärchen* (1812–15), the fairy and folk tales gathered by the brothers Grimm. With the rise of anthropology and philology as academic disciplines in the nineteenth century, scholarly folklorists interested in theorizing the lore they collected began to predominate, and the Romantic school of folklore gradually gave way to the school of comparative mythology, promoted by linguists such as Max Müller and Wilhelm Mannhardt. Müller sought to trace archetypal forms of folk stories back to what he believed were their original allegorical functions, while Mannhardt traced analogies between ancient and modern myths and tales, seeking to establish explanatory connections between ancient and contemporary cultural practices. By the late century, vast syncretic enterprises of comparative study were under way. If not quite searching for the "Key to All Mythologies" – as George Eliot satirically depicts the pedantic scholar Casaubon doing in *Middlemarch* (1872) – such projects did aspire to trace fundamental patterns of belief and of historical influence between cultures. As Yeats's own first folklore volumes appeared, Sir James Frazer in 1890 published, to widespread acclaim, the first volume of *The Golden Bough*, a comparative anthropological study of human beliefs, mythologies, and social institutions, which proposed, with late-Victorian confidence, that society progresses from the primitive and magical, to religious, and finally to scientific thought.

At the outset, Yeats identified closely with the Romantic school of folklore, emphasizing the imaginative vitality of his gatherings, and the potential of rural lore as an antidote to the sterility of what Frazer defined as evolved culture. Rather than offering "scientific" or comparative theories of the peasantry, or anthropological interpretations of stories, his focus in *Fairy and Folk Tales* is predominantly on creating literary and folkloric atmosphere. As he would stress in 1890, "imaginative impulse – the quintessence of life – is our great need from folk-lore. When we have banqueted let Learning gather the crumbs into her larder" (*UP*1 189). On being criticized by a reviewer for being "unscientific" in the volume, he countered that the folklorist who is "merely scientific" inevitably "lacks the needful subtle imaginative sympathy to tell his stories well." "The man of science" he added, "is too often a person who has exchanged his soul for a formula; and when he captures a folk-tale, nothing remains with him for all his trouble but a wretched lifeless thing" (*UP*1 174). The function of the collection as an imaginative stimulus is broadly signaled by his inclusion of topically related poems amongst the stories – by Ferguson, William Allingham, and James Clarence Mangan (writers whom Yeats at this point regarded as his key Irish precursors because of their use of legend and folklore), as well as by living writers Ellen O'Leary, A. P. Graves, and Yeats himself – thereby dramatizing the stories' value as a creative inspiration. Even at this early point, however, Yeats recognized the potential danger in advocating a purely Romantic and literary form of folklore. If to be "scientific" or to theorize involved a potentially destructive skepticism, and invited one to tabulate "all [the] tales in forms like grocers' bills – item the fairy king, item the queen," to be literary likewise raised the risk of merely indulging one's imagination. Mid-nineteenth-century Irish collectors of folklore, Yeats noted, had often heard simply what they wanted to hear, or molded it to fit their political or literary convictions, and had thus produced inauthentic stereotypes of Irish peasant life rather than capturing "the innermost heart of the Celt" (*P&I* 7–8).

The desire to be literary but also "authentic" in his own collections would prove a constant problem for Yeats. How to respond to the occult and supernatural content of the fairy tales he gathered posed a particularly awkward challenge. While he wanted to believe quite literally in the world of the supernatural himself, he recognized that most of his audience would think that in writing of fairies and spirits he was "merely trying to bring back a little of the old dead beautiful world of romance into this century of great engines" (*P&I* 58), and would regard his collections as extravagant fantasy. As a result, he worded the prefaces to his folklore volumes cautiously, typically obfuscating his own literal beliefs (which he expressed more directly in minor journal articles or when speaking to sympathetic audiences), and making only the lesser claim that "the Irish peasantry still believe in fairies" (*P&I* 58). But even this strategy could not lay to rest the question as to whether the stories he gathered embodied real belief in the supernatural, and responded to real phenomena, or represented merely imaginative play. More troublingly still, Yeats was aware that his gatherings came from only a limited area around Sligo where he was well known, whereas even "a few miles northward" where he was "a stranger" he could "find nothing" (*Myth* 94) – a fact that must have invited him to consider whether he was merely being told what it was known he wanted to hear. While he would try to dismiss his own skepticism about the status of what he gathered, suggesting that "It is better doubtless to believe much unreason and a little truth than to deny for denial's sake truth and unreason alike" (*CT* 13), a degree of caution almost always accompanies his enthusiastic reports of supernatural and occult phenomena.

In most of his folk-inspired poems of the 1880s and early 1890s, otherworldy or Romantic yearnings are likewise usually tempered by an element of skepticism. The supernatural visions of "The Man who Dreamed of Faeryland," for instance, are characterized as a questionable knowledge that brings neither "ease" nor wisdom (*VP* 126–8), while even "The Lake Isle of Innisfree" presents its incantatory vision of a mystically restorative Irish retreat as the longing of a man standing "on the roadway, or on the pavements grey" of the metropolis, rather than as an unambiguously available reality (*VP* 117). By 1893, when he published *The Celtic Twilight*, a volume of tales and anecdotes collected in Sligo, Yeats's approach to melding Romantic inspiration, literary craft, and nominally authentic anthropological study had evolved to its most artful, and evasive, form. His preface to the volume claims that it presents "accurately and candidly much that I have heard and seen, and . . . nothing that I have merely imagined," yet also acknowledges that it shows "something of the face of Ireland" only in "a vision" in which his own subjectivity and the "confused distaff of memory" have played their part (*CT* ix–x). Such careful formulations now barely masked his increasingly forceful conviction that imaginative inspiration, and not scientific authenticity, should be the true concern of the folklorist. In an essay published later in 1893 he would assert that "Folk-lore is at once the Bible, the Thirty-nine Articles, and the Book of Common Prayer, and well-nigh all the great poets have lived by its light," and professed his belief that "Imagination is God in the world of art" (*UP*1 284).

Yeats's privileging of Romantic and literary values would, however, progressively complicate his efforts to characterize folklore as an essential source of Irish identity. Inspired by mid-century comparative anthropology, pseudo-academic racial typologies of the "Celtic" races had been widely popularized in works such as Ernest Renan's *La poésie des races celtiques* (1854), and Matthew Arnold's *On the Study of Celtic Literature* (1867). Arnold's essay offers a classic marginalizing vision of the Celts as a subject race, lacking the "strong sense" and manly "genius" of English culture.[2] Depicting them as essentially "feminine" or child-like, Arnold characterizes Celts as "sentimental," "sensuous," and "quick to feel impressions," but lacking the "steadiness, patience, [and] sanity" to succeed either in practical affairs or in shaping great art. With their "extravagance and exaggeration" and affinity for "nature and the life of nature" the Celtic peoples, in his portrait, have "something romantic and attractive" about them, but remain "undisciplinable, anarchical" and – in a famous phrase – "always ready to react against the despotism of fact."[3] Written in the shadow of the Fenian bombing campaigns of 1867, his essay embodies an underlying imperial anxiety at English failure to assimilate the unruly Irish. Rather than simply seeking to uphold a traditional colonial discourse of strict racial difference, however, Arnold also offers what he probably intended as an olive branch by suggesting that the wild, imaginative Celtic temperament would be a welcome revitalizing counter to the "phlegm" and "steady humdrum habit" of the Saxon strain in English character, if the two could be commingled.[4] But it would be his marginalizing racial characterizations that gained most enduring currency, and Yeats's depictions of a primitive, visionary Irish folk culture, resistant to "the Spirit of the Age," consequently threatened merely to confirm English preconceptions about the Irish and to stereotype Yeats himself as a Celtic dreamer. Although conscious of this danger, Yeats did not publish a sustained counterblast to the "hurtful" characterizations in Arnold's essay until 1898. In "The Celtic Element in Literature" he subtly outflanks Arnold's typologies by reversing their implied hierarchy rather than rejecting them outright. Asserting that British culture has "forgotten the ancient religion" he memorably claims that "literature dwindles to a mere chronicle of circumstance, or passionless fantasies, and passionless meditation, unless it is constantly flooded with the passions and beliefs of ancient times," thereby tarring the realism predominant in contemporary British fiction and drama as imaginatively bankrupt. Of all the European races, he concluded, "the Celtic alone" had sustained "the main river" of literary inspiration (*E&I* 174, 178, 185).

This fervent proclamation, however, would effectively mark Yeats's last sustained effort to overcome the essential limitations and contradictions in his early folklore writings. Even before the publication of *The Celtic Twilight*, his work had begun to be eclipsed, notably by Douglas Hyde's bilingual volumes *Beside the Fire* (1890) and *The Love Songs of Connacht* (1893). Hyde's fluency as an Irish speaker, his intimate relationship with the country people, and his deep knowledge of Irish folk poetry contrasted markedly with Yeats's lack of Irish and limited range both as a collector and literary historian, and Yeats quickly recognized in Hyde's work an authoritative voice he could not easily match. More important, as a founder of the Gaelic League – an organization committed to the revival of the Irish language – Hyde had in 1892 begun to urge the systematic "de-anglicization" of Irish culture, a call that energized and quickly polarized contemporary debate about what constituted "authentic" Irishness. Although Hyde himself was an ideological moderate and remained on cordial terms with Yeats, his campaign for "de-anglicization" precipitated a contentious split between those who denounced what they called "West Britonism" – the corruption of Irishness by the use of the English language and customs – and nationalists like Yeats, who believed that strict cultural separatism was both impossible at the practical level and ill-advised politically.

Yeats continued to promote forms of nation-building that he hoped would unite Irish nationalists in a common cause – his manifesto launching an appeal for the "Celtic Theatre" in summer, 1897 urges the "support of all Irish people . . . in carrying out a work that is outside all the political questions that divide us" and promises the performance of "certain celtic and Irish plays" that will "bring upon the stage the deeper thoughts and emotions of Ireland" (*CL*II 123–4) – but such enterprises, and the broad, inclusive conceptions of Irish identity that animated them, came increasingly under attack. Yeats soon felt pressured to abandon the term "Celtic" as untenably vague, for instance, and even claimed disingenuously in a letter to the *Leader* that he had never used "the phrases 'Celtic note' and 'Celtic Renaissance' except as a quotation from others, if even then" (*CL*II 568). When the Irish Literary Theatre (as it was quickly re-named) was criticized for undercutting the revival of the Irish language by its promotion of English-language plays and British and European models of drama, Yeats's many years of urging that Irish literature and Irish nationalism should avoid insularity and narrow-minded patriotism briefly seemed to have been in vain. Seeking to defuse the hostility of "Irish Ireland" critics, he declared in an 1899 speech that, owing to his lack of Irish, "For good or evil, he had had to write his own books in English, and to content himself with filling them with as much Irish thought and emotion as he could, for no man can get a literary mastery of two languages in one lifetime." More humiliatingly, he felt obliged to add that "he foresaw without regret a time when these books, that were the work of his life, would be in a foreign language to a great part of the people of this country."[5]

Just as Yeats's brand of Romantic and literary folklore began to seem fatally embattled, however, timely support arrived in the form of friendship with Augusta Gregory (1852–1932). Inspired to begin collecting folklore after reading *The Celtic Twilight*, she sought him out when he was staying near her Galway home in 1896, and quickly cultivated partnership by turning over the numerous notebooks she had filled with folk materials from the region. While Lady Gregory was also motivated by fundamentally Romantic notions of nationalism, and shared Yeats's aspiration to build national identity by promoting Ireland's literary, legendary, and folkloric resources – her repeated dictum was the need to "bring dignity to Ireland"[6] – she reinvigorated his enthusiasm for folklore by bringing several distinct talents to his aid. First was her remarkable facility and energy as a collector, and the slow-working Yeats would later recall with wonder how she "brought me from cottage to cottage collecting folk-lore" and the speed with which she "wrote, if my memory does not deceive me, two hundred thousand words" (*A* 298). More valuable still were her precise habits of noting when, where, and from whom she gathered her material, and her skill in recording largely verbatim the Galway language they heard. This local dialect, which Yeats would define as "an old vivid speech with a partly Tudor vocabulary, a syntax partly moulded by men who still thought in Gaelic" (*LE* 207) would form the basis of the idiomatic "Kiltartan" speech that soon became the stylistic hallmark of her plays. By drawing word for word on her transcriptions, Yeats gained greater scientific and linguistic authenticity and anthropological specificity, thereby countering his own tendency towards abstraction and the privileging of literary effects, and he thus felt more able to compete with the daunting combination of scientific "accuracy" and literary power he had admired in Hyde's work (*UP*I 188). His partnership with Lady Gregory would yield six long folklore articles, published between 1897 and 1902, and a revised and expanded edition of *The Celtic Twilight* (1902), in which new chapters based on their Galway gatherings roughly equal in length the Sligo material Yeats retained from the first edition.

In this new work, Yeats's stress remains on the imaginative value of folklore, but a more comparative anthropological approach is evident in his sustained concern with the relationship between Christian and pagan beliefs amongst the peasantry. His implication in "The Tribes of Danu" that Catholicism merely formed a veneer over deeper-rooted pre-Christian values amongst the country people aroused clerical opposition in 1897 (*UP*II 55), but in subsequent articles he continued to insist on the underlying vitality of ancient religion amongst the folk, and increasingly stressed unsettling forms of cultural practice that still survived, rather than just highlighting romantically attractive forms of primitivism. His 1902 article "Away," for instance, mentions a case of witch-burning that had occurred as recently as 1895 (*UP*II 277). A crucial shift is also evident in his overall approach to folklore as an imaginative resource. Whereas he had previously defined folklore as the "literature of a class . . . who have steeped everything in the heart" (*P&I* 5), and folk poetry as naturally expressive of the peasant's close proximity to "the woods and hills and waters about him" (*UP*I 287), his writings of the late 1890s begin to credit the vital imaginative core of folklore to the literary genius of a few pre-eminent makers of folk poetry, rather than to the imaginative sensibilities of the country people in general. From 1899 to 1902, his paradigmatic figure for the folk artist would be the blind Irish poet and fiddler Anthony Raftery, whose verses were reputed to have the power to blight those he cursed and to give literary immortality to those he praised. Yeats's self-identification with the folk poet or bard as a figure whose linguistic mastery is both feared and venerated had already manifested itself in his folk-inspired stories of the fictional Hanrahan the Red in *The Secret Rose* (1897) and in a long-standing interest in the legendary powers of the ancient bards. In Raftery he found an appealing historical precedent for his vision of a literary maker whose creativity could voice, intensify, and transform the preoccupations of his milieu. This privileging of a "single mind" that might give "unity and design" to higher forms of art than ordinary country people could achieve is evident in "By the Roadside" (*Myth* 130), the closing essay to the revised *The Celtic Twilight* (1902); and by 1903, in his review of Lady Gregory's *Poets and Dreamers*, Yeats would quite openly dismiss "the Irish countryman" as being "prosaic enough in himself" and of most value merely as "the clay" in which the "footsteps" of the higher folk artists might still be traced (*UP*II 303). Unsurprisingly, given this shift, *The Celtic Twilight* would be Yeats's last conventional volume of folklore gatherings. With Lady Gregory's assistance, he rewrote the Hanrahan stories from *The Secret Rose* as *Stories of Red Hanrahan* (1904), a collection that confirms and intensifies his conception of the folk poet as an outcast who alone can articulate the deeper concerns of his culture; but this would also be the last volume of its kind, comprising his final effort at writing folk-inspired fiction.

After 1899 Yeats's energies were increasingly turned towards the theatre movement, and here, too, the shifting nature of his response to folk culture is evident. Though he would initially try to write "peasant" plays, his interests and aptitudes repeatedly led him away from realist representations of the Irish country people, towards symbolic dramas in which the power of the individual artist is privileged above ordinary reality. In both Douglas Hyde's *Casadh an tSugáin* (*The Twisting of the Rope*), written from Yeats's scenario in summer, 1900, and Yeats's own *Cathleen ni Houlihan*, written collaboratively with Lady Gregory in 1901 – plays set in a folk-influenced milieu of historical peasant realism – Yeats's primary interest is in the central figure of a poet-visionary whose dangerously inspiring language disturbs and disrupts a local community. In *Where There is Nothing* (1902) the theme emerges into even greater prominence, but here the poet-visionary, Paul Ruttledge, and the band of tinkers he momentarily inspires, come from jarringly separate cultural traditions, and the tinkers' "rough contemporary life," as Yeats termed it (*VPl* 1295), seems to be based more on his own imaginative needs than on any observed actualities of peasant culture. With *The King's Threshold* (1903), he abandoned peasant realism in favor of the legendary past, with the play focusing on the "high life" of a "master" poet, who starves himself to death to reassert the ancient rights of his fellow artists. In the very period when he felt most convinced that Lady Gregory's "knowledge of the country mind and country speech" had finally enabled him to escape his own tendency to "symbolise rather than to represent life" (*VPl* 1296, 1295), Yeats was already swiftly losing interest in representing peasant reality. Although his prefaces and dedications in 1902 and 1903 giddily speak of the speed with which he and Gregory worked together, and of her aptitude in supplying the right turn of phrase (*VPl* 1295–6), her knowledge seems paradoxically to have allowed him to begin to think of "peasant dialogue" as a kind of stylistic supplement that could be added to or grafted onto his own concern with "high life." Rather than conceiving of Irishness and peasant authenticity as located in actual cultural practices and beliefs that could be documented, as had hitherto been the case, his work begins instead to identify them more narrowly as located primarily in a distinctive use of language, and one that he was content to rely on another's talent to reproduce.

After 1903, Yeats's sense of art as hieratic in function, and of the artist's role as a solitary disturber-figure, progressively deepened. He continued to privilege the "ancient imagination" of the country people as embodying a rich tradition, but acknowledged that that tradition had now been virtually erased by the forces of modernity and the rise of bourgeois values. In "Poetry and Tradition" (1907), written in the wake of the protests against Synge's *The Playboy of the Western World* in 1907, he bitterly dismisses contemporary Ireland as a place where "immediate utility" has triumphed over higher idealism, and signals that, given the eclipse of "the traditions of the countryman," he will henceforth choose a life modeled on the contemplative values of medieval courts to satisfy his personal need for tradition (*E&I* 260). From this point on, his residual interest in folklore would be as much for its generic value as an ancient tradition as for its specifically Irish inflexion. In the two essays he wrote in 1914 as appendixes for Lady Gregory's two-volume collection *Visions and Beliefs in the West of Ireland* (1920), for example, his focus is overwhelmingly on "modern spiritism," Swedenborg, mediumship, and the occult, rather than on the actualities of Irish peasant belief.

In "Poetry and Tradition" Yeats regretted that "Ireland's great moment had passed" for creating the "ideal Ireland" in whose service he had labored (*E&I* 260). In his poem "The Fisherman" (1916), he would reflect further on this lost opportunity, and openly acknowledge that his earlier idealizations of the Irish peasant as a "wise and simple man" who could inspire him to "write for my own race" had been merely "a dream" (*VP* 347–8). But if the poem opens by rejecting a self-deluding Romanticism in favor of a bitter but necessary realism – a gesture of self-critical striving for self-knowledge characteristic of middle-period Yeats – it ends defiantly, unwilling to sustain that rejection. Scorning "reality," Yeats insists that rather than writing for his contemporaries he prefers to write for the countryman he has merely imagined, a solitary figure whose absorption in his craft notably parallels Yeats's own claims for the solitary priesthood of art. With "The Fisherman" his movement towards conceiving of the Irish peasantry and their folklore as an abstraction, begun with his earlier privileging of "peasant dialogue" over actual cultural practices, would be completed. The defiant neo-Romanticism reflected in the poem would endure for the remainder of his career, echoing in his extravagant claims in "Coole Park and Ballylee, 1931" that he and Lady Gregory had taken as their central theme "Whatever's written in what poets name / The book of the people" (*VP* 492), and, in "The Municipal Gallery Revisited" (1937), that "all" that they and Synge "said or sang" had come from "contact with the soil" (*VP* 603). Having moved from intense conviction in the 1880s and 1890s that folklore was a fountainhead of a specifically Irish imaginative renewal, to a more distanced wish after 1902 to draw on its "rough contemporary life" for his own increasingly hieratic aims, after 1916, if not before, Yeats began to envision folklore merely as one of many possible sources for the "soil" of tradition he saw as essential for writers. What counted, in his view, was that tradition should provide a "subject-matter . . . received from the generations" (*LE* 218), not that it should be specific to one's own culture. "Ancient salt is best packing" he would write in 1937, urging contemporary writers to access tradition wherever it could serve their needs – be it the Upanishads of India, or English Renaissance literature – and to reject every folk art "that does not go back to Olympus" (*LE* 213, 209).

Yeats's enthusiasm for heroic legend would follow a similar trajectory, moving from a defiant commitment to specifically Irish racial mythologies in the 1880s, to a generic sense of the creative value of heroic narratives, whether Irish or not, in his late writings. Initially, as with his early folklore researches, he saw Ireland's myths and legends both as an imaginative resource and as the potential locus of national identity. "The first thing needful if an Irish literature more elaborate and intense than our fine but primitive ballads and novels is to come into being" he wrote in 1890, "is that readers and writers alike should really know the imaginative periods of Irish history. It is not needful that they should understand them with scholars' accuracy, but they should know them with the heart" (*LNI* 32).

The distinction here between imaginative intensity and scholarly accuracy closely parallels the tension in his folklore work between literary value and "scientific" authenticity, and would be likewise problematic for him. While he craved heroic Irish models primarily so that they might inspire a "more elaborate and intense" Irish literature, their translation and dissemination from Gaelic manuscripts required a scholarly effort that Yeats himself was neither able nor willing to undertake. As a result, his desire for a sourcebook of foundational Irish legend was thwarted for nearly two decades. In the 1880s and 1890s, Standish O'Grady's *History of Ireland: The Heroic Period* was one of the few books of legendary history then in print that he could recommend (and even this not wholeheartedly), while the "best of all" sources – the Ulster cycle tales in the *Táin Bó Cuailnge* (*The Cattle Raid of Cooley*) – lay "untranslated and unpublished on the shelves of the Royal Irish Academy" (*LNI* 33). This lack of satisfactory published material progressively became a source of frustration for Yeats, as is suggested by the growing volume of explanatory material in his books of poetry in the 1890s. Short, glossary-style explanations of legendary backgrounds and Irish terms in *The Countess Kathleen and Various Legends and Lyrics* (1892) and *Poems* (1895), give way to a massive apparatus of notes in *The Wind Among the Reeds* (1899), in which over a thousand words of prose are keyed to the opening poem alone ("The Hosting of the Sidhe") to explain its contexts and identify the legendary figures mentioned in its sixteen lines.

Lady Gregory's translations of the Ulster cycle legends in *Cuchulain of Muirthemne* (1902), and of Fenian cycle legends in *Gods and Fighting Men* (1904), however, at last made Ireland's epic tales accessible to Yeats in a powerful form. The first of these volumes affected him so strongly, both through its subject matter and for the "dignity and simplicity and lyric ecstasy" of its "Kiltartan" style, that he acclaimed it "the best book that has come out of Ireland in my time" (*UP*II 328). When this extravagant praise for his closest friend's publication was deplored as blatant cronyism, he countered by mischievously insisting that *Gods and Fighting Men* was an even "better book," and declaring that he had found in her work "the one thing in Ireland that has stirred me to the roots – a conception of the heroic life come down from the dawn of the world" (*UP*II 238). Her volumes served to accelerate Yeats's loss of interest in collecting folklore after 1902, and inspired an immediate shift in his focus of creative attention. In summer, 1901, after reading *Cuchulain of Muirthemne* in manuscript, he began "Baile and Aillinn" – his first long poem based on Irish heroic legend since *The Wanderings of Oisin* – and declared his intention to write a cycle of heroic poems that would be "the chief work" of his life (*CL*III 91), an intention pursued the following summer with "The Old Age of Queen Maeve." The two poems, along with the play *On Baile's Strand* – likewise founded on incidents in *Cuchulain of Muirthemne* – formed the lion's share of *In the Seven Woods* (1903), a collection to which Yeats added the subtitle *Being Poems chiefly of the Irish Heroic Age* while the volume was in press. His work on *Deirdre*, a play about "Ireland's Helen," would be his chief project between 1903 and 1907. Surveying his poetic and dramatic canon in 1907, he noted that "Almost every story I have used or person I have spoken of is in one or other of" Lady Gregory's two volumes of epic legend, and charged that "If my present small Dublin audience for poetical drama grows and spreads . . . I shall owe it to these two books, masterpieces of prose, which can but make the old stories as familiar to Irishmen everywhere as are the stories of Arthur and his knights to all readers of books" (*VPl* 1282–3).

His enthusiastic absorption in Irish heroic legend would be compromised after 1907, however, with his disillusionment over the hostile reception of Synge's *Playboy* again being a predominant cause. "Words," written in mid 1908, reflects his anger at the rise of Philistinism in Ireland – "this blind bitter land" (*VP* 256) – and in "Reconciliation," written that autumn after the rekindling of his love for Maud Gonne, he resolves to jettison the "helmets, crowns, and swords" of his recent writing on heroic "half-forgotten things" in favor of more active engagement with the real world (*VP* 257). This disaffection intensified his conviction that artists must be "reborn in gaiety" (*E&I* 252) and that their task should be a defiant expression of "the joy that is themselves" rather than the creation of an external mythology or an "impersonal beauty" (*E&I* 271). His shifting conception of the hero is evident in *The Golden Helmet*, written over the winter of 1907–8, in which Cuchulain returns to a debased and fearful Ireland, and regenerates it through his reckless lack of fear. Like Christy Mahon in the *Playboy*, however, Cuchulain is a disruptive surrogate Christ, who remains mockingly distanced from the culture whose weakness he reveals, and who relishes his status as a scapegoat or combative disturber. Whereas Yeats had initially valorized Irish heroic legend as a means of grounding cultural identity for the Irish nation, his self-identification with Cuchulain in this play suggests the extent to which he had now instead begun to draw on legend predominantly to express his own sense of his conflicted relationship to contemporary Ireland.

After 1907, Irish heroic legend features progressively less in Yeats's poetry, and he began to draw widely on non-Irish sources for heroic inspiration, notably on classical mythology, particularly as his disillusionment with Ireland heightened following independence from Britain in 1923. While he would declare bitterly in "September 1913" that "Romantic Ireland's dead and gone" (*VP* 289), as with "The Fisherman," his faith in the power of his own self-created mythologies increased as his faith in the regenerative value of ancient Irish heroic legend waned. In his later plays based on the Ulster cycle – *At the Hawk's Well* (1917), *The Only Jealousy of Emer* (1919), and *The Death of Cuchulain* (1939) – his epic sources become so fully a focus for the exploration of his own autobiographical concerns that it becomes difficult to separate Yeats's myths of nationhood from his myths of self: an indication of how fully in later life he had internalized Irish heroic material as a part of his creative consciousness, even where, as in these plays, he drew predominantly on the traditions of the Japanese Noh play in determining his dramatic style. The constant in these plays, as in *The Dreaming of the Bones* (1919), is the emergence at a moment of national crisis of a hero whose passionate intensity or uncompromising self-sacrifice can redeem the sterility or loss of idealism of his culture, and this theme would be central to the writings of his final years. His last play, *The Death of Cuchulain*, and late poems such as "The Statues," insistently claim that only the vision of the master-maker can give a culture its higher ideals, and "make the truth" for its collective consciousness.

In his last works, Yeats would propose that his "boyish plan" (*VP* 577) had succeeded after all, and assert that the 1916 Easter Rising, which had made Irish independence inevitable, had been made possible by a heroism inspired by the legends of Cuchulain (and thus, in part, by his own work in popularizing them). So too, he began to insist on the heroic and quasi-legendary status of the recently dead Irish leaders of his own lifetime – his fellow artists Lady Gregory and John Synge amongst them – in having created the history of the newly independent nation. In "The Municipal Gallery Revisited," gazing on the images of these leaders and artists, he sees "not . . . / The dead Ireland of my youth, but an Ireland / The poets have imagined, terrible and gay" (*VP* 601–2). Here the regeneration of a modern Ireland deadened by "grey" rationality is figured as complete, with Yeats's "hallowed" (*VP* 604) friends having lived up to a heroic image of Irish nationality that had itself been mediated and re-shaped by the imagination of poets like Yeats. Yeats himself is thus cast not as the alienated disturber whose call, even if heeded, remains distinct from the concerns of his culture, but as part of a heroic band – "And say my glory was I had such friends" (*VP* 604) – whose words and deeds have themselves become the stuff of national legend.

NOTES

1. Lady Augusta Gregory, *Poets and Dreamers* (Gerrards Cross: Colin Smythe, 1974), p. 40.
2. Matthew Arnold, *On the Study of Celtic Literature* (London: Smith, Elder, 1867), pp. xvi, 97.
3. *Ibid.*, pp. 100–9.
4. *Ibid.*, p. 110.
5. Cited in Lady Augusta Gregory, "The language movement in Ireland," *Speaker*, 12 August, 1899, 151–2.
6. Lady Augusta Gregory, *Seventy Years* (Gerrards Cross: Colin Smythe, 1974), p. 307.

9

MARGARET MILLS HARPER

Yeats and the occult

Suppose, by some miracle or other, the essence of Yeats could be expressed in an image or figure. If by a further miracle we could ask him, Yeats would doubtless approve of such a speculative project, which would fit with his famous notion that a poet "is never the bundle of accident and incoherence that sits down to breakfast; he has been reborn as an idea, something intended, complete" (*E&I* 509). It would make sense for this idea to be imaginary rather than denotative, since Yeats's work from start to finish suggests the pre-eminence of what can be envisioned over what can be rationally explained. In a letter written a few weeks before his death, Yeats sounded a note of finality: "It seems to me that I have found what I wanted. When I try to put all into a phrase I say, 'Man can embody truth but he cannot know it'" (*L* 922). Thus, as he had asserted several years earlier, in an essay on Shelley's *Prometheus Unbound*, "the ultimate reality is not thought, for thought cannot create but 'can only perceive'"; rather, "the created world is a stream of images in the human mind" (*E&I* 419). A human being who embodied truth would also, presumably, take the form of an image or symbol. Yeats arrived early at this fundamentally religious conviction and kept it throughout his long and much changing career. Another essay on Shelley, written over three decades before the one quoted above, makes the connection between image and the soul clearly. Shelley, Yeats writes, "could hardly have helped perceiving that an image that has transcended particular time and place becomes a symbol, passes beyond death, as it were, and becomes a living soul" (*E&I* 80). Not only are people expressible through images; symbols, like emotions and ideas, may be vitalized into living beings, if of a sort that transcend mortal comprehension. Yeats regularly intertwines art and what might for lack of a better term be called religion in just such outlandishly direct ways.

If this poet were a symbol, then, what would the symbol be? For such a chameleon figure as Yeats a static shape would not do, even for the completeness and intentionality that his argument about the "bundle of accident and incoherence" might suggest. Those words, after all, come from a late essay written to introduce a deluxe edition of complete works – an edition, tellingly, that was never published but whose idea continues to haunt Yeats scholars intent on finding the intended form of their subject's final and authoritative book. Yeats is to be found sailing to Byzantium more often than living there, we might say. Indeed, as anyone who has read his poem "Byzantium" has discovered, even a destination that embodies a resolution of contraries does not itself stay still: it features "Those images that yet / Fresh images beget" (*VP* 498) in a fury of breakage and complexity. A diagram describing Yeats would need to be a moving figure, but also one whose movement is informed by pattern: Yeats certainly never proposes the natural over the artificially ordered. As the conversation in "Adam's Curse" has it, beauty must seem effortless, but it always takes work: "there is no fine thing / Since Adam's fall but needs much labouring" (*VP* 205). To indicate the dynamism of Yeats's long career it would be best to use a continually moving figure, perhaps turning or spinning rather than moving in a single direction, to indicate that movement is not necessarily progress, that favorite concept in popular thought since the beginning of the Industrial Revolution. Yeats despised the notion of progress, much preferring the countering notion that older, even ancient, was very likely better than new and improved, in most matters. The figure might also need to be double, to give the sense that oppositions or antitheses define Yeats more faithfully than single positions. The power of Yeats's poetry resides to a large degree in its willingness to make visible its internal struggles and vacillations, between such poles as self-delighting art and political conflict, public and private spheres, love and hatred, faith and doubt, natural and supernatural, the interior self and the dramatized mask, detachment and desire. The one always engages with the other, like partners in a dance.

Our figure for Yeats would need a central point, a focus of greatest intensity or center of gravity that keeps the rest of the pattern in motion. If Yeats were labeling the diagram, there are several possible forces that he would identify as such a hub. One of the most likely candidates would be his lifelong exploration of and belief in occult studies. A great many of the elements composing what is distinctively Yeatsian radiate outward from a seeming miscellany of folk-religious, psychical, spiritual, and magical ideas and practices. It is as close to a center as Yeats comes, even though, to use a metaphor from "The Second Coming," it cannot hold, in the sense of arriving either at certainty or internal consistency. Indeed, malleability is part of the attraction.

In the same introductory essay to his never-finished collected works cited above, the poet formulates a kind of *credo*, one of several that assert the crucial importance of his faith to his work. He claims that "the natural and supernatural are knit together" and that belief in a "mechanical theory" and a Christ out of "dead history" will be replaced by a reality and a religion that are "flowing, concrete, phenomenal." And he announces boldly, "I was born into this faith, have lived in it, and shall die in it; my Christ . . . is that Unity of Being Dante compared to a perfectly proportioned human body, Blake's 'Imagination,' what the Upanishads have named 'Self': nor is this unity distant and therefore intellectually understandable, but imminent, differing from man to man and age to age" (*E&I* 518). These are strong words. Yeats intended the American audience of this edition to be sure of the importance of what he called his faith to his works and to his life. However, the essay is less definitive about the specifics of just what that faith entails and on what level he expects his audience to participate in it. Allusions, to St. Patrick and Shakespeare in addition to Christ, Dante, Blake, and the Upanishads, set literary and religious texts next to each other without seeming preferences. Is this an expression of belief in art or an artistic expression of religious belief? If it entails difference from person to person, can it have enough definition to be communicated, even through art?

Sixty years later, readers of the essay and Yeats's work generally are still in the process of coming to terms with his metaphysical ideas and practices. It is not as fashionable after the turn of the recent millennium as it was a generation or two ago for mainstream Western culture to reject non-orthodox spiritualities. Even so, reading Yeats in the context of his spiritual and magical life is still problematic, despite a consensus that these beliefs are vital to and inseparable from his aesthetic concerns. Ironically, of all the poses, voices, and masks that dominate his work – Yeats the lover, the nationalist, the dramatist, the political actor of socialist or fascist leanings, the young dreamer or the wild and wicked old man – the most consistently important to him are the very personae that critics have tended over the years to make the most marginal and capricious: Yeats the hermeticist, the theosophist, the magician, the spiritualist, the occult metahistorian, or the seeker after Celtic or Indian mysteries.[1]

The reasons for this state of affairs are multiple, of course, and range from the relatively straightforward to the vaporously indirect. For example, relatively little was known for some time about Yeats's decades of involvement with the Hermetic Order of the Golden Dawn, a magical society, for the very good reason that it was a secret order. On the other hand, Yeats's love for Maud Gonne was and is widely known, especially in a popular version that does not include its occult resonances, in part because it had significant political value to her, to Yeats, and to others. Academic studies of English poetry tended for several generations to regard literary criticism as something amenable to quasi-scientific methods, so that any number of Yeats critics and teachers managed to admire the poetry but to regard the "embarrassing" beliefs as trivial and irrelevant. In an often-repeated remark, even as careful a reader as W. H. Auden could ask, "How on earth, we wonder, could a man of Yeats's gifts take such nonsense seriously?"[2] Various other issues, including literary Celticism, nationalism, revisionism, and postcoloniality have all been of greater interest to publishers and buyers of books about an Irish writer than material about philosophical and religious traditions that are difficult and predominantly English or European. In religious life, Yeats was arguably at his most bourgeois and British as well as at his silliest (to use another word Auden used to describe Yeats).

Perhaps most bothersome to many readers has been Yeats's most extensive engagement with the occult, in the automatic experiments with his wife Georgie Hyde Lees that resulted in the strange book *A Vision*. *A Vision*, especially in its second, heavily revised, and much more widely published edition (the only version more or less consistently in print), spends a significant percentage of its pages preparing readers to encounter its strange explanations of the universe through geometric symbolism. An introduction recalls the arrival of the System, as the Yeatses called it, in messages from realms beyond that were relayed by spirit Communicators through Mrs. Yeats, who practiced what might now be called channeling to receive answers to her husband's questions. Then a second introductory section tells another rambling story, obviously fictional, building on an elaborate hoax proposed in the first edition to explain where the mysterious symbols originated. This tale introduces new characters who take part in strange events that signal the operations of the System in daily life: like Yeats, apparently, they "can embody truth but . . . cannot know it." Finally, a letter from one of the characters to Yeats not only refers to the history recounted in the first introduction but also refers to events from an early story by Yeats as if those events were also, and equally, true. Truth is labyrinthine here; distinctions between matters of art and "those things that they were emblems of" (*VP* 630) are blurred beyond recognition.

The uncomfortable experience of reading *A Vision* only begins here. It is part of that book's design to unsettle its readers, and in this blur is a general truth about much of Yeats's work. As a few critics have recognized, *A Vision* mimics a number of Yeats's published positions, particularly in non-fictional prose, in anticipating and in fact encouraging the antagonistic stances of unsympathetic readers.[3] So do Mrs. Yeats's more private efforts, in another story well outside her husband's public voices. From behind the scenes, in the 1940s and 1950s, she provided help and guidance for many of the most influential critics of her husband's work and thus also promoted, or at least did not impede, narratives about *A Vision* and other matters that reduced the extent to which her years of work on occult matters were taken seriously. Despite recent studies that turn more focus on her than she has received before, George Yeats remains a somewhat occluded figure in Yeats studies, emphatically *not* one of the publicly inclined women and men whose friendships and collaborations have formed a far larger part of Yeats's reputation and definition: women like Maud Gonne, Florence Farr, Lady Gregory, or Olivia Shakespear; men like AE (George Russell), Ezra Pound, or John Millington Synge.[4]

Anyone familiar with *A Vision* will already have seen where my game of Name That Symbol has been tending, so I may as well return to it and propose that Yeats be expressed as one of his and Mrs. Yeats's own wheel- and cone-like figures, subdivided into constantly moving and inter-related Phases and doubled into a mirror image of itself, a second cone sharing a central point of greatest intensity. This double cone has a shadow other, its wide end linked to the narrow point of the other (which is turned into a diamond, with sharp points at the ends and wide middle) by means of a mysterious force of compression. (For a poetic illustration of the energy that causes this black-hole-like effect, note how the two parts of "The Second Coming" (*VP* 401–2) come together violently. The poet's lamentation about a general state of affairs suddenly turns into a moment of stark fear, triggered by the repetition of the words, "The Second Coming," as if that repeated phrase were the outer edge of one gyre and the point at the center of another.) Such a proposal is of course just as silly as Auden accused Yeats of being, with those persistent enthusiasms for occultiana, from fairies to scrying to emanations of disembodied spirits. I offer this unusual experiment for several reasons: first, to offset my suspicion that scholars like me are a bit ridiculous when we try to fit a complex and spiritually adept poet into our own pseudo-empirical-critical systems; and second, to give myself a structure within which to suggest the intricacies of Yeatsian faith. Third, it allows me room to describe and apply the System that *A Vision* uses to illuminate everything, from individual personality to history to the ways of human souls between incarnations.

The figure (see Figure 1) can be expressed both as a circle, divided into twenty-eight pie-piece sections, each representing one lunar Phase, or as an hourglass-shaped figure created by the movement into three dimensions of the two-dimensional spinning circle of Phases – spin into spiral, circle into cone. As the circle makes a round, the Phases increase and then decrease again, from the dark of the moon to the full and back again to the dark, a journey that symbolizes travel from a state of complete objectivity, with a corresponding erasure of the subject, to subjectivity and the absence of any objective reality. Like the signs of the zodiac in an astrological system, aspects of human beings, moments in time, and any actions or constructions that

The Great Wheel

Figure 1. "The Great Wheel," from *A Critical Edition of Yeats's "A Vision,"* ed. George Mills Harper and Walter Kelly Hood (London: Macmillan, 1978), p. xiv.

occur in time may all be located in a Phase and thus possess the characteristics of that Phase. Incidentally, these Phases, being abstract, do not correlate with the phases of real monthly cycles, although any practicing astrologer with a fraction of the knowledge that the Yeatses had of the art can determine the actual lunar phase that was present at a given date. Willy and George Yeats, though they loved putting people or events into Phases (the automatic script is full of dialogue between them about placement of one item or another), were not interested in factual realities underpinning their System, any more than Blake and Dante were. The point, for both husband and wife, was imaginative truth, which was inseparable from its source in spiritual questioning.

In a notebook kept to organize the automatic messages into workable form, Mrs. Yeats recorded this revelation from the Communicators: "A philosophy created from experience, burns & destroys; one which is created from search, leads."[5] The Yeatses created from search, and their System insists on the partial nature of genuine revelation.

The full-blown System of *A Vision* is the most original as well as the most complex of Yeats's spiritual pursuits, but it should not be separated from the context of the numerous other avenues of exploration that colored Yeats's life and thought from his youth until his death. Each Phase of his thought comes out of another and leads to the next, and to some degree it is important to know about them all in order to follow his movement around the wheel. Understanding Yeats's thought can be daunting because of the complexity of the various beliefs themselves as well as the nuances of the historical contexts in which they occurred, but also because reliable information about the various societies with which he was associated, or practices in which he engaged, is hard to come by. Secret societies do not leave easily discernible histories of themselves for those who are not adepts. Occult theologies also tend to be ill-defined and syncretistic, picking and choosing among doctrines of any number of schools of thought – Gnosticism, Hermeticism, Cabbalism, Neoplatonism, Manicheanism, Zoroastrianism, Freemasonry, and Rosicrucianism among others – about many of which little evidence remains, if much publicly disseminated knowledge was ever available. Moreover, magic and spiritualism are marginal religious activities, the kind that keepers of public records such as journalists and archivists tend to avoid, even in the periods during which such movements are most popular. To the extent that these movements are not officially endorsed, they are also less well funded than others, meaning that documents tend to be printed cheaply, in formats that do not preserve well; records are not kept in well-maintained locations, and so forth. At times psychic gifts have been downright dangerous: witch hunts and punishments for heresy were all too real for any number of individuals in European history. For Yeats studies, an added, less generalized wrinkle is that Mrs. Yeats was reluctant to share occult manuscript materials or information with more than a very few interested scholars. Her well-guarded privacy, as well as the fact that she lived for a scholarly generation longer than her husband, have made this area of inquiry one of the least documented.

The Phases may be divided into four quadrants (forming a tetrad, one of Yeats's favorite figures), and the progress from one quarter to the next symbolizes change from one stage of life to the next. Child-like freshness yields to youthful passion, which bends to responsible speculation and then changes into a renunciation of responsibility that can look like both wisdom and foolishness as age turns back towards infancy. (In this last revolution, our symbol for Yeats might as well reflect his tendency to propose reincarnation in one guise or another, soul into soul, state into state, mood into mood.) A little poem written directly out of George Yeats's automatic writing, "The Four Ages of Man" (*VP* 561), depicts the circular movement as a series of battles:

> He with body waged a fight,
> But body won; it walks upright.
>
> Then he struggled with the heart;
> Innocence and peace depart.
>
> Then he struggled with the mind;
> His proud heart he left behind.

The last stanza makes plain that not only is each battle lost, but the war itself is hopeless from the beginning. It will be important to remember that Yeats loved a good fight, and that he also knew that loss sometimes has more spiritual value than gain. There is a hint of wisdom in the final defeat: "Now his wars on God begin; / At stroke of midnight God shall win." I should note that Yeats's movement through the Phases as outlined below is not so much chronological as symbolic of development: the four broad areas of study and practice traced below overlap in Yeats's experience, just as they are not completely separable from each other intellectually. For example, Yeats attended séances from the 1880s, a decade that also saw his first entrancement with Indian religions, to well into the 1930s, and his interest in magic was a crucial aspect of his attraction to the Theosophical Society from the start, not supplanting it.

For the purposes of this diagram, though, the first quadrant will contain Theosophy; the second, magic, including the Golden Dawn; the third, spiritualism, including the *Vision* experiments with Mrs. Yeats; and the fourth, a cluster of religious investigations that are dominated by Indian thought and which take sex, violence, and death as controlling themes.[6] The figure as a whole is colored by what the Yeatses termed "tinctures," the subtle influences of sun or moon, elements as basic as fire and water (with which they are associated) and whose opposition forms the context for the System as a whole. For this Yeats diagram, it is tempting to label the tinctures "Pollexfen" and "Yeats" and identify them first with his deeply held sense of the immanence of a supernatural world, like the ever-present fairy people of Irish folk religion or the stories of second sight told by his mother, Susan Pollexfen, and her Sligo relations. Second would be Yeats's constant need to test spiritual ideas and phenomena with methods derived from the sciences. Like his aggressively rationalistic father, and despite their lifelong disagreements, Yeats was more inclined towards skepticism and empiricism than he liked to admit. He not only listened to stories, attended séances, and participated in magic rituals; he also made transcripts, took notes, and did historical research into the subjects that fascinated him. This wheel always includes varying proportions of the need to be subjectively engaged and the counter urge to be objectively distanced.

Theosophy

It is common to begin tracing Yeats's beliefs by recalling his lifelong interests in folk beliefs, beginning with the stories he heard as a child when the family stayed in the Sligo area. For my purposes, it is important to note that by the time Yeats collected and published collections of folk tales in 1889, 1891, and 1892, and added his own recollections in *The Celtic Twilight* (1893), his renditions of the kinds of stories that had long fascinated him already showed the totalizing impulse of the body of ideas called Theosophy. Irish myths and stories resonate beyond themselves, suggesting universality and ancient truth and not the specific practices of people from particular places. His prose sounds like a blend of reportage, story-telling, the rhetoric of contemporary anthropology in works like Frazer's *The Golden Bough* (first published in 1890), and something that gives personal spiritual and aesthetic convictions the ring of authoritative wisdom. For example, after giving several anecdotes about enchanted woods in a piece by that title, Yeats writes:

> I often entangle myself in arguments more complicated than even those paths of Inchy as to what is the true nature of apparitions. But at other times I say as Socrates said when they told him a learned opinion about a nymph of the Ilissus, 'The common opinion is enough for me'. . . . I will not of a certainty believe that there is nothing in the sunset, where our forefathers imagined the dead following their shepherd the sun, or nothing but some vague presence as little moving as nothing. If beauty is not a gateway out of the net we were taken in at our birth, it will not long be beauty. (*Myth* 63–4)

This kind of discourse underlies poetry written during this period as well. It is an interesting experiment to read short pieces from *The Celtic Twilight* in connection with early poems. "Earth, Fire and Water" (*Myth* 80), for example, complements "The Lake Isle of Innisfree" (*VP* 117), adding to the poem the suggestion that the imagined lake water has a deeper spiritual significance than personal nostalgia for one remembered place and time. The Irish landscape has lent itself to mystical interpretation by any number of writers and artists besides Yeats, of course, but it is important to remember that Yeats's western countryside from the mid 1880s is also the product of urban centers like Dublin, London, and even New York.

The founding of the Dublin Hermetic Society in 1885 (by Yeats, his friends George Russell [AE], Charles Johnston, and a few others) marked the beginning of the young poet's formal study of the occult. It did not take long for the Hermetic Society to examine and be more or less absorbed by the doctrines of Theosophy. This supposedly ancient but actually innovative mixture of Eastern mysticism and Western science with a spiritualist overlay was co-founded in 1875 in New York by Helena Petrovna Blavatsky (known to her followers as "HPB") and an American lawyer named Henry Steel Olcott. Blavatsky and Olcott discovered, or rediscovered, as their society maintained, a combination of religion, philosophy, and science that was profoundly influential among the professional classes in the United States and Great Britain, which were its primary chosen audience. When Yeats was a boy and a young man, the social world he knew was saturated with crises in faith. Profound changes in European society, coming in the wake of scientific discoveries and technological advances, had disturbed foundational beliefs in God as well as materialist paradigms, and in such divergent concepts as progress and tradition, social position and individual identity, in any number of ways. The Theosophical Society was a magnet for disaffected members of the educated public, both men and women. HPB was its mystical center and aggressive marketer of its secret powers; Olcott, a practical man, promoted the Society as a sort of religious debating society, like a number of other similar groups formed in the post Civil War period in the USA, as well as in Victorian England.

Yeats did not join the Dublin branch of the Theosophical Society (indeed, the Hermetic Society was determined to remain separate from single-minded adherence to Theosophical doctrine), but he did meet HBP and commit himself to Theosophy after he moved to London in 1887. He joined the Esoteric Section, a secret section of the Society formed in 1888 for members who wanted a "deeper study of esoteric philosophy."[7] He was deeply impressed by, if always also somewhat skeptical of, the flamboyant HPB. Yeats was dissatisfied with the materialism endorsed by discoveries in natural and applied science as well as the consolations and orthodoxies of mainstream Protestant Christianity. The Theosophical Society provided him with historical and cultural depth, the sense that his present-day acts, ideas, or images could be placed in the context of ancient and worldwide occult knowledge. Theosophy also stresses a highly elaborated doctrine of reincarnation, with the twin themes of a deterministic universe that moves souls through successive lives in a pre-ordained pattern, and a paradoxical freedom of the soul possible by means of spiritual evolution (Blavatsky's replacement for Darwinian evolution, which she denounced). Yeats was drawn intellectually to this twinning of choice and chance, among other ideas. The dialectic in Yeats of fate and will as irreconcilable opposites, and indeed his general tendency to think in antinomies or opposites, owes something to Theosophy. It also did not hurt that the Theosophical Society satisfied a few less abstract needs. It promised a young man, fresh from Ireland, uncomfortable with the trade background of his maternal family as well as the decreasing fortunes of his father's London household, a new-minted respectability among *fratres* and *sorores* who lived comfortable and influential lives. Theosophy, among other chosen teachings, enables Yeats to "walk upright" into other phases.

Magic

Yeats's interests in theurgic practice eventually alienated him from the Theosophical Society. Not only did the Society have aspirations to wide social acceptance (a common development for alternative religions), aspirations that might be impeded by wild practicing magicians, but HPB, certainly a wild character herself, had theological reasons for a firm opposition to practical occultism, including ceremonial magic. In 1890 Yeats's relationship with the Society was severed because he refused to stop pursuing "phenomena," attempting to dissolve the boundaries between spiritual and physical planes by evocation and other methods.[8] The Hermetic Order of the Golden Dawn, a secret society founded in 1888 under the principal energy of another highly unusual character, S. L. MacGregor Mathers, seemed, for some time, a perfect fit. The Golden Dawn replaced the passivity of spiritualism and respectable public-spiritedness of the Theosophical Society with the excitement of magical power. It was an irresistible lure to a young writer eager to create as well as learn, to become master in addition to scholar, and Yeats joined, and soon assumed mantles of leadership over, a group of active magicians. The enigmatic and obsessive Mathers provided Yeats with the character Michael Robartes, who plays a major role in *A Vision* as well as the early stories. Other adepts became deep influences and intimate friends, and the systematic training in symbolic systems, ritual practices, and mental discipline was formative as a kind of university-cum-seminary for Yeats's later career. Yeats's dissertation, if you will, was a project he worked on for some twelve years, the development of a distinctively Celtic mystery religion, to be based at an uninhabited castle on a lake island. The Celtic Mysteries promised an effective marriage of nationalism with esoterica by creating "an Irish Eleusis or Samothrace," as Yeats recalled in 1915. The "Castle of Heroes" would satisfy "the need of mystical rites – a ritual system of evocation and meditation – to reunite the perception of the spirit, of the divine, with natural beauty. I believed that instead of thinking of Judea as holy we should [think] our own land holy . . ." (*Mem* 123). Among the project's attractions was the interest that Maud Gonne had in spiritual collaboration, in their joint visions, and in her ritual role as High Priestess.[9]

In addition to the Celticism that the Mysteries project furthered, visible effects of this magical Phase upon Yeats's poetry include Rosicrucian and Cabbalistic sources for specific symbols, such as roses and trees, which recall the Rosy Cross and the Tree of Life among other overtones, and a general tightening of control over image. More significant is a change that affects voice in the poems written during and after the 1890s. The speaker's position shifts from receiver of experience to maker of it, a wielder of power over the material as well as the interior world, and the poetic voice makes parallel gains in authority. The idea that the empowered adept would be personally transformed as he or she progressed upward through the various grades, one of the principles of the Order, also changes Yeats's aesthetics. The intimate relation of believer to belief was congenial to Yeats's commitment to the Blakean idea (also common in Hindu and Buddhist thought) that the individual is the artist or creator of an essentially poetic universe, but a dynamic, progressive subjectivity is added to the mix: magician and magic are increasingly related, universe and maker gaining in power together. Such a magical-poetic purpose is at the heart of the volumes *The Secret Rose* and *The Wind Among the Reeds*. The poetry in these collections imposes an essentially ritualistic set of symbols over experience. *The Wind Among the Reeds* transforms even the poet's voice into mystical or occult personae, so that names like Robartes and Aedh appear in titles. (These were dropped in later editions and replaced by a generic "He.") With beautiful emblematic covers and heavily, if secretly, coded symbolism coloring the narratives of the poems, these books attempt, in Steven Putzel's words, "to close the gap between subject and object, between creator and created." The attempt to transform ritual into art is, as Putzel recognizes, an "effective yet psychologically dangerous and artistically limiting subjectivity," effective in that it imposes symbolic order on intense personal experience, but troubling in that it necessarily distances the poet from that experience.[10] These were years of considerable "[struggle] with the heart," in which love, frustration, and despair over Maud Gonne caused "Innocence and peace [to] depart," and poetic displacement is related to such personal trials.

In prose as well, the mage speaks in essays from this period, if in a form displaced into philosophy instead of lyricism. "The Philosophy of Shelley's Poetry," quoted at the beginning of this essay, joins "The Symbolism of Poetry," a contemplation influenced by Yeats's connections with French

Symbolism, and the especially declarative "Magic" (1901), as representative pieces. However, despite the concreteness of the Golden Dawn rituals and symbols and the certainty with which Yeats proclaims the power of the focused mind of the transformed self, he later described the waning of its active influence upon him by suggesting that he was lost amid confusion: "image called up image in an endless procession, and I could not always choose among them with any confidence; and when I did choose, the image lost its intensity, or changed into some other image" (*A* 215). In practice, the possibility that supreme art may result from tapping into a collective "great mind and great memory" (*E&I* 28) remains unrealized. The development of the self into divinity that ritual magic claims is not conducive to the rough beast that is literature. Indeed, were a human being to attain communion with the All, Yeats came to believe, his or her very humanity might be in danger, not merely the ability to write. A triptych of stories, "Rosa Alchemica," "The Tables of the Law," and "The Adoration of the Magi," shows the danger of allowing the self to drift beyond the realms of confusion and imperfection.

In 1901, Yeats was one of the key combatants in a controversy within the Order that led to a schism and its eventual restructuring, an ugly quarrel that played a large part in his loss of enthusiasm.[11] His integrity was questioned and his self-assurance damaged, and he distanced himself from the Order in the aftermath (his timing was sure: by the end of the year the Order made headlines after a fraudulent American couple, having infiltrated the Order, was tried and convicted for raping a young girl in a fake initiation ceremony). As he left, one of his parting shots was an essay published privately, for his magical *fratres* and *sorores* only, which betrays both his fear of dissolution into chaos and his vision of the Order as a corporate supernatural self that functions also as a symbol to enlighten a benighted world. He urgently argues that hierarchy and order must be maintained because "a Magical Order differs from a society for experiment and research in that it is an Actual Being, an organic life holding within itself the highest life of its members now and in past times," and that if its unity is preserved, it will be "a single very powerful talisman" whose "personality will be powerful, active, visible afar."[12] His charged rhetoric anticipates some of the less exalted race theory of his later years, but it also illuminates convictions about mystical marriage, supernatural collaboration, and life as timeless idea as well as temporal being. Yeats's prose is much more direct in his secret communications than in his published work, but both fear and hope are recorded in the portion of his autobiography devoted to this period. The section ends with a memory of feeling that differentiated personality was dissolving into a riot of images: "I was lost in that region a cabbalistic manuscript, shown me by MacGregor

Mathers, had warned me of; astray upon the Path of the Chameleon, upon Hodos Chameliontos" (*A* 215).

Spiritualism

Within a few years this situation shifted drastically, as the autobiography intimates by following the assertion above with a reverie about nesting birds, a favorite Yeatsian image for innate knowledge, female influence, and domesticity. Yeats wrote of the danger to self from the perspective of a less emotionally troubled quarter. "Now that I am a settled man and have many birds," he begins, joining birds to a few anecdotes about his young family (his small daughter and her pregnant mother). He then proceeds to muse on the self, not what he and his wife George came to call "daily self" but rather "that age-long memoried self, that shapes the elaborate shell of the mollusc and the child in the womb" (*A* 216). The final section of "Hodos Chameliontos," the section of the autobiography concerned with the exploration of magical images, speaks in a language of gender, complementarity, and procreation, and closes with a final quotation from the pivotal poem "Ego Dominus Tuus" about Self and Mask or Anti-Self. Autobiography has yielded to exposition of some very subtle abstractions, and these ideas have been filtered through the occult System that had been arriving automatically for several years by the time Yeats submitted this part of the manuscript to his publisher in 1922.

Between Yeats's most active commitment to the Order of the Golden Dawn and his recollections of it for *The Trembling of the Veil*, as he titled the autobiographical work about these years, he moved from image to persona, we might say, from prop to character, as a central focus. Meditations on and study of symbols, and work on rituals based upon them, yielded in Yeats's occult practice to a renewed enthusiasm for spiritualist phenomena and psychical research into the veracity of such occurrences. In his secular life, this shift was complemented by the years of work with the theatre in which, in the words of the late poem "The Circus Animals' Desertion," "Players and painted stage took all my love, / And not those things that they were emblems of" (*VP* 630). The poem exaggerates: Yeats was never far from searching out "those things" behind forms. Nonetheless, like the "painted stage," the drawing rooms of spirit mediums and the spectacular effects that often occurred in tandem with psychic experimentation were performances. Yeats was not put off by theatricality, even cheap effects. Far from it: the roles played by the self or parts of the self in exploring relationships and communication with other aspects of a single person, among selves, and between living and dead souls was a topic of infinite interest. And as with the theatre or even poetry, intellectual lines are not easy to draw between artifice and reality. For example, Yeats would not have wanted absolutely to delineate the degree to which mediumistic messages are clairvoyant or created by subconscious divisions of the personality, the level of inspiration from a collective soul in the writing of a poem, the proportion or kind of genuine emotion present in an actor's playing of a scripted role, or the way that preparation for vision makes vision possible. Nearly a century later, psychology has developed separately from the study of psychic phenomena, and the latter has been devalued as unscientific. Visual and aural technology like photography and recorded sound no longer hint at the possibilities of auras or telepathy, and mainstream Christianity emphasizes morality more than miracle. It can be difficult to imagine the heady atmosphere of a time and place in which these distinctions were not yet clearly decided upon, but the years preceding, during, and immediately following the Great War in Europe and America were such a period, and Yeats threw himself into the swirling currents of it.

From about 1909 until his marriage in 1917 Yeats attended numerous séances, investigated supposed miracles (sometimes in the company of other members of the respectable Society for Psychical Research), and spent a considerable amount of energy analyzing the automatic writing of a young woman named Elizabeth Radcliffe.[13] An account of these explorations in his published work occurs within a long essay linking spiritualism with the beliefs of Emmanuel Swedenborg and those of Irish folk belief, published as an appendix to Lady Gregory's *Visions and Beliefs in the West of Ireland.* Most significantly, Yeats developed a curious relationship with a figure he came to believe was his own daimon, alter-ego, or symbolic opposite, a voice that claimed to be the discarnate spirit of the sixteenth-century African travel writer and explorer Leo Africanus (Al Hassan Ibn-Mohammed al-Wezar Al-Fasi).[14] Leo was summoned mediumistically in séances beginning in 1912 (after a false start in 1909). By the summer of 1915, Yeats was sufficiently convinced of the value of Leo as guide to engage in an experiment with highly significant ramifications for his later work: to suspend authorial control and write as if through the personality and agency of another. He wrote an essay in the form of two letters, one from Yeats to Leo and the other from Leo to Yeats, written at Leo's suggestion, "as from him to me," as Yeats remembered the request. "He would control me ~~if he could~~ in that reply so that it would be really from him."[15] The cancelled words are significant: the process of writing the letters would open Yeats to the possibility of being controlled, but would not necessarily control him. It would put him at the borderland between traditional Western authorship, presided over by the strong myth of the stable self, and the uncharted territory of writerly mediumship with its resonances of femininity, darkness, the irrational, and the non-Western. It is furthermore no accident that Leo is identified with the Orient as an enslaved Arab only partially converted to Christian ways, and that he traveled in and wrote about Africa. His "overshadow[ing]" of Yeats from the East, as well as the importance of his book *Descrizione dell' Affrica* or *Africae descriptio* (originally written in Arabic) to the Orientalist studies of Yeats's day, suggest links with the powerful ambivalences of the exotic Other and the so-called Dark Continent, and their tantalizing and threatening promise of release from the control of the ego. Yeats would emulate the female mediums of his experience and relinquish ownership of his own pen (with all of its sexual associations) so that his words would be "but in seeming mine."

The words are still Yeats's, of course, for all his attempts to free them from his own governance. The dream of freedom from self occurs only within the framework and volition of that self; the Other exists as such only because of the subject that places it in an imagined location outside that identified with the subject. Yeats remained skeptical of his own efforts to replace consciousness with Anti-Self as he wrote. The essay is full of his doubts: "~~I think probable~~ I am not convinced that in this letter there is one sentence that has come from beyond my own imagination but I will not use a stronger phrase . . . there is no thought that has not occurred to me in some form or other for many years."[16] Leo has his doubts too, explaining that he had better stick to general topics because when he focuses on specifics "I am not even certain, that I am not certain that I did not mistake the images I discover [in Yeats's mind] for my own memories . . ." Nonetheless, the essay is distinctively bold and direct, a tonal quality which (paradoxically, given that two personages speak) derives from a less multiple authorial self than that found in *Per amica silentia lunae*, the two-part essay published in 1918 that puts forth in slippery prose the doctrine of the Anti-Self and the *anima mundi* or world soul. *Per Amica* features the poem "Ego Dominus Tuus" as its introduction. Its dedication to Iseult Gonne, Maud's daughter, is a reminder of the confused courtships of these years. The poem is set beside the stream beneath Thoor Ballylee, the Norman tower that was to be Yeats's first purchased home and to which he longed to bring his bride, but Iseult was not the woman who eventually moved there.

The investigations of spirit phenomena and the effort to find a wife both came to fruition in 1917. Georgie Hyde Lees, on whom the choice finally landed, had excellent personal and occult connections among her other virtues. In fact, Yeats had initiated her into the Order of the Golden Dawn several years before. Yeats had visited her family at the heat of his excitement about Elizabeth Radcliffe's script. The account of their marriage and the beginning of Mrs. Yeats's automatic writing has been told many times, most notably by Yeats in the introduction to the second edition of *A Vision* (at her insistence, the first edition kept her agency secret). Almost every day, in various locations, through her two pregnancies, during revolution and war in Europe and Ireland, and while he wrote poetry and plays without a reduction of pace, the Yeatses sat at table and communicated with spirits and their own daimons, he asking questions, she writing down answers as her hand was guided. By the time the "incredible experience" (as Yeats called it [*VB* 8]) was finished some two-and-a-half years later, the System of *A Vision* had been invented/received, along with many other highly personal revelations and various images and ideas that may be found in his work from this point on. The Yeatses had also established an occult marriage, meaning that in addition to the pleasures of good partnership on the secular plane, with the physical intimacy, intellectual equality, and peace of settled domestic life that the Yeatses achieved, both members of the couple had the galvanizing sense that they were chosen to accomplish profound spiritual work that neither could have achieved alone. By the mid 1920s, as George Harper notes, they were living their daily lives with the "conviction that by recognizing, or living as though, the spirit world were everywhere at hand, it becomes so."[17] Their household was a continual site of revelation and productivity.

It took years of work for the Yeatses to excerpt, order, and comprehend the raw data of the System. Yeats composed *A Vision* first as a dialogue and then in the four-part structure of the first edition, and years passed before he felt competent to correct what he felt were its inadequacies in a second version, published less than two years before his death. *A Vision* is a unique book, part cosmology, part apocalypse, part psychoanalysis, part poetry, and part confusion. It is full of wildly a-priori assumptions, unproven assertions, gross generalizations, and ahistorical pronouncements about grand narratives of history and the human condition. It is often internally inconsistent as well as sometimes repetitive. Parts are written in some of Yeats's best (and most poetic) prose, and other parts are among his more tedious. It is worth reading, and some of its anecdotes and diagrams are greatly illuminative, but it serves something of the same function that *Finnegans Wake* does for readers of Joyce: it is good to have encountered it, but it is not necessary to have understood it. Yeats explained its purpose in typically ambiguous language in the 1937 edition, writing that in the first version "I tried to interest my readers in an unexplained rule of thumb that somehow explained the world" (*VB* 81). *A Vision* is not, needless to say, a reliable rule of thumb for the late poetry and plays, any more than it is for the world. But it is not unlike Yeats's other religious ideas in some of its basic tenets, such as the subjectivity of history, the consequent parallel between history and the human soul, cyclical reincarnations, and the perpetual tension between opposites.

Yeatsian terms like Mask, Primary and Antithetical, the Daimon, Unity of Being, and Dreaming Back also receive their most elaborate exposition in *A Vision*. The most difficult work of Yeats's mature third quarter, it represents the height of his "[struggle] with the mind" in his Phasal home: he was located in Phase 17, which the System terms Daimonic Man, and he worked most conspicuously with his daimon, his personal genius, and spiritual Anti-Self, on this project. He also worked most closely with George Yeats, who was also a soul of the third quarter, belonging to Phase 18. The Creative Mind of her Phase, that is, the part of the self having to do with how one constructs one's world intellectually, is listed as Emotional Philosophy. This is as good a phrase as I can find to describe *A Vision*, perhaps the least accessible of all Yeatsiana but also unavoidable for any serious reader.

Hindu mysticism

Although earlier preoccupations, capped by the System of *A Vision*, continued to spur Yeats's thought in his last years, the poet's last religious enthusiasm was one appropriate to a period in which ill-health and the impending end of life were ever-present companions. Yeats's "wars on God" in his fourth Phase were essentially imperialistic: the desire to control his own body was allied with an imported Hindu spirituality that promised him a chance to succeed at this daunting project.[18] Yeats would not turn to the Protestant Christianity of his upbringing in his last years, but to a tradition that, in his understanding, posited a conquering and eternal Self as well as recurring lifetimes. He tried valiantly to tie that tradition to ancient Irish parallels, to psychic research, to his and George Yeats's visionary System, and to public prophecy about the nature of history and coming times. His second Indian phase was to some extent a mirror of an early infatuation, spurred by Theosophical connections and embodied in an attractive figure named Mohini Chatterjee. Similarly, Yeats's friendship and collaboration with Shri Purohit Swami, whom he met in London in 1931, re-established India in his mind as the location of truths that allowed escape from modern, materialistic, and scientific formulations of reality. This second period of interest in Hindu mysticism replaced the romantic world-weariness of the first with a much more active, even aggressive personal search accompanied by public apologetics. It should be noted that both periods are marked by a heavily orientalized sense of Asiatic spirituality, revealing more about Yeats, whose knowledge was gained at a significant remove from India, than about Hindu traditions.

In one sense, Yeats's late exploration of Indian thought can seem merely one of a series of almost determinedly outlandish episodes in his last years by which an old man could almost convince himself that he could hold onto and come to ultimate terms with life in the face of approaching death. It is the effort of a fool, and indeed the last Phase of the twenty-eight in the System of *A Vision* is called the Fool, one step beyond the Saint.[19] Like the tarot card of the same title, and with some of the same meaning as the card, Yeats consciously transformed himself in his final years to a silly old man who also, perhaps, was "the dreamer and visionary, in closer communion with God than is given to most men."[20] At the last crescent of his lunar wheel, Yeats made his life into kinship with the card that can be placed either at the beginning or the end of the sequence of trumps in the tarot deck and is, according to Richard Cavendish, often considered the "most profoundly mysterious card in the pack."[21]

From 1932 through 1936 Yeats and Shri Purohit Swami collaborated on a translation of the *Upanishads* after the publication of the latter's autobiography, for which Yeats supplied an introduction. Yeats also wrote an introduction to a translation by Shri Purohit Swami of a book by his Master, Bhagwan Shri Hamsa, recounting a pilgrimage to Mount Kailas, or Meru, a holy site in Tibet. Yeats's intense "Supernatural Songs" as well as the prose pieces "The Mandukya Upanishad" and the two introductions are a good deal more interesting than the translation of *The Ten Principal Upanishads*. In fact, the last is lackluster enough to justify Mrs. Yeats's doubts about the project from the outset. Mrs. Yeats may have had doubts about more than the literary appropriateness of her husband translating when he could have been writing poetry, in that part of Yeats's excitement over Eastern religion included the sexuality of Tantric doctrines, which dovetailed well with his personal struggles with impotence.[22] Tantrism, a marginal and radical offshoot of Buddhism, Jainism, and Hinduism, differs from the orthodoxies of these religious systems not so much in theology as in practice, in an emphasis on sensuality and eroticism as a pathway to emancipation and rebirth. The spirituality of non-orgasmic sex, an essential affirmation of the connection between body and soul, and the eternal nature of desire (as opposed to the fatality of satisfaction), are themes in the late works that are traceable to this influence.

Yet the infamous sexual quality of Yeats's later years forms part of what he would have called a phantasmagoria that has extreme asceticism as its antithesis. While he was exploring sexual encounters with a signal lack of restraint, he was also writing urgently about the highest stages of sensual deprivation. Both states concern paradoxes of loss and gain affecting the core of the personality. In love, according to Crazy Jane, it takes loss to achieve gain: "'nothing can be sole or whole / That has not been rent'" (*VP* 513). In the devotee, attainment of "absolute Self," in which "there is nothing outside his will," is achieved; those who have attained this state "are said to be physically immortal" (*E&I* 463–4). Sensualism and asceticism are not reconcilable, and to propose both at the same time is preposterous, unless the human soul is caught in an elaborate series of oppositions. Yeats believed this to be the case, but it is also true that in his last years he was more friendly to foolishness than to pretensions of wisdom. In the poem "The Pilgrim," first published in 1937, the speaker, a holy pilgrim, after an ordeal of fasting and prayer, speaks to anyone who will listen:

> Now I am in the public-house and lean upon the wall,
> So come in rags or come in silk, in cloak or country shawl,
> And come with learned lovers or with what men you may,
> For I can put the whole lot down, and all I have to say
> *Is fol de rol de rolly O.* (*VP* 593)

After a lifetime of study, practice, experimentation, and search, Yeats was content to sing, as indeed he had done all along. The verses, shaped into the whole of his *œuvre*, may not attain "'the Human Form Divine' of Blake," as Yeats claimed occurs when an initiate attains final illumination (*E&I* 483), but we may be content to envision them, along with their maker who lives only in imagined form, as ever expanding and contracting gyres, movement and counter-movement, all joined by shifting alliances and unceasing tensions. This Yeats gyre, made up of smaller gyres, joins other cones that may even reach beyond themselves to contain the lives of his readers. Once there, would it be too much to hope that, like the "stylistic arrangements of experience" of *A Vision*, they might help others as Yeats claimed they helped him to "hold in a single thought reality and justice" (*VB* 25)?

NOTES

1. By this generalization I do not intend to suggest that Yeats's occult interests have been slighted by all critics and scholars. For some of the more influential studies in this area see Virginia Moore, *The Unicorn: William Butler Yeats' Search for Reality* (New York: Macmillan, 1954 [1952]); George Mills Harper, *Yeats's Golden Dawn: The Influence of the Hermetic Order of the Golden Dawn on the Life and Art of W. B. Yeats* (London: Macmillan, 1974); Harper, ed., *Yeats and the Occult* (Toronto: Macmillan, 1975); Graham Hough, *The Mystery Religion of W. B. Yeats* (Brighton: Harvester Press; Totowa, NJ: Barnes & Noble, 1984); Kathleen Raine, *Yeats the Initiate: Essays on Certain Themes in the Work of W. B. Yeats* (Mountrath, Ireland: Dolmen Press, 1986); and George Mills Harper, *The Making of Yeats's "A Vision": A Study of the Automatic Script,* 2 vols. (London: Macmillan, 1987).
2. W. H. Auden, "Yeats as an example," in *The Permanence of Yeats: Selected Criticism,* ed. J. Hall and M. Steimann (New York: Macmillan, 1950), p. 344.

3. To date, the best treatment of this phenomenon in *A Vision* is Steven Helmling, *The Esoteric Comedies of Carlyle, Newman, and Yeats* (Cambridge: Cambridge University Press, 1988). See also Hazard Adams, *The Book of Yeats's Vision: Romantic Modernism and Antithetical Tradition* (Ann Arbor: University of Michigan Press, 1995).
4. This situation has changed utterly with the publication of the authoritative biography by Ann Saddlemyer, *Becoming George: The Life of Mrs. W. B. Yeats* (New York and Oxford: Oxford University Press, 2002). Earlier studies include David Pierce, *Yeats's Worlds: Ireland, England, and the Poetic Imagination* (New Haven and London: Yale University Press, 1995), and Brenda Maddox, *George's Ghosts: A New Life of W. B. Yeats* (London: Picador–Macmillan, 1999), published in the USA as *Yeats's Ghosts: The Secret Life of W. B. Yeats* (New York: HarperCollins, 1999). See also Bette London, *Writing Double: Women's Literary Partnerships* (Ithaca, NY, and London: Cornell University Press, 1999), especially Chapter 6.
5. George Mills Harper, ed., *Yeats's 'Vision' Papers,* 3 vols., Vol. III, ed. Robert Anthony Martinich and Margaret Mills Harper (London: Macmillan, 1992), p. 174.
6. For a similar division of Yeats's spiritual explorations into four phases see Hough, *The Mystery Religion of W. B. Yeats,* pp. 33–4. For information about the Theosophical Society it is useful to look at H. P. Blavatsky, *The Key to Theosophy* (London: Theosophical Publishing House, [1889]). Historical accounts of interest include B. F. Campbell, *Ancient Wisdom Revived: A History of the Theosophical Movement* (Berkeley: University of California Press, 1980) and K. Paul Johnson, *The Masters Revealed: Madame Blavatsky and the Myth of the Great White Lodge* (Albany: State University of New York Press, 1994). Studies of the Hermetic Order of the Golden Dawn include Ellic Howe, *The Magicians of the Golden Dawn* (London: Routledge & Kegan Paul, 1972) and Harper, *Yeats's Golden Dawn.* On Yeats's interests in spiritualism, see Arnold Goldman, "Yeats, spiritualism, and psychical research," in Harper, ed., *Yeats and the Occult*, pp. 108–29; R. F. Foster, *W. B. Yeats: A Life 1: The Apprentice Mage 1865–1914* (Oxford: Oxford University Press, 1997), sections of Chapter 17; and Terence Brown, *The Life of W. B. Yeats: A Critical Biography* (Oxford: Blackwell, 1999), Chapter 9. Indeed, Brown weaves Yeats's occult absorptions through his narrative, which suggests "that it is no longer possible simply to say that Yeats's beliefs offered him the metaphoric and symbolic means of expression for essentially humanist feelings he would have had without such 'exotic' preoccupations" (p. 379). The history of the *Vision* experiments has been traced most fully by Harper, *The Making of Yeats's "A Vision."* For the spirituality of the late period, see Richard Ellmann, *Second Puberty* (Washington: Library of Congress, 1986); Tim Armstrong, "Giving birth to oneself: Yeats's late sexuality," *Yeats Annual* 8 (London: Macmillan, 1991), pp. 39–58; and Elizabeth Butler Cullingford, *Gender and History in Yeats's Love Poetry* (Cambridge: Cambridge University Press, 1993), especially Chapter 13.
7. The announcement of its formation was carried in the fall issue of the Society's journal *Lucifer,* and is here quoted from Sylvia Cranston, *HPB: The Extraordinary Life and Influence of Helena Blavatsky, Founder of the Modern Theosophical Movement* (New York: Putnam, 1993), p. 365.

8. These methods were based on the fundamental Hermetic principle "as above, so below." They consisted of exercises focusing the mind on symbols that functioned as portals through which an adept could travel to higher truths signified by the symbols. In claiming that "things below are copies, the Great Smaragdine Tablet said," the hermit Ribh, in the poem "Ribh denounces Patrick" (*VP* 556), reiterates the maxim Yeats took from Blavatsky: "Tradition declares that on the dead body of Hermes, at Hebron, was found by an Isarim, an initiate, the tablet known as the Smaragdine. It contains, in a few sentences, the essence of the Hermetic wisdom . . . 'What is below is like that which is above, and what is above is similar to that which is below to accomplish the wonders of one thing'" (H. P. Blavatsky, *Isis Unveiled: A Master-Key to the Mysteries of Ancient and Modern Science and Theology*, 2 vols. [London and Benares: Theosophical Publishing Society, 1910], Vol. I, p. 507).
   This idea is scattered through a number of works from the esoteric tradition. For example, Yeats would have been instructed as a neophyte in the Order of the Golden Dawn that "Nature is harmonious in all her workings, and that which is above is as that which is below"; see the Neophyte Ritual in Israel Regardie, *The Golden Dawn: A Complete Course in Practical Ceremonial Magic. The Original Account of the Teachings, Rites and Ceremonies of the Hermetic Order of the Golden Dawn (Stella Matutina),* 6th edn. (St. Paul, MN: Llewellyn, 1992), p. 130. The same principle occurs in the translation and commentary of the Greek *Corpus hermeticum* and other documents by Yeats's fellow member of the Esoteric Section of the Theosophical Society, G. R. S. Mead. See Mead's version of Excerpt III by Stobaeus, "On Truth": "All things . . . that are on earth . . . are not the Truth; they're copies [only] of the True," *Thrice-Greatest Hermes: Studies in Hellenistic Theosophy and Gnosis. Being a Translation of the Extant Sermons and Fragments of the Trismegistic Literature, with Prologomena, Commentaries, and Notes,* ed. G. R. S. Mead, 3 vols. (London and Benares: Theosophical Publishing Society, 1906), Vol. III, p. 18.
9. The manuscript materials from the abortive project have been edited by Lucy Shepard Kalogera, "Yeats's Celtic mysteries" (Unpublished diss., Florida State University, 1977).
10. Steven Putzel, *Reconstructing Yeats: "The Secret Rose" and "The Wind Among the Reeds"* (Dublin: Gill and Macmillan; Totowa, NJ: Barnes & Noble, 1986), p. 3.
11. For a detailed history of this debacle see Harper, *Yeats's Golden Dawn.*
12. "Is the Order of R. R. & A. C. to remain a magical order?" In Harper, *Yeats's Golden Dawn*, pp. 261, 267.
13. For details about some of Yeats's adventures with spiritualism and psychical research, see three essays in Harper, *Yeats and the Occult*: Arnold Goldman, "Yeats, spiritualism, and psychical research," pp. 108–29; George Mills Harper, "'A subject of investigation': Miracle at Mirebeau," pp. 172–89; and George Mills Harper and John S. Kelly, "Preliminary examination of the script of E[lizabeth] R[adcliffe]," pp. 130–71. See also Christopher Blake, "Ghosts in the machine: Yeats and the metallic homunculus, with transcripts of reports by W. B. Yeats and Edmund Dulac," *Yeats Annual* 15 (London: Palgrave, 2002), pp. 69–101. Yeats was an Associate Member of the Society for Psychical Research for

some fifteen years, according to Harper, *The Making of Yeats's "A Vision,"* Vol. I, p. xii.

14. See Foster, *W. B. Yeats: A Life* I, pp. 464–7, and the introduction and notes to the manuscript by Steve L. Adams and George Mills Harper for accounts of the relationship between Yeats and Leo: Adams and Harper, eds. "The manuscript of 'Leo Africanus,'" *Yeats Annual* I (London: Macmillan, 1982), pp. 3–47.
15. *Ibid.*, p. 13.
16. *Ibid.*, pp. 33–9.
17. Harper, ed., *Yeats's "Vision" Papers*, Vol. III, p. I.
18. See John Rickard, "'Studying a new science': Yeats, Irishness, and the East," in *Representing Ireland: Gender, Class, Nationality*, ed. Susan Shaw Sailer (Gainesville: University Press of Florida, 1997), pp. 94–112. See also Declan Kiberd, *Inventing Ireland* (London: Jonathan Cape, 1995), pp. 251–3. On Yeats and Indian religion and philosophy, see Naresh Guha, *W. B. Yeats: An Indian Approach* ([Darby, PA]: Arden Library, 1978).
19. For the figure of the Fool, see the poems "The phases of the moon," "Two songs of a fool," and "Another song of a fool" from the volume *The Wild Swans at Coole* (*VP* 372–7, 380, and 381).
20. Richard Cavendish, *The Tarot* (London: Michael Joseph, 1975), p. 62.
21. *Ibid.*, p. 59.
22. For a discussion of Yeats and Tantrism, see Cullingford, *Gender and History*, pp. 245–60.

10

ELIZABETH BUTLER CULLINGFORD

Yeats and gender

The Cambridge anthropologist Jane Harrison once posed a question that remains as challenging today as when it was first framed. She asked why "women never want to write poetry about Man as a sex – why is Woman a dream and a terror to man and not the other way around?"[1] For Yeats, whose frustrated devotion to an unattainable Muse dominated his life and his poetry, women were more often a dream than a terror. Nevertheless the feminist poet Adrienne Rich sees him as exemplary of the asymmetrical power relation between male subject and female object:

> And there were all those poems about women, written by men: it seemed to be a given that men wrote poems and women frequently inhabited them. These women were almost always beautiful, but threatened with the loss of beauty, the loss of youth – the fate worse than death. Or, they were beautiful and died young, like Lucy and Lenore. Or, the woman was like Maud Gonne, cruel and disastrously mistaken, and the poem reproached her because she had refused to become a luxury for the poet.[2]

Rich describes three distinct poetic modes: the *carpe diem* genre, which threatens the mistress with the ravages of old age in order to pressure her into bed; the "cruel mistress" trope, which laments her refusal to comply; and the idealization of the dead beloved made fashionable by Dante and Petrarch. All three modes exemplify the tradition, previously noted by Jane Harrison, in which men write and women are written about.

Despite the discovery of many forgotten women poets, this tradition has until recently been the dominant one. Like it or not, male poets occupy most of the historical canon. Has feminism, in opening up to critical scrutiny the socially constructed attitudes about gender that to Yeats and to many of his contemporaries would have seemed "natural," rendered their poetry unreadable, or at least unpleasurable, to modern readers? Although their aesthetic and rhetorical appeal is seductive, some of Yeats's poems say things that jar the contemporary ear:

'To be born woman is to know –
Although they do not talk of it at school –
That we must labour to be beautiful.'
(*VP* 205)

O may she live like some green laurel
Rooted in one dear perpetual place.
(*VP* 405)

How can those terrified vague fingers push
The feathered glory from her loosening thighs?
(*VP* 441)

If we regard male representations of women as merely the verbal or visual equivalent of masculine social dominance, these lines wither. In paraphrase, Yeats says that women are decorative objects who should cultivate their looks and stay hidden quietly at home with their husbands and children, except on alarming special occasions when they are required to subject themselves to (and maybe even enjoy) the lust of the gods. Most contemporary women would not want to spend an evening with a man who thought such things, no matter how eloquent his conversation.

If paraphrase is all that interests us, then, we had better relinquish Yeats in favor of writers whose themes, attitudes, and sexual politics we find more consistently congenial. Many feminist critics have abandoned the male canon in order to study famous women, or to retrieve forgotten ones from the historical margins. But for feminists who do not wish to focus on the sins of the fathers, nor to occupy themselves exclusively with the celebration of the mothers, and for whom poetry is more than the sum of its social attitudes, the way forward is more complex. We cannot censor a few obnoxious poems and create a Yeats sanitized for feminist consumption, since he is a poet and thinker for whom sex is the supreme trope and guiding philosophical metaphor. He is, moreover, one of the most prolific Anglophone love poets of the twentieth century; and he frequently chooses to frame his most challenging insights in the persona of a woman. A Yeats shorn of sexuality would hardly be worth reading.

And indeed, reading Yeats can still be supremely pleasurable. But must it be a guilty pleasure? How do feminist critics reconcile their aesthetic and emotional enjoyment of individual male authors with their knowledge that most canonical male art is complicit with structures of power that still, even at the beginning of the twenty-first century, operate to keep women firmly in their places? If Yeats's poetry moves and delights us, what does that say about us, or about him? That we are still, despite our politics, secretly enslaved to the old games of passive female display and active male desire? Or that Yeats is a special case?

We have been helped of late by the gradual morphing of feminism into gender studies, an intellectual course correction that allows us to consider masculinity not as the universal standard against which all femininities are measured and found lacking, but as a social construction no less damaging to men than it is to women. As a writer who struggled constantly with his self-definition as a sexual being, who longed to make love but made it quite rarely, who identified the act of writing poetry with feminine sexual receptivity, and whose chosen audience was a nation stereotyped as effeminate by its colonial masters, Yeats presents a fascinating case study of the intersection between troubled masculinity, poetry, and nationality. Scholars who are primarily interested in tracing the emergence of colonial cultures from the grip of empire sometimes characterize the study of gender issues as a bourgeois luxury that can wait until more fundamental race, class, and national oppressions have been addressed. This is a false theoretical dichotomy, especially in the case of Yeats. Though it might seem incumbent upon a feminist to tease out the thread of gender from the various entanglements of Ireland's struggle for independence, or for a postcolonial critic to concentrate primarily on his work in the various literary-political societies that flourished in Dublin at the turn of the century, such a method would be unnecessarily constricting. If gender is a social construct, it is constructed differently in different times and places, and needs to be understood as a product of history.

In "Lyric poetry and society" Theodor Adorno suggests ways in which the supposedly private, subjective, and individualistic lyric mode can register social pressures for change;[3] as if to bear him out, Yeats describes himself as "a man of my time, through my poetical faculty living its history" (*LE* 198). Indeed it is history that provides a partial answer to my theoretical questions about gender and pleasurable reading. A feminist approach to the traditional canon can articulate questions of gender with questions of form and aesthetic pleasure, and situate both in their cultural context. Certainly Yeats's representations of women – as Muse, as Ideal Beauty, as Ireland – are sometimes disconcertingly conventional, but he lived during a time when the battle between convention and innovation in the construction of gender was at its height. It is naïve to suggest that works of the past can be measured exclusively by the standards of the present, or that pleasure can be derived only from texts whose content is judged to be politically progressive. The problematic of sexuality in a literary work must be mediated through a consideration of genre, audience, and history.

Yeats played a part in many intertwined histories: political, cultural, literary, and occult. Through his poetical faculty he experienced both the liberation of his country from British colonial rule and the first wave of women's emancipation. Although these two movements were distinct, and occasionally in opposition, for Yeats they were connected both through a convergence of historical personnel and through the traditional identification of Ireland as a woman. When he began to write in the 1880s, women had made significant legal advances, and the more fortunate were beginning to achieve access to higher education and to contraception. Women were not given the vote until 1918, but between 1905 and 1914 suffrage demands became increasingly vocal. The "Woman Question" and the concomitant exploration of sexual identity were among the major cultural issues of Yeats's time. As a result, Woman became increasingly a terror rather than a dream to some anxious men. Virginia Woolf wrote:

> No age can ever have been as stridently sex-conscious as our own; those innumerable books by men about women in the British Museum are a proof of it. The Suffrage campaign was no doubt to blame. It must have roused in men an extraordinary desire for self-assertion . . . when one is challenged, even by a few women in black bonnets, one retaliates, if one has never been challenged before, rather excessively.[4]

Yeats was not one of those who retaliated. Some of his best friends were feminists. Through his early involvement with the socialist group that gathered around William Morris and his friendship with actresses like Florence Farr, he met many "New Women." Although Maud Gonne put Irish nationalism first, she acted on feminist principles, founding her women's association, *Inghinidhe na hEireann*, on behalf of "all the girls who, like myself resented being excluded, as women, from National Organisations."[5]

Gonne opens her autobiography with a symbolic evocation of the figure with whom she herself was to become identified: "Cathleen ni Houlihan in all her beauty, her dark hair blowing on the wind."[6] Since the eighteenth century, Ireland "herself" had commonly been represented as a dispossessed and distraught maiden. Jacobite bards lamenting the loss of Irish political independence established this identification in their *aisling* or vision poems, which Yeats analyzed with insight and sympathy. He claimed that because of their politics, the *aisling* poets were "hated and pursued by the powerful and the rich, and loved by the poor." He noted that they habitually cloaked their meaning in the generic practices of love poetry: at dawn the poet encounters a beautiful weeping woman, whom he identifies as Ireland. "Or else he evades the law by hiding his sedition under the guise of a love-song. Then Ireland becomes his Kathleen, Ny-Houlahan, or else his Roisin Dubh, or some other name of Gaelic endearment." Yeats chooses as his example James Clarence Mangan's incendiary "Dark Rosaleen," which ends with a prophecy that "the Erne shall run red / With redundance of blood," and the glens will ring with "gun-peal and slogan cry," in defense of his Dark Rosaleen (*UP*1 149–50). In this Irish representational tradition the young Yeats located both his love for Maud Gonne and his love for his country, which became indistinguishable. The powerful nexus of politics, desire, and blood transforms the Rose of his early poems into a national Muse, whose longed-for liberation is mystically equated with Armageddon, death, or the act of love. In "The Secret Rose" the end of the world, when the stars are "blown about the sky, / Like the sparks blown out of a smithy, and die," is a coded reference to revolution: "Surely thine hour has come, thy great wind blows, / Far-off, most secret, and inviolate Rose?" (*VP* 170).

Yeats's Rose, the ubiquitous symbol of his early poetry, is therefore the focus of patriotic as well as personal desire: the desire for a free nation, represented as a beautiful woman. Through her the poet channels the cultural legacy of his country: in "To the Rose upon the Rood of Time" he summons her to preside over his evocation of the Irish past through the figures of Cuchulain, Fergus, and the Druid: "Red Rose, proud Rose, sad Rose of all my days! / Come near me, while I sing the ancient ways" (*VP* 101). Even verses that are less obviously related to "the ancient ways" of Irish history and myth or to Ireland's colonial subjection read differently in the light of the *aisling* tradition. In "The Song of Wandering Aengus," a freshly caught trout intended for the speaker's breakfast magically transforms itself into the object of a dawn love-quest:

> It had become a glimmering girl
> With apple blossom in her hair
> Who called me by my name and ran
> And faded through the brightening air.
> (*VP* 149–50)

The poem evokes Yeats's first meeting with Maud Gonne, at which he noted her "complexion like the blossom of apples" (*Mem* 40), and the *aisling* poets habitually associated the visionary maiden with apple-blossom: Yeats thus merges Gonne as his unattainable Beloved with Gonne as an image of Ireland. "The Song of Wandering Aengus" is both a love poem and a national allegory.[7]

Contemporary Irish feminists like Eavan Boland (a disciple of Adrienne Rich) reject all such uses of the female figure as a national icon, on the grounds that these static and decorative emblems both efface the material existence of real, suffering, complex Irish women, and silence the voices of aspiring women poets.[8] Certainly the visionary maiden lamenting her colonial status has little to do with the poverty-stricken rural mother watching her children die of starvation, though the political source of their grief – British imperialism – is ostensibly the same. The price of insight into one injustice may be blindness to another: the *aisling* poets, who belonged to an aristocratic tradition, were alive to the oppression of their country but could not see clearly the poor people on whom that oppression weighed most heavily.

Boland, however, is speaking from her post-independence perspective. She convincingly charts the stifling and mechanical effects of the repetition of a trope once the political circumstances that gave birth to it have been altered, and bears witness to the paralysis inflicted on contemporary women writers by use of the female figure as a nationalist icon. But in the 1890s things were different. Yeats's conflation of the Rose, his Muse, and Ireland gave an actively anti-colonial resonance to many lyrics that were ostensibly about his love for Maud Gonne. In case this resonance should be missed by readers more interested in the politics of resistance than the privacy of love, Yeats took the trouble to explain himself to nationalist readers:

> Know, that I would accounted be
> True brother of a company
> That sang, to sweeten Ireland's wrong,
> Ballad and story, rann and song;

This "company" includes Thomas Davis, the poet and cultural nationalist who led the Young Ireland rebellion in 1848; James Clarence Mangan, the author of "Dark Rosaleen"; and Sir Samuel Ferguson, a poet and antiquarian who helped to popularize the "ancient ways" of the Irish sagas by retelling them in his *Lays of the Western Gael*. Yeats stakes out his claim to belong to the masculine tradition of cultural nationalism, despite the fact that his own poetics are marked as feminine:

> Nor be I any less of them,
> Because the red-rose-bordered hem
> Of her, whose history began
> Before God made the angelic clan,
> Trails all about the written page.
> (*VP* 137–8)

His devotion to a mystical female icon of Eternal Beauty is identical with his membership in the "brotherhood" of revolutionary Irish nationalism. Occultism, sexuality, and politics, he argues, are inseparable, and are given aesthetic form under the image of the Rose.

Not everyone believed him, of course, but Gonne herself, who was an occultist as well as a committed political activist, positively encouraged his tendency to represent her as Ireland personified. In Yeats and Augusta Gregory's 1902 play *Cathleen ni Houlihan*, she incarnated the Old Woman who is metamorphosed into a young girl with "the walk of a queen" (*VPl* 231) by the blood sacrifice of a young man on the altar of Irish freedom. Such tropes were familiar to idealistic revolutionaries like Padraic Pearse, who shared Yeats's vision of Ireland as a woman. "When I was a child," he wrote, "I believed that there was actually a woman called Erin, and had Mr. Yeats's *Kathleen ni Houlihan* been then written and had I seen it, I should have taken it not as an allegory, but as a representation of a thing that might happen any day in any house."[9]

Maud Gonne was particularly fond of "Red Hanrahan's Song about Ireland," in which she achieves an iconic religious status of precisely the kind that Eavan Boland deplores:

> Our courage breaks like an old tree in a black wind and dies,
> But we have hidden in our hearts the flame out of the eyes
> Of Cathleen, the daughter of Houlihan.

Gonne saw Yeats's poems, especially those he wrote about her, as his most valuable contribution to the national struggle, and she was probably right. By rendering masculine erotic abjection indistinguishable from religious and political devotion, "Red Hanrahan's Song about Ireland" (*VP* 207–8) taps into a powerful psychological force field in which masochism provides the major affective thrust:

> Like heavy flooded waters our bodies and our blood;
> But purer than a tall candle before the Holy Rood
> Is Cathleen, the daughter of Houlihan.

Irish Catholicism, with its iconographic emphasis on the tortured male body hanging above the altar, the "Holy Rood," encouraged this emphasis on male self-sacrifice. This process is clearer in the poem, which focuses on the unworthiness of Cathleen's admirers, who have "bent low and low and kissed [her] quiet feet" (*VP* 207), and the vaguely erotic "heavy flooded waters" of their impure bodies, than in the play, where the hero Michael has almost nothing to say about his transformation from bridegroom to sacrificial victim. By saturating national politics with sexualized Christianity Yeats transforms a reasoned intellectual analysis of the need for political self-determination into the drive towards male martyrdom.

Moreover, to paraphrase Simone de Beauvoir, one is not born a man, one becomes one; and Yeats had considerable trouble becoming a man. Adrian Frazier has charted the currents of homoerotic emotion that circulated between Yeats's cousin Lionel Johnson, the repressed gay man Edward

Martyn, the sexually ambiguous George Moore, and Yeats himself, to whom persons of both sexes were regularly attracted.[10] (Always, alas, the wrong persons.) Yeats's difficulty in getting rid of his virginity (something he failed to achieve until the age of thirty-two) also suggests a certain lack of conventional male aggression. His personal character and circumstances were reflected in his philosophy and his poetics. Like many Romantic poets, he was unable to identify with the norms of masculinity dominant in the late nineteenth century. Loathing the Victorian myth of science and progress, he exalted emotion over reason; and as a young man he sought to cast out of his verse "those energetic rhythms, as of a man running" and replace them by "wavering, meditative, organic rhythms" (*E&I* 163). He espoused an organic, Keatsian, consciously essentialist and "feminine" poetics in which "words are as subtle, as complex, as full of mysterious life, as the body of a flower or of a woman" (*E&I* 164). (Jane Harrison might well have asked why women poets did not find analogies for their poetics in the mysteries of the male physique.) His horoscope showed him to be a man dominated by the moon, and in his later years he developed a philosophy based upon a lunar myth that privileged traditionally feminine symbolism: moon over sun, night over day. (His vision of life as the alternating dominance and submission of opposing principles, imaged in his gyres, is fundamentally sexual: his most important polarities were male and female.) Although his father praised active men, Yeats was sexually passive, dependent upon reverie and dreams for his poetic inspiration.

His early poem, "He wishes for the Cloths of Heaven" may stand as a paradigm of his youthful attitude of self-abnegation: despite his identification with the feminine, Woman is still a dream and even potentially a terror to him. If he could possess "the heavens' embroidered cloths" (his elaborate metaphor for the starry skies), he would use them as Sir Walter Raleigh once used his cloak: to spread under the feet of his Queen:

> But I, being poor, have only my dreams;
> I have spread my dreams under your feet;
> Tread softly because you tread on my dreams.
>
> (*VP* 176)

Such self-abasement was both literary, in that the position of the lover before the Beloved was traditionally prostrate, and personal, in that Yeats's relation to Maud Gonne, who preferred another lover, was profoundly unequal. The poetry of unrequited love preserves in its generic structures the traces of the one social power that most women could exert over most men: the power of refusal. It is the record of male dismay in the face of female resistance. To this generic imperative Yeats adds the iconography of nationalist

Ireland. A Protestant, he was nevertheless sensitive to the attractions of Mariolotry, a practice that emphasized the difference between native Catholics and Protestant colonizers. "The heavens' embroidered cloths, / Enwrought with golden and silver light" evoke the richly adorned vestments and altar cloths of Catholic ritual. "The blue and the dim and the dark cloths" (*VP* 176) remind his Irish audience that blue is Mary's color; and Mary is the ultimate object of unattainable desire. Like Kathleen, "purer than a tall candle before the Holy Rood," the female Muse addressed in "He wishes for the Cloths of Heaven" has a sacred as well as a secular dimension.

Yeats described his early poetic technique in gendered terms. Later, as his technique changed, he denigrated his own early verses as "unmanly," the "feminine" products of "a womanish introspection" (*L* 434). If "He wishes for the Cloths of Heaven" represents Yeats's so-called "feminine" style, its leading characteristics are redundancy and repetition. Exemplifying Yeats's gendered metaphor for the poetic process, "stitching and unstitching" (*VP* 204), the poem embroiders the words "cloths" and "dreams" into an elaborate formal structure that replaces rhyme by echo, and leans with self-conscious naïveté on the copula: "The blue and the dim and the dark cloths / Of night and light and the half-light" (*VP* 176). The lines are end-stopped, and the slightly irregular four-stress meter combines with the repetition to produce a hypnotic, languorously self-pitying effect. Femininity, then, is associated with minute elaboration, loosened syntax, and "wavering, meditative, organic rhythms": in other words, with decorative weakness.

Yeats's reading of Nietzsche in 1903 and his theatre experience caused him to seek "more of manful energy" (*VP* 849) in his life and his writing. In personal terms this conscious and sexist exaltation of masculinity was forced, and he knew it. He later described himself as "one that ruffled in a manly pose / For all his timid heart" (*VP* 489). Manliness, in fact, was always something of a pose for Yeats: a condition to be constructed by deliberate effort rather than taken for granted. In this he resembled Irish patriotic writers like D. P. Moran, who rejected the imperial definition of Ireland the colony as "feminine" and insisted on Irish masculinity. In poetic terms, however, his new tough-guy act paid off in sometimes surprising ways.

Yeats paradoxically employed his "manly" poetics to increase the energy of his lyric heroine. Like the New Woman herself, his Beloved casts off the stereotypes of Victorian femininity together with the rhythms of Victorian verse. If we compare "He wishes for the Cloths of Heaven" to "No Second Troy," written in December, 1908, the difference is clear. Maud Gonne had always been a political activist, but the younger Yeats preferred to represent her as a static avatar of Eternal Beauty or an un-individualized

Rose. Although "No Second Troy" celebrates her as unique, her beauty "solitary" in a banal age, Yeats's representation of femininity in the poem draws energy from women who have adopted mass protest, offering the spectacle of a world turned upside down, the little streets hurled upon the great:

> Why should I blame her that she filled my days
> With misery, or that she would of late
> Have taught to ignorant men most violent ways,
> Or hurled the little streets upon the great,
> Had they but courage equal to desire?

"No Second Troy" indicates that for Yeats as speaker, poetic "manliness" meant giving up the abject laments of the forsaken lover. Why should he blame her for rejecting him? "Manly" poetics consisted in the elliptical condensation of syntax, the replacement of parataxis by subordination, strong enjambment, stress-packed lines, colloquial diction, and emphasis on consonants rather than vowels: in the construction of an energetic spoken language. Voice, energy, and agency have traditionally been denied to women, and Yeats sees Maud Gonne as a heroic woman who lacked a tragic stage on which to speak her "mind":

> What could have made her peaceful with a mind
> That nobleness made simple as a fire,
> With beauty like a tightened bow, a kind
> That is not natural in an age like this,
> Being high and solitary and most stern?

The poetic elevation of the original sonnet heroines, Beatrice and Laura, reflected no social power. Yeats's Helen, however, has taken power into her own hands: if she is "high" above the poet it is because she has placed herself there. She transgresses all the stereotypes of femininity: she is violent, courageous, noble, fiery, solitary, and stern; her beauty is a weapon – "a tightened bow" – rather than a lure. In his closing rhetorical question, "Why, what could she have done, being what she is? / Was there another Troy for her to burn?" (*VP* 256–7), Yeats radically modifies the image of Homer's passive queen: the sex object over whom men fight their battles becomes herself a warrior, previously identified by the simile of the bow as an Amazon. Yeats's active syntax attributes to her the agency of a subject: instead of causing Troy to be destroyed, she burns it herself.

"No Second Troy" is nevertheless an ambiguous poem, in which the celebration of Amazonian female agency and power is qualified by the poet's restrictions on the exercise of that power. Gonne lives in an age that, according to Yeats, affords no fitting outlet for the energy of the heroic woman. Revolution, whether nationalist or feminist, is not an appropriate activity for a Helen. Thus the poem takes back with one hand what it gives with the other: the exceptional woman is acknowledged, but her freedom to constitute herself as a subject through political action is denied, and her frustrated power is defined as destructive. When in old age Yeats lamented the fact that he had known "A Helen of social welfare dream, / Climb on a wagonette to scream" (*VP* 626), he abandoned creative ambivalence and drew instead on anti-suffrage propaganda, which commonly deployed the nineteenth-century stereotype of the hysterical woman.

In "A Prayer for my Daughter" Yeats's patriarchal prescriptions for his daughter's sexual identity and conventional role in marriage, and his image of the ideal woman as a rooted, hidden tree inhabited by a brainless if merry linnet, directly counter the claims for female autonomy made by the suffragists. Unlike the Helen of "No Second Troy," his later Helen is limp and sullen: "Helen being chosen found life flat and dull / And later had much trouble from a fool." Her patron Aphrodite, the goddess of love, had an equally unfortunate sexual career: she "chose a bandy-leggèd smith for man." Yeats's assertion that "It's certain that fine women eat / A crazy salad with their meat" (*VP* 404) uses a witty gastronomic metaphor to mask his bitterness about the inappropriate marriages of Maud Gonne and her daughter Iseult. A beautiful woman has wrecked her life (and his) because she couldn't let go of her opinions. Rather than dismissing the poem as irritatingly conventional, however, we can appreciate its interest as a document of its time by juxtaposing the traditional interpretative strategy of close formal analysis with a consideration of the historical context.

One of the major aesthetic pleasures of this text is Yeats's complex and coherent development of the contrasting images of destroying wind and rooted tree. At the opening of the poem the storm is "howling," the wind is "levelling," the sea-wind "screams" on the tower and assaults the elm trees. "Gregory's wood" offers an inadequate protection against it. When Yeats analyzes why Maud Gonne has failed to prosper, his metaphor connects her directly with the images of storm and voice: she has rejected the virtues prized by "quiet natures" for "an old bellows full of angry wind" that will both "howl" and "burst," though it will ultimately fail to tear the linnet from the leaf. The model woman, exhorted to "think opinions are accursed," should live like a "flourishing hidden tree," safe from the wind and "rooted in one dear perpetual place" (*VP* 403–5). The lines that most emphatically reject the New Woman's demand for intellectual agency and physical mobility are also those that complete and justify the image patterns that structure the poem.

We can appreciate the intersection between metaphor and history by asking what was going on in 1919 to prompt Yeats's association of screaming sea-winds with opinionated women. For him, women's history in this period was interwoven with the history of Irish nationalism. In the aftermath of the 1916 Rising a "terrible beauty" was indeed born. The widows and bereft mothers of the revolution (Mrs. Pearse, Kathleen Clarke, Grace Plunkett, Hanna Sheehy-Skeffington), and the women of *Cumann na mBan* who had been "out" in Easter week, played a large symbolic and practical role in the electoral success of Sinn Fein. In February, 1918, the franchise was granted to British women over thirty, and in December the "rebel countess" Constance Markievicz united Irish republican, suffragist, and labor support to become the first woman to win a seat in the British Parliament. What threatens the future identity of Yeats's baby Anne, then, is not only the postwar political chaos evoked in the drafts of the poem,[11] but also the model of femininity offered by a woman who raises her voice in the service of "opinions": one who, like Markievicz in "Easter 1916," spends her nights in argument until her voice grows "shrill" (*VP* 392). In "A Prayer for my Daughter" Yeats's use of the curious legal phrase "Assault and battery of the wind" (*VP* 405) suggests that he is drawing on the anti-feminist rhetoric employed by those who opposed the "shrieking sisterhood" of the suffragists,[12] who not only raised their voices in public, but were frequently arrested on charges of attacking policemen or politicians. At the beginning of World War I Maud Gonne had written to Yeats that women would soon be "in a terrible majority, unless famine destroys them too. I always felt the wave of the woman's power was rising, the men are destroying themselves & we are looking on (*GY* 348)." Her prophetic metaphor of women's power as a rising "wave" may have prompted Yeats's vision of the "future years" as issuing "Out of the murderous innocence of the sea" (*VP* 403). The poem thus shows us Yeats living history through his poetical faculty: he is both lamenting his sexual disappointments and reacting against the re-definition of gender caused by the granting of suffrage.

Yeats's sonnet "Leda and the Swan" presents even more of a challenge to a feminist reader than "A Prayer for my Daughter." We are accustomed to hearing that it is about the violent beginnings of a historical gyre, an interpretation sanctioned by its appearance in *A Vision*. It is less often discussed as a representation of rape as potentially pleasurable for women. Again, formal and historical readings must be orchestrated. Yeats chose the sonnet, a form he rarely used and occasionally disparaged, for his depiction of a woman being violated. Originally the sonnet was the vehicle of idealized woman-worship, in which the Lady disdained the helpless male lover, who was suspended in perennially unfulfilled desire: in Yeats's poem the woman is "helpless" before "the brute blood" of her male ravisher. Having overpaid his courtly dues in his youth, Yeats swung with corresponding intensity toward the opposite extreme: rape can be construed as the dark underside of romance. Paul Fussell's analysis of the sonnet form reveals how permeated by the sexuality of male supremacy are even the supposedly abstract shapes of canonical genres. "The [octave] builds up the pressure, the [sestet] releases it; and the turn is the dramatic and climactic center of the poem . . . one of the emotional archetypes of the Petrarchan sonnet structure is the pattern of sexual pressure and release."[13] Fussell's analogy is based on the mechanics of male sexual response, with its single climactic moment. His orgasmic poetics are certainly appropriate to "Leda and the Swan," for the graphic phrase "A shudder in the loins" is placed at the "turn" between the octave and sestet, the place of maximum formal effect (*VP* 441). Yeats demonstrates both his fidelity to the male shape of the genre and, paradoxically, the way in which his attitude to the traditionally sublimated desire of the Petrarchan sonnet has been changed by the advent of the sexual revolution.

Yeats's sexual frankness provides another example of how the discussion of form can be integrated with the question of history, but in this case the historicist and the feminist readings do not dovetail neatly. After the establishment of the Irish Free State in 1922, the Catholic Church and the government cooperated to establish sexual purity as one of the essential markers of Irishness. This meant the refusal of divorce and contraception, the introduction of censorship, and the reinforcement of an already heavy Catholic emphasis on female virginity and chaste motherhood. Yeats was hostile to this culture of sexual repression: his speech in favor of divorce grounded his antagonism to the Catholic government's policies in his identity as a Protestant. In 1924, Yeats's publication of "Leda and the Swan" in the ephemeral monthly paper *To-morrow* caused outrage: he and his literary allies were referred to in the *Catholic Bulletin* not only as the New Protestant Ascendancy, but as "the Sewage School" and the "Cloacal Combine."[14]

"Leda" thus exemplifies an uncomfortable intimacy between liberation and oppression. The original title of the poem was "Annunciation." In a Catholic culture the revision of Virgin into rape victim challenges the repressive ideology of female purity, but risks re-inscribing the woman into the equally repressive category "loose" (as in "loosening thighs"). To flout religious censorship Yeats flirts with pornography. "Pornography" may seem an extreme term to apply to "Leda and the Swan," which has been protected from such judgements by its canonical status as "high" art. Artistic merit is, of course, one of the grounds on which a work can be defined in law as not pornographic. But if we strip the poem of its canonical privilege and examine it in terms of its erotic content we see a woman subordinated, dehumanized, and raped by an animal. Yeats's mythological subject is one that has been employed for centuries on the pornographic fringe of the fine arts. Bestiality is an established sub-genre of pornography: offering a visual image of female degradation, it abrogates a woman's claim to be considered human. When we encounter "Leda and the Swan" in its Norton Anthology frame as a modernist masterpiece, dirty postcards featuring women and donkeys do not suggest themselves as valid analogies, and we are likely to forget its extra-canonical pornographic pedigree. Feminist critique of "Leda," however, must negotiate the strategic problem of appearing to echo the original religious outrage. Although objections to sexism are not the same as objections to sex, they may sound alike.

One need not argue, however, that rape is unrepresentable. The first stanza of the poem, stressing as it does the absolute power of the rapist, the brutality of the attack, and the helplessness of the "staggering girl," might be read as a protest against male sexual dominance, although the full implications of the word "caressed" are disturbing. Yeats insists on the destructive historical consequences of Jove's sexual rapacity: the fall of Troy and the murder of Agamemnon. He is primarily concerned with Leda's consciousness, and ignores Jove's view of the action. Close reading of the second stanza, however, reveals certain assumptions that are often found in sexist culture. Those "vague" fingers and "loosening" thighs suggest that, although she is hurt and stunned, Leda's body, if not her will, responds to the rapist as physically erotic. Is it Leda's consciousness or the narrator's that approvingly tropes her aggressor as "the feathered glory"? Her "loosening thighs" imply a moment of consenting, mutual erotic pleasure, which may suggest to a male reader that if he behaves like the swan, women will find him emotionally as well as physically irresistible. Since centuries of cultural conditioning have constructed women's sexuality as passive and masochistic, the existence of female rape fantasies is not surprising. But the gap between fantasy (which a woman can control and which involves no actual pain) and the real thing (in which she is powerless and often suffers physical harm) makes male representations of rape as pleasurable for women extremely dangerous. For example, if the plaintiff in a rape trial appears as a sexual being in her dress, deportment, or actions; if it can be proved that she has had and enjoyed sex with other men, her consent is assumed: she must have enjoyed the rape too, and no crime has been committed.

Yeats's most famous rhetorical question re-frames the question of sexual enjoyment in intellectual terms: "Did she put on his knowledge with his power / Before the indifferent beak could let her drop?" (*VP* 441). In asking whether she "put on" his divine "knowledge" as he had carnal "knowledge" of her Yeats suggests an epiphany: the verb "put on" is ambiguous, and might suggest that she was not only "overpowered" but "empowered" by the knowledge of her engendering role in future events. But Yeats finally resists the temptation, implicit in his rhetorical question, to assume that being raped by a god must be a glamorous experience worth any amount of incidental inconvenience. The last line of the poem, although it ends with a question mark, has the force of a declarative. When the "indifferent beak" lets Leda drop we understand, as Yeats does, that she has been used, objectified, and discarded.

"Leda" can be approached formally as a revisionist love sonnet, historically as a liberal intervention in the dispute about censorship in post-Treaty Ireland, literally as a poem about rape. The poem's linguistic and emotional complexity suggests that we cannot make a tidy separation between a positive historical reading and a hostile feminist one. The lifting of sexual repression does not automatically liberate women, but the effect of Irish censorship on both literature and advertisements for contraception suggests that the virtues of transgression should not be underestimated.

In the late 1920s and early 1930s Yeats abandoned his nostalgia for the old-fashioned woman who charms her husband and keeps a quiet and ceremonious house in favor of sexually bold female speakers who carried the rhetorical weight of his challenge to the Irish status quo. Yeats constructed the erotic in opposition to the Catholic sexual ethic, and to censorship, which he feared would exclude from Ireland "all great love poetry" (*SS* 177). The arena of sexuality is always saturated by the power of the state, but the peculiar nature of post-independence Irish culture, controlled by the Church rather than by secular bureaucracies, made sexual protest both legitimate and necessary. Yeats's choice of women young and old to voice this protest represents both a return to his early identification with femininity and a realization of who would suffer most from the regressive social policies of the new state, where pressures to modernize in social and sexual life were resisted by government and clergy as emanating from the political enemy, England. The Irish idealization of the female as pure virgin or patriotic mother persisted after independence: it was maintained by the religious devotion to the Virgin Mary with which it had always been intertwined, and enshrined in de Valera's 1937 constitution, which insisted that a woman's place was in the home.

Throughout Yeats's "A Woman Young and Old" and the Crazy Jane poems, the symbiosis between the pure woman and the nation is ironized and ruptured. Jane is neither a virgin nor a mother, and she has no settled home: she is one of the disenfranchized rural poor who were largely ignored by the Catholic state. In her frank expression of post-menopausal desire she breaks taboos that still exist today. Despite her "flat and fallen" breasts, she refuses the invitation of her antagonist, the bourgeois and puritanical Bishop, to forgo earthly desire for "a heavenly mansion." Preferring the "foul sty" of human sexual experience, she nevertheless refuses to separate heaven from earth or soul from body, for "'Fair and foul are near of kin, / And fair needs foul'." Perhaps remembering the *Catholic Bulletin*'s strictures against the "Cloacal Combine," Jane rejects Manichean dualism by juxtaposing "mansion" with "sty":

'A woman can be proud and stiff
When on love intent;
But Love has pitched his mansion in
The place of excrement;
For nothing can be sole or whole
That has not been rent.' (*VP* 513)

Yeats had attacked censorship with ammunition borrowed from Aquinas: *anima est in toto corpore* [the soul inhabits all parts of the body] (*SS* 178). Throughout her sequence of poems, Jane attempts to recapture the moral high ground from the Bishops, whose hysterical tirades against the body in its Irish manifestations (cosmetics, dance halls, and immodest dress) ignore the teachings of Aquinas. In "Crazy Jane and Jack the Journeyman" Jane claims that unsatisfied desire binds us to the earth: the exhaustion of desire through its fulfillment is the precondition for union with the divine: "A lonely ghost the ghost is / That to God shall come" (*VP* 511). Yeats's rejection of the Puritan ethic of the Irish Free State leads him away from the Madonna only to precipitate him into the arms of the Whore: "Crazy Jane on God" might be spoken by a tart with a heart of gold:

That lover of a night
Came when he would,
Went in the dawning light
Whether I would or no;
Men come, men go,
All things remain in God.
(*VP* 512)

But Yeats ultimately resists reductive polarities. His Madonna is a "common woman," while his Whore is a theologian committed to the premise of the immortality of the soul.

Yeats loved, liked, collaborated with, and respected women: he certainly preferred them to men. He encouraged their intellectual and creative work, assumed their professional competence, and chose them as allies. His best friends were all women. Although these biographical facts condition his lyric representation of the feminine, the distance between poet and speaker, autobiography and creative fiction, differs from poem to poem. In "Michael Robartes and the Dancer" the overtly chauvinist Michael Robartes forbids the Dancer to put herself to school (*VP* 385–7), but Yeats tried to keep Iseult Gonne at her Sanskrit studies. The over-protective father of "A Prayer for my Daughter" urges a quiet, "rooted" life and a marriage founded in "custom" and "ceremony" (*VP* 403–6) but Yeats was delighted when his daughter Anne took up painting and started designing sets for the Abbey Theatre. He claims that "A poet writes always of his personal life," but goes on to observe that "all that is personal soon rots; it must be packed in ice or salt" (*E&I* 509, 522). Yeats's ice and salt were the conventions of the English lyric and the traditional meters and stanza forms of the English poetic tradition. His poetry demonstrates the tension between personal experience, inherited formal conventions, and the double histories of the emancipation of women and the decolonization of Ireland. A critic interested in gender must keep all these ideas in play, entertain the recuperative as well as the suspicious critical impulses, and accept contradictions as inevitable. As Yeats himself said: "All propositions . . . which set all the truth upon one side can only enter rich minds to dislocate and strain . . . and sooner or later the mind expels them by instinct" (*Mem* 151).

NOTES

1. J. G. Stewart, *Jane Ellen Harrison* (London: Martin, 1959), p. 140.
2. Adrienne Rich, *On Lies, Secrets, and Silence* (New York: Norton, 1979), p. 39.
3. Theodor W. Adorno, "Lyric poetry and society," *Telos* 20 (1974), 56–71.
4. Virginia Woolf, *A Room of One's Own* (Harmondsworth: Penguin, 1945), pp. 97–98.
5. Maud Gonne MacBride, *A Servant of the Queen* (London: Gollancz, 1938), p. 291.
6. *Ibid.*, p. 7.
7. Deirdre Toomey, "Bards of the Gael and Gall," *Yeats Annual* 5 (1987), 207–8.
8. Eavan Boland, "The woman poet in a national tradition," *Studies* 76.302 (1987), 148–58.
9. Padraic H. Pearse, *Collected Works*, 3 vols. (Dublin: Maunsel, 1918–22), Vol. III, pp. 300–1.
10. Adrian Frazier, "Queering the Irish Renaissance," in *Gender and Sexuality in Modern Ireland*, ed. Anthony Bradley and Maryann Valiulis (Amherst: University of Massachusetts Press, 1997), pp. 8–38.
11. Jon Stallworthy, *Between the Lines: Yeats's Poetry in the Making* (Oxford: Clarendon Press, 1963), pp. 29, 31.

12. Lisa Tickner, *The Spectacle of Women: Imagery of the Suffrage Campaign 1907–14* (Chicago: University of Chicago Press, 1988), pp. 199–200.
13. Paul Fussell, *Poetic Meter and Poetic Form* (New York: Random House, rev. edn, 1979), p. 116.
14. *Catholic Bulletin* (Dublin) 15.1 (1925), p. 1; 14.12 (1924), p. 1020.

11

JONATHAN ALLISON

Yeats and politics

At the age of twenty, W. B. Yeats was a nationalist and Fenian sympathizer. Being Anglo-Irish, albeit marginally so, he eventually insisted upon the Irishness of the Anglo-Irish tradition and the responsibility of the Ascendancy to Irish culture.[1] Occultist and mage, he was a mystical patriot, whose search for images involved magical visions as well as literary tropes (often they converged). After the fall of Charles Stewart Parnell in 1891, when he and others dreamed unrealistically of a radical transfer of nationalist energies from the political to cultural spheres, Yeats hoped to fill an apparent political vacuum with cultural work.[2] He was dedicated to revamping an outmoded literary nationalism that had taken its colors from the propagandist simplicities of Thomas Davis and the writers of Young Ireland. Strategically essentialist about Irish and British cultures, he argued that all Irish writers should write about indigenous places and subjects: he himself rooted his imagination in the landscapes of Sligo and the West. By contrast, he was cosmopolitan in his influences, taking lessons from French Symbolists, Swedish mystics and German philosophers. He admired powerful men like Parnell, and argued, throughout his career, for bold leadership by the few over the many.[3] He distrusted and despised the merely popular, the culture of the many, the language of newspapers, and political oratory. On the other hand, his love of ballads, early and late, seemed to be, but was not, a contradiction of this premise. His early nationalism was predicated on hatred of British utilitarianism and on the struggle with Young Ireland, but was also rooted in his marginal Anglo-Irish insecurities. Crucially, he stressed the equal importance of literature and politics. In this he was influenced by his father, but also by the old Fenian John O'Leary, who expressed reservations about Young Ireland propaganda, and said "there are things a man must not do to save a nation" (*A* 178).

Theatre work brought Yeats into conflict with nationalists who demanded Irish propaganda, not art. This led to fears that politics might curtail artistic freedom, and to a deep-seated revulsion for popular nationalism. Influenced by his friendship with Lady Gregory and by his admiration for powerful patrons of the Italian Renaissance, he turned towards a more aristocratic conception of art and culture, connected to fears of a strengthening middle class and other elements of modern social change. By the time landlord power had been eroded in Ireland (though landlords were lingering on in forgotten corners), the Anglo-Irish theme had emerged forcefully in his work. In his myth, Yeats transformed an Ascendancy he had initially despised into a dynamic intellectual group. His Irish eighteenth century was illuminated by brilliant and charismatic Protestant thinkers. Together with the peasant and the artist, the Ascendancy, inhabiting plain but imposing Georgian houses (forever emblems of oppression for the Irish majority) would contribute to a triad of cultural forces in opposition to Philistine Ireland, which just so happened to be middle-class and Catholic. Emphatically insisting on the need for enlightened leadership, and denigrating influential figures in the new Irish Free State, caricatured as "Paudeen," Yeats longed for a spiritual and intellectual unity of self, to be achieved by seeking one's opposite – the Anti-Self, as he terms it in his esoteric System. As with other modernist authors who lamented social malaise and "the dissociation of sensibility,"[4] all of this would be delivered in the name of cultural regeneration, in the face of degeneracy. Fearing for posterity, he argued that social decline would be hastened by exogamous reproduction, hence his strictures against marrying outside one's class – the consequences of which are savagely figured forth in his final play and essay: *Purgatory* and *On the Boiler*. In response to the rise of de Valera, the renewal of IRA activity, and the apparent threat of communism, he gave support for several months in 1933 to the Irish Blueshirts, as a bulwark, as he saw it, against anticipated chaos. He wrote marching songs for them, but soon, realizing his mistake, he revised them so they could not be sung.

Politically, Yeats has been described variously as fascist,[5] patriotic Tory,[6] colonial,[7] postcolonial,[8] and "establishment" nationalist.[9] For Charles Ferral, he had "essentially three political identities: radical nationalist, defender of Anglo-Irish or Ascendancy culture, and fascist."[10] For Terence Brown, he was a fusion of contradictory impulses: the rage for order vying with his "instinctive libertarianism."[11] For Hazard Adams, he was an antithetical nationalist, "antithetical in the sense of critical opposition to forms of nationalism that tended toward superficiality and suppression."[12] A. Norman Jeffares and others depict him as a kind of inclusivist nationalist, aiming at a synthesis of Anglo-Irish and native Irish elements. Michael North argues that, in the course of repudiating liberalism, Yeats espoused a form of civic nationalism ("pluralism") because he realized that ethnic nationalism would exclude Protestants from leadership and representation.[13] In the

1980s, Elizabeth Butler Cullingford portrayed Yeats as an aristocratic liberal, a Burkean Tory, a "nationalist of the school of John O'Leary."[14] In the 1990s, she claimed his growing political conservatism should be seen in light of or in contradistinction from his sympathy with suffragism and the revolutionary sexual politics embodied in his late poetry. Valorizing "pollution over purity," he "constructed the erotic in opposition to the Catholic sexual ethic and censorship."[15]

Although a political poet, Yeats often expressed distaste for the word "political." Politics were among those things – disguised in "All Things can Tempt me" as "the seeming needs of my fool-driven land" – that distracted him from poetry (*VP* 267). They were associated with rhetoric, oratory, and the forces that stay or guide the hand of the artist. Although clearly embroiled in cultural politics, Yeats was suspicious of the political milieu and, as John S. Kelly has noted, "saw his enterprise as cultural. He therefore supposed that it was not 'political' since he habitually defined 'politics' in a narrowly party or sectarian sense."[16]

Disdain for politics, in his usage of the term, is a recurrent theme. To Lady Gregory, in October 1897, after chairing a long meeting, he wrote that he found the "infinite triviality of politics more trying than ever. We tare each others characters in peices for things that dont matter to anybody" (*sic*; *CL*II 135). Politics were trivial, relative to the imperatives of cultural work, and after the turn of the century, certainly by the year 1907, Yeats believed that Irish political life had become dominated by fools. He complained in 1909 that Ireland's "political class" (he meant the lower middle classes), "have suffered through the cultivation of hatred as the one energy of their movement, a deprivation which is the intellectual equivalent to a certain surgical operation. Hence the shrillness of their voices" (*A* 359). By now, his thought was dominated by fears that the *embourgeoisement* of sections of Irish culture had "emasculated" the nation, severing ancient links between landlords and peasants and in other ways re-shaping the culture. If Paudeen had become political, politics were beneath the dignity of the creative mind. Accordingly, he portrays John Millington Synge, who "seemed by nature unfitted to think a political thought," as the antithesis of this new class (*E&I* 319). After the 1916 Rising, writing to Lady Gregory, he uses the word "politics" to convey something inimical to artistic freedom: "All the work of years has been overturned . . . the freeing of literature from politics" (*L* 613). Similarly, in "On a Political Prisoner," the mind of the republican Constance Markievicz has become "a bitter, an abstract thing" (*VP* 397). By the late 1930s, his disgust with politics has reached new heights; he writes to Dorothy Wellesley and Ethel Mannin: "Politics as the game is played today, are so much foul lying," and "I suppose we have had too much politics in the past," and "I have a horror of modern politics," and (decisively) "not for politics – I'm finished with that for ever" (*L* 880–4). There is a grim continuity to be discerned: during the period 1907–16, he associates politics with the emergent middle class, Young Ireland, and militant republicanism; in old age, despite having served successfully as Senator in the 1920s, he considers politics to be completely mendacious and destructive.

While Yeats disliked politics, he frequently became embroiled in them. As he wrote to Lord Haldane, in October, 1918, "I have no part in politics and no liking for politics, but there are moments when one cannot keep out of them."[17] Yeats joined C. H. Oldham's Contemporary Club in 1885, a broadly nationalist talking shop that included among its members his father, J. F. Taylor, T. W. Rolleston, Maud Gonne, and John O'Leary. He became a regular patron of Young Ireland Society meetings in Dublin, joining the York Street membership in October, 1885. The ethos of these meetings has been described as "distinctly armchair-Fenian" suggesting a degree of radical thought unmixed with devotion to action.[18] Yeats probably took the Fenian oath at one such meeting, a prerequisite for membership in the Irish Republican Brotherhood. He flirted with socialism, often visiting the home of William Morris ("there were moments when I thought myself a Socialist"), but soon tired of the anti-religious fervor and hyperbole, as he heard it, of his fellow discussants (*Mem* 20). Socialism was not for him, despite his high regard for Morris: "I remember old O'Leary saying 'No gentleman can be a socialist though he might be an anarchist'" (*L* 869). Socialism was also tainted by association with that English materialism and mechanistic thought that Yeats despised. Early influences included Shelley, Blake, Spenser, and, among writers of prose, Ruskin, Morris, and "the Homericised Carlylese of Standish O'Grady."[19] O'Grady suggested the waning aristocracy might forge allegiances with the peasantry; through him Yeats absorbed Carlylesque ideas about heroes.

Although Yeats's Fenian sympathies were established by 1886, the effect of meeting Maud Gonne in 1889 was (as he later construed it) to increase his desire to be seen as "political": "it was natural to commend myself by claiming a very public talent, for her beauty as I saw it in those days seemed incompatible with private, intimate life" (*Mem* 41). "Public talent" involved work on committees, including the Dublin and London committees for the 1798 centenary celebrations. He protested against the 1900 royal visit to Dublin, and made numerous pro-Boer pronouncements. Famously, he was a founding member of the Irish Literary Society (London), and the National Literary Society (Dublin), and fought against Charles Gavan Duffy to establish a series of books on Irish history and literature free of Young Ireland influence (*A* 187). Despite his enthusiasms, Maud Gonne made clear in her letters that she wished to protect him from politicking: "Be true to yourself & let nothing interfere with your literary work" she urged, in the protective tone common in the letters (*GY* 55). He matched this protectiveness by physically restraining her, against her will, from joining a riotous Dublin mob during Queen Victoria's Diamond Jubilee in 1897, an occasion that confirmed his aversion to physical violence.

His fascination with occultism (despite his father's disapproval) pre-dated his meeting with Gonne. A founding member of the Dublin Hermetic Society in 1885, which later became the Theosophical Society, in 1890 he joined the Order of the Golden Dawn, in which he began to practice ritual magic. As a letter to O'Leary in 1892 reveals, a deep commitment to the occult dominated his thoughts: "If I had not made magic my constant study I could not have written my Blake book nor would 'The Countess Kathleen' have ever come to exist. The mystical life is the centre of all that I do & all that I think & all that I write" (*CL*I 303). There was always an overlap between nationalist and occultist interests, and his attempts at visionary experiences sometimes involved efforts to invoke specifically national spirits or gods. He took from Irish folklore a mass of beliefs involving the supernatural life of Ireland, especially in the remoter parts of the country. Underlying all this was his profound belief in the spiritual superiority of Ireland to godless, industrialized Britain.

The early poetry reflects his fascination with ancient beliefs and legends recorded in the oral tradition, recently translated by antiquarians. The recuperative cultural politics of the Literary Revival find expression in poems about Cuchulain, Fergus and the Druid, King Goll, and the visionary apocalypse of the Valley of the Black Pig. His poems deploying the imagery of the mystical Rose, partly borrowed from Rosicrucian tradition, affirm an early love of Spenser and Shelley, while also gesturing towards the rose of nationalist literary tradition. Only very rarely, as in his lackluster Parnell elegy, did the early Yeats allude directly to current affairs (*VP* 737–8).

"To Ireland in the Coming Times" brings together occultist and nationalist passions in a manifesto-like poetic statement about the poet's sense of the national literary past and his hopes for the future (*VP* 137–9). The poem appeared in *The Countess Kathleen and Various Legends and Lyrics* (1892), and combines, as Foster notes, "occultism and advanced nationalism in a manner calculated to appeal to Maud Gonne, and to irritate nearly everyone else."[20] The poem's brisk tetrameters and rhyming couplets announce fidelity to the ballad tradition of Young Ireland. However, this poem not only advertises aspirations to be a national poet ("true brother of a company"); it also suggests this ambitious writer's intention of exceeding the talent of his precursors. He claims to be a patriot, despite his repeated deployment of the mystical imagery of the rose of Ireland, invoked here in terms of the skirt-hem of that most characteristic of Yeatsian figures, a dancer. In Irish tradition, the *aisling* is a dream or vision poem in which the nation is personified as female. All-pervasive in Yeats's poetry, the symbolic dancer is an *aisling* figure of Ireland, an eroticizing of nationality, and, in the rhythmic quality of her movements ("the measure of her flying feet"), a figure of poetry itself.

During the first decade of the new century, he directed much of his energy towards theatre work, co-founding with Lady Gregory the Irish Literary Theatre in 1899 and later the Abbey Theatre. At once aesthetic and political in its aims, the national theatre would be patriotic but produce works of the highest artistic merit. Crucial to the project was finding or creating the right kind of audience: "There is no feeling, except religious feeling, which moves masses of men so powerfully as national feeling, and upon this, more widely spread among all classes in Ireland to-day than at any time this century, we build our principal hopes" (*UP*II 140). Echoing O'Leary's belief in the intimacy between literature and nationality, he argued that "All literature and all art is national" (*UP*II 141). How precisely drama should express the national became a subject of controversy during subsequent years however, resulting in conflict with nationalist audiences who found Synge's plays offensive, and with Arthur Griffith, founder of Sinn Fein, who demanded propagandist drama for the national theatre.

Disillusionment with popular nationalism is readily discernible in Yeats's 1907 essay, "Poetry and Tradition" (*E&I* 246–60). In stark contrast to his earlier hopes for the theatre, he has lost faith in audiences and his power to cultivate them. He praises O'Leary as an embodiment of a romantic nationalism based on respect for artistic distinctiveness and on personal integrity, and he reiterates O'Leary's limited regard for Young Ireland poetry: after all, those who had opposed Synge were "the wreckage of Young Ireland" (*A* 349). He decries the emergence of a mediocre culture of bourgeois prudence: "We had opposing us from the first, though not strongly from the first, a type of mind which had been without influence in the generation of Grattan, and almost without it in that of Davis, and which has made a new nation out of Ireland, that was once old and full of memories" (*E&I* 250). Degeneracy of various kinds has atrophied the political movement, and deprived it of distinguished leadership. These opinions would be played out in various ways for the rest of his life. His later theory of a unified culture is rooted in the tripartite model introduced here, comprising aristocrat, peasant, and artist, linked together by passionate recklessness, long tradition, and the capacity to create "beautiful things" (*E&I* 251).

This model found expression in various poems about the Big House, the first of which, "Upon a House Shaken by the Land Agitation," was an anxious response to the reduction of tenants' rents at Coole by the Irish Land Commission (*VP* 264).[21] The house becomes an emblem of Anglo-Irish power, and a source of cultural energy: "This house has enriched my soul out of measure because here life moves within restraint through gracious forms," he wrote in 1910.[22]

> How should the world be luckier if this house,
> Where passion and precision have been one
> Time out of mind, became too ruinous
> To breed the lidless eye that loves the sun?

The power of the poem is located in the familiar force of Yeats's controlled rhetorical questioning, but also in a phrase like "time out of mind," which vaguely invokes ancient traditions, playing the colloquial against the sonorous, suggesting that the origins are mythic and beyond history. The house synthesizes passion and intellect, implicit in Yeatsian ideas of Unity of Being. The image of the eagle's lidless eye attributes to the Anglo-Irish certain qualities understood to be natural attributes (though the eyes may also suggest the cold stasis of Greek statuary). Suggesting vision and dominance, the image relies on the Blakean distinction, attractive toYeats, between eagle and gregarious crow.

If the decline of landed power offered signs of national enervation, similar fears would dominate the 1914 collection, *Responsibilities*. In a note, Yeats explains the impact certain public events have had on him, illuminating the political background of the sequence beginning with "To a Wealthy Man . . ." and ending with "To a Shade." Three events had "stirred" his imagination: the Parnell, *Playboy*, and Hugh Lane bequest controversies, and he complains of the "lying accusations forgetful of past service," which marked the first (*VP* 818). The word "service" is important, since his heroes are patrons who have served the nation in political or cultural terms. He paves the way for the satirical thrust of "September 1913" by attacking all kinds of devotions not "of the whole being": "Religious Ireland – and the pious Protestants of my childhood were signal examples – thinks of divine things as a round of duties separated from life and not as an element that may be discovered in all circumstance and emotion, while political Ireland sees the good citizen but as a man who holds to certain opinions and not as a man of good will" (*VP* 819). It is a comprehensive vision incorporating both religious traditions, and observing inextricable ties between various branches of culture, each infected with enervating orthodoxies.

In "To a Wealthy Man . . ." he argued for the responsibilities of the aristocracy to offer patronage, independent of popular opinion, citing the examples of Italian Renaissance benefactors, such as Cosimo de Medici (*VP* 287–8). Such patrons might help to "breed the best" in the culture, his diction evincing faith in "good breeding" – a theme he developed insistently, but which emerged forcefully during the 1930s.[23] Elsewhere in the volume, a person is "honour bred" and "Bred to a harder thing," ("To a Friend whose Work has come to Nothing"); in "Pardon, Old Fathers," the speaker boasts he has no blood from a "huckster's loin" (*VP* 291, 269).

Linked to this preoccupation with "breeding," and underlying the collection generally, is an anxiety about the decline of traditions deemed necessary to stem the tide of mediocrity. "September 1913," partly responding to the Hugh Lane crisis, to the machinations of newspaper editor William Martin Murphy, and to the Dublin lockout, concerns the breaking with a noble political tradition, represented variously by O'Leary and the martyrs of 1798 and 1803 (*VP* 289–90).[24] By elegizing "Romantic Ireland," Yeats revives the tradition in literary terms, and vital agents, presumed dead, are re-introduced to the culture:

> What need you, being come to sense,
> But fumble in a greasy till
> And add the halfpence to the pence
> And prayer to shivering prayer, until
> You have dried the marrow from the bone?

The phrase "come to sense" connotes the caricatured shopkeeper's self-interested prudence, suggesting a chilling absence of vitality. Prayer is totted up in a grotesque economy of religious observance. The dutiful, shivering prayers imply a dubious combination of piety and mercantilism.

Yeats was notoriously silent about the subject of the Great War, apart from a couple of lyrics, including "On being asked for a War Poem" (*VP* 359).[25] Though estranged from extreme nationalism by 1914, he saw the war as primarily a British imperial venture, and strove to distance the speaker of "An Irish Airman Foresees his Death" from any note of jingoism (*VP* 328). Despite large numbers of Irish casualties on the Western Front, the confrontation that stirred his imagination was not the battle of the Somme, but Dublin's Easter Rebellion. "Easter 1916" celebrates the romantic energy of revolution, but does so ambiguously (*VP* 391–4). Having lamented the lack of revolutionary spirit in "September 1913," he now witnesses a modern manifestation of it and does not wholly approve. He responded initially to news of the rebellion with dismay ("the Dublin tragedy has been a great sorrow and anxiety"), a dismay that left its mark on the poem (*L* 612). He criticizes the chief participants, implying that by concentrating on a physical force solution, they have turned themselves into stone, and contrasts their petrified state with the active, organic life of nature. He questions the wisdom of self-sacrificial martyrdom ("Was it needless death after all?"), and that holy of holies, the Irish right to strike for freedom, by suggesting that "England may keep faith / For all that is done and said." In important ways, the poem departs from the formulaic conventions of the Davisite tradition.

All of the leaders are commemorated precisely because they have become changed; yet paradoxically, it is that fundamental change that the poet questions. This idea of transformation is central, a miraculous release of energy, and a revelation of Anti-Selves. "All had seemed to him ordinary people," writes Richard Ellmann, "but they had suddenly found their heroic opposites, not like Yeats by effort and discipline, but by the sudden violence of a great action."[26] Yet the poet's ambivalence is clear. Stone hearts represent ideological fixity, perhaps venerated as self-transcendence, but also regretted. The phrase "Hearts with one purpose alone" implies they might reasonably be expected to have more than one purpose. While all around them nature changes, they seem unnaturally rendered into the cold stillness of sculpture. The poem is the opposite of conversational and expansive in tone and syntax, and its insistent rhymes and short trimeters lend an effect of stately but troubled meditation. The final instance of the oxymoron "terrible beauty" might suggest admiration and renewed hopes of redemption, but the poem suggests revolutionary action has been achieved at too high a price. Yeats seems to imply there are values more important than national freedom, that "there are things a man must not do to save a nation."

Not all of Yeats's 1916 poems (not to mention his play of 1919, also a response to the Rising, *The Dreaming of the Bones*) express this degree of ambiguity. "The Rose Tree" offers a stark celebration of the blood sacrifice associated with Pearse's brand of political martyrology, and "Sixteen Dead Men" suggests something similar (*VP* 396, 395). The variety of Yeats's responses to the Rising suggests that the poet's viewpoint is not single and definitive; at the very least, it suggests that individual lyrics cannot be relied upon to reveal his opinions. Skepticism about republican martyrology resurfaces in "On a Political Prisoner" (*VP* 397). The poem, which pictures Markievicz in prison, relies on the same kind of contrast we find in "Easter 1916" between a brilliant past and a degraded present. However, in this poem, there is no transformation of terror into something beautiful. In the past, Markievicz was "clean and sweet" like a seabird, qualities ironically invoked in the grey gull that eats from her hand through the barred window of the cell. Focusing primarily on the woman's decline and fall (as he sees it), the poet ignores her courage and deeply held political convictions, dismissing her as withered and degenerate. Implicitly, the poem is anti-revolutionary, perhaps misogynist, conveying the poet's abhorrence of a generation of insurrectionist women, from whose politics he had grown increasingly distant. This notion that his revolutionary women friends destroyed themselves through hatred recurs in his poetry of this period (perhaps most memorably in "A Prayer for my Daughter" [*VP* 403–6]). Again, it is striking that poems like these appear adjacent to unabashedly revolutionary lyrics like "The Rose Tree," pointing to a capacity to explore a range of positions within the same period.

In 1919, Yeats announced a longing to "hammer [his] thoughts into unity," and wished he could begin a new epoch, based on his doctrine of Unity of Being ("If I Were Four-and-Twenty," *Ex* 263–80). The opposite of Unity of Being was abstraction – "meaning by abstraction not the distinction but the isolation of occupation, or class or faculty" (*A* 164). He used the word "abstraction" and its cognates with notable frequency after 1916, as when the political prisoner's mind is an "abstract thing" (*VP* 397). The heroes of "Easter 1916" suffer an abstraction; marrow is separated from bone in the abstract prayer of "September 1913." Yeats associated the abstract with modernity, logic, and materialism, but also rhetoric, propaganda, Marxism, and much else. He fought against all this with an aesthetic of linguistic vitality associated with Synge and Lady Gregory. For Yeats, "abstract" did not mean merely aesthetic failure, but connoted fundamental poverty at cognitive and political levels. Culture entailed the struggle between the urges for rejuvenation and degeneration by abstract thought. He responded to this perceived degeneration with his doctrines of Unity of Culture and Unity of Being.

In 1917, the year he married, his wife George began doing automatic writing, supposedly dictated by spirit "instructors," which provided Yeats with the data for his occult book, *A Vision* (1925, second version 1937). Variously considered a sacred book, a philosophical analysis of history and personality, or a joke, it has been described in this volume by Margaret Mills Harper as "part cosmology, part apocalypse, part psychoanalysis, part poetry, and part confusion" (p. 160). *A Vision* offers a reading of history, as portrayed in the inter-penetrating gyres or cones, as eternal cyclical recurrence of opposing political dispensations, the rule of the few following the rule of the many. Yeats argued that Bolsheviks had used utopian hopes in order to justify, as in 1917, political massacre: the end was used to justify the means. Marxism for Yeats, with its teleological structure, was "an instrument of destruction and persecution": "men will die and murder for an abstract synthesis" (*VB* 161). Unlike Marxist utopianism, there is no end of history in Yeats's System, each apocalypse giving birth to a new epoch. Hence, the System does not necessarily entail allegiance to either aristocratic or democratic rule, but supposes a viewpoint transcending that dichotomy. (Generally though, the poet favored the former.) The current gyre was "primary," objective, and democratic: "All our scientific, democratic, fact-accumulating, heterogeneous civilization belongs to the outward gyre and prepares not the continuance of itself but the revelation as in a lightning flash . . . of the civilization that must slowly take its place" (*VP* 825). The next gyre would be "antithetical," subjective, and aristocratic. Ireland, he urged, must prepare for the future, rejecting the democratic thinking of the primary gyre. He believed democracy was dying or dead, and would be replaced, unless something was done, by anarchy or by Bolshevism. As a bulwark against these, Yeats affirmed a conservative theory based on oligarchy and an idealized Ascendancy, associated in particular with figures like Burke, Grattan, Swift, Goldsmith, and Berkeley, seen as radical individualists, and opposed to "Whiggery," as he writes in "The Seven Sages" (*VP* 486).

The executions of 1916 hardened nationalist opinion; in 1918, Sinn Fein came to power, ousting the constitutional nationalists under John Redmond. By mid 1920, IRA activity was widespread; Black and Tan atrocities were widely reported (the Black and Tans were an auxiliary force of some 9,500 men, recruited by the Royal Irish Constabulary from the ranks of the British Army and Royal Navy). Exasperated, Yeats complained that Ireland had a "lunatic faculty of going against everything which it believes England to affirm" (*L* 656). He struck a more sympathetic note in his speech to the Oxford Union in February, 1921, when he criticized the Black and Tan war, claiming Sinn Fein had justice on their side. Writing to a correspondent that "we shall have a pleasant life if the treaty is accepted," Yeats was in favor of the 1921 Treaty, but was apprehensive of the hatred and turmoil that might ensue (*L* 678).

When Liam Cosgrave appointed him to the Senate, Yeats was at last able to influence policy. Despite a commendable record of Senate work (including several high-level government missions to London) Yeats could be self-deprecating about his role as politician – he claimed that poetry and the theatre are "matters in which I felt I had a greater right to an opinion than I have in politics" (*SS* 48). He confessed: "In the senate I speak as little about politics as is possible" (*L* 704). Again: "You will forgive me if I forget that I am occasionally a politician, and remember that I am always a man of letters and speak less diplomatically and with less respect for institutions and great names than is, perhaps, usual in public life" (*SS* 47).

Most of his speeches addressed cultural and artistic matters. He was concerned about the preservation of historic and ancient monuments, Irish manuscripts, national treasures and artifacts in the National Museum (at a time when the ruins of many Big Houses were still smoldering, he voiced inquiries about fire safety in the Museum building).[27] He sought to preserve the architectural heritage, and made numerous petitions on behalf of the French paintings of the Lane bequest. Early on, he struck a high Tory note in a speech on the preservation of a "leisured class" (*SS* 38–9). He wished to promote new forms of representation in several spheres – he chaired the committee to design a new national coinage – but disapproved of the adoption of Irish as a national language, arguing that it would be imposed from above, not spoken naturally. He thought it deceptive and impractical to use Irish in Senate prayers, street signs, railway tickets, and so on, since relatively few spoke it. The new father expressed his concern for the rights of children in his efforts to preserve a park in Merrion Square for use by children at play (daughter Anne was born in 1919, son Michael in 1921), and, inspired by Italian social theorists like Gentile, he gave notable speeches on the need to improve the nation's schools. Protective of artistic freedom, he spoke against censorship and, fearing the increasing influence of the Catholic clergy, he fought for the separation of Church and state. In an unusual moment of recognition of Northern Unionists, he suggested Irish unity would be delayed if an independent Ireland became too Catholic.

In his 1925 speech on divorce, he argued for the rights of the Protestant minority, explicitly defending the Anglo-Irish tradition: "We against whom you have done this thing are no petty people. We are one of the great stocks of Europe" (*SS* 99). He predicted, however, that Ireland would slowly become more tolerant, finding encouragement in the Dublin statues of those adulterers, Nelson, O'Connell, and Parnell.[28] He feared that the narrow nationalism he earlier identified with "Paudeen" was helping to shape a rigid, confessional state controlled by a triumphalist Church guided by moralistic zeal. He himself felt the force of all this during the 1920s, when the Catholic press condemned him and his circle as "pagan" and (more hurtfully) "un-Irish."[29]

Partly in response to the government's Censorship Bill of 1928, and in anticipation of further incursions on artistic freedom under a new Fianna Fail administration (victorious in the general election of February, 1932), Yeats established, with George Bernard Shaw, the Irish Academy of Letters, in September, 1932. The foundation of the Academy, like his Senate speeches, exemplifies the lengths to which the poet would go, in the last decade of his life, to offer a leadership role in defending free speech. At the same time, the situation is of course complicated by the fact that his fight against censorship cast him in the role of defender not only of struggling artists but also of Anglo-Irish Protestants, formerly a very powerful class, against the reforms of clergy acting supposedly on behalf of the native Irish majority.

In a 1921 letter to AE, Yeats wrote "We writers are not politicians, the present is not in our charge, but some part of the future is" (*L* 667). A sense of responsibility for posterity is obvious in his speeches, but it is also discernible in the poetry of *The Tower*, dominated by fears of personal and national decline. Yeats noted that the volume expressed great bitterness, yet depended for its power on just that quality (*L* 742). This bitterness is tied to anxieties about the future in the face of the destruction of the Civil War and that greater violence Yeats associated with the forthcoming gyre. In his search for "emblems of adversity" (*VP* 420) the poet expresses a longing for lasting things, balanced with the knowledge of inevitable decline – "And what if my descendants lose the flower . . .?" (*VP* 423). He longs for the continuance of traditional values: "I declare / They shall inherit my pride" (*VP* 414).

Do we regard this as a celebration of the Anglo-Irish alone? Probably not: the title poem itself, in its use of folklore and local legend (Mrs. French, Mary Hynes, Hanrahan), combined with its recognition of the history of Thoor Ballylee and its planter-occupants ("Rough men-at-arms" [*VP* 412]), offers the kind of synthesis between Gaelic, Norman, and Planter cultures undergirding much Revival ideology.[30] *The Tower*, like the Senate speeches, reflects anxiety about the fate of Irish Protestants – not regarded as tyrants but mythologized as passionate individualists, freethinkers, and, in that respect, images of the poet. But we should recognize the degree to which the poet admired the Ascendancy in all its "bloody, arrogant power" (as he would later put it in "Blood and the Moon" [*VP* 480]), defending it with a pugilist's violence, writing with what George Watson has called "a Nietzschean sort of swagger."[31] The desire for cultural synthesis in *The Tower* vies with the affirmation of raw power, in the face of its demise.

Yeats measured the distance between his hero Parnell and modern Ireland's political leaders, including Cosgrave, in his great, bitter poem, "Parnell's Funeral" (*VP* 541–3). They had failed because (as he wrote in the poem's second section, published in 1934) they had not "eaten Parnell's heart." Nevertheless, he praised the Cosgrave administration in an essay written two years earlier, on the eve of the 1932 Fianna Fail electoral victory ("Ireland, 1921–1931"). The government, he then wrote, had had the moral courage, under the influence of Minister of Justice Kevin O'Higgins, to execute seventy-seven republican prisoners: "The Government of the Free State has been proved legitimate by the only effective test; it has been permitted to take life" (*LAR* 231). As before, the idea of public order is paramount, this time achieved by the ruthless shedding of blood. Above all, he applauds the government because "its mere existence delivered us from obsession. No sooner was it established, the civil war behind it, than the musician, the artist, the dramatist, the poet, the student, found – perhaps for the first time – that he could give his whole heart to his work" (*LAR* 232). Political arrangements are viewed as the framework in which the arts can flourish. "Freedom from obsession" is all-important, echoing his concerns about the narrowing of imagination and the descent into abstraction. Yeats had his own obsessions, of course, not least of which in the early 1930s was the need for "public order," which brought him strange bedfellows, including the Blueshirt General Eoin O'Duffy, in the most damaging and futile episode in Yeats's political career.

In February, 1932, a group of former Free State soldiers founded the Army Comrades Association in response to a marked increase in IRA activity and fears of the spread of communism in Ireland – the IRA was bent on denying free speech for pro-Treaty "traitors." By fall, 1932, the ACA had 30,000 members.[32] Convinced that communists in IRA circles might destabilize the government, Yeats and others feared a *coup d'état*, until de Valera began to crack down on IRA activities, which he had formerly tolerated. By April, 1933, he was discussing "a social theory which can be used against communism in Ireland – what looks like emerging is Fascism modified by religion" (*L* 808). Elizabeth Butler Cullingford, responding to Conor Cruise O'Brien's accusing Yeats of fascism, points out that Yeats's ideology as described in this letter, "fascism modified by religion," is unlikely to be fascism at all. Maybe so. But Yeats's attraction to the Blueshirts was more to do with widespread fears of an overthrow of legitimate government by the losing side in the recent Civil War than any ambitions for a European fascist state. Public order, again, was the driving force: "In politics I have but one passion and one thought, rancour against all who, except under the most dire necessity, disturb public order, a conviction that public order cannot long persist without the rule of educated and able men" (*VP* 543). Irish fascism, in Cullingford's words, "was always far more Irish than fascist."[33] It is tempting, but erroneous, to compare Irish fascism with that of Hitler or Mussolini. It would be wrong to deny the anti-democratic precepts of Yeats's thinking at this time, but irresponsible to blur the distinctions between Blueshirt ideology in 1933 and the racist, expansionist worldview, based upon anti-Semitic hatred, of Corporal Hitler.

Yeats was disillusioned when in July, 1933 he met O'Duffy, who was clearly unsympathetic to the poet's dream of a Unity of Culture. By September, Yeats wrote bemusedly about the series of events as a misguided escapade, as "our political comedy" (*L* 815). He attributed his hundred days of fascism to a wayward and poetic passion, which "laid hold upon me with the violence which unfits the poet for all politics but his own" (*VP* 543). This seems to be a recognition of the role of the irrational in his thought and conduct; of the limits of his political sagacity; and of the fact, as Denis Donoghue observed, that Yeats "derived a politics from an aesthetic," recognizing this derivation (in this case) just in time.[34] Frank Kermode made a similar point when he argued Yeats "was sceptical of the nonsense with which he satisfied what we can call his lust for commitment. Now and again he believed some of it, but in so far as his true commitment was to poetry he recognized his fictions as heuristic and dispensable, 'consciously false.'"[35]

Indeed, the fictiveness of Yeats's Irish Enlightenment period is a critical commonplace. Many of his so-called historical personages resemble the figure in the poem "The Fisherman" – "A man who does not exist, / A man who is but a dream" (*VP* 348). Symbolic, diagrammatic, and reduced in portraiture, they have certain values bestowed on them, which they are taken to embody. In this sense, his poetic is linked to his ambitions in *A Vision*, where he attempted to present "stylistic arrangements of experience" (*VB* 25), no more. The same might be said of his image of Parnell (recurrent in the poetry from "Mourn – and Then Onward!" to "Come Gather Round Me, Parnellites"), which differs markedly from the figure historians have given us (*VP* 737, 586). Lyons wrote: "In all of this, it is necessary to insist, there was little enough resemblance to the real Parnell. Or rather, myth and symbol fastened only upon one facet of his character, one aspect of his career, to produce a portrait which, while recognizable, was manifestly distorted."[36]

There are continuities between "The Tower" and the Big House poems of *The Winding Stair and Other Poems* (1933), in how they mythologize the Anglo-Irish, with particular reference to the Gore-Booth home, Lissadell, and Coole Park. If elegy affirms faith in a lasting principle, what is consolatory in poems like "Coole Park, 1929" and "Coole Park and Ballylee, 1931" is the possibility that aristocratic nationalist values might survive (if only in the mind of the reader) the rise of Irish democracy (*VP* 488–92). "In Memory of Eva Gore-Booth and Con Markiewicz" (*VP* 475–6) opens with a golden image of Lissadell, when the named women, scions of the house, were at the height of their beauty. The "light of evening" in the opening scene is recalled ironically in the speaker's final proclamation: "Bid me strike a match and blow." The desire to burn the "great gazebo" and all it represents suggests a mood of exhaustion. The image is reminiscent of the poet's anxiety about fire, revealed in Senate speeches when he lamented the lack of fire precautions in the National Museum, and in letters in which he remarked upon the burning of old homes by the IRA. His proposal to strike the match, however, gestures towards ritualistic cremation, as though lighting a funeral pyre. In these terms, the promised burning is a ritual of purgation, a final gesture of commemoration. If this suggests resignation to defeat and destruction, it accords with the implicit argument of a number of late poems that look upon the coming antithetical gyre with resignation, if not with mounting ecstasy. Indeed, so readily is destruction embraced in certain poems that critics have found them wanting in pity. In "The Gyres," Yeats embraces the prophesied violence of the next epoch with discomfiting boldness. It is possible to feel that the man who flirted with the Blueshirts in 1933 cannot with impunity celebrate with such abandon the bloodshed envisaged here: "What matter though numb nightmare ride on top, / And blood and mire the sensitive body stain? / What matter? Heave no sigh, let no tear drop" (*VP* 564). The poem expresses a belief in the inevitable transformation of society, in the principles of eternal recurrence and conflict, and demonstrates Yeats's notion of tragic joy, that "tragedy is a joy to the man who dies." The reckless tone is at a far remove from the so-called "passive suffering," in Yeats's phrase, of Wilfred Owen (*LE* 199). It differs notably from the elegiac strain found in Yeats's great lamentations for the end of things, "Meditations in Time of Civil War" and "Nineteen Hundred and Nineteen," and from the quasi-exhilarated but fearful, awe-struck note of "The Second Coming" (*VP* 417–33, 401–2). Again, the poet takes different, sometimes self-contradictory positions, expressing different moods, exploring Self and Anti-Self, producing a body of work of great range.

In its celebration of romantic desire, the short lyric "Politics" (*VP* 631) challenges the Thomas Mann quotation cited as epigraph: "In our time the destiny of man presents its meaning in political terms." The poem responds to Archibald MacLeish's view that, while Yeats's language was admirably "public," he had isolated himself in old age, and had failed to deliver his full potential. "Politics" is also a valorization of romantic desire as an appropriate subject for modern poetry: "How can I, that girl standing there, / My attention fix / On Roman or on Russian / Or on Spanish politics?" The lines imply he has at some time tried to focus on international politics (Mussolini, Stalin, Franco), but has failed (at this moment) to do so, or does not care to do so. As the terminal point of the lyric *œuvre*, and so placed, "Politics" is a final rejection of the claim that modern destiny (or poetry) is best understood in light of political processes.[37] However, there is little reason to suppose this was Yeats's definitive opinion on these matters in 1939, the year of publication.

"Under Ben Bulben" (*VP* 636–40) was for a while, but is no more, considered the final poem in Yeats's collected poems. Daunting and imperious, it voices characteristic concerns that modernity has instigated processes of degeneration that might be reversed by the arts. "Do we altogether assent to the samurai stare and certainty . . .?" asks Seamus Heaney; "Do we say yes to this high-stepping tread?"[38] It begins with the word "Swear," in which critics have heard an echo of Hamlet's ghost, as though the whole poem is spoken from beyond the grave.[39] Certainly, this must be how it felt for the readers of Dublin's three main newspapers where the poem was first published, posthumously, on 3 February, 1939. The poem's fourth section hints at a eugenic theme in the address to future poets and sculptors: "Bring the soul of man to God, / Make him fill the cradles right." Eugenics became a paramount concern to Yeats in the 1930s, as the rant in *On the Boiler* indicates.[40] In the poem's fifth section, he addresses Irish poets in particular ("Sing whatever is well made"), managing to combine eugenic theory, snobbery, and distaste for the contemporary. Primarily, he scorns bad poets, but he also implies disdain for those of low social rank. Donoghue wrote of the later poetry: "the political rant is tolerable when we receive it as a poet's rage for order, a revolt against formlessness, vagueness, mess."[41] On the other hand, Terence Brown writes of this poem in particular: "The rant of such a poem, with its obnoxious denunciation of 'Base-born products of base beds' could perhaps be tolerated easily enough along with the foolishness of *On the Boiler*, were it not so mesmeric a performance."[42] Its power to mesmerize can seem unforgivable. We are left with the paradox that the poetry can seem intolerable because, as poetry, it is so powerful. The poet's irrationality, part of his power, is dangerous when he most seems to believe in it.

The obsession with what Jon Stallworthy calls "dynastic continuity," evident in "The Tower," "Under Ben Bulben," and other poems, helped to shape Yeats's final grim, relentless tract, *On the Boiler.*[43] He feared he might lose friends over it, but nonetheless embraced its severity gleefully: "I must lay aside the pleasant paths I have built up for years and seek the brutality, the ill breeding, the barbarism of truth" (*L* 903). It is not clear whether we should treat this fiercely reactionary document as a definitive statement of the poet's beliefs, or as a hyperbolic expression of temporary feelings. It certainly reflects a rage for order, projected onto a public dimension; yet the order envisaged is decidedly non-systemic, anti-corporatist, and romantically individualistic. Yeats returns to the Revival trope of an essential Ireland:

> If ever Ireland again seems molten wax, reverse the process of revolution. Do not try to pour Ireland into any political system. Think first how many able men with public minds the country has, how many it can hope to have in the near future, and mould your system upon those men. It does not matter how you get them, but get them. Republics, Kingdoms, Soviets, Corporate States, Parliaments, are trash, as Hugo said of something else "not worth one blade of grass that God gives for the nest of the linnet." These men, whether six or six thousand, are the core of Ireland, are Ireland itself. (*OTB* 13)

Outrageous and impractical, the proposal is a naïve fantasy of elitist control, perhaps a vision of the sort of order the next gyre would see established. Furthermore, in language borrowed from Raymond B. Cattell's influential 1937 work, *The Fight for Our National Intelligence*, and fueled by recent correspondence with the Eugenics Society, Yeats expresses fears that Europe's uneducated majority will reproduce themselves more effectively than the minority, propagating stupidity and "mob rule." The terms are not unfamiliar, though the tone, dissociated from poetic form, expresses something close to despair.

Yeats was a pre-Holocaust fascist for a season, but only in local terms. He favored leadership of the few, emphatically so in the 1930s, in the face of a democracy that was or seemed to be in collusion with the Church. Yet, he was frequently skeptical of his role as public man, partly because politics would dilute his artistic vision and waste his energy (at which times he would curse politics), and partly because he felt himself unfitted to be a political thinker. At such times, he would make self-deprecating remarks about his abilities, as he did in the 1920s, or (as in 1934) beg pardon for his folly.

In a letter of April, 1936, Yeats responded to his communist friend Ethel Mannin, who, with Ernst Toller, had asked him to write a letter nominating the German poet Ossietsky for the Nobel Prize, as a method of securing his release from a Nazi concentration camp in which he was incarcerated and suffering from tuberculosis. Partly wishing to distance himself from Mannin's communism, Yeats refused, claiming he no longer took part in international politics:

> Do not try to make a politician out of me, even in Ireland I shall never I think be that again – as my sense of reality deepens, and I think it does with age, my horror at the cruelty of governments grows greater, and if I did what you want, I would seem to hold one form of government more responsible than any other, and that would betray my convictions. Communist, Fascist, nationalist, clerical, anti-clerical, are all responsible according to the number of their victims. I have not been silent; I have used the only vehicle I possess – verse. (*L* 850–1)

We are familiar with his aversion to the political domain. Yet the letter contains some of the contradictions that pervade the later politics. In retrospect, given what we know about Nazi concentration camps (although that is certainly not what anyone in Ireland in 1936 could have known) the refusal seems monstrous. On the other hand, he takes a stand on his principles, arguing that all governments are more or less corrupt. His condemnation of various beliefs is understandable, in light of his disillusionment with nationalism and fascism, his hatred of communism, his vendetta with clericalism, although it seems unconvincing to tar all "-isms" with the same brush. Without budging on the issue of this prisoner in particular, he expresses humanitarian concern for all victims of state cruelty, making a plea for the power of poetry.

NOTES

1. In his *W. B. Yeats: A Life I: The Apprentice Mage 1865–1914* (Oxford and New York: Oxford University Press, 1997), R. F. Foster has portrayed the Anglo-Irish community as becoming increasingly marginal in relation to the center of Irish political and cultural life during this period. Yeats's family, related to trade on the maternal side, and to dwindling property on the impecunious, bohemian, nationalist father's side, is portrayed as marginal in relation to the center of propertied, Unionist, Church of Ireland Anglo-Ireland.
2. Yeats came to think of the death of Parnell in 1891 as a watershed for his movement and sought to fill the apparent political vacuum with cultural work. However, historians have questioned Yeats's poetic rendition of the period, arguing that he exaggerated the extent of this "vacuum." See F. S. L. Lyons, "Yeats and Victorian Ireland," in *Yeats, Sligo and Ireland*, ed. A. Norman Jeffares (Totowa, NJ: Barnes & Noble, 1980), pp. 115–38; Foster, *Yeats: A life I*, p. 41; and Alvin Jackson, *Ireland 1798–1998* (Oxford: Blackwell, 1999), p. 174.
3. John S. Kelly, "The fifth bell: race and class in Yeats's political thought," in *Irish Writers and Politics*, ed. Okifumi Komesu and Masaru Sekine (Savage, MD: Barnes & Noble, 1990), p. 114.
4. The phrase is T. S. Eliot's from his well-known essay, "The metaphysical poets."
5. Conor Cruise O'Brien, "Passion and cunning: an essay on the politics of W. B.Yeats," in *In Excited Reverie*, ed. A. Norman Jeffares and K. G. W. Cross (London: Macmillan, 1965), pp. 207–78; George Orwell, "W. B.Yeats," *Horizon* (January, 1943), reprinted in *Collected Essays, Journalism and Letters of George Orwell: My Country Left or Right, 1940–43*, Vol. II, ed. Sonia Orwell and Ian Angus (New York: Harcourt, Brace & World, 1968), pp. 271–6.
6. Denis Donoghue, *We Irish: Essays on Irish Literature and Society* (New York: Knopf, 1986); Patrick Maume, "Yeats, William Butler," in *The Oxford Companion to Irish History*, ed. S. J. Connolly (Oxford: Oxford University Press, 1999), p. 601.
7. Seamus Deane, *Celtic Revivals: Essays in Modern Irish Literature 1880–1980* (London and Boston: Faber and Faber, 1985).
8. Declan Kiberd, *Inventing Ireland: The Literature of the Modern Nation* (Cambridge, MA: Harvard University Press, 1995); Edward Said, *Orientalism* (New York: Vintage Books, 1979 [1978]).
9. R. F. Foster, "Yeats at war: poetic strategies and political reconstruction," in *The Irish Story: Telling Tales and Making It Up in Ireland* (London: Allen Lane; Penguin, 2001), p. 60.
10. Charles Ferral, *Modernist Writing and Reactionary Politics* (Cambridge: Cambridge University Press, 2001), p. 21.
11. Terence Brown, *Ireland: A Social and Cultural History, 1922–1979* (London: Fontana, 1981), p. 341.

12. Hazard Adams, "Yeats and antithetical nationalism," reprinted in *Yeats's Political Identities*, ed. Jonathan Allison (Ann Arbor: University of Michigan Press, 1996), p. 310.
13. Michael North, *The Political Aesthetic of Yeats, Eliot, and Pound* (New York and Cambridge: Cambridge University Press, 1991), pp. 54–5.
14. Elizabeth Butler Cullingford, *Yeats, Ireland and Fascism* (London: Macmillan, 1980), p. 235.
15. Elizabeth Butler Cullingford, *Gender and History in Yeats's Love Poetry* (Cambridge: Cambridge University Press, 1993), p. 8.
16. Kelly, "The fifth bell," p. 117.
17. Foster, "Yeats at war," p. 70.
18. Foster, *Yeats: A Life* I, p. 43.
19. John Eglinton, *Irish Literary Portraits* (London: Macmillan, 1935), p. 23.
20. Foster, *Yeats: A Life* I, p. 122.
21. The poem responds to the Land Commission's granting a 20 percent reduction in rents to tenants on the Coole estate. Behind this lay the Wyndham Act, 1903, and the Irish Land Bill, 1908, which evidenced the government's determination to transfer land ownership. See Donoghue, *We Irish*, pp. 53–4.
22. Quoted in A. Norman Jeffares, *A New Commentary on the Poems of W. B. Yeats* (London: Macmillan, 1984), p. 93.
23. Kelly has argued that conservative ideas of "good breeding" and careful sexual selection became increasingly important to Yeats, associated in his mind with the maintenance of social order and the continuity of the Ascendancy (p. 145). Also on this topic, see Marjorie Howes, *Yeats's Nations: Gender, Class, and Irishness* (Cambridge: Cambridge University Press, 1996), pp. 115–20.
24. William Martin Murphy opposed the construction of a Dublin gallery designed to house the Hugh Lane pictures, and supported the employers who locked out the Dublin tramway workers who had joined Jim Larkin's Irish Trade Union. In a public letter, Yeats supported the trade unionists, in the face of massive capitalist and clerical opposition to Larkin's socialist mission. See Cullingford, *Yeats, Ireland and Fascism*, pp. 80–2.
25. On Yeats and the Great War, see Fran Brearton, *The Great War in Irish Poetry: W. B. Yeats to Michael Longley* (Oxford: Oxford University Press, 2000), pp. 43–82, and Foster, "Yeats at war." Foster argues the poet "practiced a deliberate amnesia about the 1914–18 war" (p. 78).
26. Richard Ellmann, *Yeats: The Man and the Masks*, 2nd edn. (New York: Norton, 1978), pp. 220–1.
27. Between December, 1921 and March, 1923, 192 Big Houses were burnt in Ireland (Brown, *Ireland*, p. 110).
28. These provide the theme of his 1925 poem "The Three Monuments" (*VP* 460), in which he imagines the amorous "rascals" defying pious claims that "purity" was a founding value of the Free State.
29. Yeats was vilified by the Irish *Catholic Bulletin* and other journals for alleged obscenity, anti-Catholicism, and plain snobbery. See Cullingford, *Gender and History*, pp. 140–50.
30. Brown, *Ireland*, p. 122.
31. George J. Watson, *Irish Identity and the Literary Revival: Synge, Yeats, Joyce, and O'Casey* (London: Croom Helm, 1979), p. 129.

32. Cullingford, *Yeats, Ireland and Fascism*, p. 201.
33. *Ibid.*, p. 200.
34. Denis Donoghue, *Yeats* (London: Fontana, 1971), p. 125.
35. Frank Kermode, *The Sense of an Ending: Studies in the Theory of Fiction* (New York: Oxford University Press, 1967), p. 104.
36. F. S. L. Lyons, *Charles Stewart Parnell* (London: Fontana, 1978), p. 611.
37. For discussion of the order of the last poems, see Warwick Gould, "The definitive edition: a history of the final arrangements of Yeats's work," in *Yeats's Poems*, ed. A. Norman Jeffares (Dublin: Gill and Macmillan, 1989), pp. 706–49.
38. Seamus Heaney, *Preoccupations: Selected Prose, 1968–1978* (London and Boston: Faber and Faber, 1980), p. 100.
39. Hugh Kenner, "The three deaths of Yeats," in *Yeats: An Annual of Critical and Textual Studies*, 5 (1987), p. 92.
40. Other critics, particularly Howes, and Paul Scott Stanfield, *Yeats and Politics in the 1930s* (London: Macmillan, 1988), have explored the eugenics theme in greater depth.
41. Donoghue, *Yeats*, p. 122.
42. Brown, *Ireland*, p. 369.
43. Jon Stallworthy, *Vision and Revision in Yeats's Last Poems* (Oxford: Clarendon Press, 1969), p. 9.

12

MARJORIE HOWES

Yeats and the postcolonial

Any reader of Yeats who begins to investigate the topic of "Yeats and the postcolonial" will quickly encounter a problem: there is very little agreement among scholars about what "postcolonial" means. As a result, the reader will realize that she will have trouble approaching this topic in what might have seemed like an obvious manner: by trying to determine whether or not Yeats is a postcolonial writer or by trying to determine whether or not Ireland is a postcolonial nation. I think this apparent difficulty is a good thing; rather than being an obstacle in the reader's way, it is precisely what makes it useful to explore the relationship between Yeats's writings and postcolonial studies. This exploration may raise more questions than it answers, and the reader may find this frustrating, but if she can adjust her expectations, she will also find that there are varieties of uncertainty that are more illuminating, and even more enjoyable, than certainty. Yeats himself repeatedly emphasized the important and productive nature of such experiences. In 1898, while considering one of his perennial dilemmas, the question of whether the "visions" he saw were reflections of some eternal reality or merely the products of his own mind, he concluded, "To answer is to take sides in the only controversy in which it is greatly worth taking sides, and in the only controversy which may never be decided" (*E&I* 152). I am not, of course, arguing for the singular importance of postcolonial studies or postcolonial questions for Yeats; as the other essays in this volume attest, there are many controversies about Yeats's works that are worth engaging in. But I think the idea that it is the really interesting questions that are the most difficult to settle, so characteristic of Yeats, indicates a fruitful approach to the topic of this chapter. In what follows I will offer some ideas about how the issues, debates, and uncertainties that animate contemporary postcolonial studies can enrich the experience of reading Yeats.

In the broadest terms, postcolonial studies investigates the relationship between politics and culture in the context of the historical processes associated with colonization, decolonization, and globalization. These historical processes involve hybridizing, fluid cultural exchanges among nations, and unequal, often brutal, power relationships among them as well. Postcolonial scholars draw their theoretical frameworks and methods of investigation from a number of intellectual traditions, such as Marxism, feminism, poststructuralism, and psychoanalysis. They also identify, analyze, and employ various alternative intellectual traditions, local or indigenous knowledges, and counter-memories, such as religion and occultism, folklore, and popular culture. They are often based in literature departments, and their work is also often interdisciplinary to some extent, spanning literary and cultural studies, history, political economy, anthropology, and other fields. Postcolonial scholarship includes several general kinds of intellectual project: analyses of colonialism, investigations of nationalism and other forms of anti-colonial resistance, and recoveries of the subaltern cultural practices, experiences, and histories that are often erased by colonialism and anticolonialism alike.

The political opinions, value, and implications of Yeats's writings have been the subject of lively academic discussion for some time.[1] In recent years, scholars interested in postcolonial studies have continued this conversation by taking up that field's intellectual projects in relation to Yeats, whose life and writings offer numerous, and often confusing, opportunities for pursuing each one. Predictably enough, the results have varied widely. For example, Seamus Deane has read Yeats as "an almost perfect example of the colonialist mentality."[2] In response, Edward Said has suggested we could "more accurately see in Yeats a particularly exacerbated example of the nativist (e.g. negritude) phenomenon."[3] Nativism is a form of nationalism that is anti-imperialist yet derived from imperial structures of thought; like imperialism, it insists on an absolute distinction between the colonizer and the colonized, but it praises the colonized rather than denigrating them. The term enables Said to acknowledge Yeats's debt to imperialism and still praise his "considerable achievement in decolonization."[4] Depending on which texts or periods of his career we focus on and what methods of analysis we employ, Yeats can appear as a trenchant critic of imperialism, a closet imperialist, an apologist for the colonial ruling class in Ireland (the Protestant Anglo-Irish), a committed member of the first postcolonial Irish government, or a fierce opponent of that government's policies and its conception of national identity. His commitment to several varieties of Irish nationalism can appear as an influential means of national liberation, an Irish Protestant's attempt to dissolve or evade sectarian conflict through an appeal to a shared Irish culture, or a colonialist appropriation of decolonizing, nationalist tropes. And his interest in Irish folklore, the Irish peasantry, and the occult can be read as commitments to the subaltern cultures and resistances of the colonized, or as forms of orientalism, in which Yeats projected onto "others" various exotic qualities and forms of knowledge that fascinated him. Jahan Ramazani's "W. B. Yeats: a postcolonial poet?" points out that claims for or against each of these readings will necessarily invoke particular definitions of the postcolonial, and his essay helpfully "parses multiple definitions of postcoloniality in relation to Yeats."[5] I will also examine multiple definitions of the postcolonial in relation to Yeats. I find this approach the most useful, not simply because many individual and competing definitions of the postcolonial can be applied to Yeats, but, further, because Yeats's writings and the field of postcolonial studies as a whole share many of the same commitments, issues, and questions.

Scholars in postcolonial studies use the term "postcolonial" all the time, and they frequently discuss the pros and cons of its various definitions. But no consensus has emerged about which definition of the postcolonial is best. Each current usage has strengths and limitations; it clarifies some issues and muddies others. One reason for this is that different scholars have approached the problem of definition through different kinds of questions. Some ask: where is the postcolonial? Others ask: when is the postcolonial? And still others ask: what is the postcolonial? There are several related terms that could help us distinguish among these questions and possible answers to them: "postcolonialism," "postcoloniality," "postcolonial" as an adjective, and the term I've chosen to use in this chapter, "the postcolonial" as a noun. But this has not happened in any systematic way in the critical literature. For example, postcolonial studies has no clear analogue to the distinction between the term "modern," which usually denotes a historical period, and "Modernism," which usually refers to a particular literary movement that produced particular kinds of writing. Students of history will be quick to point out that, depending on who we ask, the modern period can begin anytime between the Renaissance and the early twentieth century. And students of literature will be equally quick to point out that recent scholarship has expanded the definition of literary Modernism to include an ever increasing proportion of the literature written in the first half of the twentieth century, a shift indicated by the use of terms like the plural "Modernisms," or "alternative Modernisms." But the vocabulary that enables a general distinction between issues of periodization and those of literary production remains fairly stable, even though its terms are constantly debated and revised. In postcolonial studies, on the other hand, questions of when, what, or where the postcolonial "is" are often tangled together.

To begin our investigation of how these questions can illuminate Yeats's writings, it will be helpful to disentangle them – to the extent that we can. We will take the question of "where" first. Postcolonial studies asserts that colonization and decolonization exert formative influences on literatures and cultures – but which literatures and cultures? For some scholars the answer is "all of them"; they define the postcolonial as a global condition or era, and insist that we should re-read everything, including the literature of Western, metropolitan, imperial powers, to uncover how colonialism and its aftermath shaped them. Their work often defines the postcolonial as the moment when the West could no longer think of itself as the unquestioned center of the world, and demonstrates how the foundations of Western philosophy, history, and literature – concepts like Reason, Progress, Humanity, the Sublime, the Beautiful – are thoroughly implicated in and even dependent upon imperialism.[6] Other scholars claim that some parts of the globe are postcolonial and others are not. Some make this distinction by taking "postcolonial" to mean "Third World," a term that was originally coined during the Cold War to name the parts of the globe not included in either the First World (the United States and its allies) or the Second World (the Soviet bloc). This definition encompasses virtually all non-Western nations: those the West dominated through colonial conquest and those it dominated by other means, like economic influence. One problem with it is that it gives us no way to describe what was specific or different about colonization as a means of control. An alternative definition of the postcolonial that addresses this problem rests on the sheer fact of colonization, characterizing any nation that was once ruled by another as postcolonial. But under this definition the United States, which currently dominates the rest of the globe in a number of ways, becomes a postcolonial nation, and this clearly violates some scholars' sense of what the postcolonial means.[7]

Some nations, like India, fall easily into the category of the postcolonial no matter which geographical definition we cite. But Ireland is a different matter. In terms of culture, religion, social structures, and living standards, twentieth-century Ireland is far more reasonably classified as part of the West or First World than as part of the non-West or Third World. In addition, nineteenth-century Ireland, or parts of it, helped build and maintain the British Empire. Scores of Irish men, many (but by no means all) of them Protestants, became British soldiers or colonial administrators. And much of Catholic Ireland enthusiastically endorsed the Christian missionary projects that were an important part of European imperial ideology and practice. On the other hand, if we emphasize the fact of colonization Ireland begins to look more postcolonial. Ireland waged a long and at least partially successful struggle to free itself from British control, and many, though not all, people involved in or affected by that struggle have seen it as an anti-colonial one. There is some disagreement among scholars about whether or not we should call British control of Ireland colonization.[8] But many features of that control do fit well with colonial models of domination: a native population distinguished from the ruling classes, in this case by religion, and denied the full rights of citizenship on that basis; a native language that the colonial authorities tried to eradicate; a native culture whose difference from British culture became a nationalist rallying point. Ireland, then, was both a partner in the British imperial project and a victim of it. The fascinating complexity of Ireland's historical relation to colonization and decolonization becomes visible only if we keep several competing definitions of the postcolonial in mind rather than trying to choose one. The most adequate way to represent Ireland's relation to the question of where we should locate the postcolonial might be a series of transparent maps laid over one another.

When we turn to Yeats's writings, we find that a similarly complex, and even confusing, geographical imagination structures his representations of Ireland's relation to the political and cultural results of colonization, decolonization, and globalization. One Yeatsian map would show the whole earth from space. It would cast Ireland, or certain elements of Irish culture, as just one point of access among many to the eternal truths, beauties, or conflicts whose essences were constant throughout the world, though they might reveal themselves through different forms in different places. Rather than being Eurocentric, this global perspective is often radically equalizing. In his 1900 essay on Shelley, for example, Yeats lists the "ministering spirits" of Intellectual Beauty as "the Devas of the East, and the Elemental Spirits of mediaeval Europe, and the Sidhe of ancient Ireland" (*E&I* 74), and his 1902 critique of Matthew Arnold's *On the Study of Celtic Literature* insists that the properties Arnold identifies as specifically Celtic originally belonged to all ancient, "primitive" peoples. In his autobiography, he speculates that "In Christianity what was philosophy in Eastern Asia became life, biography and drama" (*A* 346), and asks "Was the *Bhagavad Gita* the 'scenario' from which the Gospels were made?" (*A* 346). Later in his career, this map would also suggest that the rise and fall of empires, Eastern or Western, ancient or modern, was all part of the global, cyclical, historical process he outlined in *A Vision*. In *A Vision*, Yeats rejects the Eurocentrism of much Western philosophy, commenting, "Hegel identifies Asia with Nature; he sees the whole process of civilisation as an escape from Nature, partly achieved by Greece, fully achieved by Christianity" (*VB* 202). Instead, Yeats's System denies Hegelian theories of progress, and impartially asserts that human civilization is dominated alternately by East and West. Civilization does not advance, it merely undergoes cyclical change, and all stages are of equal value: "The historian thinks of Greece as an advance on Persia, of Rome as in something or other an advance of Greece, and thinks it impossible that any man could prefer the hunter's age to the agricultural. I, upon the other hand, must think all civilisations equal at their best; every phase returns, therefore in some sense every civilisation" (*VB* 206).

Another map offered by Yeats's writings would conflict with the global perspective; it would show Ireland as part of Europe or the West generally, and the West as opposed to the rest of the world. It would reveal Yeats as a cultural and even a military imperialist, convinced of the West's superiority and bent on drawing Ireland into it. Yeats described writers like Shelley, Blake, Shakespeare, Dante, and Balzac as his formative influences, and repeatedly traced the genealogy of all that was best in his own work and in Irish civilization to Western traditions, such as the European Renaissance and ancient Greece. In "To a Wealthy Man who promised a second Subscription to the Dublin Municipal Gallery if it were proved the People wanted Pictures" (*VP* 287), for example, the speaker looks to the model of Renaissance Italy, whose art drew inspiration from "the dugs of Greece" and flourished under the patronage of cultured aristocrats. And the speaker of "To a Young Beauty" (*VP* 335) asserts that one reward of the difficult life of an artist will be that he "may dine at journey's end / With Landor and with Donne." Some aspects of Yeats's lifelong fascination with India fit into this map as forms of orientalism. For both the early and the late Yeats, India was the alluring embodiment of states of unity and wisdom unavailable in Western culture, but it was also feminine, infantile, and even threatening. While *A Vision*'s *literal* geography insists that Asian civilizations were just as potentially worthy as Western civilizations, it also employs a *symbolic* geography that valued the qualities Yeats labeled Western or Hellenic over those it designated as Eastern or Asiatic. Thus Yeats equates "Asiatic" with "barbaric" (*VB* 269) and describes "an Asiatic and anarchic Europe" (*VB* 283) during (roughly) the eighth, ninth, and tenth centuries CE. Similarly, the late poem "The Statues" (*VP* 610–11) combines European cultural and military might, praising the European victory over "All Asiatic vague immensities" at the battle of Salamis and, more important, through the intellect and calculation of Greek sculpture. Occasionally, when it suited him, Yeats also attacked this Eurocentric map of the world precisely for the imperialist violence it implied. When, in 1925, he argued against the Irish Free State's plan to prohibit divorce among all Irish citizens, Catholics and Protestants alike, he compared such an effort to make Catholic social teachings law with the imperialist arrogance of missionaries and the tyrannies of the Spanish Inquisition (*UP*II 450).

Still another Yeatsian map would emphasize Ireland's colonial subjugation to Great Britain and its potential affinities with other colonized peoples. As a young man, Yeats moved in nationalist circles, particularly under the influence of John O'Leary and Maud Gonne, and joined the Irish Republican Brotherhood. His 1902 essay on the English poet Edmund Spenser, who was a major influence on Yeats's early writings and who spent part of his life as a colonial administrator in Ireland, argues that Spenser's artistic and intellectual limitations spring from his loyalty to the Elizabethan colonial state. Spenser experienced and wrote about Ireland "as an official" rather than "as a poet merely" (*E&I* 372). As a result, he "never understood the people he lived among" (*E&I* 361) and saw "nothing but disorder" (*E&I* 373) in Ireland, instead of comprehending the richness and creative potential of the Irish landscape and folk imagination. Yeats offers an acute analysis of the flawed "logic" of colonialist ideology: "Like an hysterical patient he drew a complicated web of inhuman logic out of the bowels of an insufficient premise – there was no right, no law, but that of Elizabeth, and all that opposed her opposed themselves to God, to civilisation, and to all inherited wisdom and courtesy, and should be put to death" (*E&I* 361). His comment also anticipates the work of postcolonial scholars like Frantz Fanon in suggesting that colonialism produces psychosis in the colonizer, not just in the colonized.[9]

The bitter late poem "The Ghost of Roger Casement" (*VP* 583–4) also belongs to this map. Born in Ireland, Casement joined the British diplomatic service, and was knighted in 1911 for his work exposing imperialist atrocities in the Belgian Congo and the Putumayo region of Peru. He joined the Irish nationalist movement in 1913, tried to drum up German support for an Irish rising during World War I, and arranged to have German weapons shipped to Irish rebels. He was arrested by the British in 1916 and hanged for treason. In the poem, the ghost of Casement, who combined a commitment to Irish nationalism with opposition to imperialist violence in Africa and South America, also indicts British imperialism in India:

John Bull has gone to India
And all must pay him heed,
For histories are there to prove
That none of another breed
Has had a like inheritance,
Or sucked such milk as he,
And there's no luck about a house
If it lack honesty.

The poem glances ironically back towards "To a Wealthy Man . . ." and mocks Britain's claim that it sucked from the dugs of a superior civilization. It points out that such claims are part of an imperial strategy to justify colonialism by writing "histories" to "prove" that the colonized are barbarians in need of civilization. Postcolonial studies critiques such histories and works to write or uncover alternatives to them. The ghost of the executed Casement performs both those functions here, haunting the British empire with its own brutality and dishonesty, and bodying forth the people, narratives, and memories it sought to erase. The refrain, "*The ghost of Roger Casement / Is beating on the door*," suggests that the recovery of those ghosts inaugurates the empire's disintegration, and every stanza figures the empire's weakness or eventual demise in some way.

The point I would like to emphasize about these maps is not that Yeats's writings or his political thinking were contradictory or inconsistent, though that is true enough in some respects. Rather, I wish to stress the idea that colonization, decolonization, Eurocentrism, and globalizing cultural relativism – as historical realities, as possible outcomes to be feared or desired, as figures or tropes – offered Yeats a number of different intellectual and rhetorical possibilities. They provided him with various ways of thinking and talking about Ireland (and other places, for that matter). The fact that these various ways were sometimes conflicting indicates that, faced with the complexities of Irish history, his particular origins, and the traditions that enabled his own work, Yeats shared some of the geographical hesitations that we also find in the field of postcolonial studies. In addition, claims that Ireland "is" or "is not" postcolonial are often as much political statements as they are intellectual conclusions. And as Ramazani observes, "the issue of Yeats's 'eligibility' for postcolonial status depends not merely on questions of definition; it inevitably gets entangled in institutional interests,"[10] as some scholars rush to include Yeats in the category of the postcolonial, which is privileged in much contemporary scholarship, while others want to defend him from being taken up, inappropriately and opportunistically, by the latest academic fad. Here geography and our map metaphor prove insufficient by themselves; each of our maps should come with two keys: one indicating which aspects of Yeats's works or Ireland it helps illuminate, the other describing whose political or institutional interests it might support and why.

When we move from the question of "where" the postcolonial might be to the question of "when," a different set of uncertainties presents itself.[11] The postcolonial appears to demand a temporal definition: the literal meaning of "post" in this and other terms like "postmodern" is "after." But defining the postcolonial as after the colonial turns out to be more complicated than one might think. For one thing, it is not always easy to tell when colonialism ends, even if we take formal independence as the major criterion. If Ireland was once a colonized nation, when did the colonial period give way to the postcolonial? A case could be made for the Easter Rising of 1916, the Treaty of 1921, the 1937 constitution, the 1949 repeal of the External Relations Act, the recent Good Friday peace accords, or some future resolution of the Northern Irish problem. Another question that has caused some debate among scholars concerns the precise connotations of "post." To what extent does the postcolonial represent a new departure from the colonial? To what extent should we think of it as the aftermath of the colonial, marked by the legacy and effects of colonialism? Too much emphasis on the first risks being naïve and premature and assuming that colonialism is over and done with. It can make it harder to recognize neo-colonialism – in which former colonial powers continue to dominate nominally independent countries through indirect economic influence – and the persistence of other oppressive structures within postcolonial nations. Too much emphasis on the second runs the opposite risk of reductively conceptualizing the complex social, cultural, and political life of newly independent nations primarily in terms of the colonial legacy. In addition, in the context of decolonization, the new ruling classes often place a political premium on declaring the new state fully independent and eradicating (or, at a minimum, concealing) continuities with the colonial period or power, while their opponents seek to declare the revolution unfinished and to expose the lingering colonial elements. Thus here again, judgements about when the colonial gives way to the postcolonial, about postcolonial change and postcolonial continuity, are bound up with political and institutional interests.

In Ireland, where violent political revolution went along with social and economic conservatism that was anything but revolutionary, and where partition led to a continuing British presence in the North, questions of postcolonial change versus continuity were highly contentious. As a Senator from 1922 to 1928, Yeats participated in the process of forming the Irish Free State. He had long found theories characterizing historical change as violent rupture appealing, and during this period in particular he was both interested in the notion that a postcolonial Ireland should be or had been transformed, and acutely aware that this notion had a wide currency in Irish public opinion. As a result, we cannot reliably separate his personal opinions from the rhetorical strategies he hoped to employ persuasively as a "smiling public man" (*VP* 443), as he described himself in "Among School Children." That poem was prompted in part by Yeats's visits to Irish primary schools as part of his Senatorial work. In a resulting 1925 article on the state of those schools, he expressed a sense of postcolonial potential and creativity: "Ireland has been put into our hands that we may shape it, and I find all about me in Ireland to-day a new overflowing life" (*UP*II 455), even though he also found that "the schools in Ireland are not fit places for children" (*UP*II 456). In "Ireland, 1921–1931" Yeats organized his assessment of the

Free State's first decade around a series of postcolonial transformations. The article begins:

> I walked along the south side of the Dublin quays a couple of years ago; looked at the funnels of certain Dublin steamers and found that something incredible had happened; I had not shuddered with disgust though they were painted green on patriotic grounds; that deep olive green seemed beautiful. I hurried to the Parnell Monument and looked at the harp. Yes, that too was transfigured; it was a most beautiful symbol; it had ascended out of sentimentality, out of insincere rhetoric, out of mob emotion . . . Our Government has not been afraid to govern, and that has changed the symbols, and not for my eyes only.
> (*UP*II 486–7)

Yeats traces a transformation from the nominally postcolonial to the truly postcolonial, or from aftermath to new departure, through a change in the meaning of nationalist symbols. Because the new state has proved itself capable of governing, the color green and the harp no longer embody a nationalism that is insincere and sentimental. Freed from the overwhelming necessity of resisting British rule, Irish national feeling has entered a new, more liberating phase. The issue Yeats addresses here is an important topic of debate in postcolonial studies: is narrow nationalism a necessary stage in anti-colonial struggles, one that can then give way to more liberal and more genuinely postcolonial conceptions of national community and culture after independence? Yeats answers yes, and emphasizes the sudden, "incredible," almost magical nature of the transformation. He also notes that on a personal level, "Freedom from obsession brought me a transformation akin to religious conversion" (*UP*II 488). It is natural to want to speculate about the extent to which such utterances may or may not have reflected Yeats's sincere beliefs. Even if we could answer that question, for my purposes here that would be less important than observing that Yeats inhabited and spoke to a historical and cultural situation that was structured by the temporal issues that are central to postcolonial studies.

As we have already seen, in other moods and other moments during the 1920s, and especially the 1930s, Yeats was a fierce critic of the new nation. His critiques often denied the Irish Free State's claims to just the sort of transformation he gave them credit for in "Ireland, 1921–1931," and asserted postcolonial Ireland's crippling continuities with the injustices of the colonial period. In "The Great Day" (*VP* 590), written in 1937, the poem's title makes fun of the very notion of a transformative moment or a "great day" when Ireland left the oppression of the colonial and entered the liberation of the postcolonial:

Hurrah for revolution and more cannon shot!
A beggar upon horseback lashes a beggar upon foot.
Hurrah for revolution and cannon come again!
The beggars have changed places, but the lash goes on.

The postcolonial reveals itself as a repetition, with one small inversion, of the colonial: "The beggars have changed places but the lash goes on." The poem's structure, based on repetition and parallelism, also embodies this negative reading of the postcolonial as the damaged aftermath or continuation of the colonial. "Parnell" and "Church and State" .conduct similar critiques.

"Easter 1916" (*VP* 391–4) is a postcolonial poem, in the sense that it grapples with the temptations, dangers, and ambiguities of defining the postcolonial in temporal terms and casting a particular event as a transformative or foundational moment. The poem is driven by a tension between the speaker's certainty that the Easter Rising represents such a moment: "All changed, changed utterly," and his anxious uncertainty about what that change means. Or, as David Lloyd has put it, "the question posed is the relation between the singular moment in which a nation is founded or constituted and the future history of the citizens it brings into being."[12] The speaker stands poised, as it were, on the edge of the postcolonial, and tries to peer into the darkness ahead. Like many of Yeats's poems, "Easter 1916" progresses, not from uncertainty to certainty, but from some uncertainty to even more. The speaker begins by acknowledging that he must revise his previous attitude towards the rebels. Whatever they are now, political martyrs, tragic victims, foolish children (all ideas the poem tries at some point), they are no longer what they were for the speaker: the objects of class-based elitism, condescending politeness, and secret scorn. This rejection of a previous (colonial) state is the poem's closest approach to a firm conclusion or position. The "terrible beauty" is unresolvably contradictory, and the speaker remains ambivalent about the rebels, the Rising, and the human cost involved.

In the final stanza, the uncertainties multiply. The speaker asks and cannot answer a series of questions about the relationship between the current moment and future outcomes and judgements: "when may it suffice?" and "Was it needless death after all?" and "what if excess of love / Bewildered them till they died?" The declaration that follows, "I write it out in a verse," which sounds so assertive and certain, and seems to give the poet a clear role as official memorialist for the rebels, actually marks the point where he abandons the attempt to answer questions or reach conclusions about how the rebels should be judged or what may lie ahead.[13] Instead, he simply lists the names:

MacDonagh and MacBride
And Connolly and Pearse
Now and in time to be,
Wherever green is worn,
Are changed, changed utterly:
A terrible beauty is born.

At the beginning of the poem, the refrain seemed revolutionary, revelatory. By the end, however, what strikes the reader about these lines is how little they tell her.[14] In contrast to "Ireland, 1921–1931," here the color green indicates a nationalism, and a way of remembering the rebels, that make the speaker uncomfortable because there is something insincere, sentimental, or rhetorical about them. The very last line of the poem is actually "*September 25, 1916*," emphasizing the speaker's particular location in history, immersed in the moment of possible change rather than viewing it with the knowledge and clarity of hindsight. The poem enacts a discovery; it discovers the relative emptiness of claims about revolutionary or decolonizing moments, temporal transitions from the colonial to the postcolonial. It discovers, in other words, a problem that has been central to discussions in postcolonial studies about "when" the postcolonial might occur and what that might mean. Like the geographical, the temporal approach to defining the postcolonial proves insufficient by itself, and demands other approaches as its necessary supplements.

This brings us to the question of "what." Many scholars who take this approach define the postcolonial as resistance to colonialism. In this view, the postcolonial begins with colonization and is always present alongside and within it. Some concentrate on the instabilities and contradictions within the colonial project itself, stressing that colonialism is a messy, incoherent, and ambivalent business, offering numerous toeholds to those who resist it.[15] Yeats's critique of Spenser's ignorance about Ireland and bad colonialist logic might fall into this category. Other scholars emphasize that this definition enables us to analyze the active agency of the colonized, rather than simply pitying them as helpless victims. It makes visible the history of how the colonized find resources, methods, and opportunities to survive and combat their oppression. Often they find resources in native culture, language, and religion, particularly if those things have been prohibited by the colonial power and are, as a result, already politicized. Methods can include organized anti-colonial movements, the everyday practices of individuals, defiance, evasion, and mimicry. Obviously, many of these resources and methods do not fall squarely into traditional conceptions of politics. Earlier I observed that postcolonial studies assumes colonization and decolonization shape literature and culture in important ways. Now I need to add a further observation about the culturalism of postcolonial studies. Culturalism is the privileging of culture, rather than, for example, economics or military force, as an instrument of colonization and as a vehicle of resistance to it. For most postcolonial scholars, culture does not simply describe or reflect the forces that make things happen. Culture itself is a political and historical agent; culture can make things happen. Culturalism is also a subject of debate in contemporary postcolonial studies. Many colonized people have little access to conventional means of acquiring agency, expressing political demands, or gaining political power such as political institutions, weapons, or money. So culturalism – ranging from the study of literature to the analysis of everyday beliefs and practices – has enabled scholars to examine the means that the colonized do have access to, and, through them, to reveal their sufferings, resistances, and counter-narratives. On the other hand, many scholars now see culturalism as a problem, a way of thinking that wishfully exaggerates culture's importance in shaping power relations and historical processes. In doing so, it can romanticize the lives of the oppressed, the very people whose struggles it originally sought to bring to light.

In Yeats, too, we find both a commitment to culturalism and a set of anxieties about its founding principles. For Yeats, the costs of British rule in Ireland were material in a conventionally political sense, involving "wars of extermination" and "persecution" (*E&I* 519). They were also cultural, and importantly so; colonialism crippled Irish culture by suppressing the native traditions, importing a vulgar English popular culture to Ireland, and ensuring that much Irish art would serve nationalist propaganda rather than the vision of the individual artist. Yeats frequently read the didactic nationalist poetry of Thomas Davis, and its massive popularity, as one of these costs, as an unfortunate colonial necessity. This enabled him to negotiate between his disdain for Davis's verse and his interest in and sympathy for the nationalist feelings it aroused. For example, in a 1910 essay on "J. M. Synge and the Ireland of his Time," Yeats claims that Davis "had understood that a country which has no national institutions must show its young men images for the affections, although they be but diagrams of what should be or may be" (*E&I* 312–13) and confesses that although he criticizes his mediocre verse, "I have felt in my body the affections I disturb" (*E&I* 318).

This kind of negotiation was central to Yeats's version of culturalism, which differed from contemporary postcolonial studies in its commitment to a firm distinction between art and propaganda. Throughout his career, Yeats disapproved of propaganda and insisted that Irish writers should not try to appeal to popular tastes or advocate political causes in their work; they should have "no propaganda but that of good art" (*Ex* 100). But he believed, at least for part of that career, that good art could achieve the goals nationalist propaganda ultimately sought – to create and re-invigorate national community. In 1901 he wrote in "Ireland and the Arts" that he wanted to "re-create the ancient arts, the arts as they were understood . . . when they moved a whole people" (*E&I* 206). Yeats's cultural nationalism during the Literary Revival was devoted to producing art that moved a whole people as Davis's poetry had done, but that did so precisely because it was trying to do something else: express the artist's personal vision and artistic principles. According to this theory, art was art because it was not propaganda, but in a sense it was also art because, in its public functions, it was more effective propaganda than propaganda was. One foundation for this theory was Yeats's immense faith in the non-rational basis of national community and human subjectivity generally. In the essay on Synge he claimed, "Only that which does not teach, which does not persuade, which does not condescend, which does not explain, is irresistible" (*E&I* 341). "To Ireland in the Coming Times" (*VP* 137–9) makes a related argument, asking that Yeats be included in the nationalist brotherhood of "Davis, Mangan, Ferguson" even though "My rhymes more than their rhyming tell," a line that suggests both Yeats's greater aesthetic skill and his occult interests.

But the notion that the significant public effects of good art would by definition be in excess of the artist's intentions proved true in unexpected and disturbing ways for Yeats, as he confronted over and over again the Irish public's refusal to like the plays he liked or to re-imagine themselves as a national community in the terms he offered them. In his comments on the "hysterical patriots" (*Ex* 232) and the "mobs" who rioted at Synge's plays, art's capacity to produce national feeling and the non-rational basis of human collectivities assumed very different meanings: important elements of his culturalism had, in effect, turned against him. "At the Abbey Theatre" (*VP* 264–5) complains of audiences as unmanageable and changeable as Proteus. "The Fisherman" (*VP* 347–8) expresses disillusionment with the actual nationalist communities that made up his audiences, and confronts the gap between "What I had hoped 'twould be / To write for my own race / And the reality." The poem invents an alternative audience that is the antithesis of the real, re-invigorated national collective Yeats originally hoped cultural revival could spark: the fisherman is solitary and imagined. And "The Road at my Door" (*VP* 423–4) takes up a distinction Yeats was interested in throughout most of his career, the difference between the poet and the man of action, and records the speaker's "envy" of the soldiers on either side of the Irish Civil War. Although Yeats's culturalism was not identical to the culturalism of contemporary postcolonial studies, it was a meditation on the relationship between politics and culture in the context of Ireland's colonial relationship to Britain and its aftermath. His belief in the public, collective, transformative power of culture proved to be both a creatively enabling way of connecting to the Irish people and a reminder of his ultimate separation from them. I think it is worth noting that postcolonial scholars who analyze his writings are often working in intellectual traditions that have not resolved this dilemma.

Another way of approaching the question of "what" the postcolonial is involves anti-colonial nationalism, and, indeed, scholars of Yeats's cultural nationalism have traditionally emphasized its nationalism over its culturalism. Postcolonial studies is characterized by an enormous ambivalence about nationalism. Postcolonial scholars critique nationalism on a number of grounds. Some claim that nationalism's intellectual structures simply invert and mirror those of imperialism. Others emphasize that nationalism is often homogenizing; it ignores or tries to erase differences among members of the nation. Subaltern, feminist, and Marxist critiques point out that nationalism usually articulates the political grievances and aspirations of the middle classes. At the same time, postcolonial studies remains obsessed with the nation, for several reasons. For one thing, culturalism tends to think in terms of national cultures. In addition, because historically, most (though not all) anti-colonial struggles have been versions of nationalism, nationalism is an important aspect of the conditions and aspirations that postcolonial scholars study. Is Yeats's nationalism (in its various incarnations) part of a colonial problem, or part of a postcolonial solution? As we saw earlier, critics like Seamus Deane and Edward Said arrive at different conclusions. And to make the obvious answer – "it can be both" – is both true and, like the refrain from "Easter 1916," relatively empty. The devil is in the details.

Rather than trying to elaborate on these details to arrive at a judgement about how postcolonial studies might definitively read Yeats's nationalisms, I would like to point out that the question that would provide the structure for this elaboration – nationalism as derivative colonial problem versus nationalism as liberatory postcolonial movement – provided the basis on which Yeats distinguished his own nationalism from other nationalisms. Further, it also gave him the terms with which he tried to defend himself against the charge that his conceptions of nationalism and of the national theatre were not genuinely national and were, in fact, Anglo-Irish imperialisms. Again and again, he accused the Catholic nationalists who opposed him of an unconscious and slavish devotion to English imperial values and culture. For example, in a 1908 *Samhain* he defended his cosmopolitan ideal of an Irish theatre that drew on the best of other national traditions as well by commenting, "English provincialism shouts through the lips of Irish patriots who have no knowledge of other countries to give them a standard of comparison"

(*Ex* 232), and claimed that "the English influence which runs through the patriotic reading of the people is not noticed because it is everywhere" (*Ex* 243). Postcolonial studies should obviously consider the question of whether we should call Yeats's nationalism more colonial or postcolonial. But this distinction is not merely an analytic tool that we can apply to Yeats's works; we should also recognize that Yeats himself was using it, in his own way, to think about his own nationalism and competing nationalisms.

Still another way to think about "what" the postcolonial might be would define it through concepts of hybridity. Because postcolonial studies imagines the colonial encounter as both political domination and cultural exchange, scholars frequently trace the way different cultures interact and combine to produce new hybrid cultural forms. In postcolonial studies, hybridity is often seen as an adaptive, appropriative response to cultural contact, particularly on the part of the colonized. It can be experienced as both painful and enabling – and this was certainly true for Yeats. Yeats's entire career could be characterized as a search for a hybrid poetic form that would combine English and Irish, personal and collective. From very early on, he was consciously searching for ways to appropriate and revise the English language and English literary traditions in which he worked, to cross them with the Irish traditions, forms, and cadences he found so inspiring. In 1901 he spoke of it as a way of writing in English "which would not be an English style and yet would be musical and full of colour" (*E&I* 3). When he looked back over his career in "A General Introduction for my Work" (1937), he returned repeatedly to the various hybridities that structured his life and work. The essay records his search for a way of writing poetry that had the personal cadence of "passionate prose" but that also retained a "ghostly voice" which displayed the collective cadences of "the folk song" (*E&I* 524). He observes "Gaelic is my national language, but it is not my mother tongue" (*E&I* 520). He invokes the colonial "persecution" of the Irish and the hatred for England that its memory produces in him: "No people hate as we do in whom that past is always alive, there are moments when hatred poisons my life and I accuse myself of effeminacy because I have not given it adequate expression" (*E&I* 519). But as a hybrid colonial subject, Yeats also loves England:

> Then I remind myself that though mine is the first English marriage I know of in the direct line, all my family names are English, and that I owe my soul to Shakespeare, to Spenser and to Blake, perhaps to William Morris, and to the English language in which I think, speak, and write, that everything I love has come to me through English; my hatred tortures me with love, my love with hate. (*E&I* 519)

As Yeats's relative helplessness in the face of his conflicting emotions about England in this passage suggests, he was also interested in exploring the predicaments of colonial subjects who were less self-conscious and articulate about their hybrid status – an interest he shared with James Joyce. For example, in "The Ballad of Father O'Hart" (*VP* 91–3), first published in 1888, he employs the ballad form to tell the story of an eighteenth-century priest whose lands were stolen by a Protestant "shoneen," or upstart, who had agreed to take the lands in trust for him. The poem and Yeats's notes to it deplore this injustice and emphasize that Father O'Hart was much beloved by the country people.[16] But the poem also casts this loving relation as politically ambiguous, and Father O'Hart as an agent of imperialism. He has tried to regularize the Catholic devotional practices of his flock and to suppress traditional practices like keening: "He bade them give over their keening; / For he was a man of books." This invokes the "devotional revolution" of the nineteenth century, in which the hierarchy worked to centralize Church authority and to discourage the popular rituals, associated with wakes, patterns, and holy wells, which were often fairly rowdy social occasions and drew on pagan or folk beliefs, in favor of more orthodox forms of Catholic worship. Despite the fact that "All loved him," the priest's effort to civilize and educate his flock on the assumption that his book-learning is superior to traditional Irish ways is rejected by nature itself. When he dies, the birds keen for him, and the poem concludes, "This way were all reproved / Who dig old customs up." The end of the poem places Father O'Hart, beloved and trusted though he was, alongside the shoneen who betrayed his trust and stole his lands. As the inclusive "all" suggests, both were to be "reproved" for helping Britain dominate Ireland "In penal days" and eradicate old Irish customs. Father O'Hart's hybridity lies in the larger political ambiguity of his commitments, commitments that are sincere and unambiguous for him on a personal level. It places him between two cultures – the Irish peasantry he loves but helps to suppress, and the English or Protestant imperial classes whom he hates but in some respects emulates in ways that he cannot see.

Despite this defense of "old customs" and Yeats's commitment to the Literary Revival's retrieval of them, it would be a mistake to assume that Yeats routinely cast hybridity as a violation of cultural integrity. Some postcolonial scholars have suggested that cultural hybridity can produce the desire for, and the fantasy of, cultural purity, simplicity, or wholeness on the part of colonizer or colonized. "The Lake Isle of Innisfree" (*VP* 117), with its contrast between the "pavements grey" of the speaker's actual location and the "peace" and beauty of Innisfree, analyzes this kind of dynamic rather than simply capitulating to it. The poem was inspired by the sight of a fountain in a London shop window; the homesick Irish poet returns to an idealized

Ireland in his imagination. The text emphasizes the speaker's willful creation of an imaginary place through assertive phrases like "I will," and "I shall." The speaker's actual journey to Innisfree does not occur during the poem; indeed, it seems clear that it will never occur, and that the only journey he will make there is the one he makes in his mind. At the end of the poem, he is still standing "on the roadway" listening to the lapping waters in his "deep heart's core." The poem is about the speaker's desire to escape London and to construct an imaginary Ireland, but the intellectual tools available to Yeats were various and mixed, so even that imaginary Ireland is inescapably hybrid. The poem invokes both the biblical story of the Prodigal Son (Luke 15.18) and the work of the American writer Henry David Thoreau. It is, of course, written in English, and, as Hugh Kenner has pointed out, the word "wattles," originally a term that outside observers used to characterize the way the rude native Irish made their houses, gestures towards "the long story of English condescension to things Irish."[17] Yeats himself may or may not have known that last bit of etymology, and he may have cursed or chuckled about his poem's other hybridities, but he was surely aware that the idealized Irish world the speaker loves is only available through the material and intellectual English world he hates, and the poem draws its energy from this tension rather than articulating it clearly as Yeats does in "A General Introduction for my Work."

The fact that we do not know which of the hybridities of "The Lake Isle of Innisfree" were intentional on Yeats's part, which were forced upon him by the traditions he wrote in, and which may have escaped his consciousness altogether, begins to suggest that defining the postcolonial through the question of "what" it is also has limitations. The poem's hybrid character can appear as ironic self-analysis, clever appropriation of an English tradition, or helpless subordination to it, and the distinction between these possibilities could be made (and made differently) by appealing to Yeats's intentions, to the cultural and historical contexts in which he originally wrote, or to the current contexts in which the poem is read. The poem is now famous for being Yeats's most well-known, well-beloved, and requested poem at readings; just as famous are the stories about how much this irritated him.[18] Perhaps later in his life its hybridities, and their attendant ironies and complications, became clearer to him than they had been when he composed it, or perhaps they had always been clear to him, and he realized some time later that they had never become clear to his readers, and that, indeed, his readers may have loved the poem precisely for that reason. Ultimately, the meaning of hybridity is inseparable from the contexts of "where" and "when," and the end of our discussion of "what" the postcolonial might be demands that we return to those categories. I began this chapter by saying that it would be helpful to disentangle these questions about how we define the postcolonial. By now it should be clear that we can only do so in temporary and incomplete fashion. The basic entanglement among them is fundamental, for better and worse, to postcolonial studies. I hope that this exercise has provided a useful way of investigating the enormous range of work that falls under the general heading of postcolonial studies, and outlining the multiple ways that scholars have gone about defining the postcolonial. I have also been trying to suggest that this extremely varied, contradictory, and uncertain body of work can yield a great deal of insight into Yeats's works, less because the individual paradigms or theories it offers can apply to or explain Yeats than because Yeats's writings reveal many of the same frustrating, fascinating variations and uncertainties.

NOTES

1. See Conor Cruise O'Brien, "Passion and cunning: an essay on the politics of W. B. Yeats," in *In Excited Reverie: A Centenary Tribute to W. B. Yeats, 1865–1939*, ed. A. Norman Jeffares and K. G. W. Cross (New York: St. Martin's Press, 1965); Elizabeth Butler Cullingford, *W. B. Yeats, Ireland and Fascism* (New York and London: New York University Press, 1981); Grattan Freyer, *W. B. Yeats and the Anti-Democratic Tradition* (Dublin: Gill and Macmillan; Totowa, NJ: Barnes & Noble, 1981); Jonathan Allison, ed., *Yeats's Political Identities: Selected Essays* (Ann Arbor: University of Michigan Press, 1996).
2. Seamus Deane, "Yeats and the idea of revolution," in *Celtic Revivals: Essays in Modern Irish Literature 1880–1980* (London and Boston: Faber and Faber, 1985), p. 49.
3. Edward Said, "Yeats and decolonization," in *Nationalism, Colonialism, and Literature*, ed. Seamus Deane (Minneapolis: University of Minnesota Press, 1990), p. 81.
4. *Ibid.*, p. 94. This combination also appeals to Declan Kiberd in his *Inventing Ireland: The Literature of the Modern Nation* (Cambridge, MA: Harvard University Press, 1996), especially pp. 99–165, 286–326, 438–53. See also Marjorie Howes, *Yeats's Nations: Gender, Class, and Irishness* (Cambridge: Cambridge University Press, 1996), and David Lloyd, "The poetics of politics: Yeats and the founding of the New State," in *Anomalous States: Irish Writing and the Post-Colonial Moment* (Durham, NC: Duke University Press, 1993).
5. Jahan Ramazani, *The Hybrid Muse: Postcolonial Poetry in English* (Chicago and London: University of Chicago Press, 2001), p. 22.
6. Robert Young's *White Mythologies* (London: Routledge, 1990) is a good example here.
7. An exception here is Bill Ashcroft, Gareth Griffiths, and Helen Tiffin's *The Empire Writes Back* (London and New York: Routledge, 1989); they argue that "because of its current position of power, and the neo-colonizing role it has played, its post-colonial nature has not been generally recognized" (p. 2) but that the USA should in fact be considered postcolonial.

8. For example, some Irish historians offer an "archipelago" model, which casts Ireland as one of several peripheral regions that gradually became absorbed into the centralizing state (See Tom Dunne, "New histories: beyond revisionism," *Irish Review* 13 [Winter, 1992–3]), and Liam Kennedy has suggested the word "secession" rather than "decolonization" as a term for what happened when Ireland broke away from Britain ("Modern Ireland: post-colonial society or post-colonial pretensions?" *Irish Review* 12 [Spring/Summer, 1992], p. 116).
9. See Frantz Fanon, *Black Skin, White Masks* (New York: Grove Weidenfeld, 1967 [1952]).
10. Ramazani, *The Hybrid Muse*, p. 22.
11. For a useful consideration of some debates over temporal definitions of the postcolonial, see Stuart Hall, "When was 'the post-colonial'? Thinking at the limit," in *The Post-Colonial Question: Common Skies, Divided Horizons*, ed. Iain Chambers and Lidia Curti (London and New York: Routledge, 1996).
12. Lloyd, "The poetics of politics," p. 71.
13. Terry Eagleton has observed that "'Easter 1916' is much more at a loss than it would like to appear" and that therefore "Yeats is involved here in a kind of performative contradiction between what he says and the way he says it" (*Crazy John and the Bishop* [Cork: Cork University Press, 1998], p. 276).
14. Declan Kiberd remarks that the refrain "comes back shamefacedly, as an admittedly rhetorical device to suppress the terrifying interrogation" (*Inventing Ireland*, p. 216).
15. Homi K. Bhabha's works are often thought to exemplify this approach. See, for example, *The Location of Culture* (London and New York: Routledge, 1994).
16. A. Norman Jeffares helpfully collects all the various notes Yeats appended to the poem at different times in *A Commentary on the Collected Poems of W. B. Yeats* (Stanford: Stanford University Press, 1968), pp. 16–17.
17. Hugh Kenner, *A Colder Eye: The Modern Irish Writers* (New York: Knopf, 1983), p. 73.
18. See R. F. Foster, *W. B. Yeats: A Life II: The Arch-Poet 1915–1939* (Oxford and New York: Oxford University Press, 2003), pp. 303, 362, 418.

SELECT BIBLIOGRAPHY

Adams, Hazard. *Blake and Yeats: The Contrary Vision*. Ithaca, NY: Cornell University Press, 1955.

The Book of Yeats's "Vision": Romantic Modernism and Antithetical Tradition. Ann Arbor: University of Michigan Press, 1995.

Albright, Daniel. *Quantum Poetics: Yeats, Pound, Eliot, and the Science of Modernism*. New York: Cambridge University Press, 1997.

Allison, Jonathan, ed. *Yeats's Political Identities*. Ann Arbor: University of Michigan Press, 1996.

Archibald, Douglas. *Yeats*. Syracuse, NY: Syracuse University Press, 1983.

Bloom, Harold. *Yeats*. Oxford and New York: Oxford University Press, 1970.

Bornstein, George. *Material Modernism: The Politics of the Page*. Cambridge and New York: Cambridge University Press, 2001.

Poetic Remaking: The Art of Browning, Yeats, and Pound. University Park, PA: Pennsylvania State University Press, 1988.

Transformations of Romanticism in Yeats, Eliot, and Stevens. Chicago: University of Chicago Press, 1976.

Yeats and Shelley. Chicago: University of Chicago Press, 1970.

Bradford, Curtis. *Yeats at Work*. Carbondale, IL: Southern Illinois University Press, 1965.

Bradley, Anthony. *William Butler Yeats*. New York: Ungar, 1979.

Bramsbäck, Birgit. *Folklore and W. B. Yeats: The Function of Folklore Elements in Three Early Plays*. Stockholm: Almqvist & Wiksell, 1984.

Brearton, Fran. *The Great War in Irish Poetry: W. B. Yeats to Michael Longley*. New York: Oxford University Press, 2000.

Brown, Malcolm. *The Politics of Irish Literature: From Thomas Davis to W. B. Yeats*. Seattle, WA: University of Washington Press, 1972.

Brown, Terence. *The Life of W. B. Yeats: A Critical Biography*. Oxford: Blackwell, 1999.

Bushrui, Suheil. *An International Companion to the Poetry of W. B. Yeats*. Savage, MD: Barnes & Noble, 1990.

Cairns, David and Shaun Richards, eds. *Writing Ireland: Colonialism, Nationalism and Culture*. Manchester: Manchester University Press, 1988.

Castle, Gregory. *Modernism and the Celtic Revival*. New York and Cambridge: Cambridge University Press, 2001.

Chapman, Wayne. *Yeats and English Renaissance Literature*. New York: St. Martin's Press, 1991.

Chaudhry, Yug Mohit. *Yeats, the Irish Literary Revival and the Politics of Print*. Cork: Cork University Press, 2001.

Clark, David. *W. B. Yeats and the Theatre of Desolate Reality*. Chester Springs, PA: Dufour Editions, 1965.

Yeats at Songs and Choruses. Amherst, MA: University of Massachusetts Press, 1983.

Cullingford, Elizabeth Butler. *Gender and History in Yeats's Love Poetry*. Cambridge: Cambridge University Press, 1993.

Yeats, Ireland and Fascism. New York and London: New York University Press, 1981.

Dawe, Gerald and Edna Longley, eds. *Across a Roaring Hill: The Protestant Imagination in Modern Ireland*. Belfast: Blackstaff Press, 1985.

Deane, Seamus. *Celtic Revivals: Essays in Modern Irish Literature 1880–1980*. London and Boston: Faber and Faber, 1985.

Desae, Rupin. *W. B. Yeats's Shakespeare*. Evanston, IL: Northwestern University Press, 1971.

Donoghue, Denis, ed. *An Honoured Guest: New Essays on W. B. Yeats*. London: Edward Arnold, 1965.

ed. *The Integrity of Yeats*. Cork: Mercier Press, 1964.

Yeats. London: Fontana, 1971.

Eagleton, Terry. *Crazy John and the Bishop and Other Essays on Irish Culture*. Notre Dame, IN: University of Notre Dame Press, 1998.

Eddins, Dwight. *Yeats: The Nineteenth Century Matrix*. University, AL: University of Alabama Press, 1971.

Ellis-Fermor, Una. *The Irish Dramatic Movement*. London: Methuen, 1964 [1939].

Ellmann, Richard. *Eminent Domain: Yeats among Wilde, Joyce, Pound, Eliot, and Auden*. New York: Oxford University Press, 1967.

Four Dubliners. Washington: Library of Congress, 1986.

The Identity of Yeats. New York: Oxford University Press, 1964 [1954].

Yeats and Joyce. Dublin: Dolmen Press, 1968.

Yeats: The Man and the Masks, 2nd edn. New York: Norton, 1978.

Engelberg, Edward. *The Vast Design: Patterns in W. B. Yeats's Aesthetic*. Toronto: University of Toronto Press, 1965 [1964].

Finneran, Richard, ed. *Critical Essays on W. B. Yeats*. Boston: Hall, 1986.

Editing Yeats's Poems. London: Macmillan, 1983.

Flannery, James W. *W. B. Yeats and the Idea of a Theatre: The Early Abbey Theatre in Theory and Practice*. New Haven: Yale University Press, 1976.

Fleming, Deborah, ed. *W. B. Yeats and Postcolonialism*. West Cornwall, CT: Locust Hill Press, 2001.

Foster, R. F. *The Irish Story: Telling Tales and Making It Up in Ireland*. Oxford: Oxford University Press, 2000.

W. B. Yeats: A Life I: The Apprentice Mage 1865–1914. Oxford and New York: Oxford University Press, 1997.

W. B. Yeats: A Life II: The Arch-Poet 1915–1939. Oxford and New York: Oxford University Press, 2003.

Frazier, Adrian. *Behind the Scenes: Yeats, Horniman, and the Struggle for the Abbey Theatre*. Berkeley: University of California Press, 1990.
Freyer, Grattan. *W. B. Yeats and the Anti-Democratic Tradition*. Dublin: Gill and Macmillan; Totowa, NJ: Barnes & Noble, 1981.
Garratt, Robert. *Modern Irish Poetry: Tradition and Continuity from Yeats to Heaney*. Berkeley: University of California Press, 1986.
Hall, James, ed. *The Permanence of Yeats*. New York: Collier Books, 1961 [1950].
Harper, George Mills. *The Making of Yeats's "A Vision": A Study of the Automatic Script, Volume 1*. Carbondale and Edwardsville, IL: Southern Illinois University Press, 1987.
ed. *Yeats and the Occult*. Toronto: Macmillan, 1975.
Yeats's Golden Dawn: The Influence of the Hermetic Order of the Golden Dawn on the Life and Art of W. B. Yeats. London: Macmillan, 1974.
ed. *Yeats's "Vision" Papers*, 4 vols. London: Macmillan, 1992.
Harrington, John. *Modern Irish Drama*. New York: Norton, 1991.
Harris, Daniel. *Yeats: Coole Park and Ballylee*. Baltimore, MD: Johns Hopkins University Press, 1974.
Harris, Susan C. *Gender and Modern Irish Drama*. Bloomington, IN: Indiana University Press, 2002.
Hassett, Joseph M. *Yeats and the Poetics of Hate*. Dublin: Gill and Macmillan; New York: St. Martin's Press, 1986.
Henn, T. R. *Last Essays*. Gerrards Cross: Smythe, 1976.
The Lonely Tower: Studies in the Poetry of W. B. Yeats. Rev. edn. London: Methuen; New York: Barnes & Noble, 1965.
W. B. Yeats and the Poetry of War. Oxford: Oxford University Press, 1965.
Holdeman, David. *Much Labouring: The Texts and Authors of Yeats's First Modernist Books*. Ann Arbor: University of Michigan Press, 1997.
Holdridge, Jefferson. *Those Mingled Seas: The Poetry of W. B. Yeats, the Beautiful and the Sublime*. Dublin: University College Dublin Press, 2000.
Hough, Graham. *The Mystery Religion of W. B. Yeats*. Brighton: Harvester Press; New Jersey: Barnes & Noble, 1984.
Howes, Marjorie. *Yeats's Nations: Gender, Class, and Irishness*. Cambridge: Cambridge University Press, 1996.
Jeffares, A. Norman. *The Circus Animals: Essays on W. B. Yeats*. London: Macmillan, 1970.
A New Commentary on the Collected Poems of W. B. Yeats. London: Macmillan, 1984.
ed. *In Excited Reverie: A Centenary Tribute to William Butler Yeats*. New York: Macmillan, 1965.
W. B. Yeats. London: Routledge & Kegan Paul, 1971.
ed. *W. B. Yeats: The Critical Heritage*. London: Routledge & Kegan Paul, 1977.
Jeffares, A. Norman and A. S. Knowland. *A Commentary on the Collected Plays of W. B. Yeats*. London: Macmillan, 1975.
Jochum, K. P. S. *W. B. Yeats: A Classified Bibliography of Criticism*. Urbana and Chicago: University of Illinois Press, 1990.
Keane, Patrick J. *Terrible Beauty: Yeats, Joyce, Ireland, and the Myth of the Devouring Female*. Columbia: University of Missouri Press, 1988.
Yeats's Interactions with Tradition. Columbia: University of Missouri Press, 1987.

Kelleher, John V. "Yeats's use of Irish materials." *Tri-Quarterly* 4 (Fall 1965), 115–25.

Kelly, John S. *A W. B. Yeats Chronology*. New York: Palgrave Macmillan, 2003.

Kenner, Hugh. *A Colder Eye: The Modern Irish Writers*. New York: Knopf, 1983.

Kermode, Frank. *Romantic Image*. New York: Vintage Books, 1964 [1957].

Kiberd, Declan. *Inventing Ireland: The Literature of the Modern Nation*. Cambridge, MA: Harvard University Press, 1996.

Irish Classics. Cambridge, MA: Harvard University Press, 2001.

Kinahan, Frank. *Yeats, Folklore, and Occultism: Contexts of the Early Work and Thought*. Boston: Unwin Hyman, 1988.

Kline, Gloria C. *The Last Courtly Lover: Yeats and the Idea of Woman*. Ann Arbor: UMI Research Press, 1983.

Knowland, A. S. *W. B. Yeats: Dramatist of Vision*. Gerrards Cross: Colin Smythe, 1983.

Koch, Vivienne. *W. B. Yeats, the Tragic Phase: A Study of the Last Poems*. London: Routledge & Kegan Paul, 1951.

Komesu, Okifumi. *The Double Perspective of Yeats's Aesthetic*. Gerrards Cross: Smythe, 1984.

Krimm, Bernard. *W. B. Yeats and the Emergence of the Irish Free State 1918–1939: Living in the Explosion*. Troy, NY: Whitson, 1981.

Loizeaux, Elizabeth Bergmann. *Yeats and the Visual Arts*. New Brunswick: Rutgers University Press, 1986.

Longenbach, James. *Stone Cottage: Pound, Yeats, and Modernism*. New York: Oxford University Press, 1988.

Lynch, David. *Yeats: The Poetics of the Self*. Chicago: University of Chicago Press, 1979.

MacNeice, Louis. *The Poetry of W. B. Yeats*. London and New York: Oxford University Press, 1941.

Macrae, Alasdair. *W. B. Yeats: A Literary Life*. New York: St. Martin's Press, 1995.

Maddox, Brenda. *George's Ghosts: A New Life of W. B. Yeats*. London: Picador–Macmillan, 1999.

Mahaffey, Vicki. *States of Desire: Wilde, Yeats, Joyce, and the Irish Experiment*. New York: Oxford University Press, 1998.

Marcus, Philip. *Yeats and Artistic Power*. New York: New York University Press, 1992.

Yeats and the Beginning of the Irish Renaissance. Ithaca, NY: Cornell University Press, 1970.

Martin, Augustine. *W. B. Yeats*. Gerrards Cross: Smythe, 1990.

McCormack, W. J. *Ascendancy and Tradition in Anglo-Irish Literary History from 1798 to 1939*. Oxford: Clarendon Press, 1985.

McCready, Sam. *A William Butler Yeats Encyclopedia*. Westport, CT: Greenwood Press, 1997.

McDiarmid, Lucy. *Saving Civilization: Yeats, Eliot, and Auden between the Wars*. Cambridge: Cambridge University Press, 1984.

Melchiori, Giorgio. *The Whole Mystery of Art: Pattern into Poetry in the Work of W. B. Yeats*. London: Routledge & Kegan Paul, 1960.

Mikhail, E. H., ed. *W. B. Yeats: Interviews and Recollections*. New York: Barnes & Noble, 1977.

Miller, Joseph Hillis. *Poets of Reality: Six Twentieth-Century Writers*. Cambridge, MA: Harvard University Press, 1965.

Miller, Liam. *The Noble Drama of W. B. Yeats*. Dublin: Dolmen Press; Atlantic Heights, NJ: Humanities Press, 1977.

Miller, Nicholas. *Modernism, Ireland and the Erotics of Memory*. Cambridge: Cambridge University Press, 2002.

Moore, Virginia. *The Unicorn: William Butler Yeats' Search for Reality*. New York: Macmillan, 1954 [1952].

North, Michael. *The Political Aesthetic of Yeats, Eliot, and Pound*. New York and Cambridge: Cambridge University Press, 1991.

O'Driscoll, Robert, ed. *Theatre and Nationalism in Twentieth-Century Ireland*. Toronto: University of Toronto Press, 1971.

Olney, James. *The Rhizome and the Flower: The Perennial Philosophy – Yeats and Jung*. Berkeley: University of California Press, 1980.

Orr, Leonard. *Yeats and Postmodernism*. Syracuse, NY: Syracuse University Press, 1991.

Parkin, Andrew. *The Dramatic Imagination of W. B. Yeats*. Dublin: Gill and Macmillan; New York: Barnes & Noble, 1978.

Parkinson, Thomas. *W. B. Yeats: The Later Poetry*. Berkeley: University of California Press, 1964.

W. B. Yeats, Self-Critic: A Study of his Early Verse. Berkeley: University of California Press, 1951.

Perloff, Marjorie. *Rhyme and Meaning in the Poetry of Yeats*. The Hague: Mouton, 1970.

Pierce, David. *Yeats's Worlds: Ireland, England, and the Poetic Imagination*. New Haven and London: Yale University Press, 1995.

Pritchard, William H., ed. *W. B. Yeats: A Critical Anthology*. Harmondsworth: Penguin, 1972.

Putzel, Steven. *Reconstructing Yeats: "The Secret Rose" and "The Wind among the Reeds."* Dublin: Gill and Macmillan; Totowa, NJ: Barnes & Noble, 1986.

Raine, Kathleen. *Yeats the Initiate: Essays on Certain Themes in the Work of W. B. Yeats*. Mountrath: Dolmen Press; London: Allen & Unwin, 1986.

Ramazani, Jahan. *The Hybrid Muse: Postcolonial Poetry in English*. Chicago and London: University of Chicago Press, 2001.

Yeats and the Poetry of Death: Elegy, Self-Elegy, and the Sublime. New Haven: Yale University Press, 1990.

Rosenthal, M. L. and Sally M. Gall. *The Modern Poetic Sequence: The Genius of Modern Poetry*. New York: Oxford University Press, 1983.

Running to Paradise: Yeats's Poetic Art. New York: Oxford University Press, 1994.

Saddlemyer, Ann. *Becoming George: The Life of Mrs. W. B. Yeats*. New York and Oxford: Oxford University Press, 2002.

Said, Edward. *Culture and Imperialism*. New York: Knopf, 1993.

Sekine, Masaru, ed. *Irish Writers and the Theatre*. Gerrards Cross: Smythe, 1986.

Yeats and the Noh: A Comparative Study. Savage, MD: Barnes & Noble, 1990.

Sena, Vinod. *The Poet as Critic: W. B. Yeats on Poetry, Drama, and Tradition*. Delhi: Macmillan of India, 1980.

Sidnell, Michael J. *Yeats's Poetry and Poetics*. New York: St. Martin's Press, 1996.

Sikka, Shalini. *W. B. Yeats and the Upanisads*. New York: P. Lang, 2002.

Smith, Stan. *W. B. Yeats: A Critical Introduction*. Dublin: Gill and Macmillan, 1990.
Snukal, Robert M. *High Talk: The Philosophical Poetry of W. B. Yeats*. Cambridge: Cambridge University Press, 1973.
Stallworthy, Jon. *Between the Lines: Yeats's Poetry in the Making*. Oxford: Clarendon Press, 1963.
Vision and Revision in Yeats's Last Poems. Oxford: Clarendon Press, 1969.
Yeats' Last Poems: A Casebook. London: Macmillan, 1968.
Stanfield, Paul Scott. *Yeats and Politics in the 1930s*. London: Macmillan, 1988.
Surette, Leon. *The Birth of Modernism: Ezra Pound, T. S. Eliot, W. B. Yeats, and the Occult*. Montreal and Buffalo: McGill-Queen's University Press, 1993.
Taylor, Richard. *The Drama of W. B. Yeats: Irish Myth and the Japanese Nō*. New Haven: Yale University Press, 1976.
A Reader's Guide to the Plays of W. B. Yeats. London: Macmillan, 1984.
Thuente, Mary Helen. *W. B. Yeats and Irish Folklore*. Dublin: Gill and Macmillan, 1980.
Torchiana, Donald T. *W. B. Yeats and Georgian Ireland*. Evanston, IL: Northwestern University Press; London: Oxford University Press, 1966.
Tratner, Michael. *Modernism and Mass Politics: Joyce, Woolf, Eliot, Yeats*. Stanford: Stanford University Press, 1995.
Tuohy, Frank. *Yeats*. New York: Macmillan, 1976.
Unterecker, John. *A Reader's Guide to William Butler Yeats*. New York: Noonday Press, 1963 [1959].
ed. *Yeats: A Collection of Critical Essays*. Englewood Cliffs, NJ: Prentice Hall, 1963.
Ure, Peter. *Yeats*. New York: Barnes & Noble, 1963.
Yeats and Anglo-Irish Literature: Critical Essays, ed. C. J. Rawson. Liverpool: Liverpool University Press, 1974.
Yeats the Playwright: A Commentary on Character and Design in the Major Plays. London: Routledge & Kegan Paul, 1963.
Vendler, Helen Hennessy. *Yeats's "Vision" and the Later Plays*. Cambridge, MA: Harvard University Press, 1963.
Watson, George. *Irish Identity and the Literary Revival: Synge, Yeats, Joyce, and O'Casey*. London: Croom Helm, 1979.
Webster, Brenda. *Yeats: A Psychoanalytic Study*. Stanford: Stanford University Press, 1973.
Welch, Robert. *Irish Poetry from Moore to Yeats*. Gerrards Cross: Smythe, 1980.
Whitaker, Thomas R. *Swan and Shadow: Yeats's Dialogue with History*. Chapel Hill: University of North Carolina Press, 1964.
Wilson, F. A. C. *W. B. Yeats and Tradition*. London: Gollancz, 1958.
Yeats's Iconography. London: Gollancz, 1960.
Worth, Katharine. *The Irish Drama of Europe from Yeats to Beckett*. London: Athlone Press, 1978.
Wright, David G. *Yeats's Myth of Self: The Autobiographical Prose*. Dublin: Gill and Macmillan; Totowa, NJ: Barnes & Noble, 1987.
Yao, Steven, G. *Translation and the Languages of Modernism: Gender, Politics, Language*. New York: Palgrave, 2002.

INDEX

Abbey Theatre 8, 10, 14, 102, 104, 125, 126, 183, 190, 219
Adams, Hazard 186
Adorno, Theodor
  "Lyric poetry and society" 169
AE *see* Russell, George
Aedh 6, 155
Aesthetic movement *see* Decadence
Africanus, Leo 158–9, 161, 166
  Descrizione dell' Affrica 159
aisling poetry 170, 171, 172, 190
Allingham, William 132
Anglo-Irish Treaty 77, 100, 195, 196, 214
Anglo-Irish War 13, 23, 77, 195, 209
Antheil, George
  Golden Bird 73
Apollinaire, Guillaume 72–3
Aquinas, St. Thomas 182
Aristotle 84
Army Comrades Association 198
Arnold, Matthew 36, 38, 40–5, 50, 115, 124, 126
  Culture and Anarchy 44
  "Empedocles on Etna" 41
  On the Study of Celtic Literature 41–5, 134, 210
  "Preface to First Edition of *Poems* (1853)" 41
  "Scholar Gypsy, The" 40–1
Auden, W. H. 59–60, 61, 62, 65, 147, 148
  "In Memory of W. B. Yeats" 59–60, 61
  "Public v. the Late Mr. William Butler Yeats, The" 59–60
automatic writing 11, 14, 74, 77, 147, 149, 150, 151, 157, 158, 159–60, 194
Baillie, Joanna 20
Balla, Giacomo
  Street Lamp 70
ballads 17, 89, 97, 100, 140, 185, 189, 222
Balzac, Honoré de 211
Barbauld, Anna 20
Bartók, Béla 65
Bastien-Lepage, Jules 37
Baudelaire, Charles 65, 68
  "Correspondences" 65–6
  Painter of Modern Life, The 65
Beckett, Samuel 103, 105, 111
  Endgame 111
  Waiting for Godot 103, 110, 111, 113
Behan, Brendan 124
Bentley, Eric 104
Berg, Alban 65
Berkeley, George 88, 195
Bhagavad Gita 210
Bible, the 120, 133, 210, 223
bibliographic codes 26–7, 30–1
Black and Tans 78, 195
Blackmur, R. P. 117
Blake, William 20, 21–2, 24–7, 31, 32, 37, 38, 47, 49, 53, 70, 71, 93, 125, 146, 149, 155, 163, 188, 189, 191, 211, 221
  Island in the Moon, An 24
  "Tyger, The" 26
Blavatsky, Helena Petrovna 70, 153–4
Bloom, Harold 52–3, 62, 104, 106
Blueshirts 16, 95, 186, 198–9, 200
Boer War 188
Boland, Eavan 171, 172, 173
Bradley, Anthony 108
Brecht, Bertholt 111

Breton, André 72–4
  Immaculate Conception, The 74
  Surrealist Manifesto 72–3
Brown, Terence 103, 104, 105, 186, 201
Browning, Robert 36, 48
Buddhism 96, 155, 162
  Esoteric 130
Burke, Edmund 88, 195
Burne-Jones, Edward 45
Bushrui, S. B. 106, 108
Byron, Lord George 20, 21, 51, 82

Cabbalism 150, 155, 156
Čapek, Karel
  R. U. R. 69
Carlyle, Thomas 66, 188
Casement, Roger 212–13
Catholic Bulletin 179, 182, 204
Catholicism 36, 47, 209
  Catholic press 14, 186, 196
  in Yeats's poetry 8–9, 173, 175, 222
  Yeats's attitude towards 28, 94, 186, 187, 196, 202
  Yeats's conflicts with 136, 179, 181–2, 196, 197, 204, 211, 220–1
Cattell, Raymond B.
  Fight for Our National Intelligence, The 202
Cavendish, Richard 162
Celtic Mysteries 47, 154–5, 161, 165
Celticism 41–5, 134, 147
censorship 14, 179, 181, 187, 196
Chatterjee, Mohini 2, 161, 165–6
Chaucer, Geoffrey 62
Church of Ireland 37
Civil War, Irish 14, 20, 24, 77–8, 100, 197, 198, 219
Clarke, Kathleen 178
class, Yeats's ideas of 8–9, 14, 28, 85, 94, 186, 187–8, 190, 196
Claudel, Paul 59
Cold War 209
Coleridge, Samuel Taylor 20, 92, 100, 127
  "Eolian Harp, The" 29
  "Frost at Midnight" 29
  "Kubla Khan" 93
  "Rime of the Ancient Mariner, The" 121
colonialism *see* imperialism
Columcille 27
communism 202
Connolly, James 79, 217
constitution, Irish 214
Contemporary Club 2, 188
Coole 7, 10, 15, 16, 19, 82, 118, 191, 199
Cosgrove, Liam 195, 197–8
Craig, Gordon 67, 103, 107, 109, 113
Crazy Jane 16, 25, 89, 112, 162–3, 181–2
Cromwell, Oliver 85
Crookes, Sir William 70
Cuala Press 6, 17, 26–7, 30–1
Cubism 67, 75, 103, 109
Cuchulain 4, 19, 23, 32, 78, 96, 100, 103–4, 105, 107–8, 113, 124, 141–2, 171, 189
Cullingford, Elizabeth Butler 186, 187, 198
culturalism 218–20
Cumann na mBan 178

Dadaism 71–2
Dante Alighieri 20, 24, 31–2, 33, 97, 100, 146, 149, 167, 211
Darwin, Charles 154
Davis, Thomas 23, 27, 55–6, 172, 185, 190, 193, 218, 219
Deane, Seamus 126, 207, 220
de Beauvoir, Simone 173
Debussy, Claude 65
Decadence 2, 3–4, 47–56, 61
decolonization *see* postcolonial issues
de Valera, Eamon 181, 186, 198
de Vere, Aubrey
  "Little Black Rose, The" 27
dialogue 2, 105
Dickens, Charles
  Dombey and Son 39
Dickinson, Emily 26
divorce 14, 179, 196, 211
Donne, John 92, 211
Donoghue, Denis 199, 201
Dowden, Edward 39, 122–3, 124–5
Dowson, Ernest 47, 50, 52, 57
Dryden, John 63
Dublin Hermetic Society 2, 153, 189
Duffy, Sir Charles Gavan 5, 45, 188
Dulac, Edmund 109
Dun Emer Press 6, 26–7
Duran, Carolus 37

Eagleton, Terry 44
Easter Rising 10, 12, 23, 24, 77, 78, 79, 80, 96, 97, 100, 142, 178, 187, 192–4, 195, 213, 216–17
Edward VII, King 7
Edwards, Philip 125
elegy 15, 59–60, 61, 78, 93–5, 100, 118, 192, 199, 200

Eliot, George 38
Middlemarch 131
Eliot, T. S. 21, 60–1, 62, 63, 65, 66, 101, 103, 107
"Little Gidding" 60–1
"metaphysical poets, The" 203
"Tradition and the individual talent" 61
Waste Land, The 60, 61, 66, 67, 70
Elizabeth I, Queen 32, 174, 212
Ellis, Edwin 24
Ellis-Fermor, Una 104
Ellmann, Richard 107, 108–10, 111
eugenics 17–8, 201–2, 204, 205
External Relations Act 214

Fanon, Frantz 212
Farr, Florence 24, 148, 170
fascism 16, 59, 95, 186, 198–9, 202
femininity 46, 51, 167–8, 169, 174–7, 181
feminism 167–9, 171–2, 179–81, 207, 220
during Yeats's lifetime 170, 177, 178, 183
Fenian cycle tales 140–1
Fenianism 2, 6, 10, 19, 134, 185, 188
Fenollosa, Ernest 105
Fergus 3, 4, 23, 171, 189
Ferguson, Sir Samuel 23, 27, 40, 43, 130, 132, 219
Lays of the Western Gael 172
Ferral, Charles 186
Fianna Fail 196, 197
Figaro, Le 68
Finn 27
Finneran, Richard 106
First World War see World War I
Fitzgerald, F. Scott 123
Flannery, James 103–4, 105, 107–8
Flaubert, Gustav 2 116
folklore 3, 4, 5, 19, 129–40, 152, 197, 207–8
Foster, R. F. 11, 23, 109, 189
Franco, Francisco 200
Frazer, Sir James
Golden Bough, The 132, 152
Frazier, Adrian 173–4
Freemasonry 150
Fuller, Loie 85
Fussell, Paul 179
Frayne, John 43
Freud, Sigmund 73
Futurism 68–71

Gaelic League 135
Gentile, Giovanni 196
Gnosticism 150
Goethe, Johann Wolfgang von 33
Goldsmith, Oliver 88, 195
Gonne, Iseult 11, 159, 177, 183
Gonne, Maud 8, 13, 22, 71, 90, 108, 141, 148, 155, 167, 174, 188–9, 212
in Yeats's poetry 9, 11, 81–2, 83, 84, 95, 159, 171, 172, 175–8
marriage to MacBride 7, 177
meets Yeats 2, 107, 171, 188–9
occult interests 47, 146, 172–3
political activities and beliefs 108, 170, 172–3, 175–8, 188–9
rejects Yeats 7, 11, 20, 77, 155
Good Friday Agreement 214
Gore-Booth, Eva 15
Gould, Warwick 106
Government of Ireland Act 77
Grattan, Henry 190, 195
Graves, A. P. 132
Greater Romantic Lyric 29–30
Gregory, Lady Augusta 5, 6, 9, 13, 16, 19–20, 31, 32, 77, 78, 82, 108, 113, 130, 138, 142, 148, 177, 186, 187, 190
Cathleen ni Houlihan 138, 173
Cuchulain of Muirthemne 140–1
Gods and Fighting Men 140–1
Poets and Dreamers 137
Visions and Beliefs in the West of Ireland 138, 139, 158
Gregory, Robert 13, 77
Griffith, Arthur 190
Grimm, brothers 131

Haldane, Lord 188
Hallam, A. H. 48–50
Hamsa, Bhagwan Shri 162
Harper, George Mills 160
Harper, Margaret Mills 194
Harrison, Jane 167, 174
Heaney, Seamus 115, 200
Crediting Poetry 32–3
Hegel, G. W. F. , 210
Helen of Troy 11, 81, 141, 176–7
Hemans, Felicia 20
Henn, T. R. 126
Herder, Johann von 131
Hermeticism 150
Hermetic Order of the Golden Dawn 5, 47, 146, 151, 154–7, 159, 189
Hindu mysticism 161–3

Hinkson, Katharine Tynan *see* Tynan, Katharine
Hitler, Adolf 198
Home Rule 10, 13, 20, 23
Homer 188
Odyssey, The 66
Hugo, Victor 201
Huxley, T. H. 37
hybridity 207, 221–3
Hyde, Douglas 125, 135, 136
Beside the Fire 135
Love Songs of Connacht, The 135
Twisting of the Rope, The 138
Hyde Lees, George *see* Yeats, George

Ibsen, Henrik 102
imperialism 42, 130, 169, 171, 172, 175, 206–24 *passim*
impressionism 50–2
India 56, 96, 125, 139, 146, 162, 209, 211, 212
Indian religious thought 151, 161–3
Inghinidhe na hEireann 170
Irish Academy of Letters 196
Irish Free State 14, 179, 182, 186, 197, 198, 204, 211, 214–16
Irish independence 142, 170, 172
Irish Land Commission 191
Irish language 125, 130, 135, 195, 196, 221
Irish Literary Revival 41, 197, 201, 222
Yeats's engagement with 4, 6, 43, 54–6, 125–6, 189, 219
see also Celticism
Irish Literary Society 188
Irish Literary Theatre 5, 6, 8, 102, 107, 135, 190
Irish Renaissance *see* Irish Literary Revival
Irish Republican Army (IRA) 186, 195, 199
Irish Republican Brotherhood (IRB) 188, 212
Irish Times 60
Irish War of Independence *see* Anglo-Irish War

Jainism 162
Jeffares, A. Norman 126, 186
Johnson, Lionel 47, 50, 51, 52, 57, 173
Joyce, James 65, 66, 221, 222
Finnegans Wake 160
Ulysses 66, 124, 126

Kandinsky, Vassily 65
Kavanagh, Patrick 115
Keats, John 20, 32, 49, 71, 174
"Eve of St. Agnes, The" 26
"Ode to a Nightingale" 29
"Ode on a Grecian Urn" 94
"To Autumn" 86
Kelly, John 187
Kenner, Hugh 223
Kermode, Frank 199
Kipling, Rudyard 59
Kirchner, Ludwig 65
Klee, Paul
Twittering Machine 73
Klimt, Gustav 65
Judith 67
Knowland, A. S. 105

Landor, Walter Savage 211
Lane, Hugh 8, 10, 20, 23, 45, 191, 192, 195, 196, 204
Lang, Fritz
Metropolis 69
Lawrence, D. H. 65
Leader, The 42, 135
legends, Irish 140–3
see also Cuchulain; Fenian cycle tales; Fergus; Finn; Oisin; Ulster cycle tales
Leicester, Earl of 32
Lewis, Wyndham 75
Library of Ireland (later New Irish Library) 5, 45, 58
Linnell, John 24
Lloyd, David 216
Lyons, F. S. L. 199

MacBride, John 7, 11, 79, 217
MacDonagh, Thomas 79, 217
MacLeish, Archibald 200
MacNeice, Louis 104
Macpherson, James 131
Maeterlinck, Maurice 52, 102, 103, 107, 111
magic 151, 152, 154–7, 189
Mallarmé, Stéphane 52
Mangan, James Clarence 23, 27, 132, 219
"My Dark Rosaleen" 27, 170–1, 172
Manicheanism 150
Mann, Thomas 200
Mannhardt, Wilhelm 131
Mannin, Ethel 187–8, 202
Marconi, Guglielmo 70
Marinetti, Filippo Tommaso 68–9, 70
"Technical Manifesto of Futurist Painting" 68

Markievicz, Constance 15, 60, 178, 187, 193–4
Martin, Henri
Histoire de France 42
Martyn, Edward 173
Heather Field, The 5
Marx, Karl 32
Marxism 194, 207, 220
masculinity 169, 172, 173–6, 187
Mathers, MacGregor 73, 154, 156
Matisse, Henri 65
McCready, Sam 110
Miller, Liam 105
Millevoye, Lucien 2
Milton, John 20, 29, 33
Modernism 1, 9, 20–1, 28, 49, 59–75, 79, 85, 86, 100, 103, 105, 110, 113, 121, 186
Moore, George 174
Diarmuid and Grania 6, 108
Moore, T. Sturge 27, 31
Moran, D. P. 42, 57, 175
Moréas, Jean 66
Morris, William 20, 26, 45, 126, 170, 188, 221, 222
Morrison, Toni 119
Müller, Max 131
Murphy, William Martin 192
Mussolini, Benito 198, 200

Nation, The 55
National Literary Society 188
nationalism 2, 4, 12, 60, 147, 185–7, 188, 207, 220–1
cultural 23–4, 26, 27–8, 55–6, 118–22, 125, 130, 135, 172, 185–7, 218, 219
in Yeats's plays 108, 173
in Yeats's poetry 171–2, 173, 211–13
relationship to Yeats's occult interests 3, 185
relationship to women and gender 178
Yeats's changing views of 2, 10, 20, 22–4, 185–7, 199, 202, 211–13, 214–15, 217
Yeats's conflicts with 6, 121, 123, 135, 185, 190, 196
see also Easter Rising; Fenianism; Home Rule; postcolonial issues
nativism 207
naturalism 37
in the theatre 102–4
Nelson, Admiral Lord 196
Neoplatonism 150
Nietzsche, Friedrich 53, 95, 175, 197
Use and Abuse of History, The 56
Nobel Prize for Literature 14, 23, 32, 106, 112, 202
Noh drama 67, 105, 107, 109, 112, 113, 142
North, Michael 186

O'Brien, Conor Cruise 198–9
O'Brien, Flann 124
O'Casey, Sean 105
occult, the 1, 2, 10, 25, 129, 130, 144–63, 207–8
as theatre 157–8
critical neglect of 146–8, 161, 163
relationship to folklore and peasant belief 132–4, 138, 139, 189
relationship to nationalism 3, 172, 185, 189, 219
see also automatic writing; Hermetic Order of the Golden Dawn; Theosophy; Theosophical Society; *A Vision*
O'Connell, Daniel 43, 123, 196
O'Duffy, Eoin 198–9
O'Grady, Standish 188
History of Ireland: The Heroic Period 140
O'Hara, Daniel T. 123
O'Higgins, Kevin 197
Oisin 4, 27
Olcott, Henry Steel 153
Oldham, C. H. 188
O'Leary, Ellen 132
O'Leary, John 2, 19–20, 25, 27–8, 31, 55, 101, 130, 185, 187, 188, 189, 190, 192, 193, 212
oral culture 131, 189
Ossietsky, Carl von 202
Owen, Wilfred 200

Parkinson, Thomas 106
Parnell, Charles Stuart 20, 21, 23, 43, 95, 123, 185, 189, 191, 196, 197, 199, 203, 215
Partisan Review 59
Pascal, Blaise 71
Pater, Walter 47, 48–52, 53, 57, 125
Marius the Epicurean 48
Studies in the History of the Renaissance 48, 50
Patrick, St. 27, 93, 146
Pearse, Mrs. 178
Pearse, Padraic 60, 79, 96, 173, 217
peasant plays 137–8

Pethica, James 5, 112
Petrarch 167, 179
Phidias 96
Picasso, Pablo 65, 67
Pirandello, Luigi 66
  Henry IV 66
Plato 84, 105
Plunkett, Grace 178
postcolonial issues 119–20, 125, 147, 169, 183, 186, 206–24
  see also imperialism
poststructuralism 207
Pound, Ezra 9, 10, 21, 64, 65, 66, 69, 107, 109, 148
  "Canto LXXXIII" 62–3
  "Return, The" 63, 64
Pre-Raphaelite movement 45–7
Protestant Ascendancy 14, 85, 94, 179, 185, 186, 195, 197
Protestant burial service 123
Protestant Home Rule Association 20, 23
psychoanalysis 207
Purohit Swami, Shri 161, 162, 166
  Upanishads 162
Putzel, Steven 155
Pythagoras 84, 96, 126

questions in Yeats's poetry 12–13, 18, 180–1, 216

Radcliffe, Elizabeth 10, 158, 159
Raftery, Anthony 137
Raleigh, Sir Walter 174
Ramazani, Jahan 208, 213
realism 134
  in the theatre 102–4, 111
Red Hanrahan 30, 137
Redmond, John 195
Renan, Ernest
  La poésie des races celtiques 134
revisionism 147
Rhymers' Club 2, 47, 50, 56, 57, 58
Ribh 93
Rich, Adrienne 167, 171
Ricketts, Charles 27
ritual 46, 47, 57, 152, 155, 156, 157, 189, 199
Robartes, Michael 154, 155
Rolleston, T. W. 188
Romanticism 1, 2, 19–34, 38, 51, 63, 71, 79, 94, 106, 120, 121, 129, 136, 139
  and folklore 131–2, 133, 134, 136
Roosevelt, Theodore 7
Rose, Nathan 80
Rose, the 2–3, 16, 21, 22–3, 27, 171, 172, 189
Rosicrucianism 150, 155, 189
Rossiter, A. P. 125
  Lilith 46, 47
  Sibylla Palmifera 46, 47
  Venus Syriaca 46
Rossetti, Dante Gabriel 26, 31, 45, 46, 47
Royal Irish Academy 140
Ruskin, John 188
Russell, George 101, 148, 196, 197
Russian Revolution 78
Russolo, Luigi
  Music 70

Said, Edward 207, 220
  Orientalism 42
Salome 67
Savoy, The 5
Schoenberg, Arnold 64
scientific rationalism 36–8, 129
séances 151, 152, 158
Second World War *see* World War II
Senate, Irish 14, 30, 188, 195–6, 197, 214
sexuality 168, 169, 172, 199
  desire 1–2, 7–8, 9, 18, 162, 181, 200
  love poetry 3–4, 100, 168, 170–1, 172, 174, 181
  relationship to politics 187
  relationship to religion 16, 162–3
  sexual frankness 16, 178–82
  see also aisling poetry; Gonne, Maud; Gonne, Iseult; vasectomy; Yeats, George
Shakespear, Olivia 5, 90, 91, 148
Shakespeare, William 25, 33, 34, 38–9, 85, 94, 95, 112, 125, 126, 146, 211, 221
  Hamlet 87, 122, 200
  Henry V 39
  King Lear 25, 122
  Richard II 39, 124–5
  Timon of Athens 25
Shaw, George Bernard 101, 102, 103, 119–20, 196
Sheehy-Skeffington, Hanna 178
Shelley, Percy Bysshe 20, 21–2, 24, 25, 26, 27, 29, 31–2, 37, 38, 49, 82, 88, 126, 144, 188, 189, 210, 211
  Alastor 22
  "Defence of Poetry, A" 21, 32
  Prometheus Unbound 24, 27, 29, 32, 144
  Sensitive Plant, The 23

Sinn Fein 12, 178, 190, 195, 196
Skene, Reg 103, 107
Smart, Christopher
  "Song to David" 51
socialism 188
Society for Psychical Research 158
Socrates 71, 152
Sophocles 110
Spenser, Edmund 20, 22, 31, 32, 33, 34, 39, 46, 118, 125, 188, 189, 221
  Faerie Queene, The 32
  View of the Present State of Ireland, A 32, 212, 217
spiritualism 2, 157–61, 165–6
Stalin, Joseph 200
Stanislawski, Konstantin 103, 110
Steinach operation 16
Stevens, Wallace 21, 28
  "Sailing after Lunch" 3
Stone Cottage 9, 10, 63
Strauss, Richard 65, 67
Stravinsky, Igor 64, 65
  Nightingale, The 73
Strindberg, August 116
Surrealism 72–5
Swami, Shri Purohit *see* Purohit Swami, Shri
Swedenborg, Emmanuel 158
Swift, Jonathan 88, 195
Swinburne, Algernon Charles 36
Symbolism 2, 22, 26, 27, 56, 65, 66–8, 117, 118, 155, 174, 185
  in *A Vision* 147, 148–9
  in the theatre 6, 102–4, 107, 109, 111, 113, 137–8
  occult 156, 157
  symbols in Yeats's poetry 10, 155
    birds 157
    dancers 85
    nationalist iconography 174, 214–5
    roses 155
    towers 15, 17, 22, 28–9, 31, 88
    trees 155, 177
    see also Rose, the
Symons, Arthur 51, 52, 57, 103
Synge, J. M. 5–6, 8, 32, 102, 112, 116, 122–3, 126, 139, 142, 148, 187, 190, 218, 219
  In the Shadow of the Glen 6, 104
  Playboy of the Western World, The 6, 20, 21, 23, 45, 101, 123, 138, 139, 141, 191
  Riders to the Sea 104, 120–1

Tagore, Rabindranath 126
Táin Bó Cuailnge 140
Tantrism 162, 166
Taylor, John F. 188
Tennyson, Alfred Lord 48, 51
Theosophical Society 5, 151, 152–4, 189
  Esoteric Section 153
Theosophy 2, 130, 151, 152–4, 161, 165
Thomas, Dylan 21
Thoreau, Henry David 223
Thoor Ballylee 12, 14, 28, 29, 30–1, 33, 77, 78, 159, 197
Times Literary Supplement 113
Toller, Ernst 202
Tom the Lunatic 16, 89
To-morrow 14, 179
Trilling, Lionel 43, 44
Tynan, Katharine 5, 23
Tyndall, John 37
Tzara, Tristan 71, 72

Ulster cycle tales 140–1, 142
unionism 20, 23, 123, 196
United Ireland 44
United Irishman 54
Unterecker, John 127
Upanishads 139, 146, 162
Ure, Peter 104, 105, 108, 110

vasectomy 16
Vendler, Helen 104, 105, 106, 126
Verhaeren, Emile 52
Victoria, Queen 7, 36, 189
Villiers de l'Isle Adam, Philippe-Auguste 52, 56
Virgil 71, 92

Walker, Alice 119
Walker, Emery 26
Watson, George 4, 197
Webern, Anton 65
Wellesley, Dorothy 187–8
Whitaker, Thomas 126
Wilde, Oscar 5, 47, 116, 126
  Salomé 67
Wilson, Edmund 103
women's movement *see* feminism
Woolf, Virginia 65, 68, 121, 170
Wordsworth, William 20, 48, 49, 90
  "Ode: Intimations of Immortality" 85
  "Tintern Abbey" 29
World War I 10, 13, 41, 71, 77, 78, 100, 158, 178, 192, 204, 212

World War II 93, 100
Worth, Katharine 102–3, 110–11

Yeats, Anne Butler (Yeats's daughter) 12, 77, 81–2, 111, 157, 178, 183, 196
Yeats, Elizabeth Corbet ('Lolly') (Yeats's sister) 6, 26–7, 30
Yeats, George (Yeats's wife) 11–12, 14, 30, 77, 147–8, 149–50, 151, 157, 159–60, 161, 164, 194
Yeats, John Butler (Yeats's father) 77, 82, 93, 116, 119, 122, 130, 152, 154, 174, 188, 203
Yeats, Michael Butler (Yeats's son) 196
Yeats, Susan (Yeats's mother) 81–2, 151, 154, 203
Yeats, Susan Mary ('Lily') (Yeats's sister) 6, 26–7
Yeats, W. B.
  plays
    At the Hawk's Well 64, 101, 103, 107–8, 109, 112, 113, 142
    Calvary 72
    Cat and the Moon, The 104, 110
    Cathleen ni Houlihan 6, 104, 105, 108, 113, 138, 173
    Countess Cathleen, The 5, 6, 101, 106, 108, 189
    Death of Cuchulain, The 67–8, 107–8, 110, 142
    Deirdre 108, 121, 141
    Diarmuid and Grania 6, 108
    Dreaming of the Bones, The 109, 142, 193
    Full Moon in March, A 67
    Golden Helmet, The 106, 141–2
    Green Helmet, The 106, 107–8, 109
    Herne's Egg, The 74, 104, 105
    Hour-Glass, The 103, 110
    Island of Statues, The 2, 46, 101
    King of the Great Clock Tower, The 67
    King's Threshold, The 106, 108, 111, 126, 138
    Land of Heart's Desire, The 108
    Mosada 105
    On Baile's Strand 105, 107–8, 110, 124, 141
    Only Jealousy of Emer, The 107–8, 142
    Player Queen, The 104, 105, 106, 111
    Purgatory 102, 104, 105, 107, 110, 111, 112, 113, 186
    Resurrection, The 110
    Shadowy Waters, The 106, 112
    Where There Is Nothing 108, 110, 111, 138
    Words upon the Window-Pane, The 111
  poems
    "Acre of Grass, An" 1, 25
    "Adam's Curse" 8, 39, 54, 91, 145, 168, 175
    "After Long Silence" 90–1
    "All Souls' Night" 15
    "All Things can Tempt me" 187
    "Among School Children" 15, 82, 83–5, 214
    "Ancestral Houses" 85, 87
    "Are You Content?" 17
    "At Galway Races" 8, 39–40
    "At the Abbey Theatre" 219
    "Baile and Aillinn" 141
    "Ballad of Father Gilligan, The" 4
    "Ballad of Father O'Hart, The" 4, 222
    "Ballad of Moll Magee, The" 4
    "Black Tower, The" 17, 97, 98
    "Blood and the Moon" 15, 28, 29, 88–9, 197
    "Bronze Head, A" 95
    "Byzantium" 91–3, 94, 96, 145
    "Cap and Bells, The" 4
    "Chambermaid's Second Song, The" 63
    "Church and State" 216
    "Circus Animals' Desertion, The" 81, 82, 95–6, 100, 101, 104, 105, 112, 117, 147, 157
    "Cloak, the Boat, and the Shoes, The" 46
    "Cold Heaven, The" 9–10
    "Come Gather Round Me, Parnellites" 199
    "Coming of Wisdom with Time, The" 8
    "Coole Park, 1929" 15, 25, 82, 112, 175, 199
    "Coole Park and Ballylee, 1931" 9, 15, 19, 20, 28, 31, 50, 82, 112, 139, 199
    "Crazy Jane and Jack the Journeyman" 182
    "Crazy Jane on God" 182
    "Crazy Jane talks with the Bishop" 25, 89, 162–3, 182
    "Cuchulain Comforted" 32, 78, 97–8
    "Delphic Oracle upon Plotinus, The" 17
    "Demon and Beast" 81
    "Dialogue of Self and Soul, A" 15

"Double Vision of Michael Robartes The" 11
"Easter 1916" 10, 12, 44, 78–80, 98, 109, 126–7, 178, 192–3, 194, 216–17, 220
"Ego Dominus Tuus" 31, 51, 123, 157, 159
"Ephemera" 3, 16
"Falling of the Leaves, The" 3
"Fascination of What's Difficult, The" 8, 101, 102, 108
"Fergus and the Druid" 3
"Fisherman, The" 13, 118, 139, 199, 219
"Folly of Being Comforted, The" 7–8
"Four Ages of Man, The" 151, 161, 164
"Fragments" 70
"Ghost of Roger Casement, The" 212–13
"Great Day, The" 215–16
"Grey Rock, The" 56
"Gyres, The" 17, 94–5, 96, 200
"Happy Shepherd, The" 129
"He gives his Beloved certain Rhymes" 46
"He reproves the Curlew" 49
"He wishes for the Cloths of Heaven" 3–4, 6, 47, 174–5
"His Dream" 64
"High Talk" 74, 112
"Hosting of the Sidhe, The" 3, 53, 140
"I See Phantoms of Hatred and of the Heart's Fullness and of the Coming Emptiness" 68, 87
"In Memory of Eva Gore-Booth and Con Markiewicz" 15, 199
"In Memory of Major Robert Gregory" 28, 78
"In the Seven Woods" 6–7
"Into the Twilight" 4
"Irish Airman Foresees his Death, An" 40, 78
"Lake Isle of Innisfree, The" 3, 6–7, 133, 152, 222–23
"Lapis Lazuli" 69, 94–5, 118, 122
"Leda and the Swan" 12, 14, 52, 168, 178–82
"Lines Written in Dejection" 10
"Long-legged Fly" 17
"Magi, The" 52
"Man and the Echo, The" 18, 98, 104, 105
"Man who Dreamed of Faeryland, The" 3, 133
"Man Young and Old, A" 16, 89
"Meditations in Time of Civil War" 13–14, 28, 33, 82, 85–7, 126, 200
"Meru" 52, 94
"Michael Robartes and the Dancer" 117, 183
"Moods, The" 82
"Mourn – And Then Onward!" 189, 199
"Municipal Gallery Revisited, The" 32, 97, 118, 139, 142–3
"My Descendants" 87, 197
"My House" 15, 85–6, 197
"My Table" 86
"News for the Delphic Oracle" 17, 63–4
"Nineteen Hundred and Nineteen" 13–14, 52, 78, 80, 82, 88, 200
"No Second Troy" 175–7
"Old Age of Queen Maeve, The" 141
"Old Stone Cross, The" 122
"On a Political Prisoner" 187, 193–4
"On being asked for a War Poem" 78, 192
"Pardon, Old Fathers" 8, 9, 40, 192
"Parnell" 216
"Parnell's Funeral" 95
"Paudeen" 9
"Peacock, The" 63
"People, The" 13
"Phases of the Moon, The" 11, 28, 29
"Pilgrim, The" 163
"Politics" 18, 112, 200
"Prayer for my Daughter, A" 12, 81–2, 111, 168, 177–8, 183, 194
"Prayer for Old Age, A" 117–18
"Reconciliation" 141
"Red Hanrahan's Song About Ireland" 173, 175
"Reprisals" 13, 78
"Ribh at the Tomb of Baile and Aillinn" 93
"Ribh considers Christian Love insufficient" 93
"Ribh Denounces Patrick" 93
"Road at my Door, The" 86–7, 219
"Rose Tree, The" 193, 194
"Sad Shepherd, The" 2
"Sailing to Byzantium" 25, 30, 73, 82–3, 91

"Second Coming, The" 12, 19, 52, 73, 79, 145, 148, 200
"Secret Rose, The" 171
"September 1913" 8–9, 10, 27–8, 31, 40, 192, 194
"Seven Sages, The" 195
"Shepherd and Goatherd" 78
"Sixteen Dead Men" 12, 193
"Solomon and the Witch" 11
"Solomon to Sheba" 11
"Song of the Happy Shepherd, The" 37, 46
"Song of Wandering Aengus, The" 3, 46–7, 171
"Spur, The" 1–2
"Stare's Nest by my Window, The" 33, 64
"Statues, The" 50, 96, 126, 142, 211
"Stolen Child, The" 3
"Supernatural Songs" 88, 93–4, 162
"These are the Clouds" 8
"Three Bushes, The" 89
"Three Monuments, The" 204
"Three Movements" 34
"To a Friend whose Work has come to Nothing" 9, 192
"To a Shade" 191
"To a Wealthy Man . . ." 9, 191, 192, 211, 212
"To a Young Beauty" 211
"To be Carved on a Stone at Thoor Ballylee" 30–1
"To Ireland in the Coming Times" 3, 23, 44, 55, 172, 189–90, 219
"To the Rose upon the Rood of Time" 3, 22–3, 171
"Tom at Cruachan" 89
"Tower, The" 12, 15, 28–31, 88, 98–9, 197, 199, 201
"Travail of Passion, The" 1
"Two Songs from a Play" 52
"Under Ben Bulben" 17–18, 24, 60, 63, 69, 71, 97, 99–100, 200–1
"Upon a House Shaken by the Land Agitation" 8, 191
"Vacillation" 40, 88
"Wanderings of Oisin, The" 52–3, 141
"What Magic Drum?" 94
"What Then?" 17
"While I, from that reed-throated whisperer" 8, 9
"Why should not Old Men be Mad?" 111, 177
"Wild Swans at Coole, The" 77
"Woman Young and Old, A" 16, 89, 112, 181
"Words" 141
"Words for Music Perhaps" 89–91
essays and short stories
"Adoration of the Magi, The" 53–54, 156
"Art and Ideas" 40, 49–51
"At Stratford-on-Avon" 38–40, 124–5
"Autumn of the Body, The" 48
"Away" 137
"Binding of the Hair, The" 67
"By the Roadside" 137
"Celtic Element in Literature, The" 41–2, 134–5, 210
"Certain Noble Plays of Japan" 107, 109
"Earth, Fire and Water" 152
"Edmund Spenser" 39, 212, 217
"General Introduction for my Work, A" 55, 144, 145–6, 221, 223
"Hopes and Fears for Irish Literature" 54
"If I Were Four-and-Twenty" 194
"Ireland, 1921–1931" 197–8, 214–15, 217
"Ireland and the Arts" 56, 219
"Irish Dramatic Movement, The" 102, 106
"Irish National Theatre and Three Sorts of Ignorance, The" 121
"Is the Order of R. R. & A. C. to remain a Magical Order?" 165
"J. M. Synge and the Ireland of his Time" 218, 219
"John Eglinton and Spiritual Art" 48
"Magic" 41, 156
"Mandukya Upanishad, The" 162
"Moods, The" 58
"New National Library, The" 58
"Philosophy of Shelley's Poetry, The" 22, 144, 155, 210
"Poetry and Tradition" 138–9, 190
"*Prometheus Unbound*" 24, 144
"Rosa Alchemica" 53, 54, 156
"Rhymers' Club, The" 58
"Symbolism of Poetry, The" 155
"Tables of the Law, The" 53, 54, 156
"Theatre, The" 49, 107
"Tomorrow's Revolution" 111
"Tribes of Danu, The" 136

"What is 'Popular Poetry'?" 56
"William Blake and his Illustrations to *The Divine Comedy*" 24
"William Blake and the Imagination" 24
prose works and edited volumes
Autobiographies 10, 20, 27, 37, 45, 47, 49, 50, 51, 52, 77, 116–17, 119, 123, 156–7, 210
Beltaine 102, 126
Celtic Twilight, The 5, 129–30, 133, 135, 136, 137, 152
Essays and Introductions 125–6
Explorations 107, 126
Fairy and Folk Tales of the Irish Peasantry 5, 129–30, 131, 132
Ideas of Good and Evil 24, 107
Irish Fairy Tales 5, 129–30
John Sherman 5
Letters to the New Island 58
Memoirs 20
On the Boiler 17, 95, 102, 111, 186, 201–2
Oxford Book of Modern Verse, The 17, 21, 36, 41, 51–2, 63, 64
Per Amica Silentia Lunae 77
Plays and Controversies 113
Representative Irish Tales 129–30
Samhain 102, 126, 220–1
Secret Rose, The 47, 52–3, 55, 137, 155
Stories from Carleton 129–30
Stories of Red Hanrahan 137
Vision, A 11, 14, 16, 20, 25, 31–2, 39, 66, 69, 71–2, 74–5, 77, 97, 110, 147, 148–9, 151, 154, 160–1, 163, 163, 178, 194–5, 199, 210–1
Works of William Blake: Poetic, Symbolic, and Critical 24–5, 26
volumes of poetry
Countess Kathleen and Various Legends and Lyrics, The 140, 189
Crossways 46
Green Helmet and Other Poems, The 101, 121
In the Seven Woods 6–7, 8, 141
Michael Robartes and the Dancer 12, 30, 78–9
Last Poems 17, 89
Last Poems and Two Plays 102
October Blast 30–1
Poems (1895) 5, 26, 129–30
Responsibilities 8, 9, 191–2
Rose, The 2
Tower, The 14, 28, 30–1, 81, 82, 89, 110, 197
Wild Swans at Coole, The 11, 78
Wind Among the Reeds, The 2, 6, 46, 140, 155
Winding Stair and Other Poems, The 15, 28, 29, 34, 89, 91, 110, 199
Young Ireland 55–6, 130, 172, 185, 188, 189, 190
Young Ireland Society 2, 130

Zoroastrianism 150